CAPTAIN
REB

Writer
ED BRUBAKER

Artists
BRYAN HITCH
BUTCH GUICE

Prologue Pencils
LUKE ROSS

Prologue Inks
RICK MAGYAR

Colors
PAUL MOUNTS

Prologue Colors
JUSTIN PONSOR

Letters
VC's JOE CARAMAGNA

Cover Art
BRYAN HITCH
BUTCH GUICE
PAUL MOUNTS

AMERICA

ORN

Associate Editors
LAUREN SANKOVITCH
JEANINE SCHAEFER

Editor
TOM BREVOORT

Captain America created by
JOE SIMON
& JACK KIRBY

Collection Editor
JENNIFER GRÜNWALD

Assistant Editor
ALEX STARBUCK

Associate Editor
JOHN DENNING

Editor, Special Projects
MARK D. BEAZLEY

Senior Editor, Special Projects
JEFF YOUNGQUIST

Senior Vice President of Sales
DAVID GABRIEL

Book Design
RIAN HUGHES at DEVICE

Editor in Chief
JOE QUESADA

Publisher
DAN BUCKLEY

Executive Producer
ALAN FINE

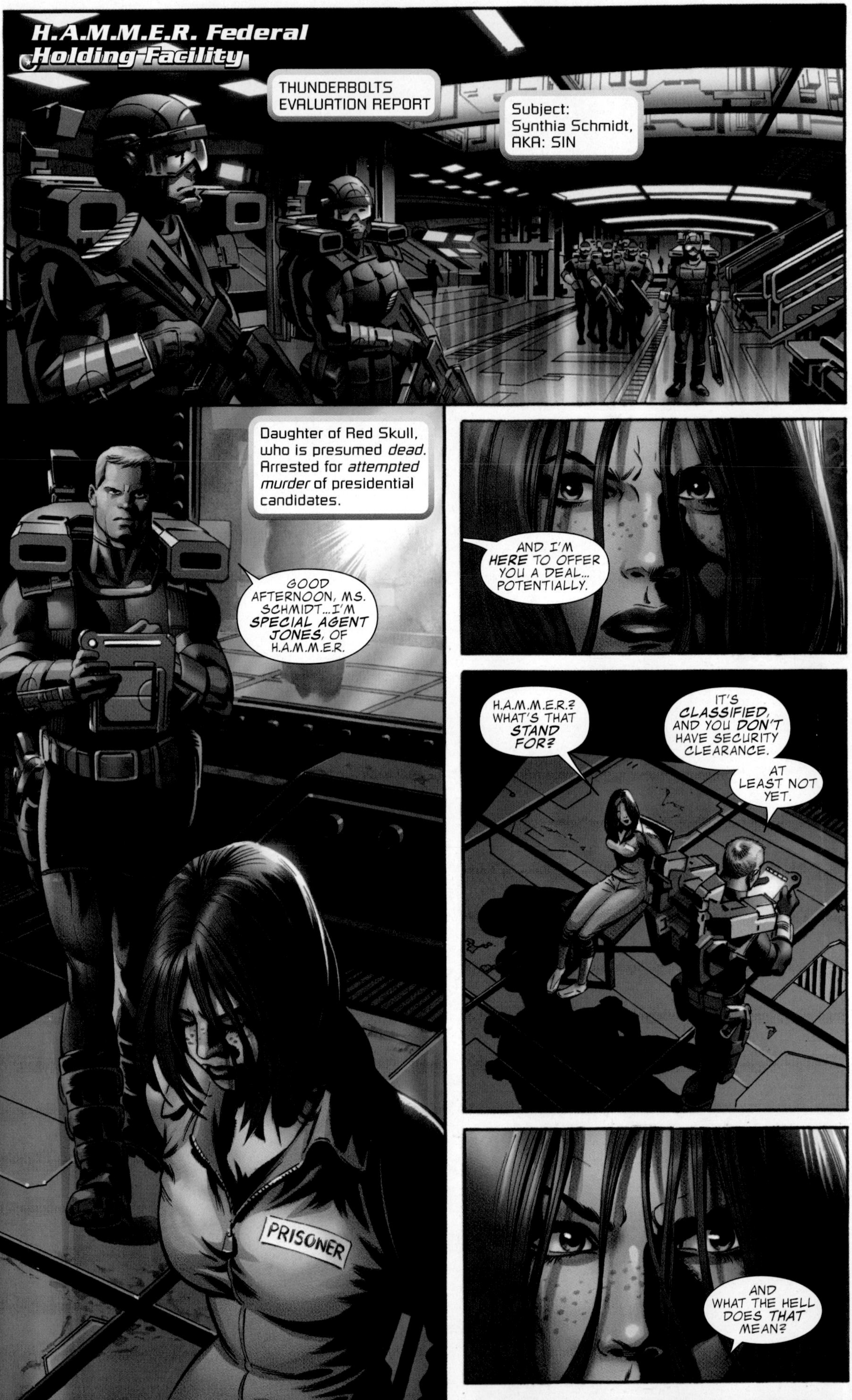
H.A.M.M.E.R. Federal Holding Facility
THUNDERBOLTS EVALUATION REPORT
Subject: Synthia Schmidt, AKA: SIN
Daughter of Red Skull, who is presumed *dead*. Arrested for *attempted murder* of presidential candidates.
GOOD AFTERNOON, MS. SCHMIDT...I'M **SPECIAL AGENT JONES**, OF H.A.M.M.E.R.
PRISONER
AND I'M **HERE** TO OFFER YOU A DEAL... POTENTIALLY.
H.A.M.M.E.R.? WHAT'S THAT **STAND FOR?**
IT'S **CLASSIFIED**, AND YOU **DON'T** HAVE SECURITY CLEARANCE.
AT LEAST NOT YET.
AND WHAT THE HELL DOES **THAT** MEAN?

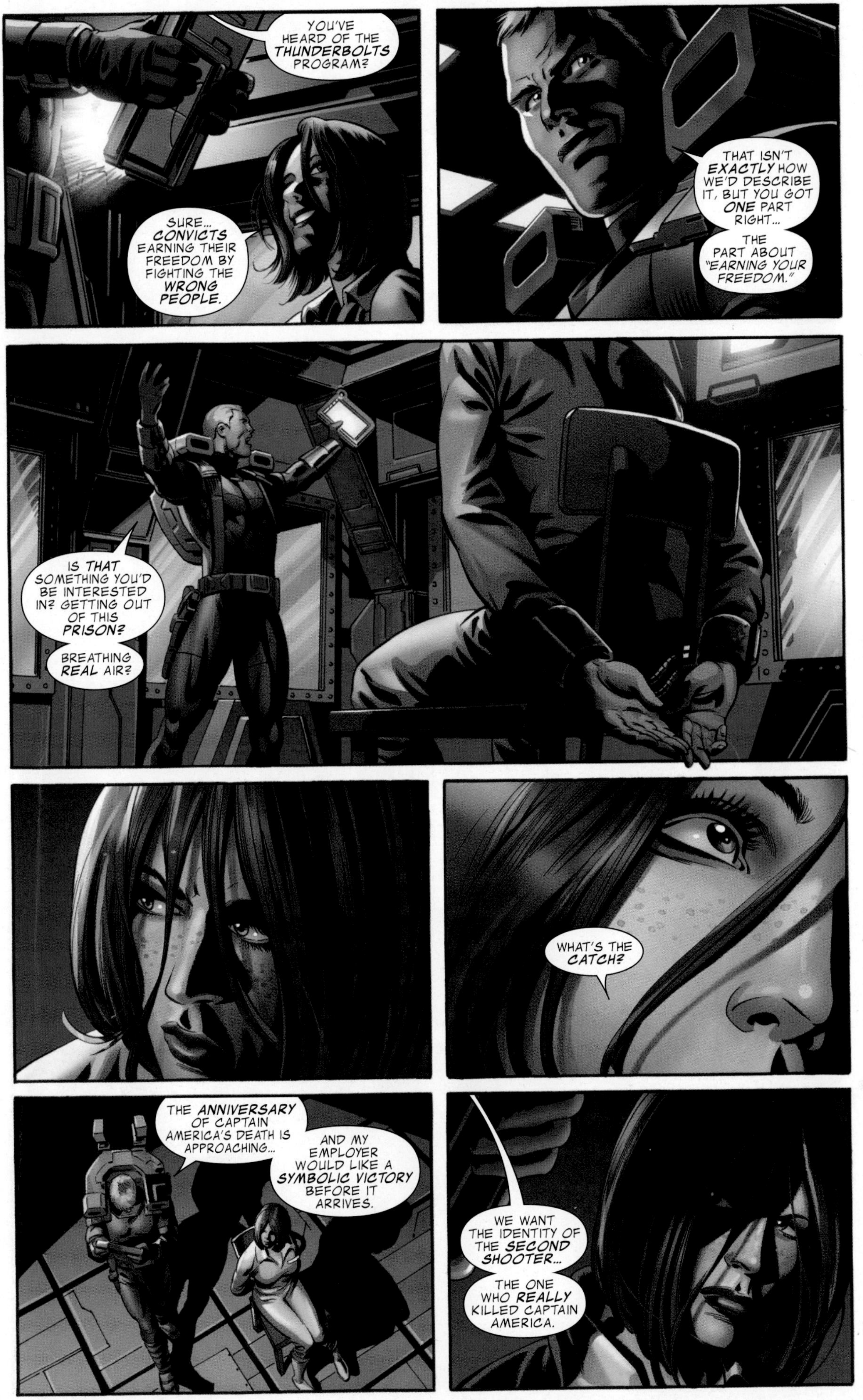

YOU'VE HEARD OF THE THUNDERBOLTS PROGRAM?
SURE... CONVICTS EARNING THEIR FREEDOM BY FIGHTING THE WRONG PEOPLE.
THAT ISN'T EXACTLY HOW WE'D DESCRIBE IT, BUT YOU GOT ONE PART RIGHT...
THE PART ABOUT "EARNING YOUR FREEDOM."
IS THAT SOMETHING YOU'D BE INTERESTED IN? GETTING OUT OF THIS PRISON?
BREATHING REAL AIR?
WHAT'S THE CATCH?
THE ANNIVERSARY OF CAPTAIN AMERICA'S DEATH IS APPROACHING...
AND MY EMPLOYER WOULD LIKE A SYMBOLIC VICTORY BEFORE IT ARRIVES.
WE WANT THE IDENTITY OF THE SECOND SHOOTER...
THE ONE WHO REALLY KILLED CAPTAIN AMERICA.

SEE, WE'VE EXAMINED ALL THE *SURVEILLANCE FOOTAGE* FROM THE DAY OF THE *ASSASSINATION...*

...AS WE'RE SURE *S.H.I.E.L.D.* DID, TOO...

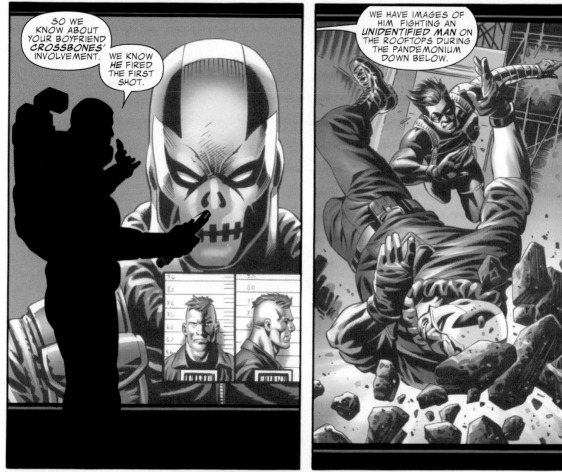

SO WE KNOW ABOUT YOUR BOYFRIEND *CROSSBONES'* INVOLVEMENT. WE KNOW *HE* FIRED THE FIRST SHOT.

WE HAVE IMAGES OF HIM FIGHTING AN *UNIDENTIFIED MAN* ON THE ROOFTOPS DURING THE PANDEMONIUM DOWN BELOW.

AND WE KNOW *THE FALCON* WAS THERE...BUT *THAT* WAS TO BE EXPECTED.

SEVERAL *S.H.I.E.L.D. AGENTS* WERE ON THE SCENE, AS WELL--AGAINST *ORDERS,* MIND YOU...

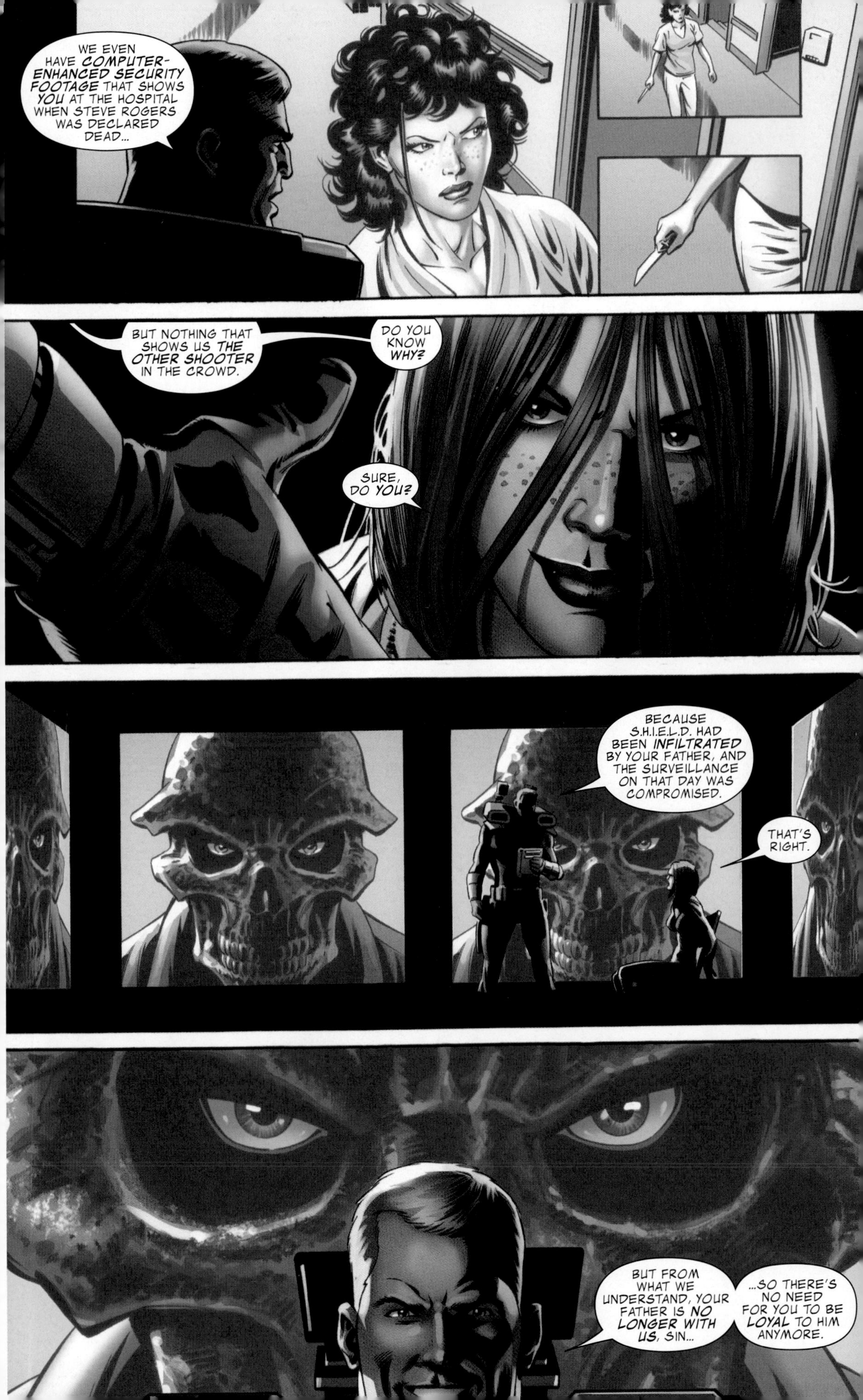
WE EVEN HAVE COMPUTER-ENHANCED SECURITY FOOTAGE THAT SHOWS YOU AT THE HOSPITAL WHEN STEVE ROGERS WAS DECLARED DEAD...
BUT NOTHING THAT SHOWS US THE OTHER SHOOTER IN THE CROWD.
DO YOU KNOW WHY?
SURE, DO YOU?
BECAUSE S.H.I.E.L.D. HAD BEEN INFILTRATED BY YOUR FATHER, AND THE SURVEILLANCE ON THAT DAY WAS COMPROMISED.
THAT'S RIGHT.
BUT FROM WHAT WE UNDERSTAND, YOUR FATHER IS NO LONGER WITH US, SIN...
...SO THERE'S NO NEED FOR YOU TO BE LOYAL TO HIM ANYMORE.

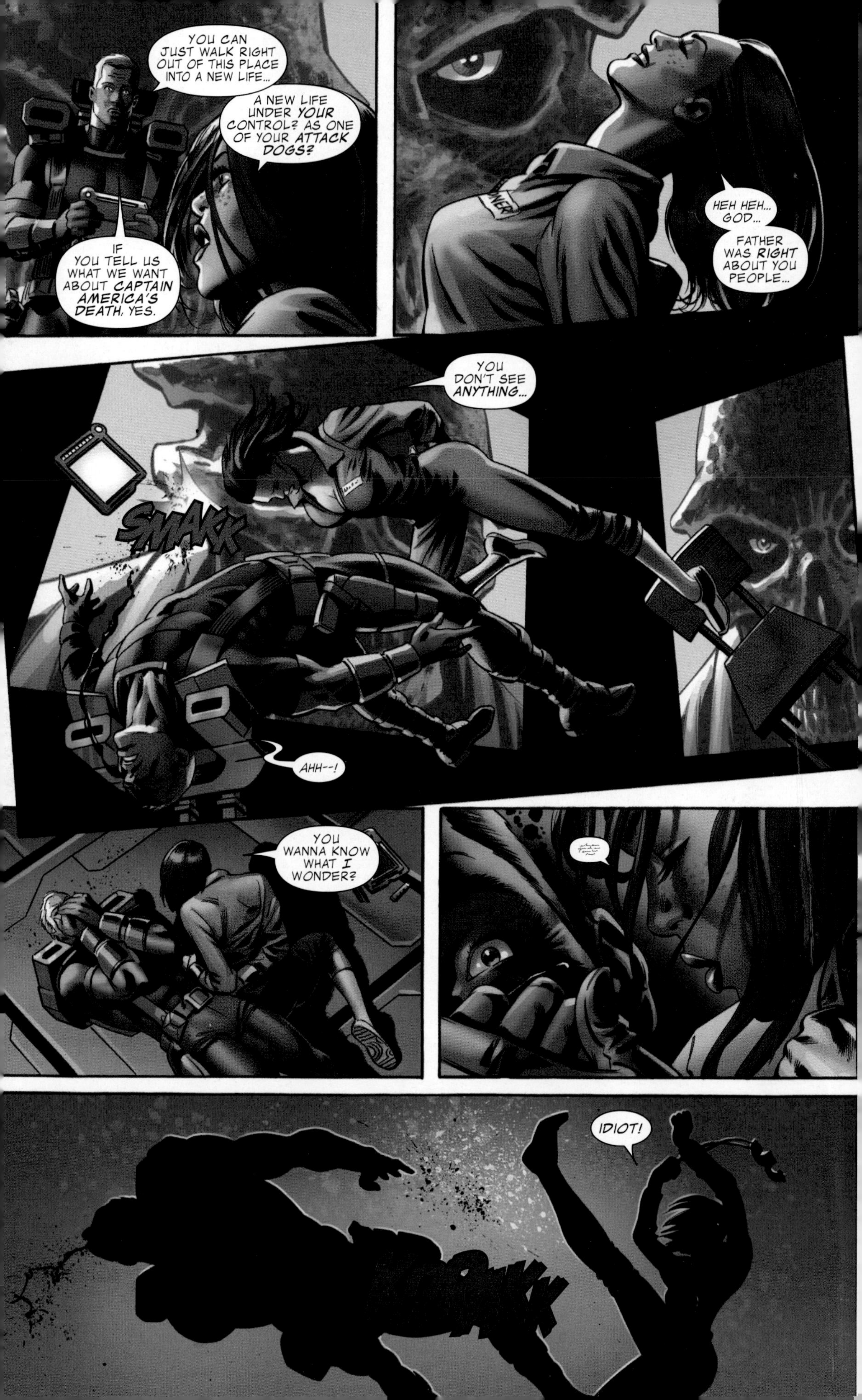
YOU CAN JUST WALK RIGHT OUT OF THIS PLACE INTO A NEW LIFE...
A NEW LIFE UNDER YOUR CONTROL? AS ONE OF YOUR ATTACK DOGS?
IF YOU TELL US WHAT WE WANT ABOUT CAPTAIN AMERICA'S DEATH, YES.
HEH HEH... GOD...
FATHER WAS RIGHT ABOUT YOU PEOPLE...
YOU DON'T SEE ANYTHING...
SMAKK
AHH--!
YOU WANNA KNOW WHAT I WONDER?
IDIOT!

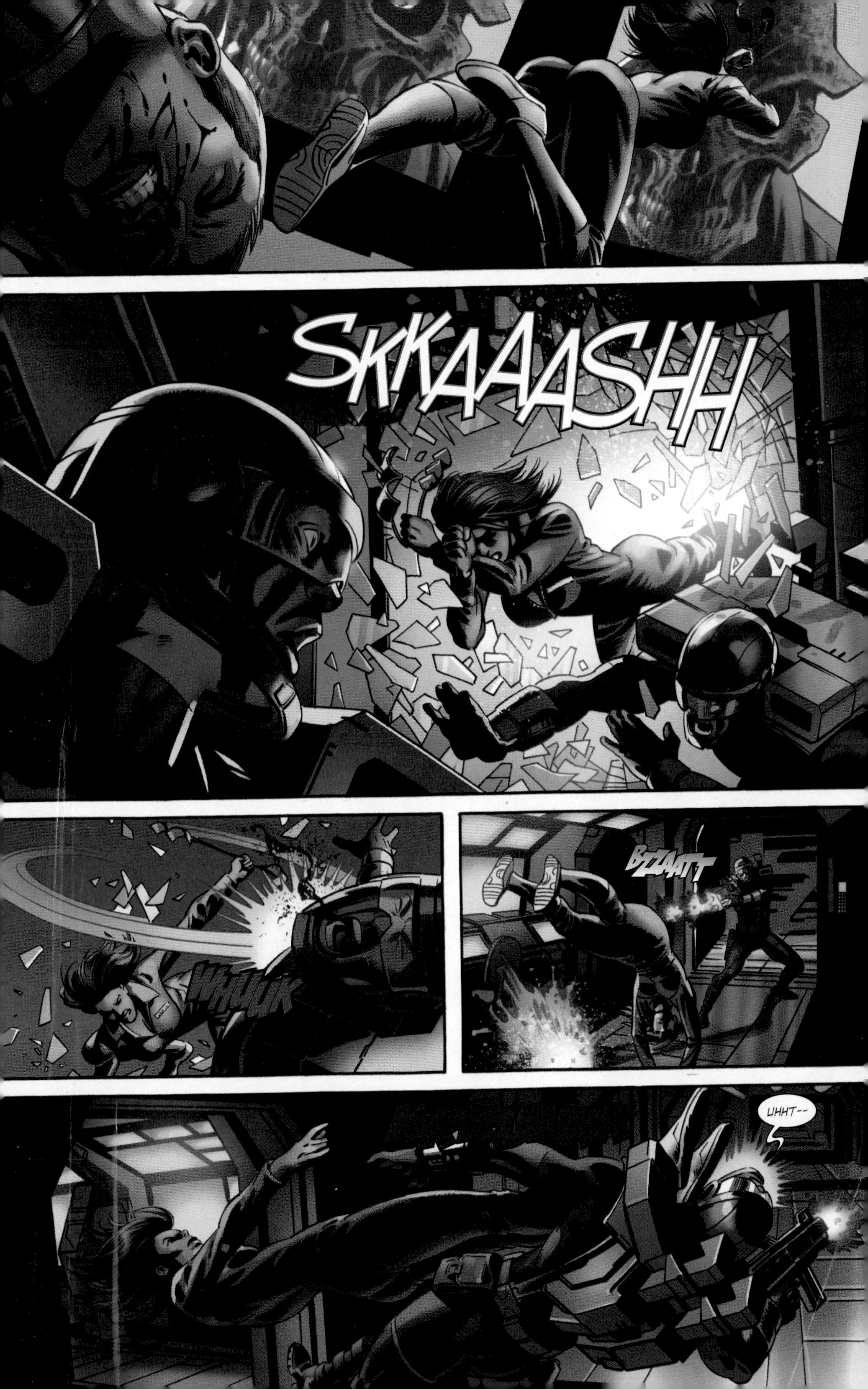
SKKAAASHH
WHUUK
BZZAATT
UHHT--

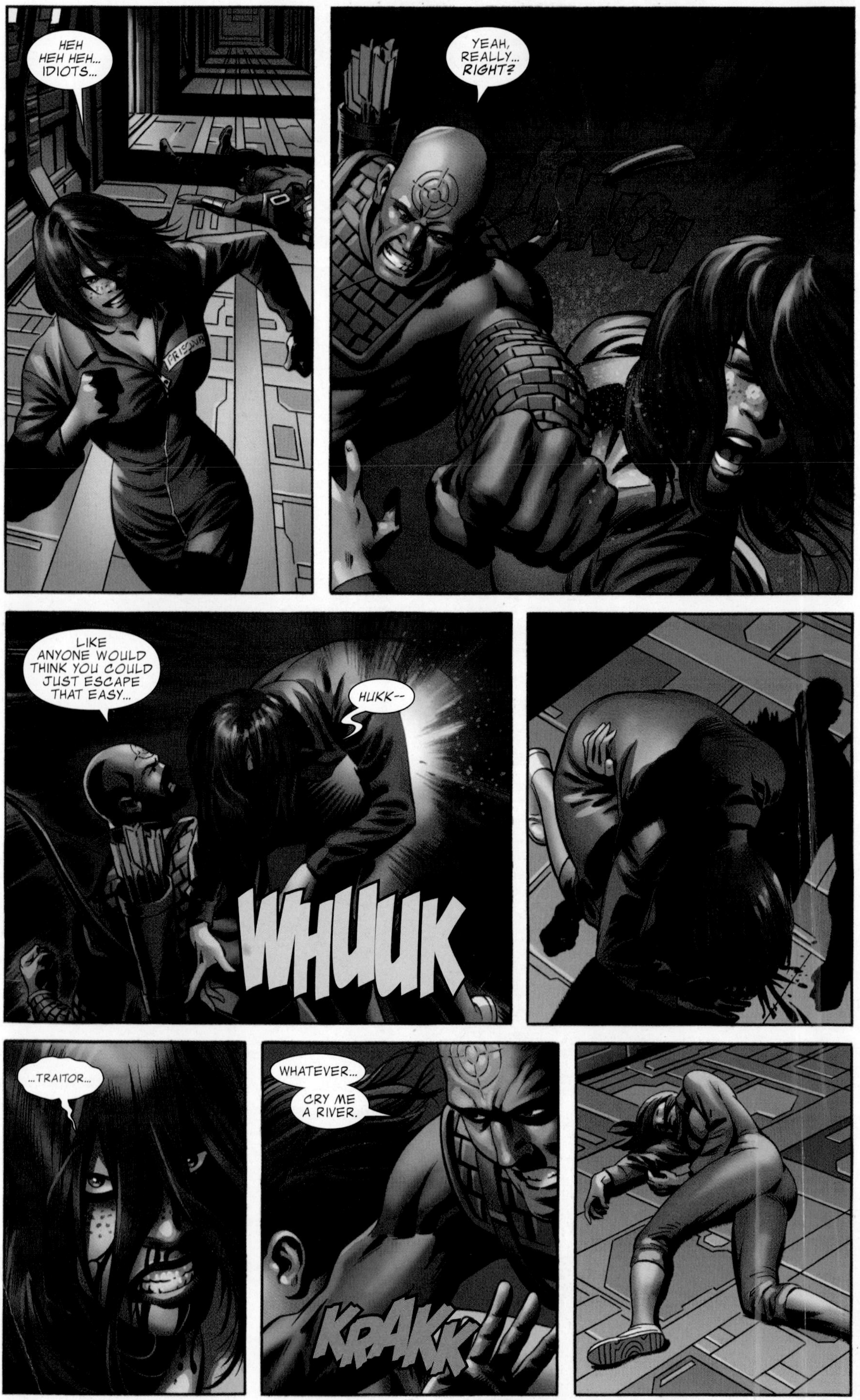
HEH HEH HEH... IDIOTS...
YEAH, REALLY... RIGHT?
PRISONR
LIKE ANYONE WOULD THINK YOU COULD JUST ESCAPE THAT EASY...
HUKK--
WHUUK
...TRAITOR...
WHATEVER...
CRY ME A RIVER.
KRAKK

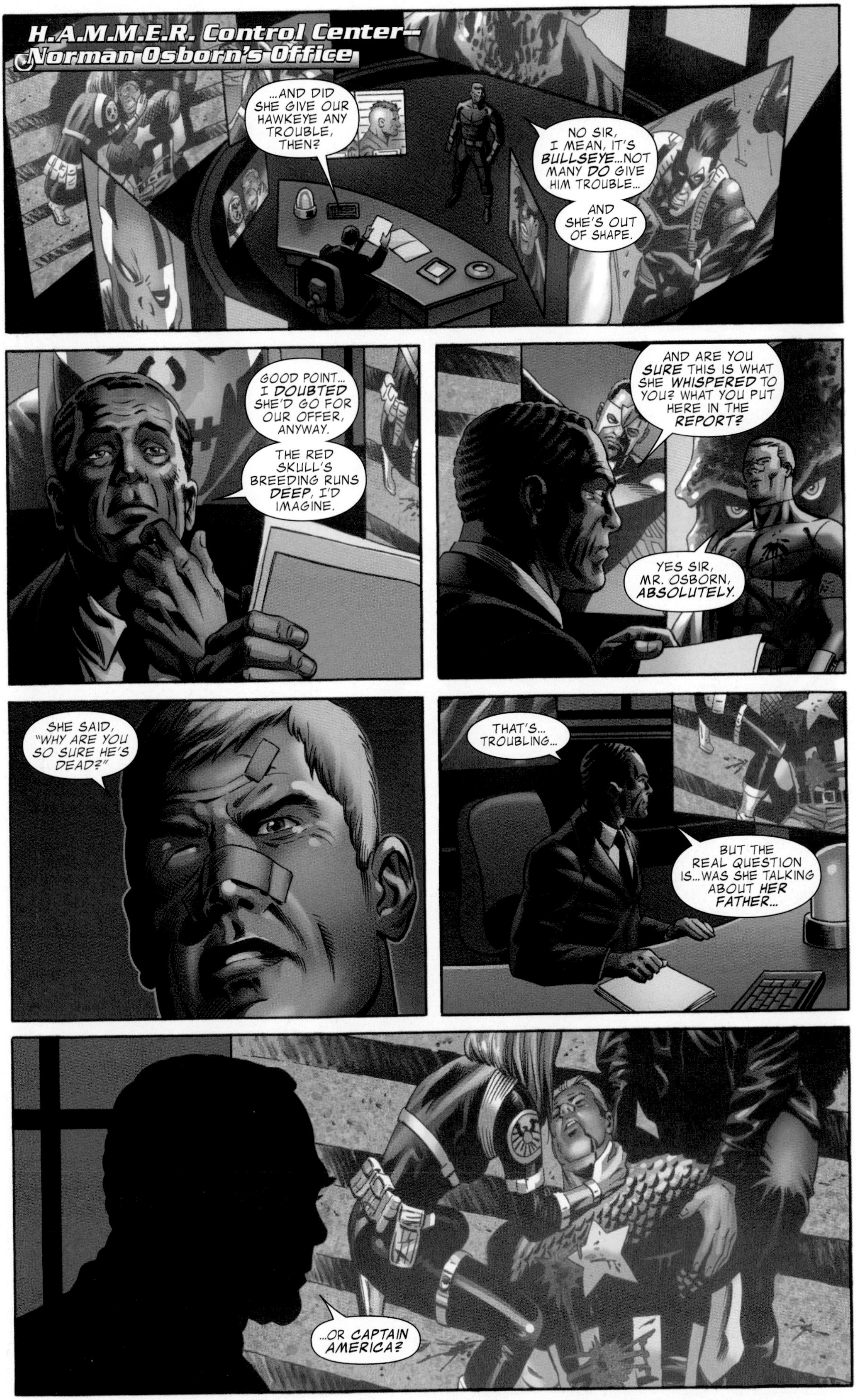
H.A.M.M.E.R. Control Center--
Norman Osborn's Office
...AND DID SHE GIVE OUR HAWKEYE ANY TROUBLE, THEN?
NO SIR, I MEAN, IT'S BULLSEYE...NOT MANY DO GIVE HIM TROUBLE...
AND SHE'S OUT OF SHAPE.
GOOD POINT... I DOUBTED SHE'D GO FOR OUR OFFER, ANYWAY.
THE RED SKULL'S BREEDING RUNS DEEP, I'D IMAGINE.
AND ARE YOU SURE THIS IS WHAT SHE WHISPERED TO YOU? WHAT YOU PUT HERE IN THE REPORT?
YES SIR, MR. OSBORN, ABSOLUTELY.
SHE SAID, "WHY ARE YOU SO SURE HE'S DEAD?"
THAT'S... TROUBLING...
BUT THE REAL QUESTION IS...WAS SHE TALKING ABOUT HER FATHER...
...OR CAPTAIN AMERICA?

"No bastard ever won a war by dying for his country"

– *Patton*

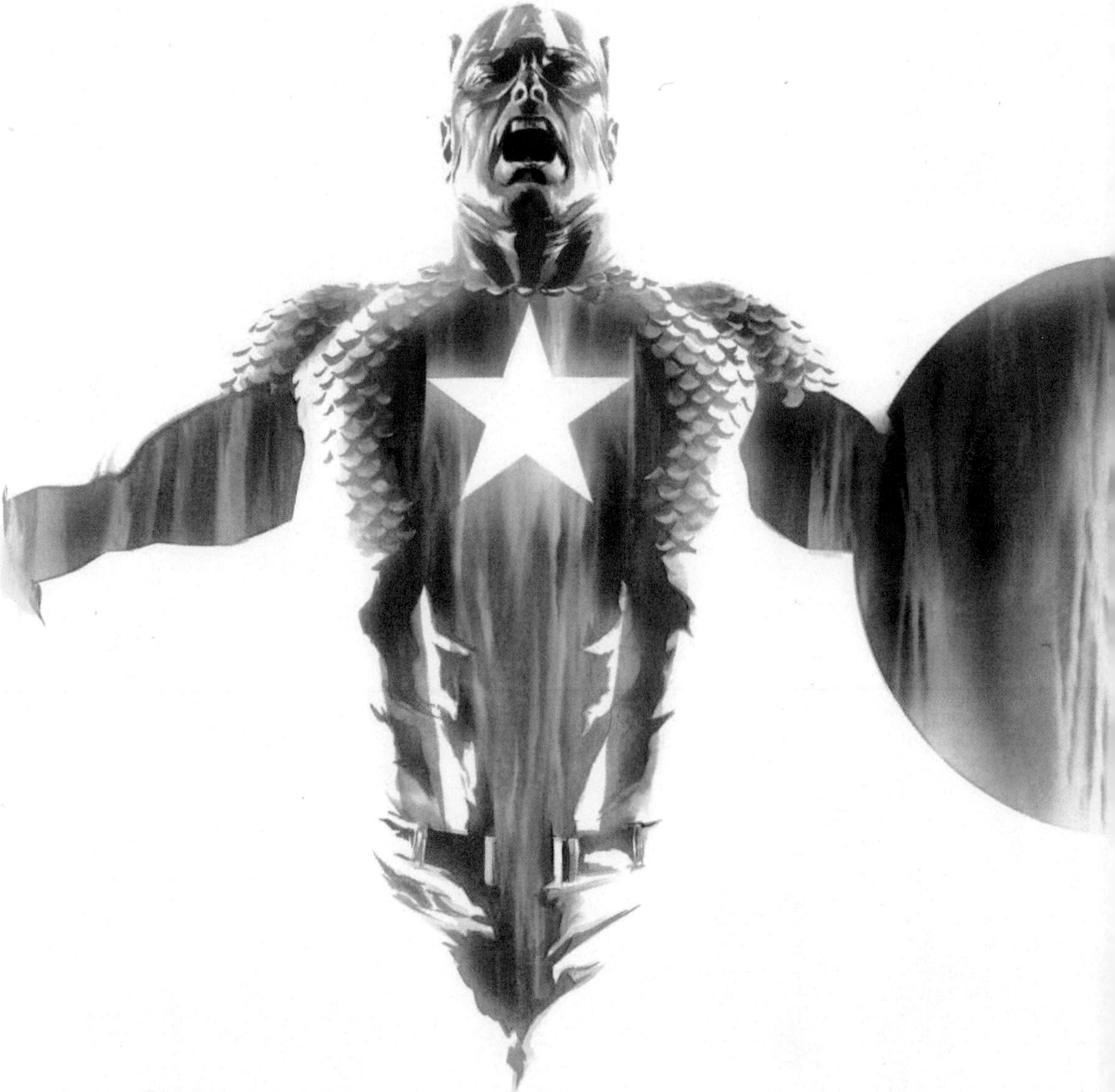

Issue 1 variant cover by **ALEX ROSS**

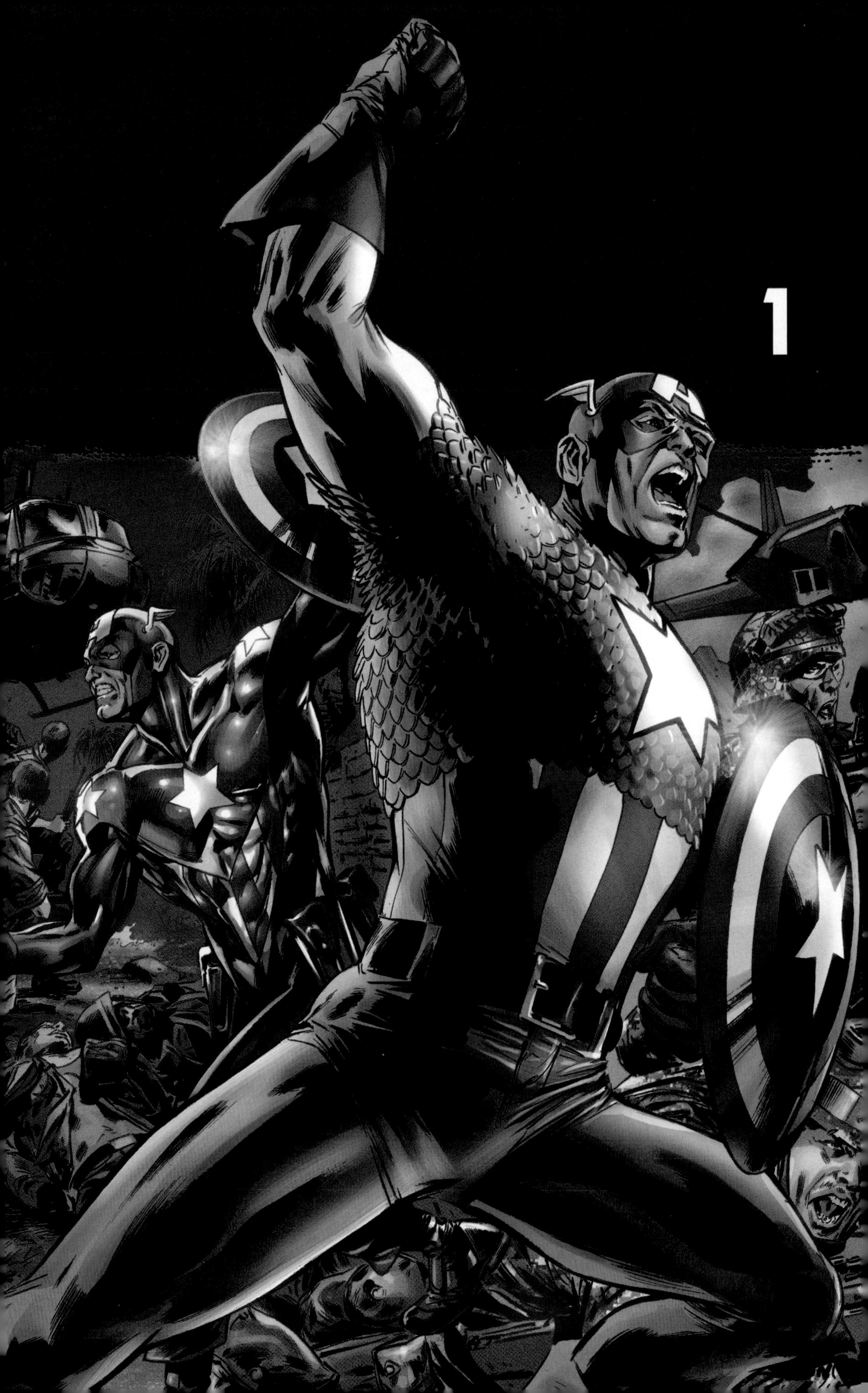
1

CAPTAIN AMERICA
REBORN

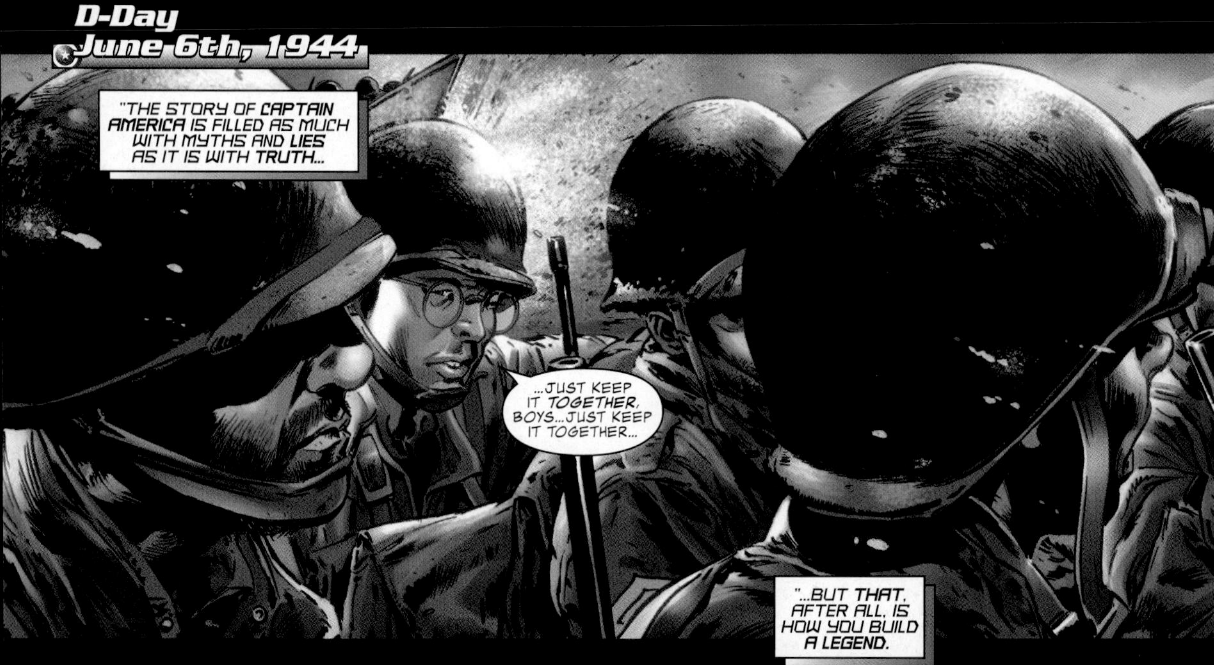
D-Day
June 6th, 1944
"THE STORY OF CAPTAIN AMERICA IS FILLED AS MUCH WITH MYTHS AND LIES AS IT IS WITH TRUTH...
...JUST KEEP IT TOGETHER, BOYS...JUST KEEP IT TOGETHER...
"...BUT THAT, AFTER ALL, IS HOW YOU BUILD A LEGEND.

"YOU LEAVE OUT THE UGLY BITS, THE DEATH AND HARDSHIP...

"...AND YOU FOCUS ON THE PARTS EVERYONE CAN DIGEST EASILY.

OKAY, MEN...BE READY...

"THE NATURAL BORN HERO...

...THIS IS GOING TO BE THE HARDEST DAY OF YOUR LIVES.

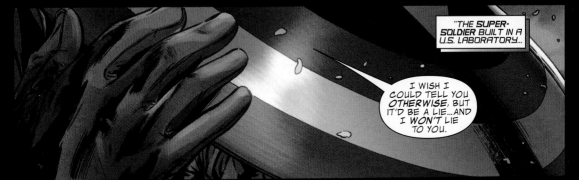

"THE SUPER-SOLDIER BUILT IN A U.S. LABORATORY...

I WISH I COULD TELL YOU OTHERWISE, BUT IT'D BE A LIE...AND I WON'T LIE TO YOU.

"THE FINEST OF HIS GENERATION...

SO KEEP YOUR HEADS LOW...FOLLOW MY LEAD...

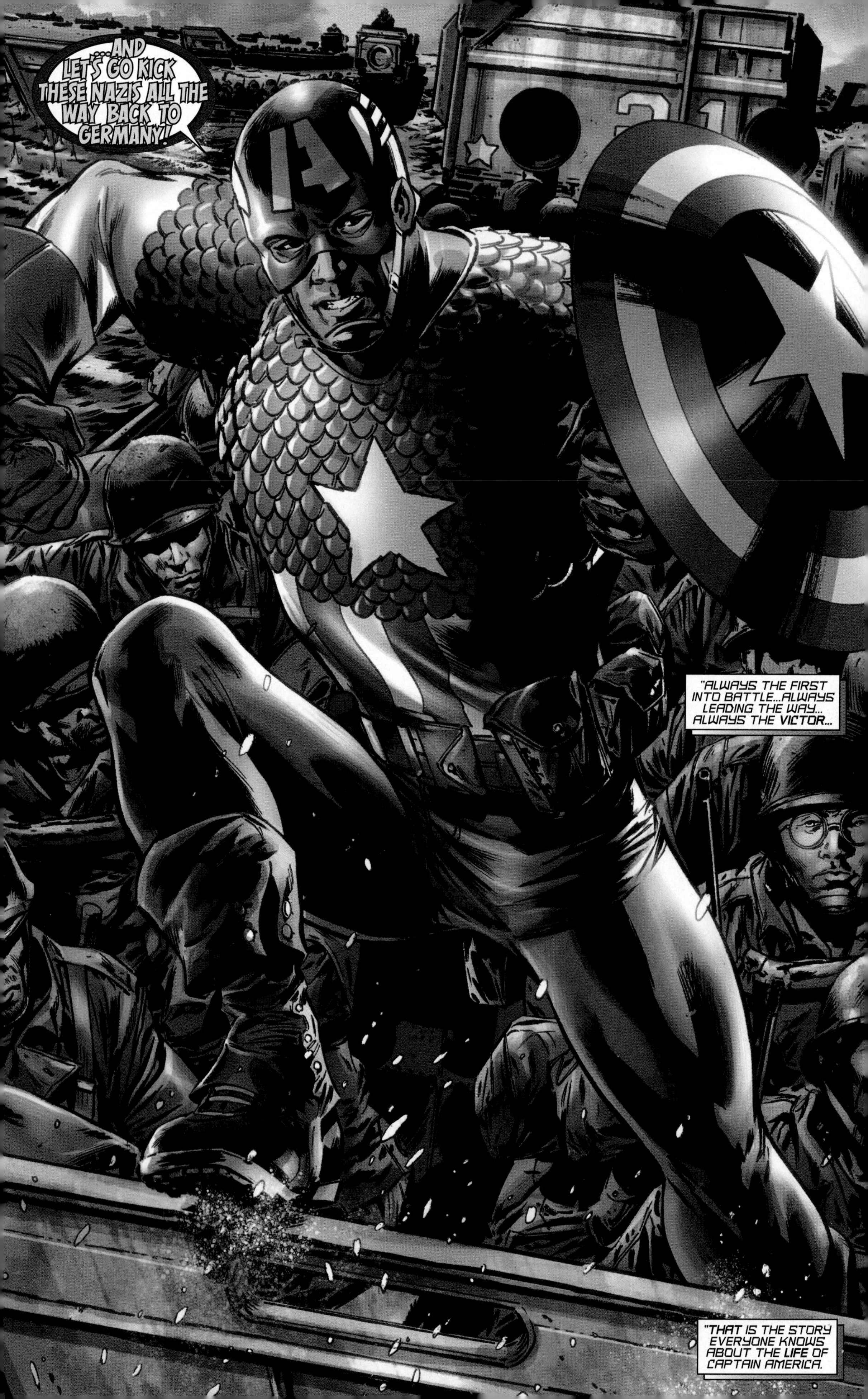
...AND LET'S GO KICK THESE NAZIS ALL THE WAY BACK TO GERMANY!
"ALWAYS THE FIRST INTO BATTLE...ALWAYS LEADING THE WAY... ALWAYS THE VICTOR...
"THAT IS THE STORY EVERYONE KNOWS ABOUT THE LIFE OF CAPTAIN AMERICA.

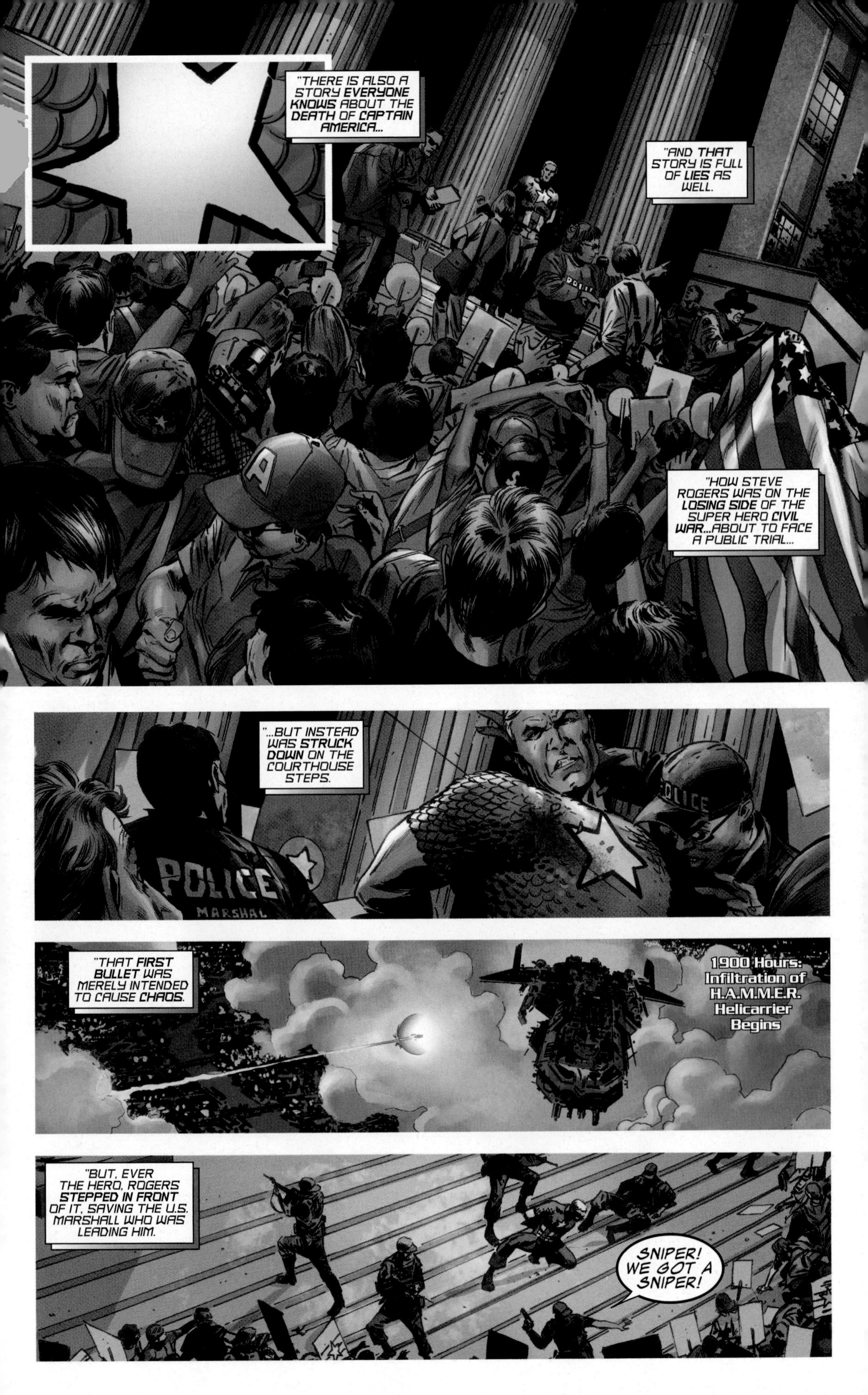
"THERE IS ALSO A STORY EVERYONE KNOWS ABOUT THE DEATH OF CAPTAIN AMERICA...
"AND THAT STORY IS FULL OF LIES AS WELL.
"HOW STEVE ROGERS WAS ON THE LOSING SIDE OF THE SUPER HERO CIVIL WAR...ABOUT TO FACE A PUBLIC TRIAL...
"...BUT INSTEAD WAS STRUCK DOWN ON THE COURTHOUSE STEPS.
POLICE
POLICE
MARSHAL
"THAT FIRST BULLET WAS MERELY INTENDED TO CAUSE CHAOS.
1900 Hours: Infiltration of H.A.M.M.E.R. Helicarrier Begins
"BUT, EVER THE HERO, ROGERS STEPPED IN FRONT OF IT, SAVING THE U.S. MARSHALL WHO WAS LEADING HIM.
SNIPER! WE GOT A SNIPER!

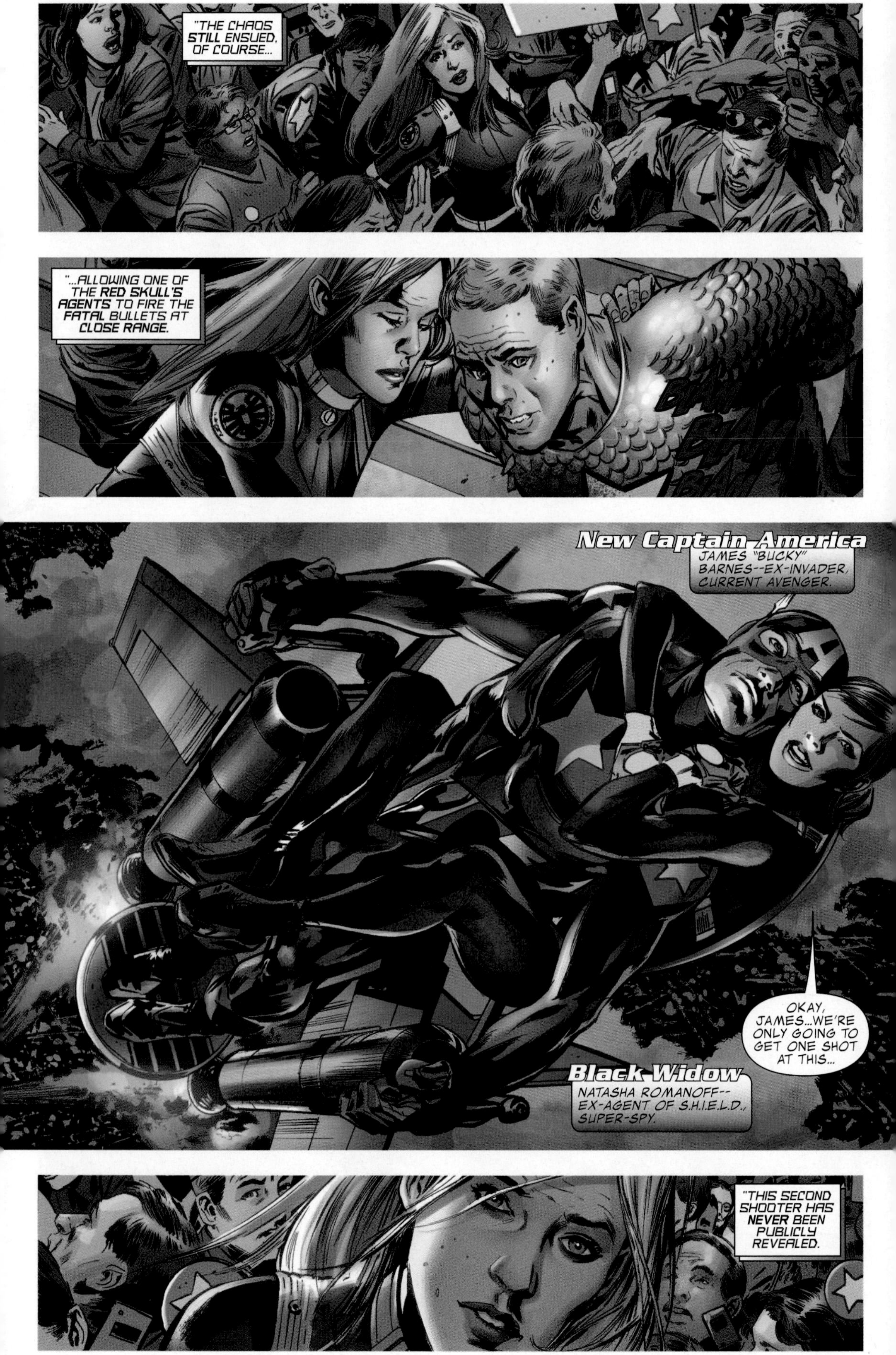
"THE CHAOS STILL ENSUED, OF COURSE...
"...ALLOWING ONE OF THE RED SKULL'S AGENTS TO FIRE THE FATAL BULLETS AT CLOSE RANGE.
New Captain America
JAMES "BUCKY" BARNES--EX-INVADER, CURRENT AVENGER.
OKAY, JAMES...WE'RE ONLY GOING TO GET ONE SHOT AT THIS...
Black Widow
NATASHA ROMANOFF--EX-AGENT OF S.H.I.E.L.D., SUPER-SPY.
"THIS SECOND SHOOTER HAS NEVER BEEN PUBLICLY REVEALED.

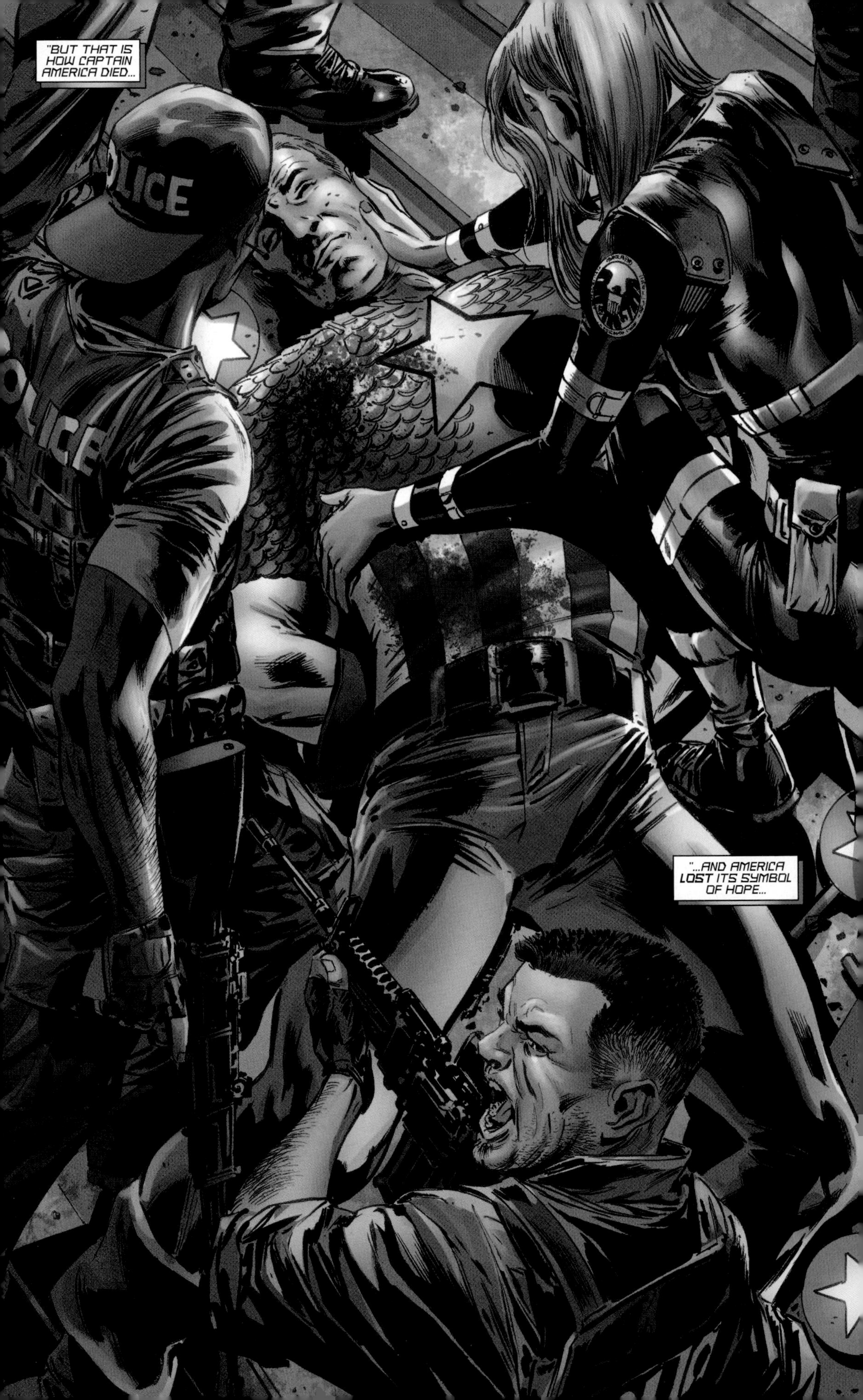
"BUT THAT IS HOW CAPTAIN AMERICA DIED...
"...AND AMERICA LOST ITS SYMBOL OF HOPE...

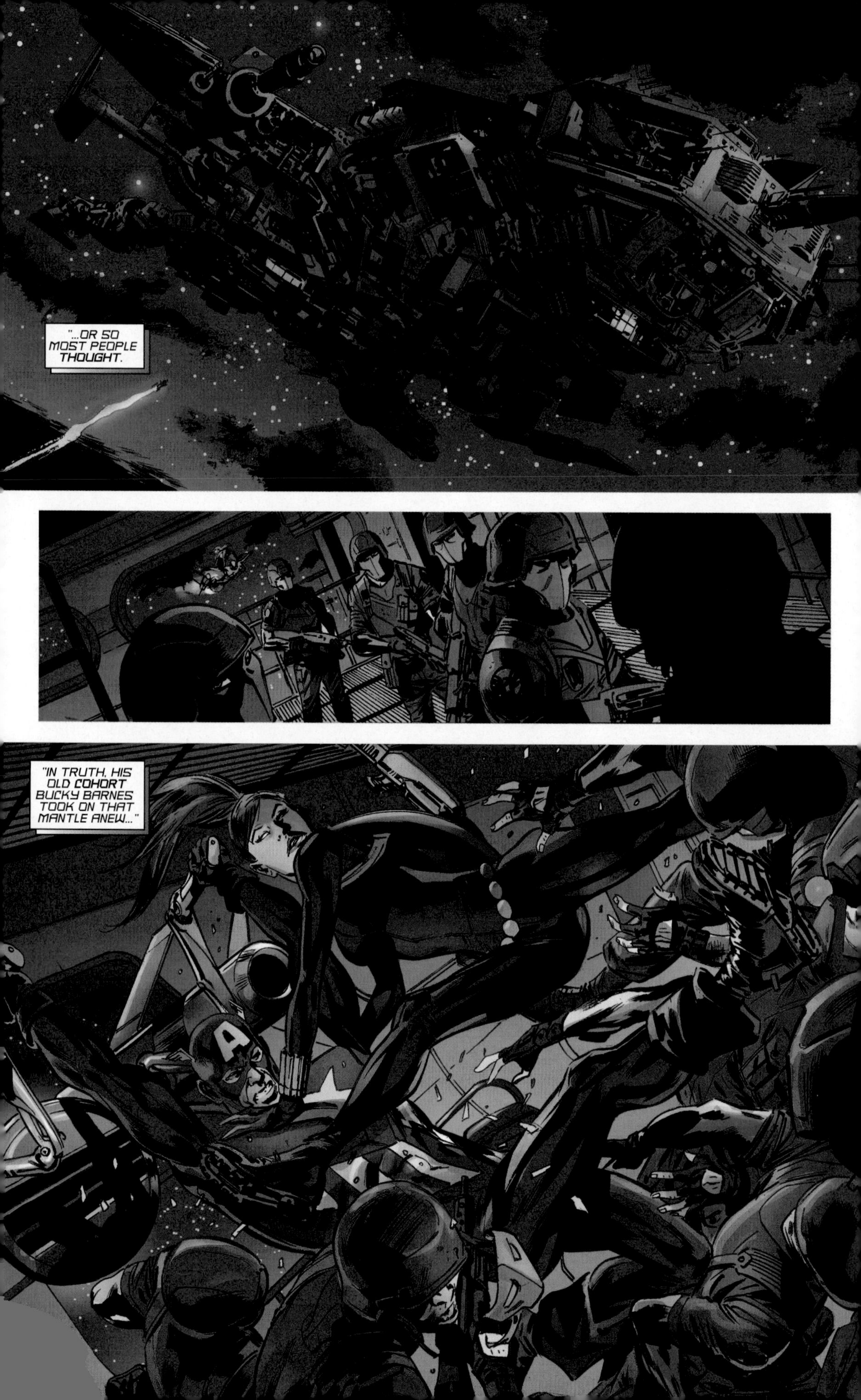
"...OR SO MOST PEOPLE THOUGHT.
"IN TRUTH, HIS OLD COHORT BUCKY BARNES TOOK ON THAT MANTLE ANEW..."

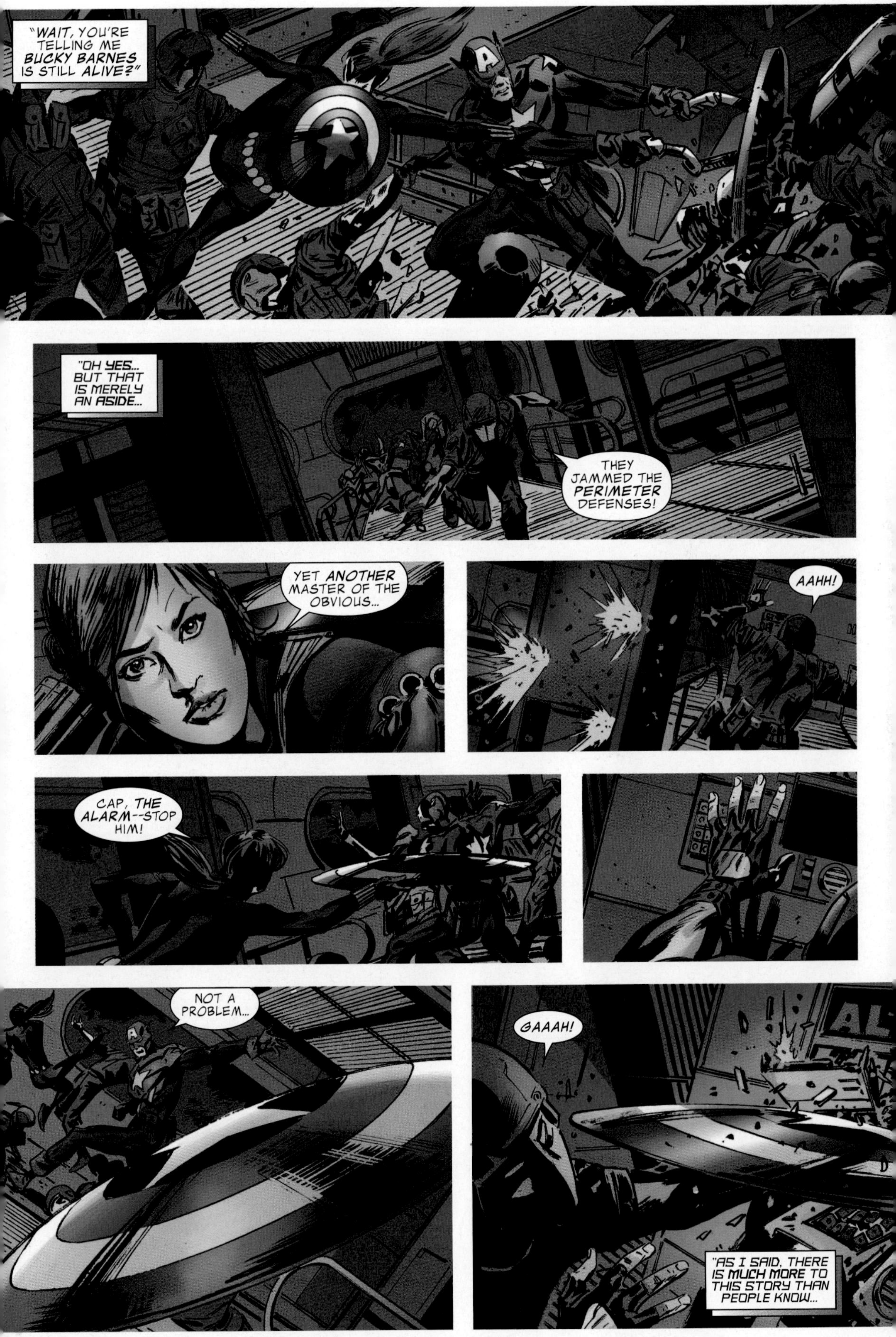
"WAIT, YOU'RE TELLING ME BUCKY BARNES IS STILL ALIVE?"
"OH YES... BUT THAT IS MERELY AN ASIDE...
THEY JAMMED THE PERIMETER DEFENSES!
YET ANOTHER MASTER OF THE OBVIOUS...
AAHH!
CAP, THE ALARM--STOP HIM!
NOT A PROBLEM...
GAAAH!
"AS I SAID, THERE IS MUCH MORE TO THIS STORY THAN PEOPLE KNOW...

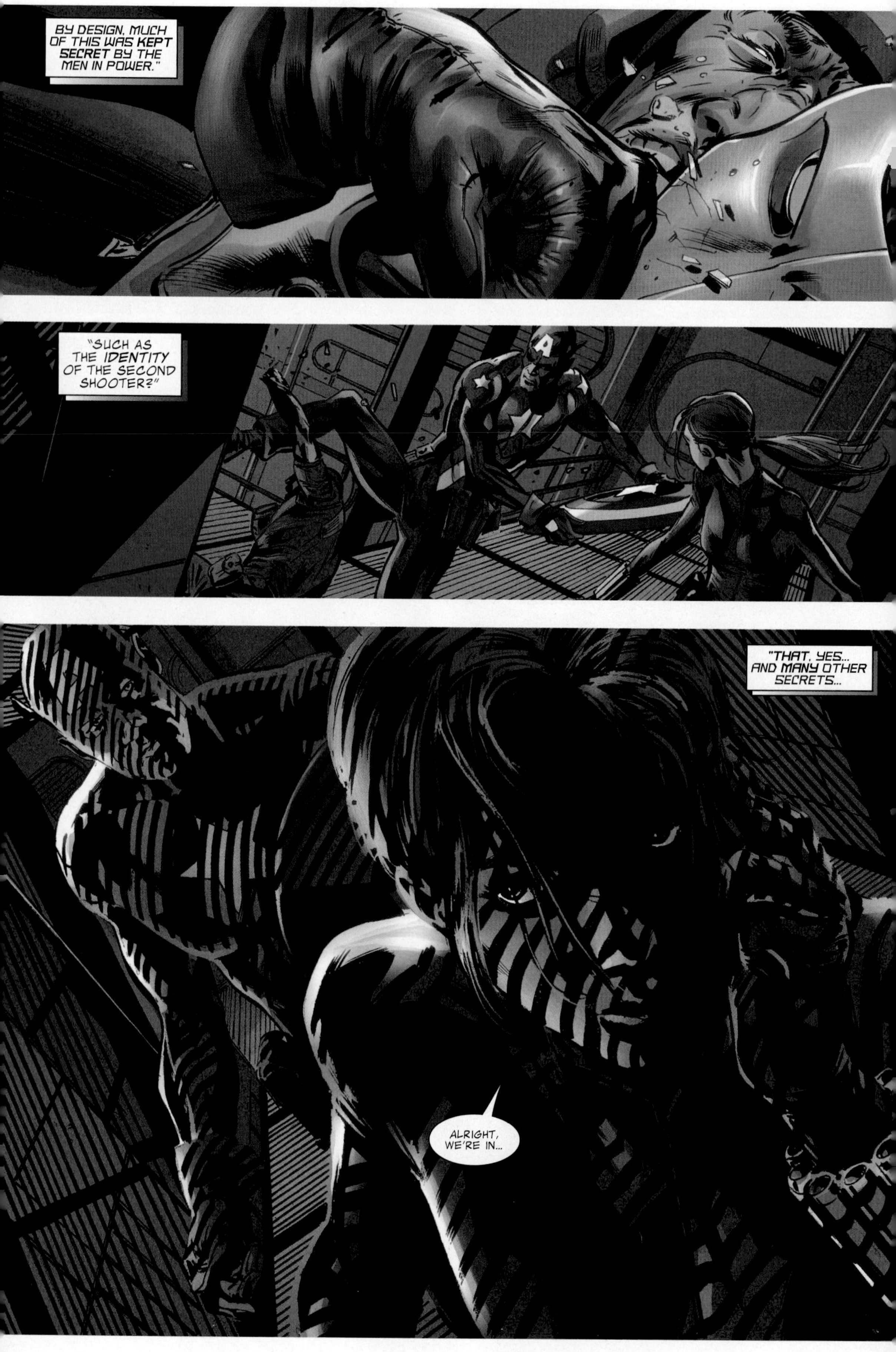
BY DESIGN, MUCH OF THIS WAS KEPT SECRET BY THE MEN IN POWER."
"SUCH AS THE IDENTITY OF THE SECOND SHOOTER?"
"THAT, YES... AND MANY OTHER SECRETS...
ALRIGHT, WE'RE IN...

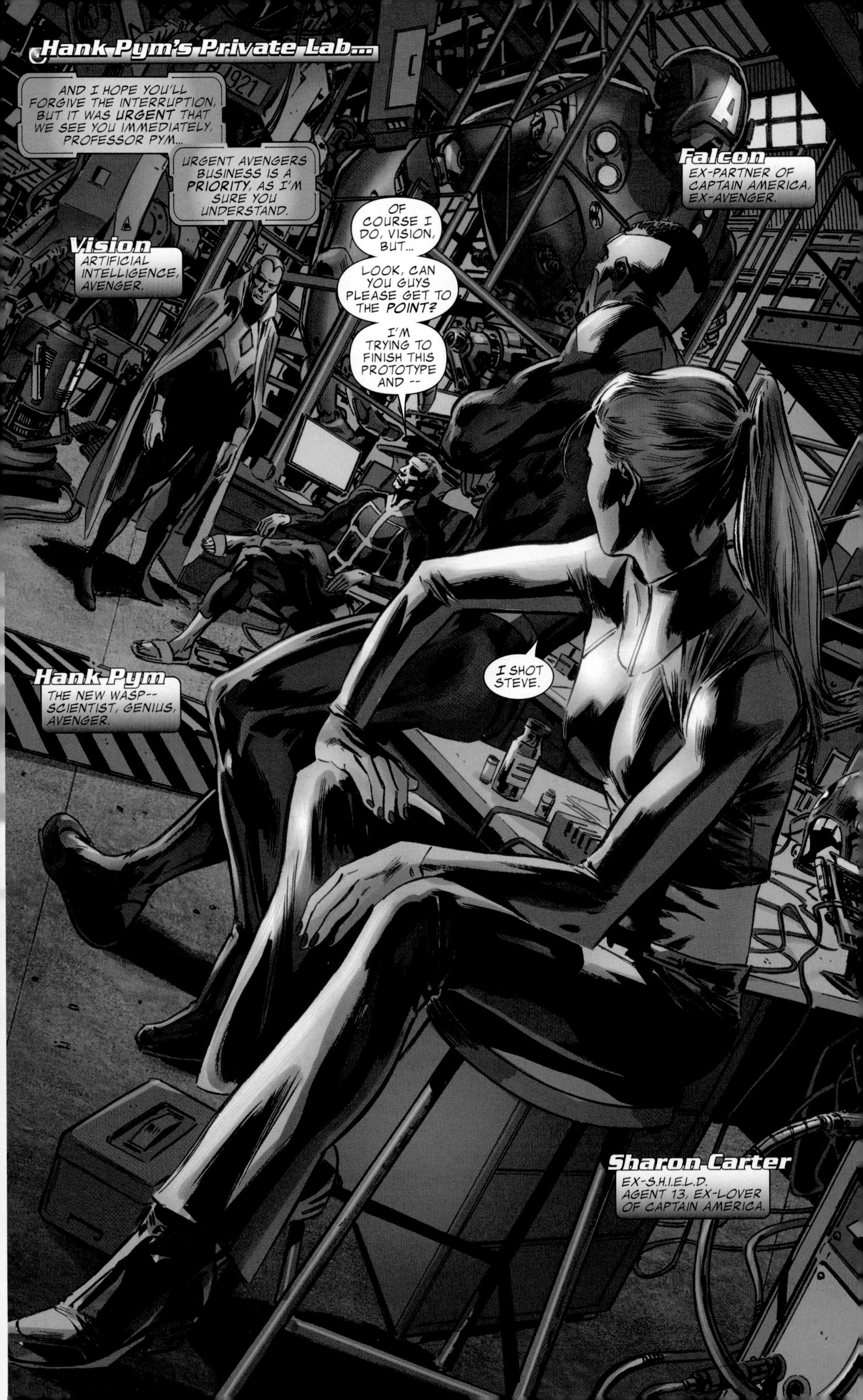

Hank Pym's Private Lab...
AND I HOPE YOU'LL FORGIVE THE INTERRUPTION, BUT IT WAS URGENT THAT WE SEE YOU IMMEDIATELY, PROFESSOR PYM...
URGENT AVENGERS BUSINESS IS A PRIORITY, AS I'M SURE YOU UNDERSTAND.
Vision
ARTIFICIAL INTELLIGENCE, AVENGER.
OF COURSE I DO, VISION, BUT...
LOOK, CAN YOU GUYS PLEASE GET TO THE POINT?
I'M TRYING TO FINISH THIS PROTOTYPE AND --
Falcon
EX-PARTNER OF CAPTAIN AMERICA, EX-AVENGER.
Hank Pym
THE NEW WASP-- SCIENTIST, GENIUS, AVENGER.
I SHOT STEVE.
Sharon Carter
EX-S.H.I.E.L.D. AGENT 13. EX-LOVER OF CAPTAIN AMERICA.

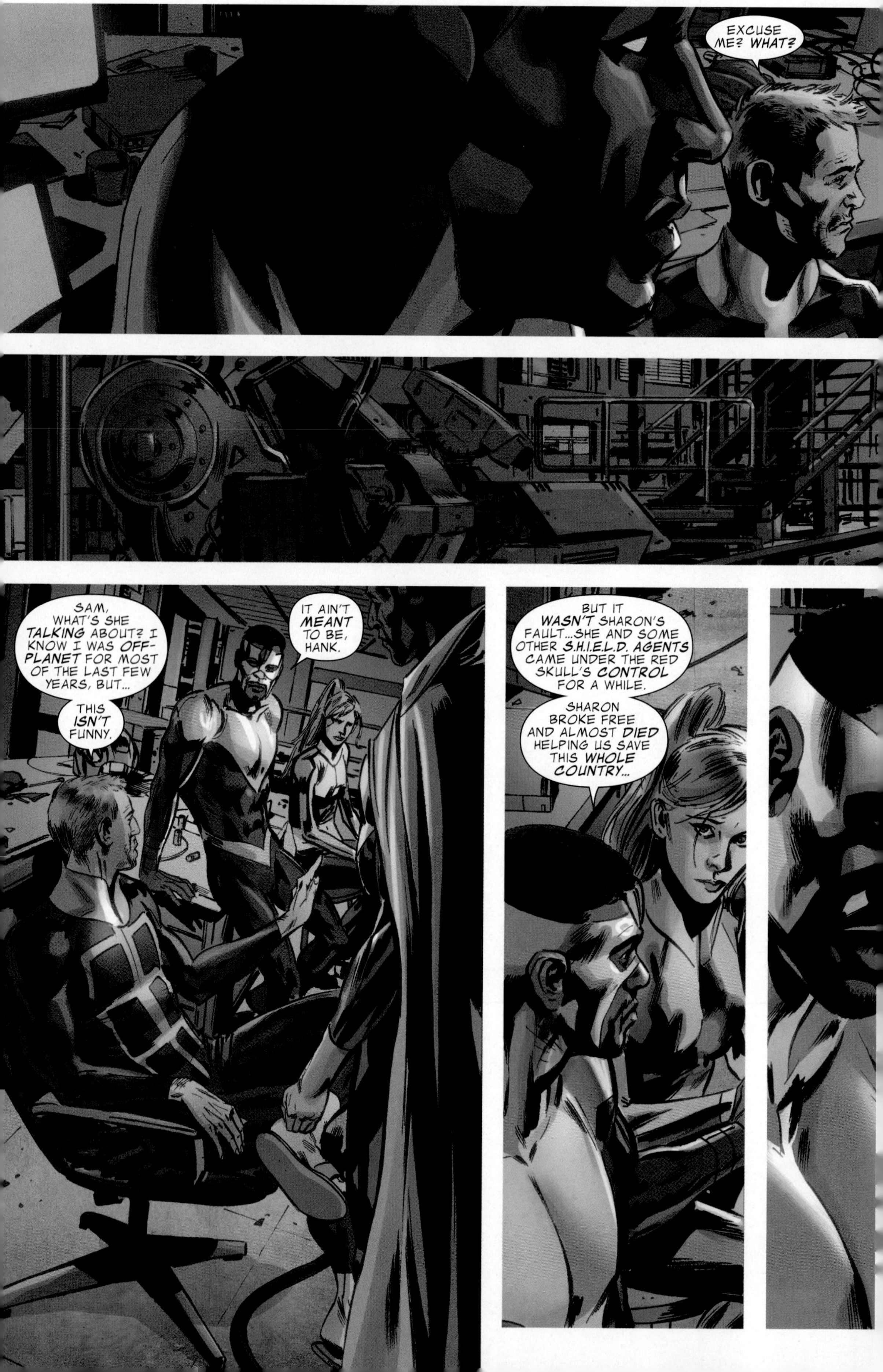
EXCUSE ME? WHAT?
SAM, WHAT'S SHE TALKING ABOUT? I KNOW I WAS OFF-PLANET FOR MOST OF THE LAST FEW YEARS, BUT...
THIS ISN'T FUNNY.
IT AIN'T MEANT TO BE, HANK.
BUT IT WASN'T SHARON'S FAULT...SHE AND SOME OTHER S.H.I.E.L.D. AGENTS CAME UNDER THE RED SKULL'S CONTROL FOR A WHILE.
SHARON BROKE FREE AND ALMOST DIED HELPING US SAVE THIS WHOLE COUNTRY...

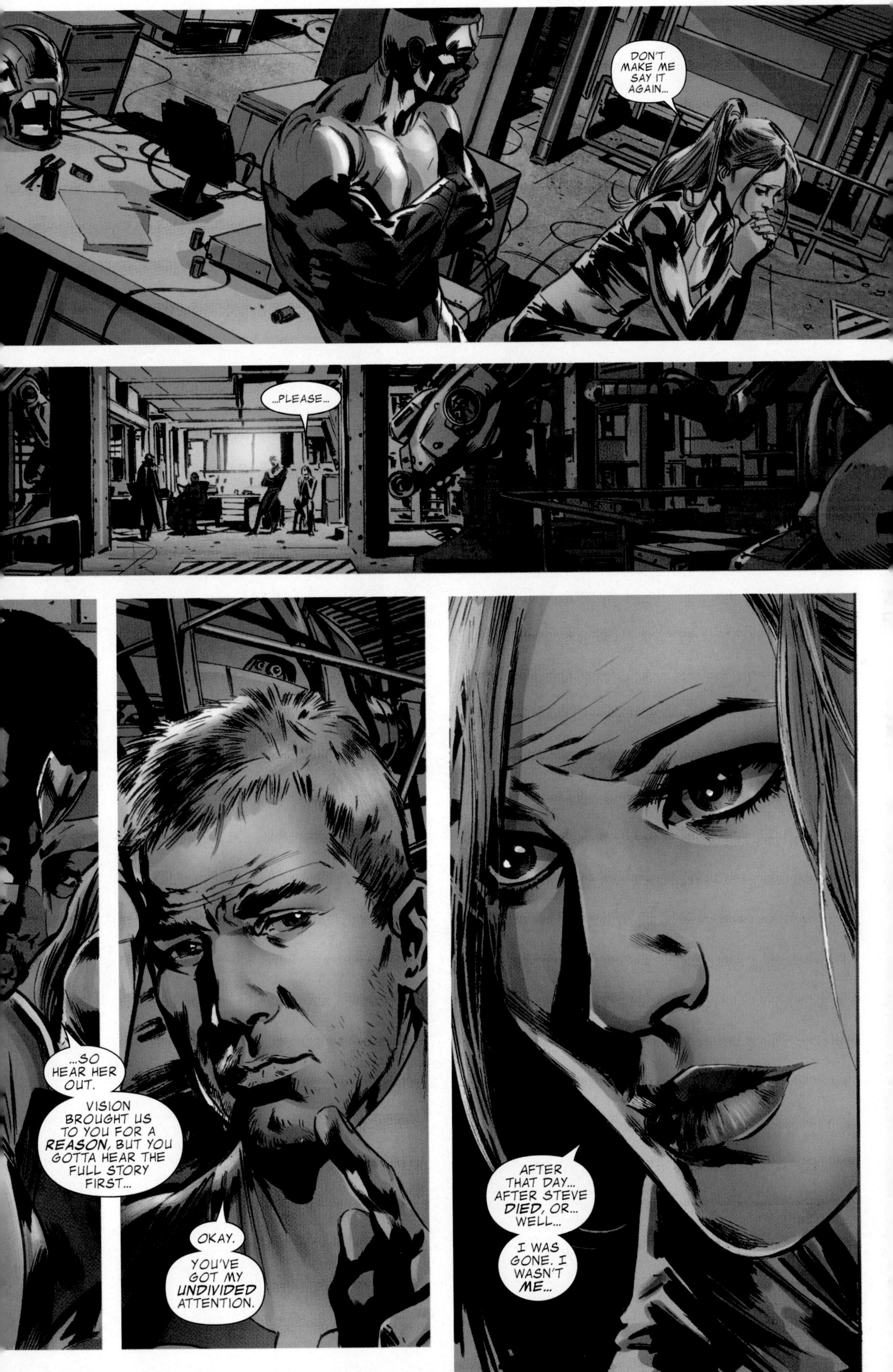
DON'T MAKE ME SAY IT AGAIN...
...PLEASE...
...SO HEAR HER OUT.
VISION BROUGHT US TO YOU FOR A REASON, BUT YOU GOTTA HEAR THE FULL STORY FIRST...
OKAY.
YOU'VE GOT MY UNDIVIDED ATTENTION.
AFTER THAT DAY... AFTER STEVE DIED, OR... WELL...
I WAS GONE. I WASN'T ME...

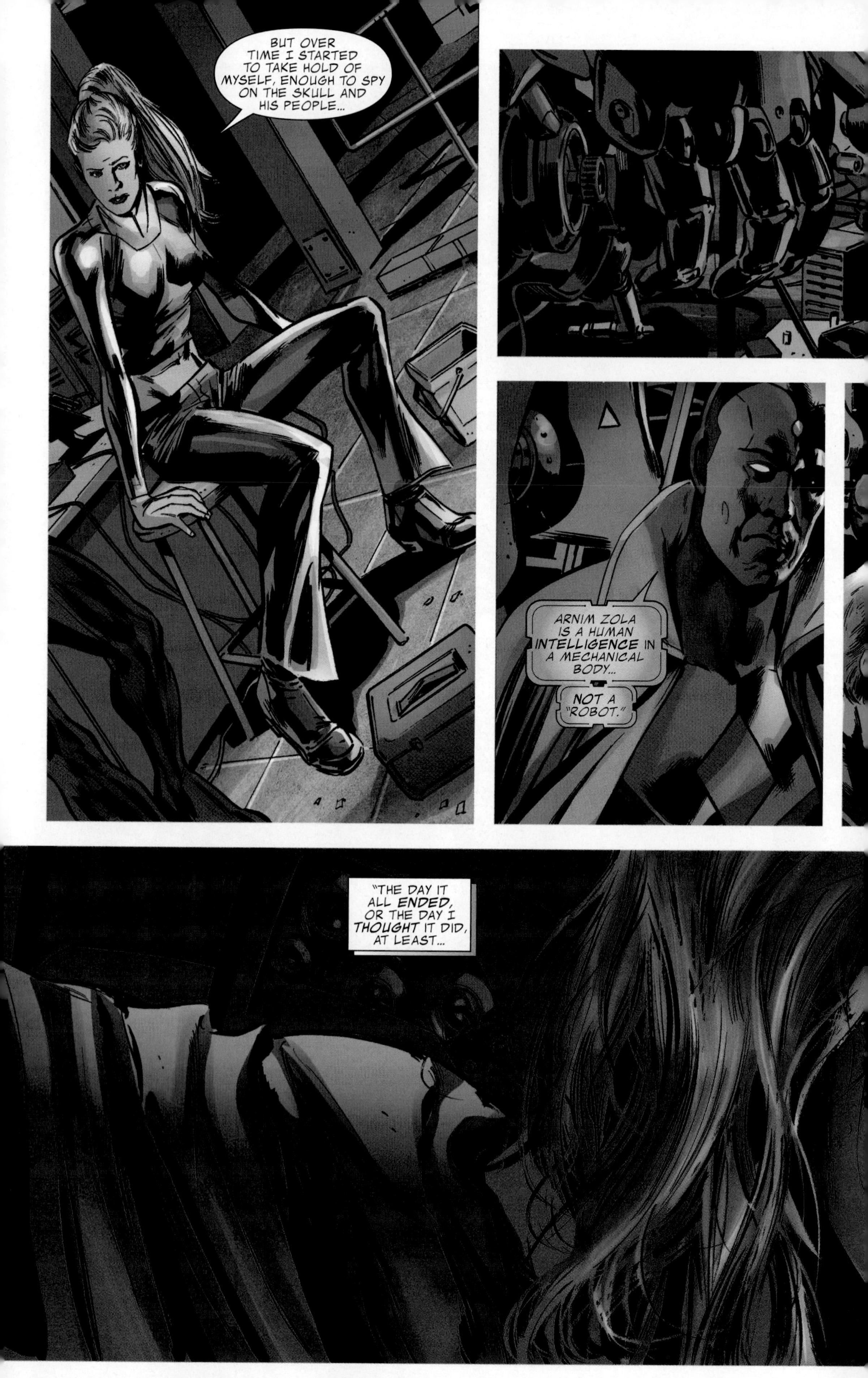

BUT OVER TIME I STARTED TO TAKE HOLD OF MYSELF, ENOUGH TO SPY ON THE SKULL AND HIS PEOPLE...
ARNIM ZOLA IS A HUMAN INTELLIGENCE IN A MECHANICAL BODY...
NOT A "ROBOT."
"THE DAY IT ALL ENDED, OR THE DAY I THOUGHT IT DID, AT LEAST...

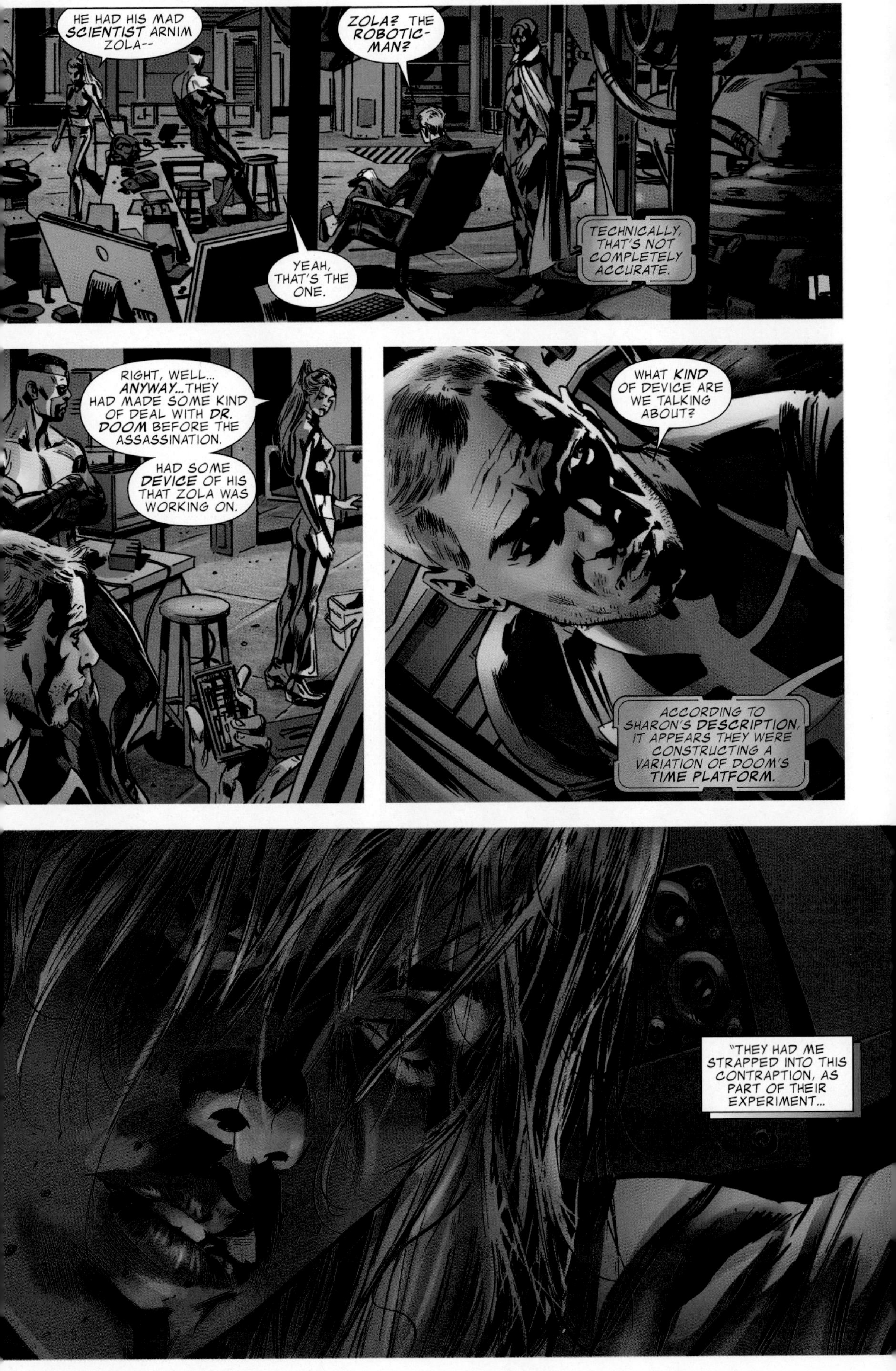
HE HAD HIS MAD SCIENTIST ARNIM ZOLA--
ZOLA? THE ROBOTIC-MAN?
YEAH, THAT'S THE ONE.
TECHNICALLY, THAT'S NOT COMPLETELY ACCURATE.
RIGHT, WELL... ANYWAY... THEY HAD MADE SOME KIND OF DEAL WITH DR. DOOM BEFORE THE ASSASSINATION.
HAD SOME DEVICE OF HIS THAT ZOLA WAS WORKING ON.
WHAT KIND OF DEVICE ARE WE TALKING ABOUT?
ACCORDING TO SHARON'S DESCRIPTION, IT APPEARS THEY WERE CONSTRUCTING A VARIATION OF DOOM'S TIME PLATFORM.
"THEY HAD ME STRAPPED INTO THIS CONTRAPTION, AS PART OF THEIR EXPERIMENT...

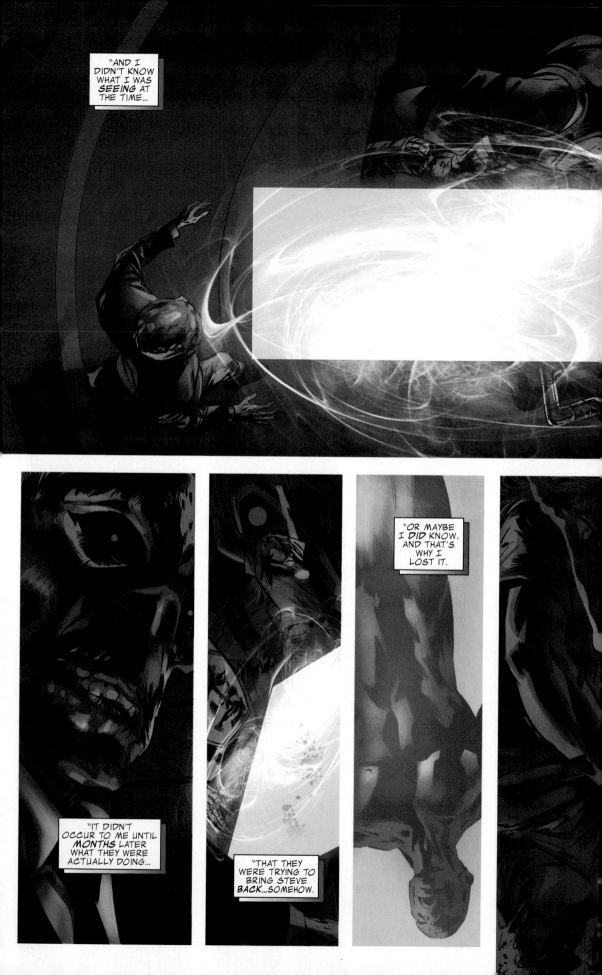

"AND I DIDN'T KNOW WHAT I WAS *SEEING* AT THE TIME...

"OR MAYBE I *DID* KNOW, AND THAT'S WHY I LOST IT.

"IT DIDN'T OCCUR TO ME UNTIL *MONTHS* LATER WHAT THEY WERE ACTUALLY DOING...

"THAT THEY WERE TRYING TO BRING STEVE *BACK*...SOMEHOW.

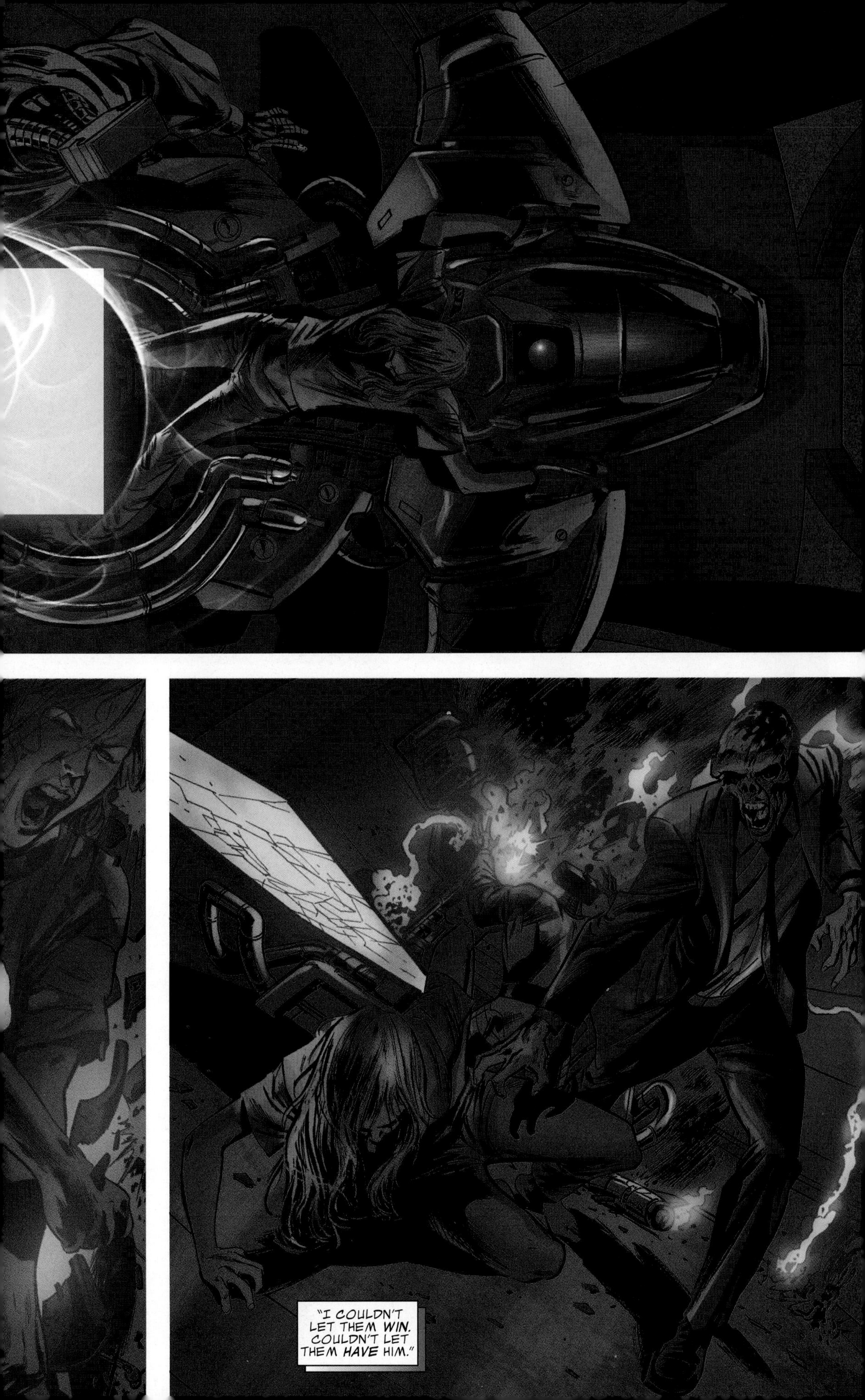
"I COULDN'T LET THEM WIN. COULDN'T LET THEM HAVE HIM."

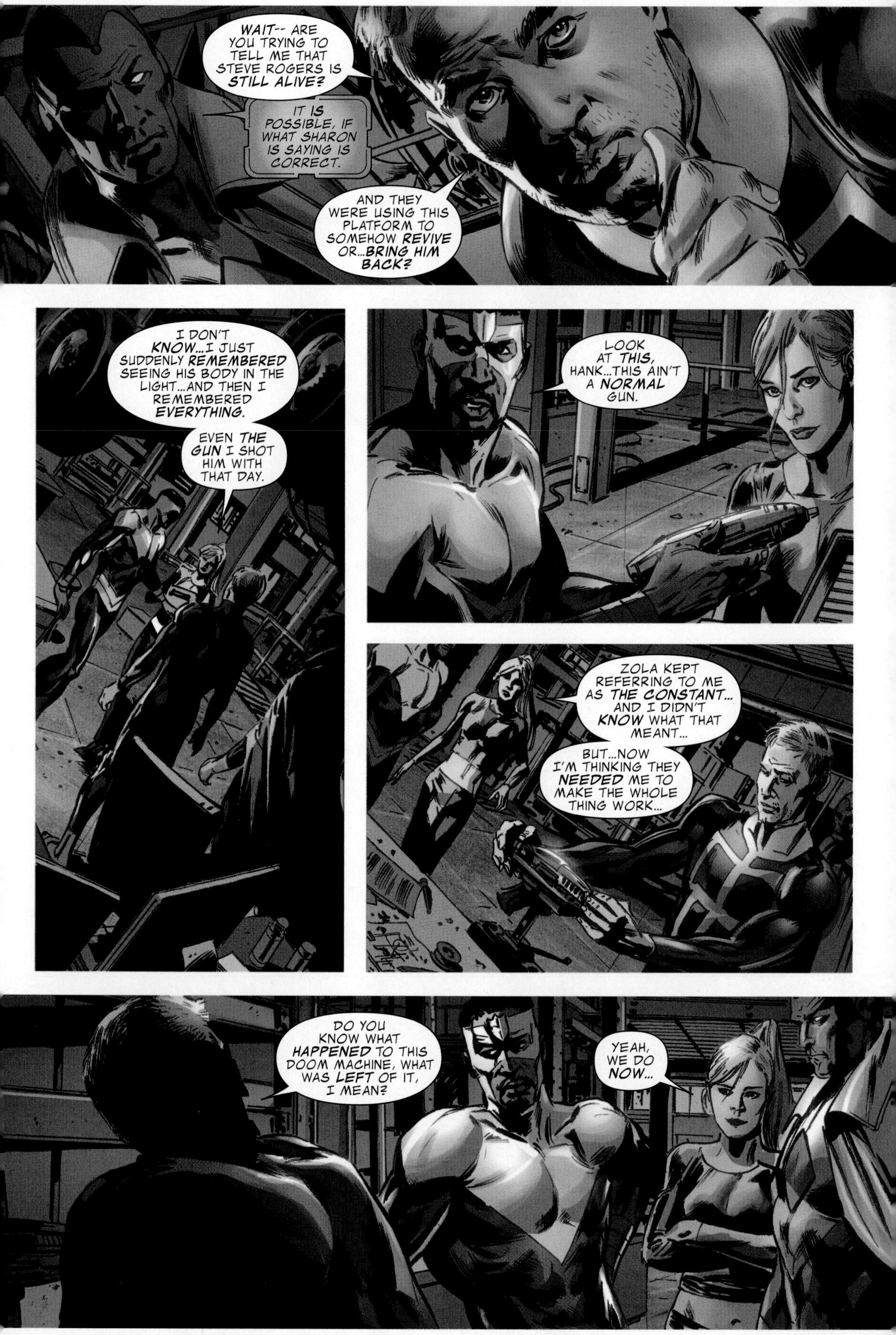
WAIT-- ARE YOU TRYING TO TELL ME THAT STEVE ROGERS IS STILL ALIVE?
IT IS POSSIBLE, IF WHAT SHARON IS SAYING IS CORRECT.
AND THEY WERE USING THIS PLATFORM TO SOMEHOW REVIVE OR...BRING HIM BACK?
I DON'T KNOW...I JUST SUDDENLY REMEMBERED SEEING HIS BODY IN THE LIGHT...AND THEN I REMEMBERED EVERYTHING.
EVEN THE GUN I SHOT HIM WITH THAT DAY.
LOOK AT THIS, HANK...THIS AIN'T A NORMAL GUN.
ZOLA KEPT REFERRING TO ME AS THE CONSTANT... AND I DIDN'T KNOW WHAT THAT MEANT...
BUT...NOW I'M THINKING THEY NEEDED ME TO MAKE THE WHOLE THING WORK...
DO YOU KNOW WHAT HAPPENED TO THIS DOOM MACHINE, WHAT WAS LEFT OF IT, I MEAN?
YEAH, WE DO NOW...

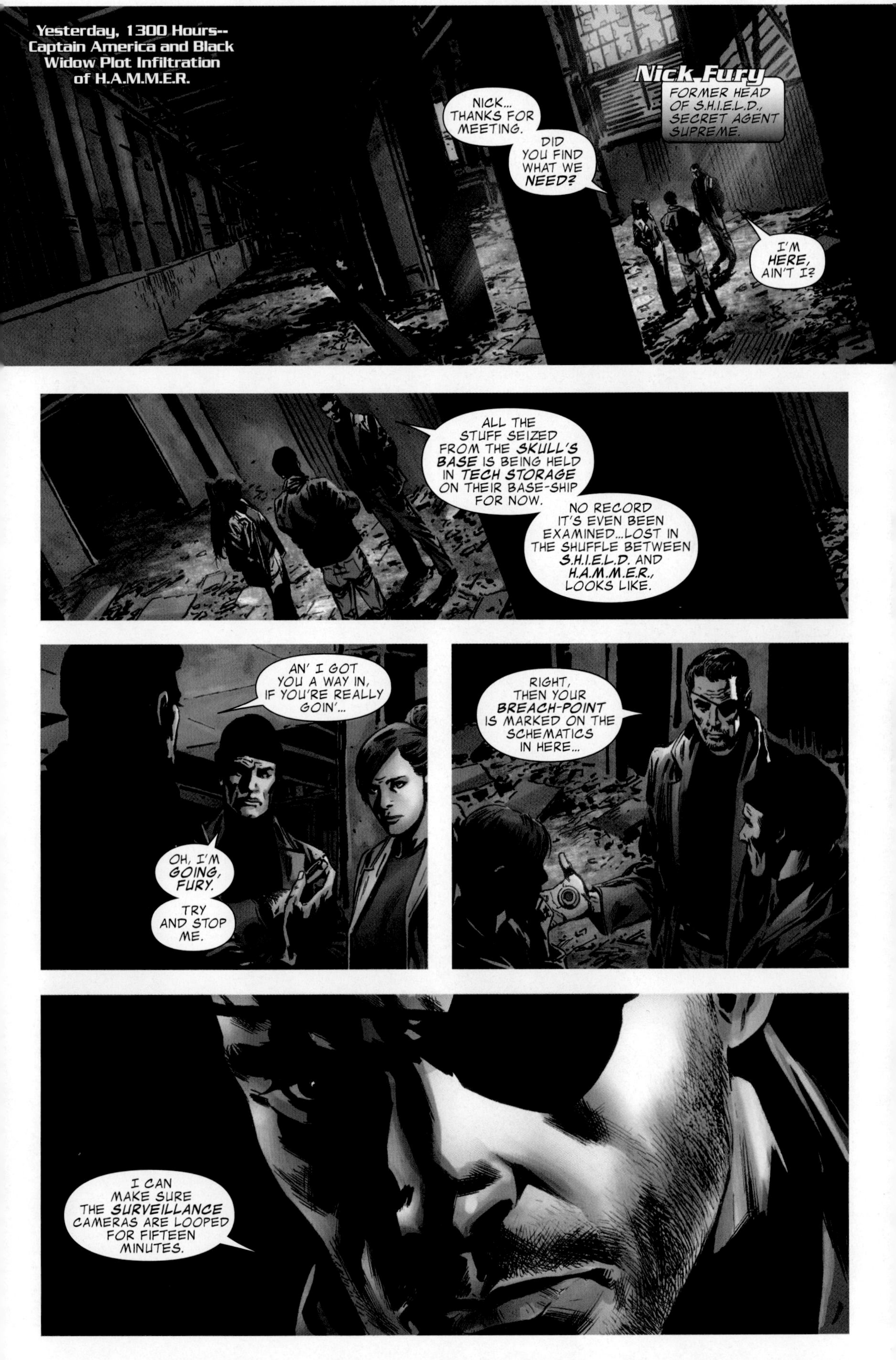
Yesterday, 1300 Hours--
Captain America and Black Widow Plot Infiltration of H.A.M.M.E.R.
Nick Fury
FORMER HEAD OF S.H.I.E.L.D., SECRET AGENT SUPREME.
NICK... THANKS FOR MEETING.
DID YOU FIND WHAT WE NEED?
I'M HERE, AIN'T I?
ALL THE STUFF SEIZED FROM THE SKULL'S BASE IS BEING HELD IN TECH STORAGE ON THEIR BASE-SHIP FOR NOW.
NO RECORD IT'S EVEN BEEN EXAMINED...LOST IN THE SHUFFLE BETWEEN S.H.I.E.L.D. AND H.A.M.M.E.R., LOOKS LIKE.
AN' I GOT YOU A WAY IN, IF YOU'RE REALLY GOIN'...
OH, I'M GOING, FURY.
TRY AND STOP ME.
RIGHT, THEN YOUR BREACH-POINT IS MARKED ON THE SCHEMATICS IN HERE...
I CAN MAKE SURE THE SURVEILLANCE CAMERAS ARE LOOPED FOR FIFTEEN MINUTES.

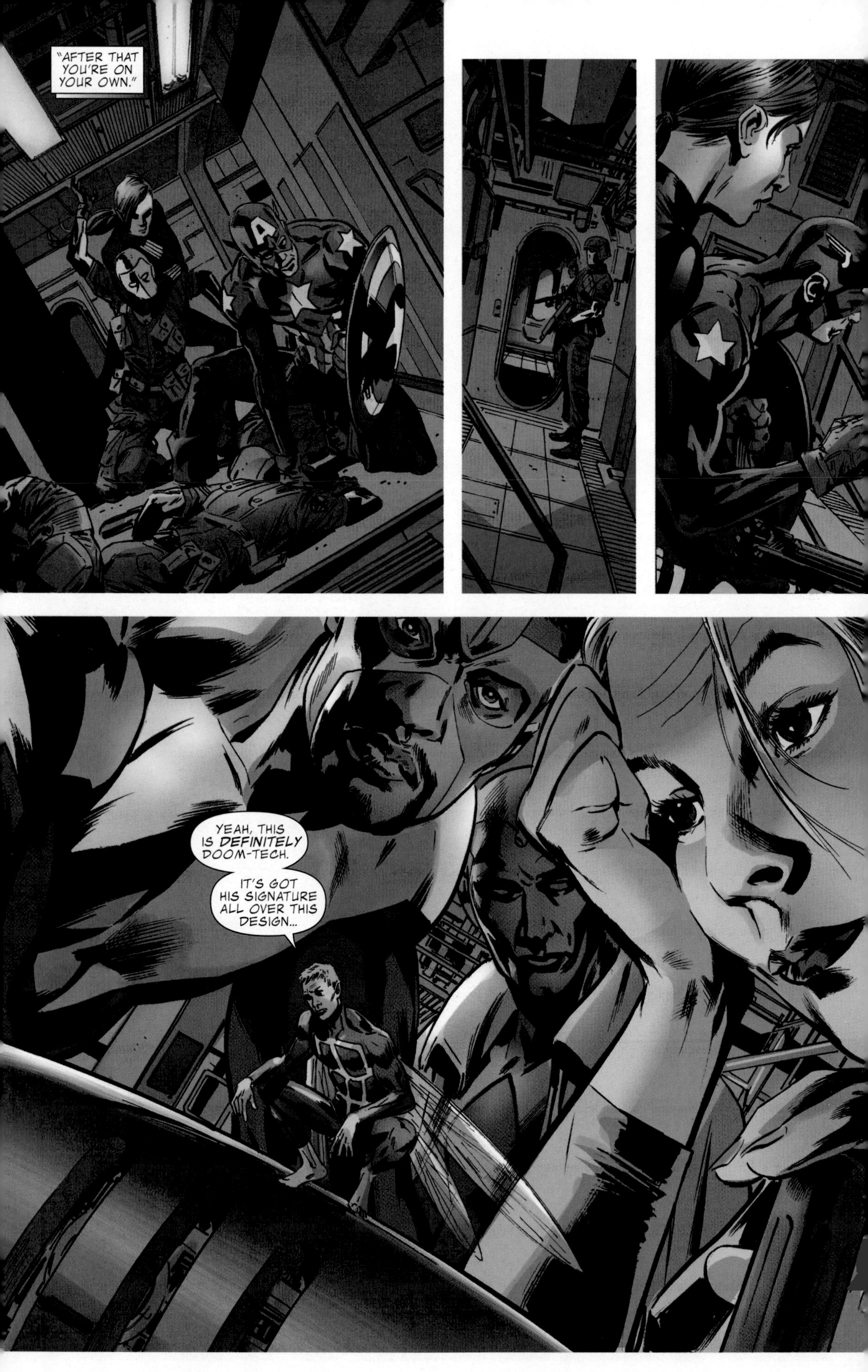
"AFTER THAT YOU'RE ON YOUR OWN."
YEAH, THIS IS *DEFINITELY* DOOM-TECH.
IT'S GOT HIS SIGNATURE ALL OVER THIS DESIGN...

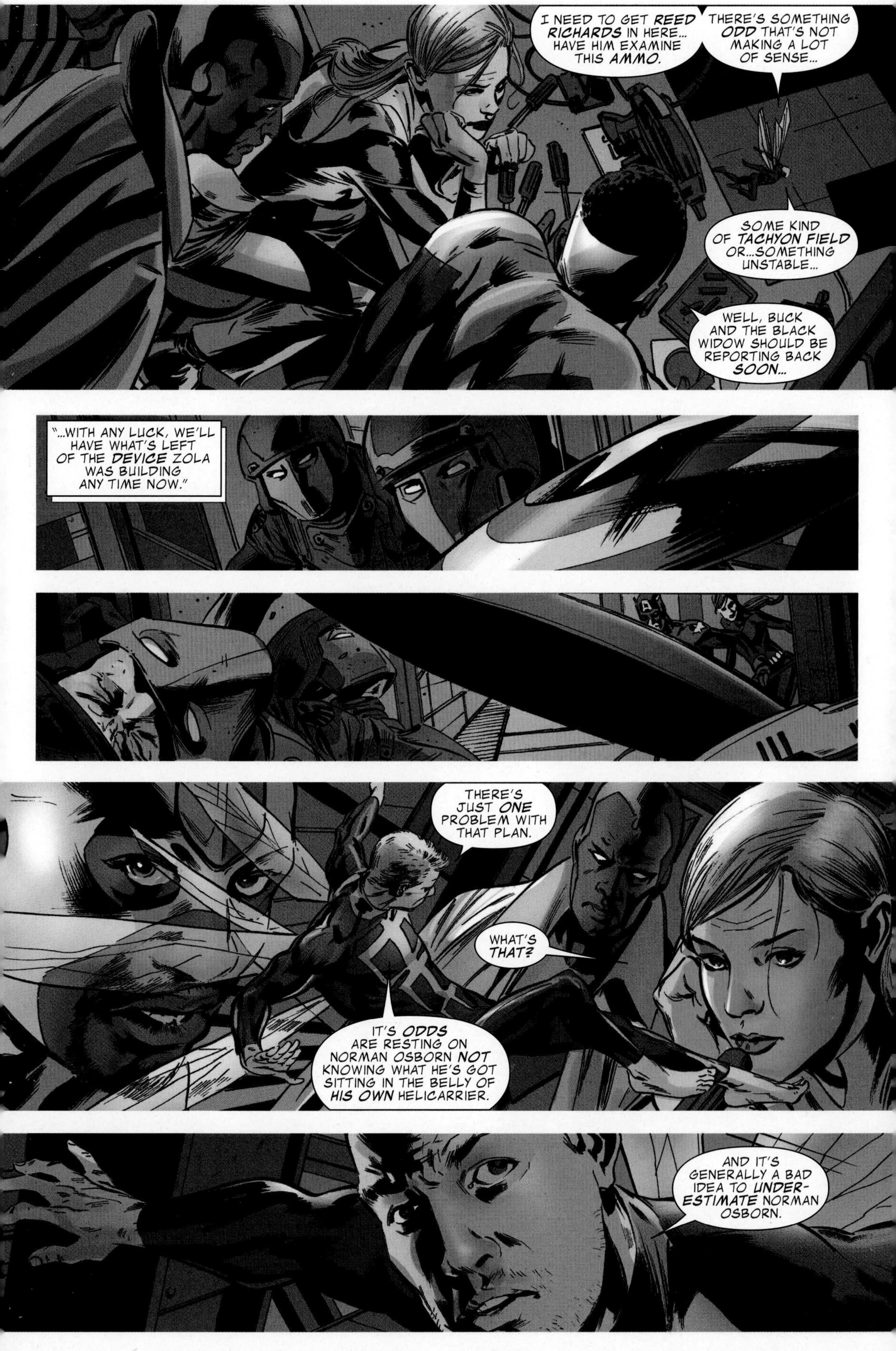
I NEED TO GET REED RICHARDS IN HERE... HAVE HIM EXAMINE THIS AMMO.
THERE'S SOMETHING ODD THAT'S NOT MAKING A LOT OF SENSE...
SOME KIND OF TACHYON FIELD OR...SOMETHING UNSTABLE...
WELL, BUCK AND THE BLACK WIDOW SHOULD BE REPORTING BACK SOON...
"...WITH ANY LUCK, WE'LL HAVE WHAT'S LEFT OF THE DEVICE ZOLA WAS BUILDING ANY TIME NOW."
THERE'S JUST ONE PROBLEM WITH THAT PLAN.
WHAT'S THAT?
IT'S ODDS ARE RESTING ON NORMAN OSBORN NOT KNOWING WHAT HE'S GOT SITTING IN THE BELLY OF HIS OWN HELICARRIER.
AND IT'S GENERALLY A BAD IDEA TO UNDER-ESTIMATE NORMAN OSBORN.

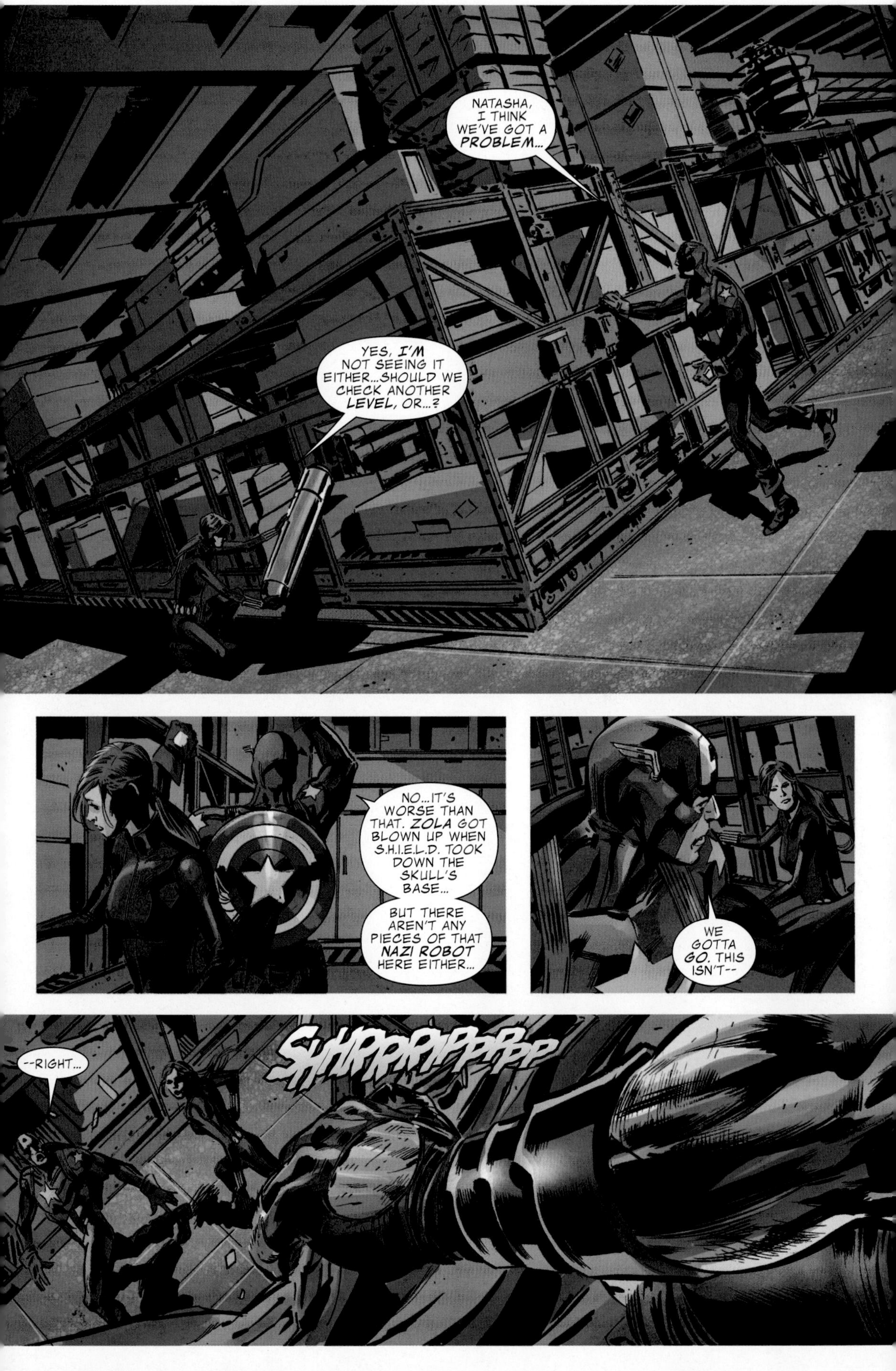
NATASHA, I THINK WE'VE GOT A PROBLEM...
YES, I'M NOT SEEING IT EITHER...SHOULD WE CHECK ANOTHER LEVEL, OR...?
NO...IT'S WORSE THAN THAT. ZOLA GOT BLOWN UP WHEN S.H.I.E.L.D. TOOK DOWN THE SKULL'S BASE...
BUT THERE AREN'T ANY PIECES OF THAT NAZI ROBOT HERE EITHER...
WE GOTTA GO. THIS ISN'T--
SHHRRRIPPPPP
--RIGHT...

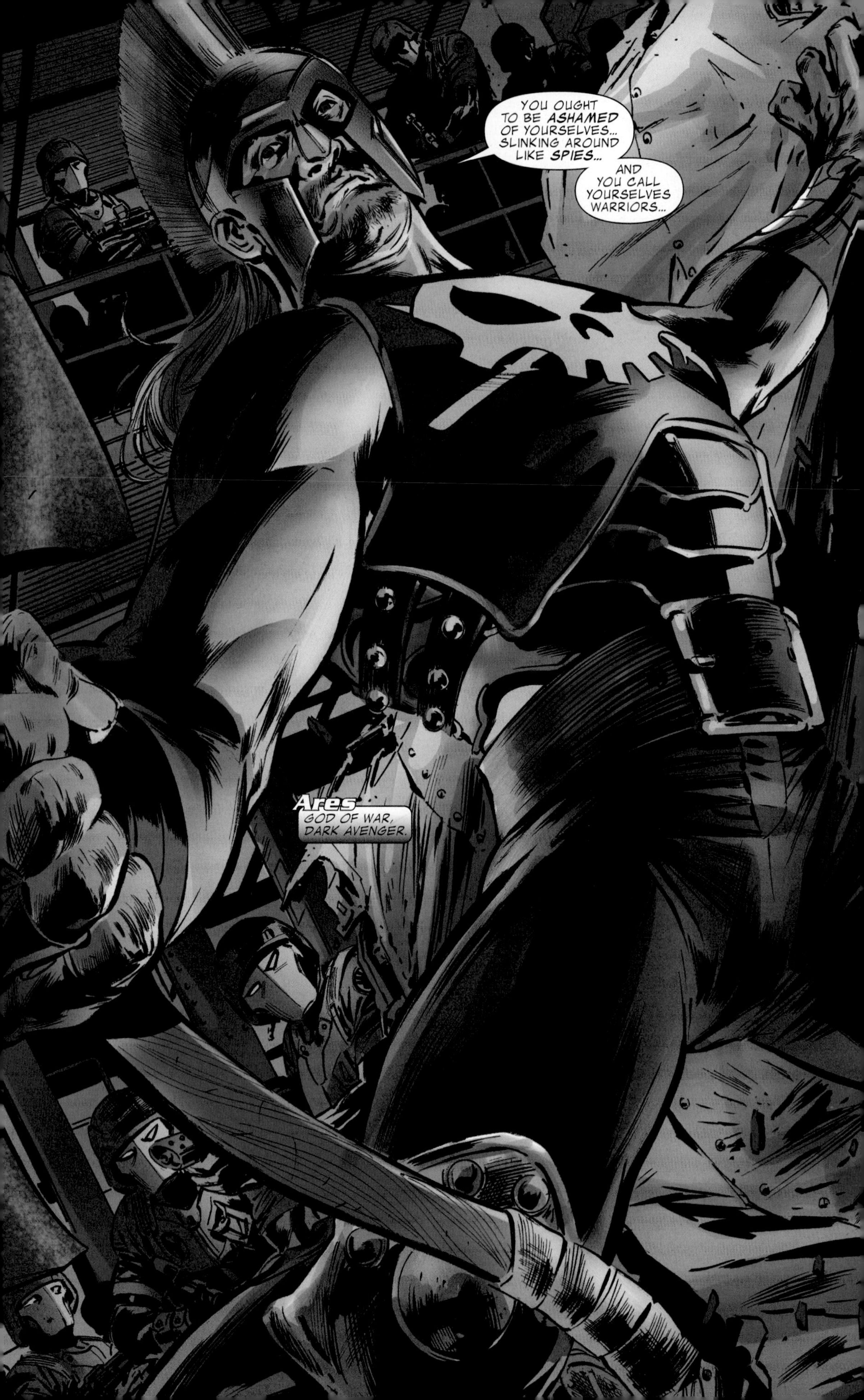
YOU OUGHT TO BE ASHAMED OF YOURSELVES... SLINKING AROUND LIKE SPIES...
AND YOU CALL YOURSELVES WARRIORS...
Ares
GOD OF WAR, DARK AVENGER.

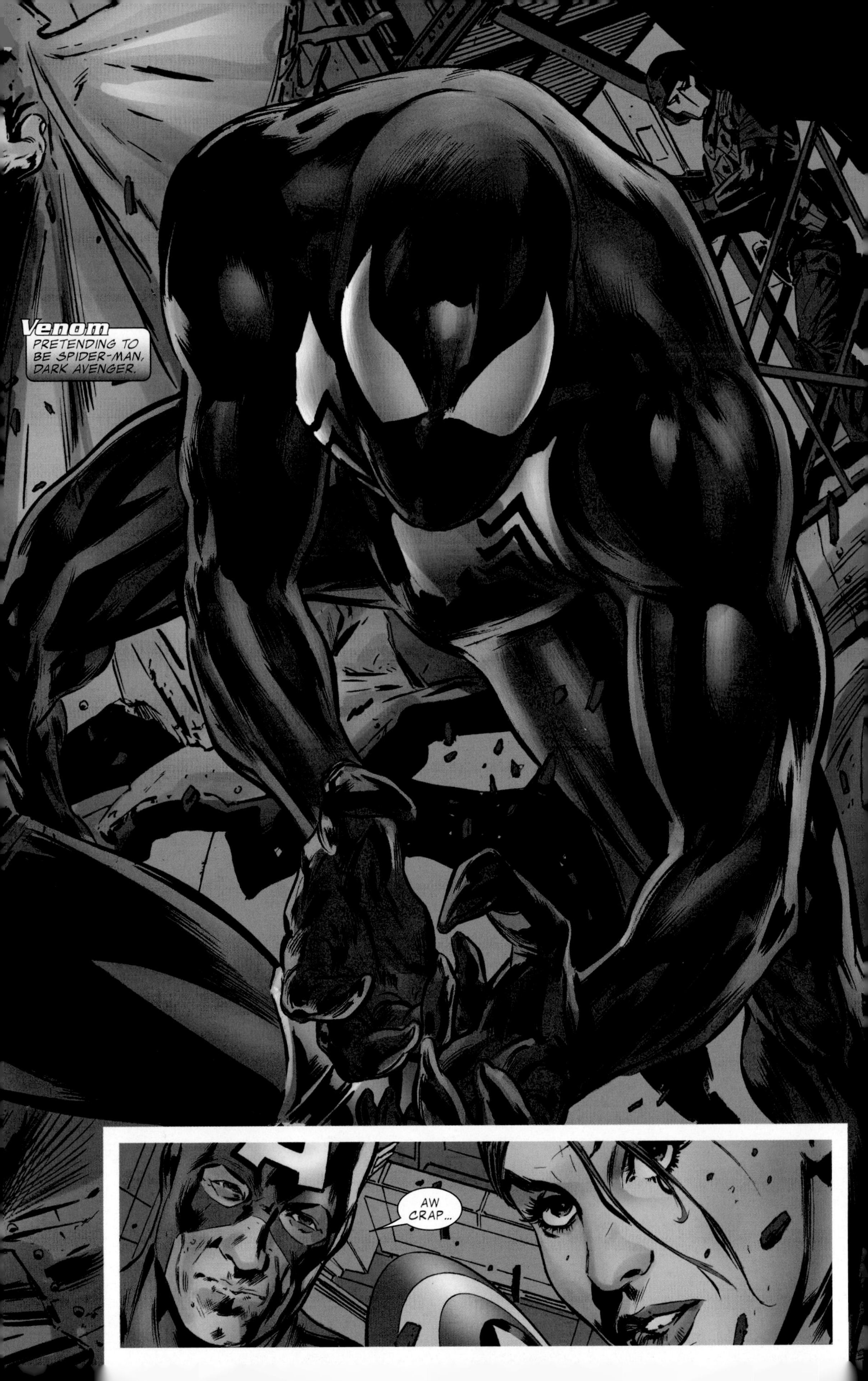
Venom
PRETENDING TO BE SPIDER-MAN, DARK AVENGER.
AW CRAP...

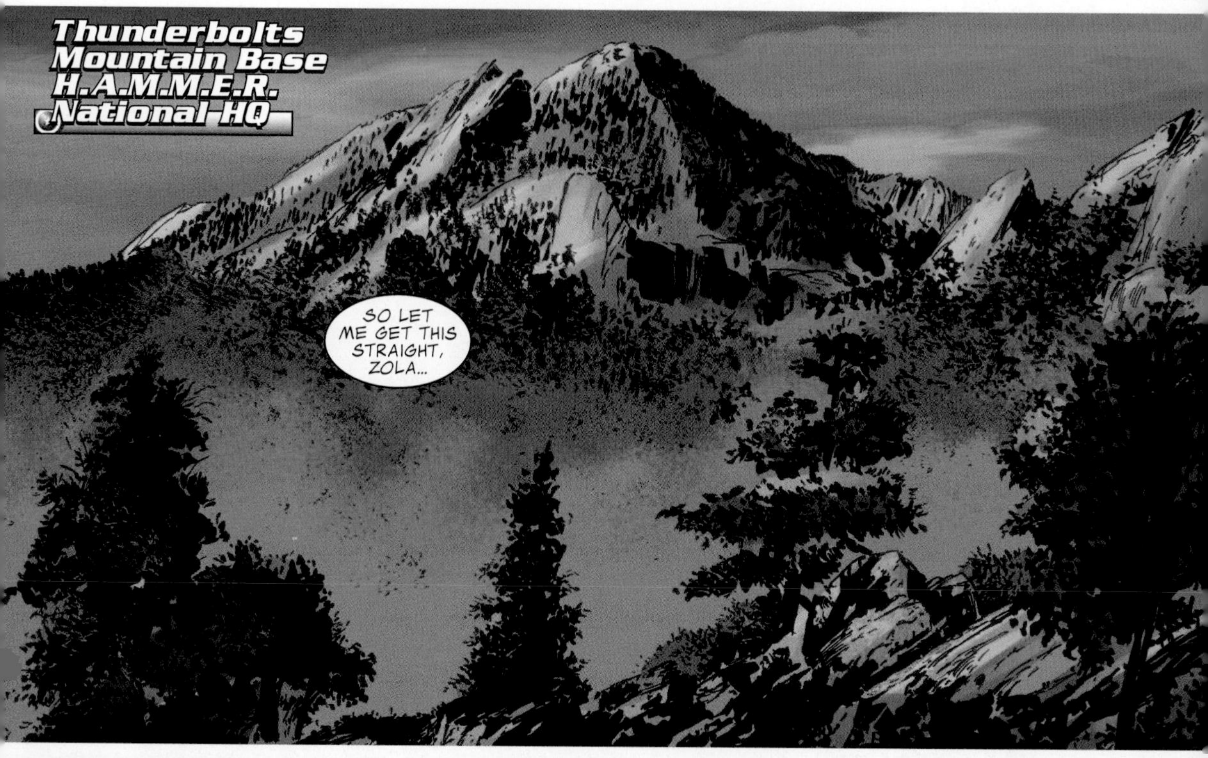
Thunderbolts Mountain Base H.A.M.M.E.R. National HQ
SO LET ME GET THIS STRAIGHT, ZOLA...

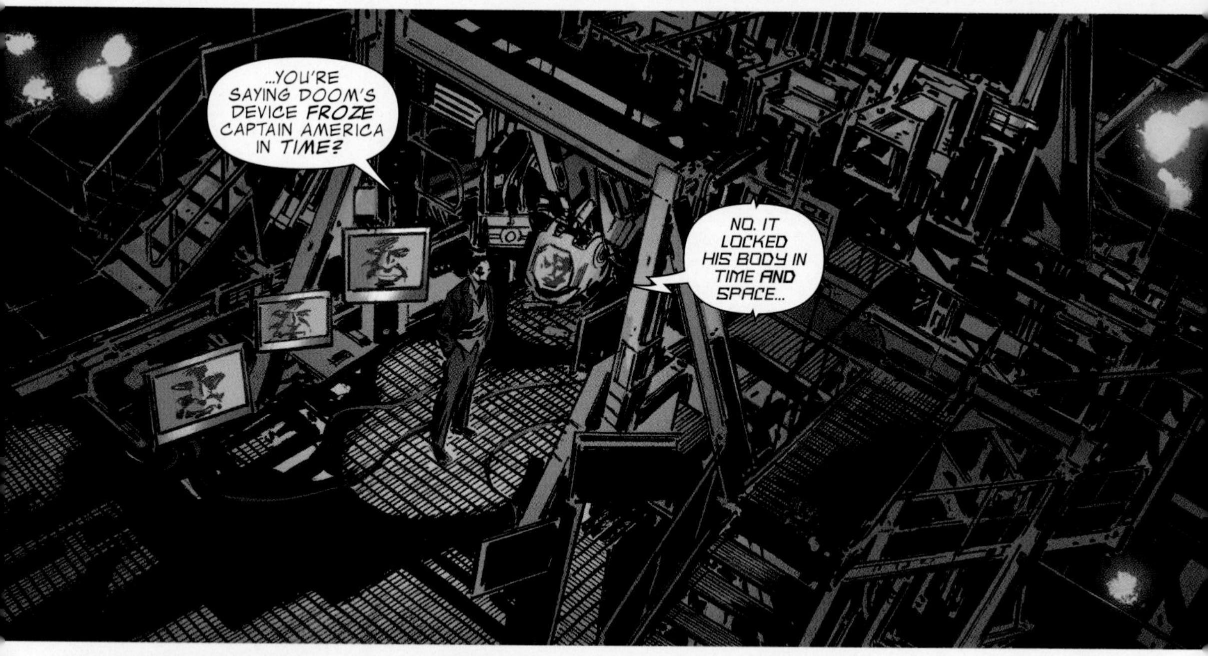
...YOU'RE SAYING DOOM'S DEVICE FROZE CAPTAIN AMERICA IN TIME?
NO. IT LOCKED HIS BODY IN TIME AND SPACE...

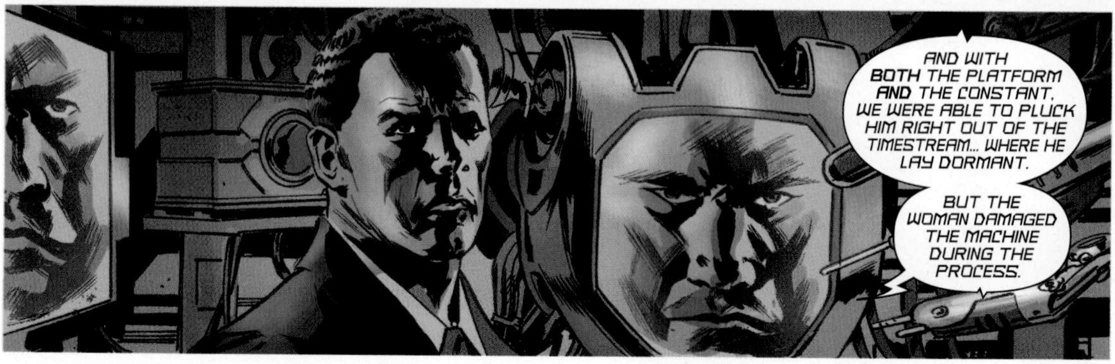
AND WITH BOTH THE PLATFORM AND THE CONSTANT, WE WERE ABLE TO PLUCK HIM RIGHT OUT OF THE TIMESTREAM... WHERE HE LAY DORMANT.
BUT THE WOMAN DAMAGED THE MACHINE DURING THE PROCESS.

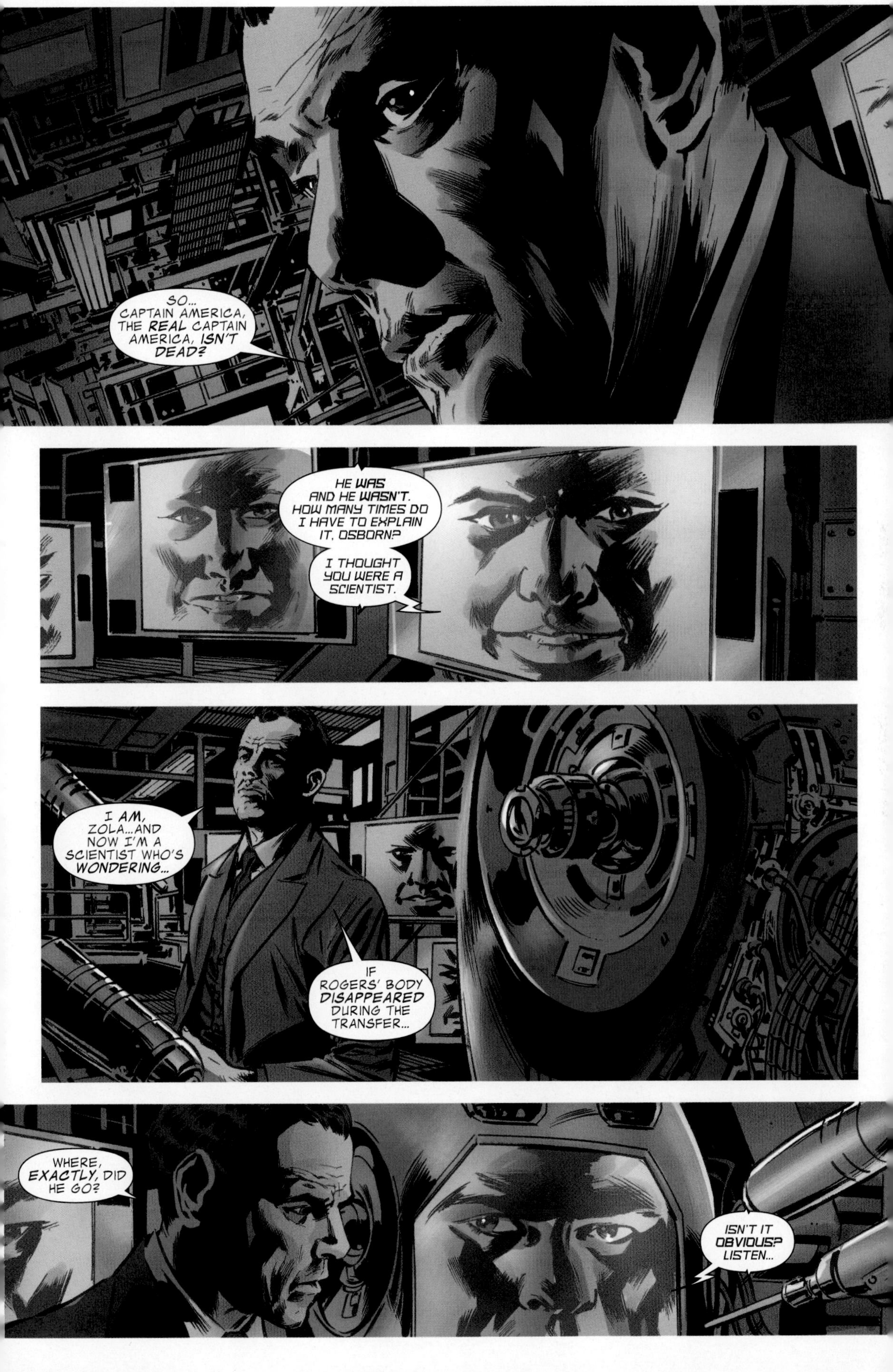
SO... CAPTAIN AMERICA, THE REAL CAPTAIN AMERICA, ISN'T DEAD?
HE WAS AND HE WASN'T. HOW MANY TIMES DO I HAVE TO EXPLAIN IT, OSBORN?
I THOUGHT YOU WERE A SCIENTIST.
I AM, ZOLA...AND NOW I'M A SCIENTIST WHO'S WONDERING...
IF ROGERS' BODY DISAPPEARED DURING THE TRANSFER...
WHERE, EXACTLY, DID HE GO?
ISN'T IT OBVIOUS? LISTEN...

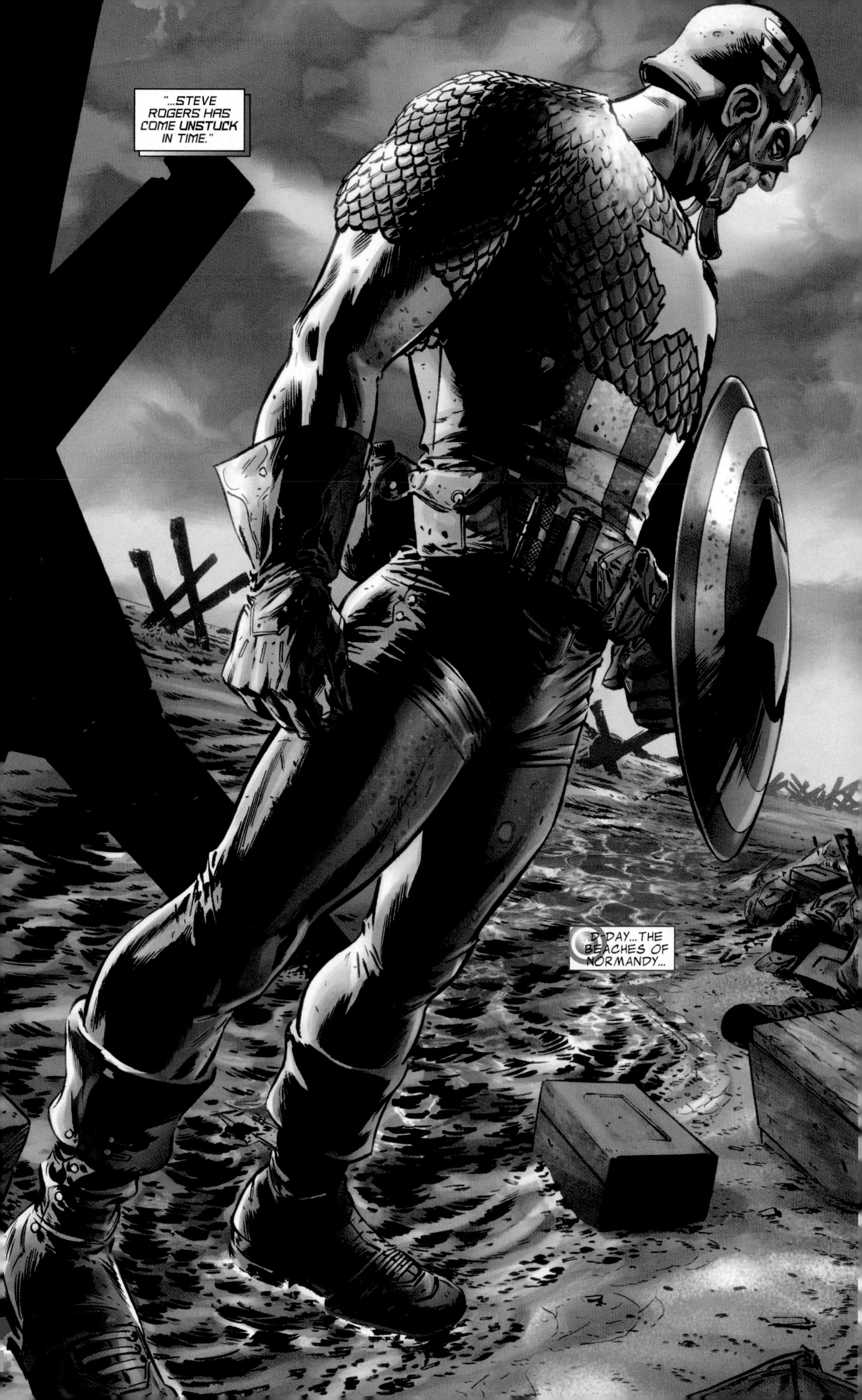
"...STEVE ROGERS HAS COME UNSTUCK IN TIME."
D-DAY... THE BEACHES OF NORMANDY...

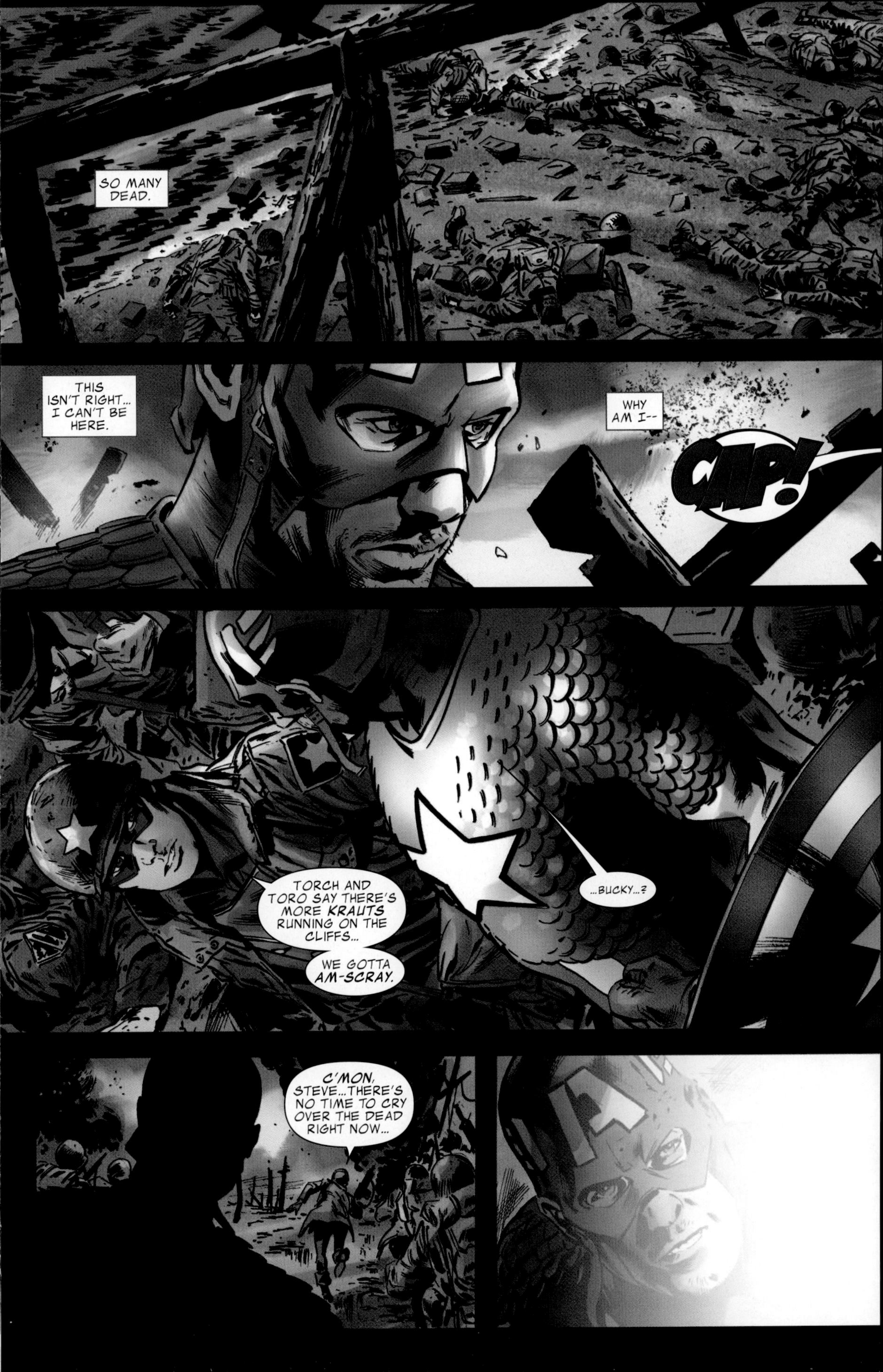
SO MANY DEAD.
THIS ISN'T RIGHT... I CAN'T BE HERE.
WHY AM I--
CAP!
TORCH AND TORO SAY THERE'S MORE KRAUTS RUNNING ON THE CLIFFS...
WE GOTTA AM-SCRAY.
...BUCKY...?
C'MON, STEVE...THERE'S NO TIME TO CRY OVER THE DEAD RIGHT NOW...

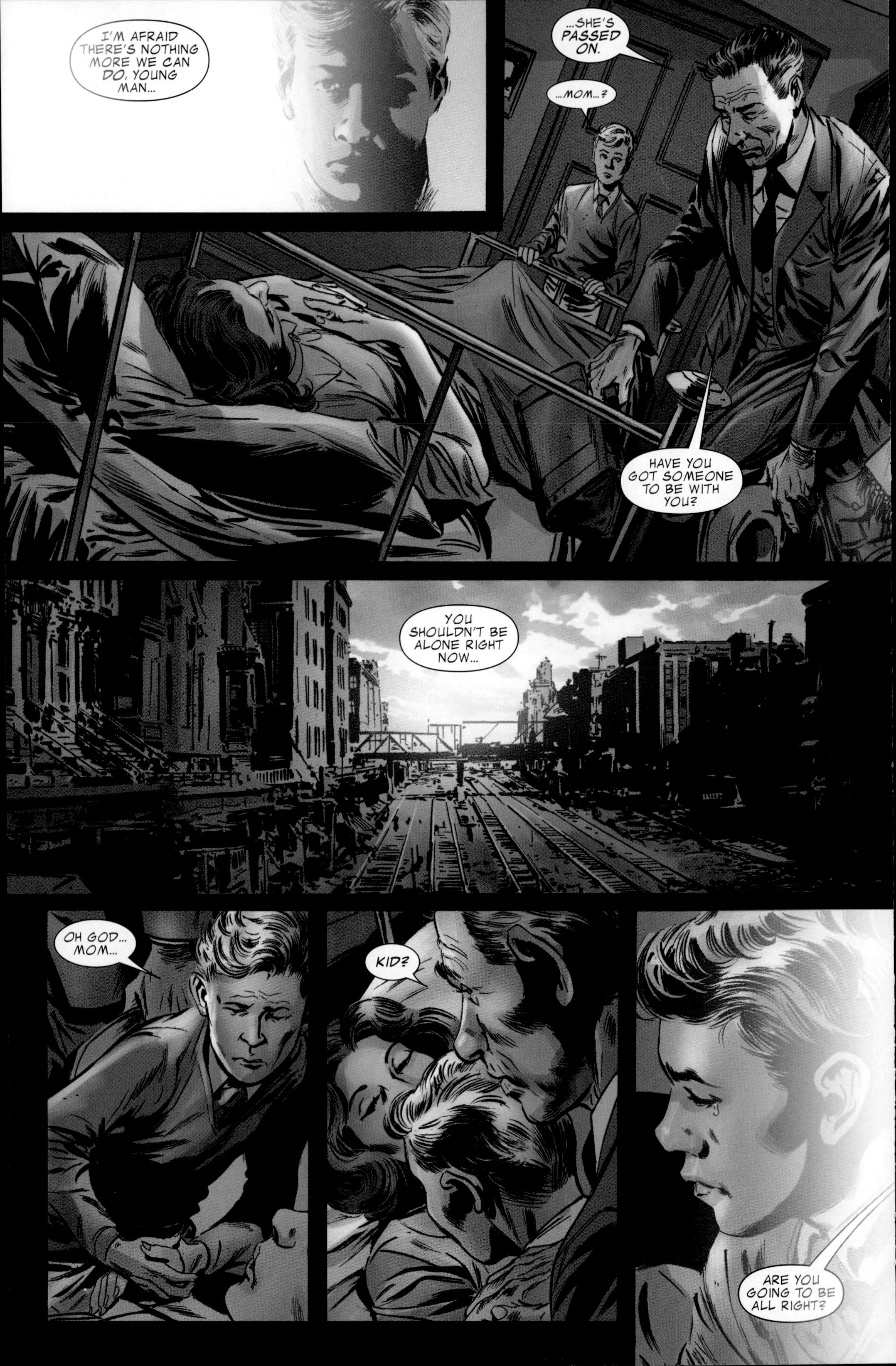
I'M AFRAID THERE'S NOTHING MORE WE CAN DO, YOUNG MAN...
...SHE'S PASSED ON.
...MOM...?
HAVE YOU GOT SOMEONE TO BE WITH YOU?
YOU SHOULDN'T BE ALONE RIGHT NOW...
OH GOD... MOM...
KID?
ARE YOU GOING TO BE ALL RIGHT?

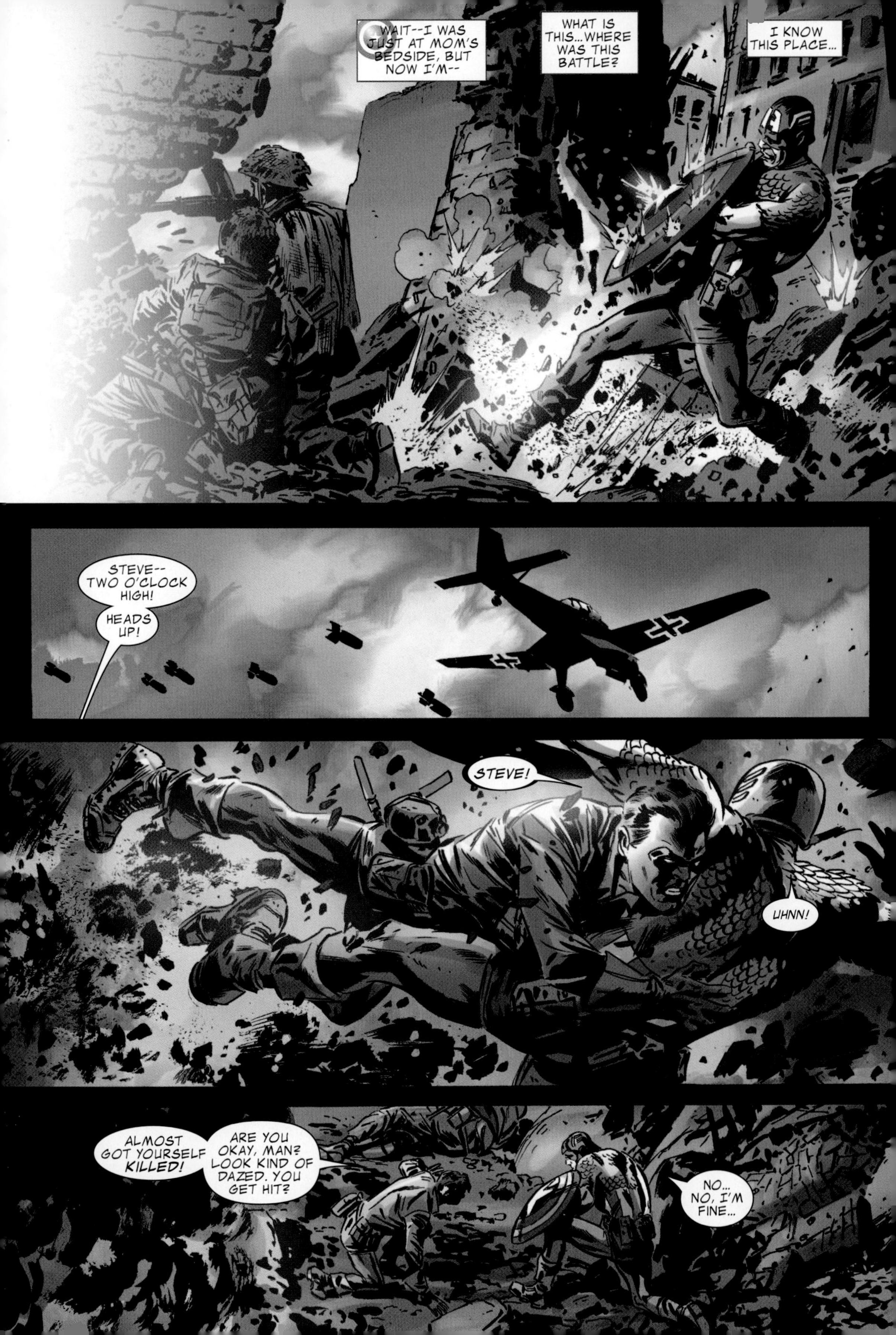
WAIT--I WAS JUST AT MOM'S BEDSIDE, BUT NOW I'M--
WHAT IS THIS...WHERE WAS THIS BATTLE?
I KNOW THIS PLACE...
STEVE-- TWO O'CLOCK HIGH!
HEADS UP!
STEVE!
UHNN!
ALMOST GOT YOURSELF **KILLED!**
ARE YOU OKAY, MAN? LOOK KIND OF DAZED. YOU GET HIT?
NO... NO, I'M FINE...

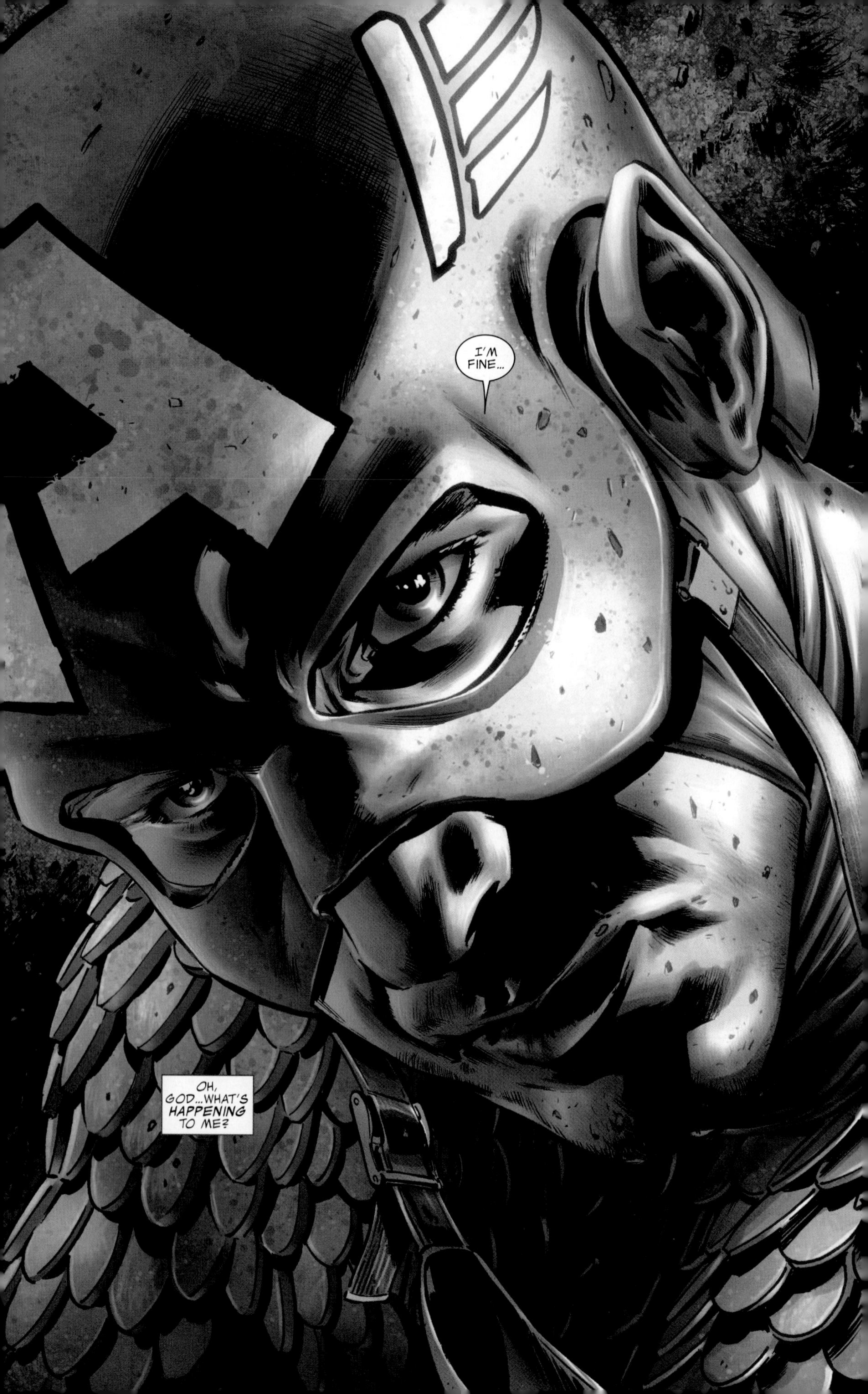
I'M FINE...
OH, GOD...WHAT'S HAPPENING TO ME?

"We have it in our power to begin the world again"

– *Thomas Paine*

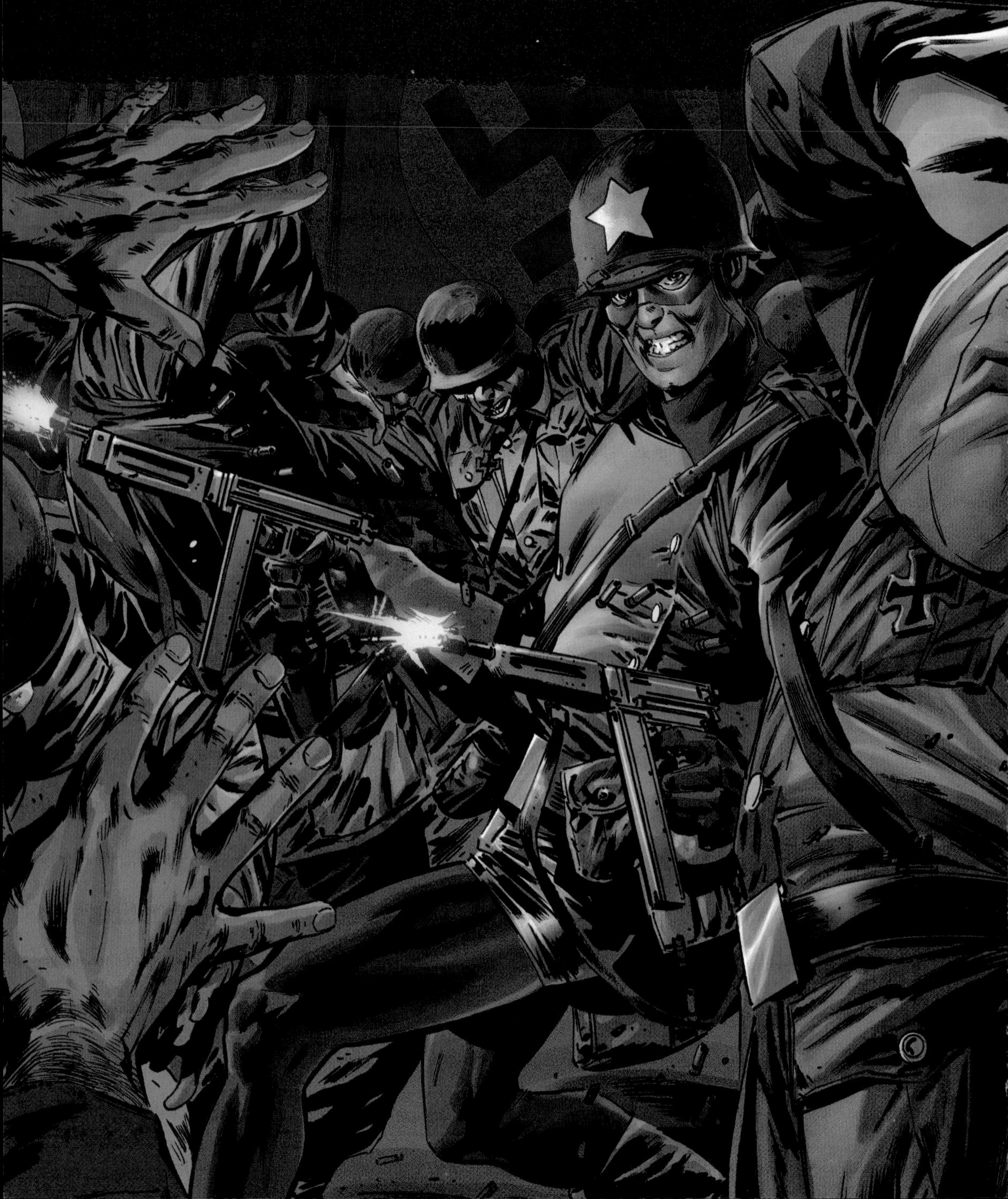

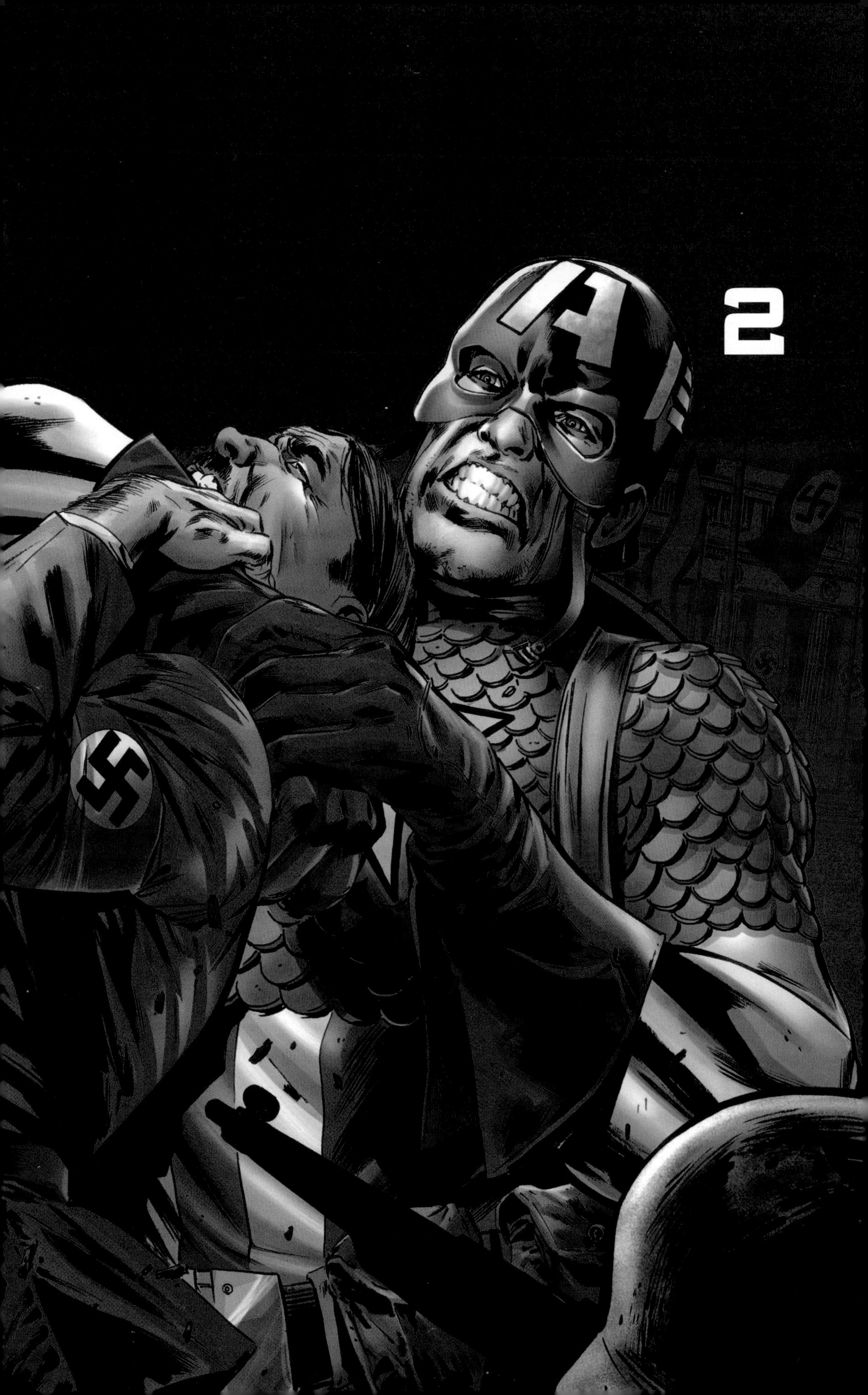
2

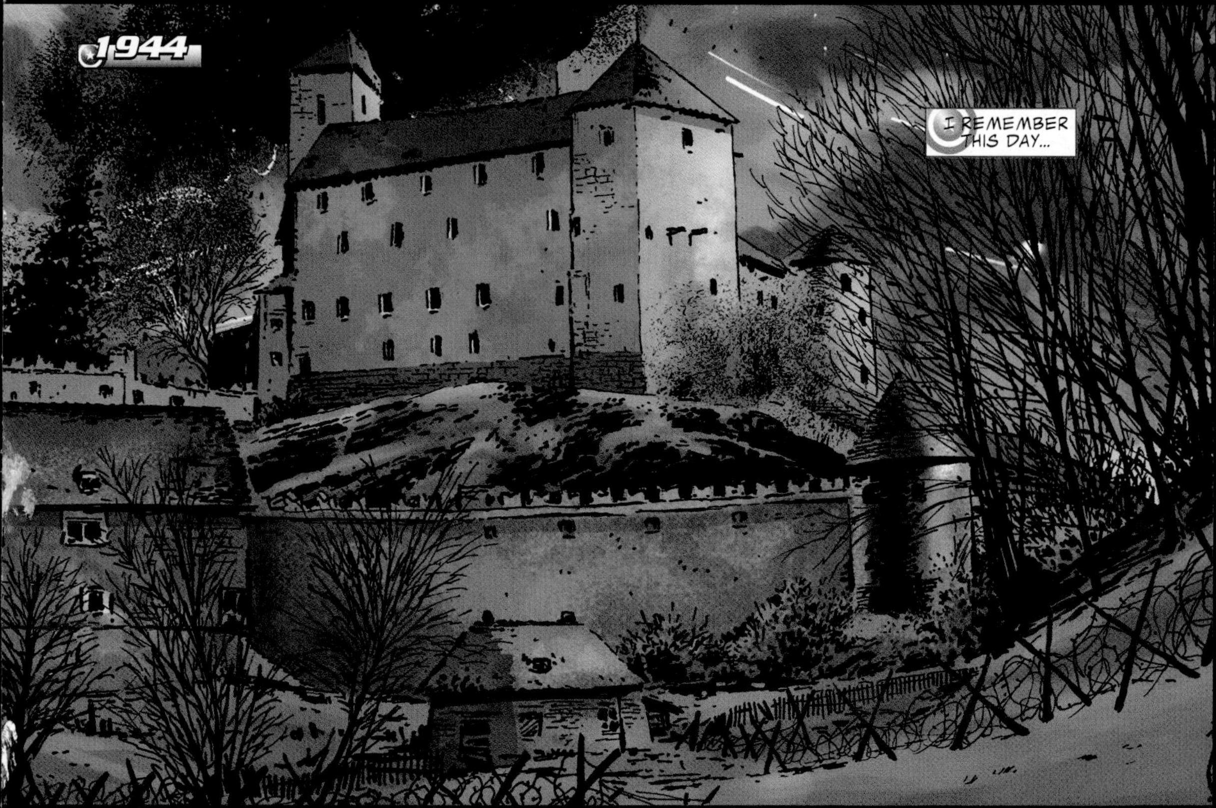
1944
I REMEMBER THIS DAY...

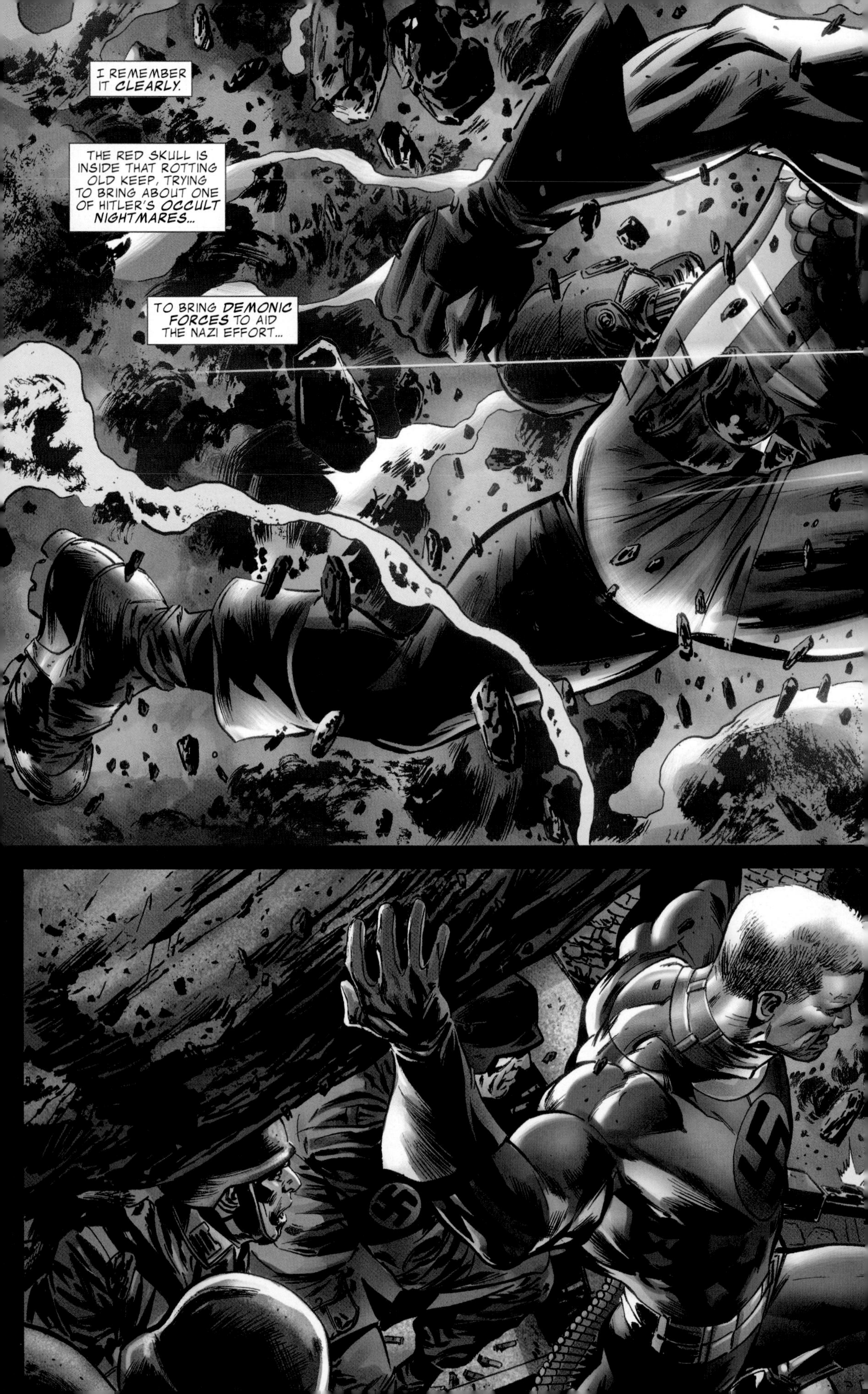
I REMEMBER IT CLEARLY.
THE RED SKULL IS INSIDE THAT ROTTING OLD KEEP, TRYING TO BRING ABOUT ONE OF HITLER'S OCCULT NIGHTMARES...
TO BRING DEMONIC FORCES TO AID THE NAZI EFFORT...

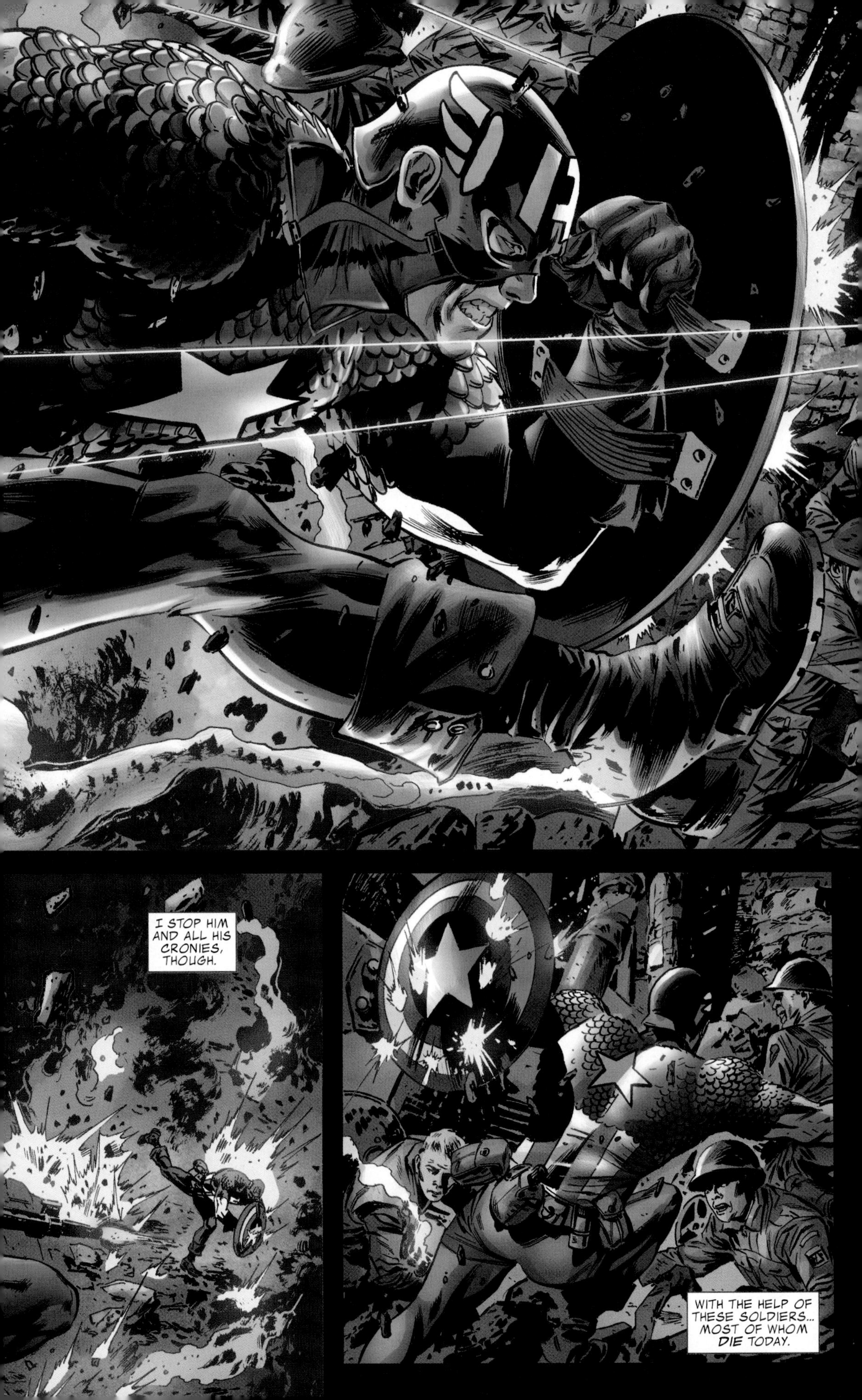
I STOP HIM AND ALL HIS CRONIES, THOUGH.
WITH THE HELP OF THESE SOLDIERS... MOST OF WHOM DIE TODAY.

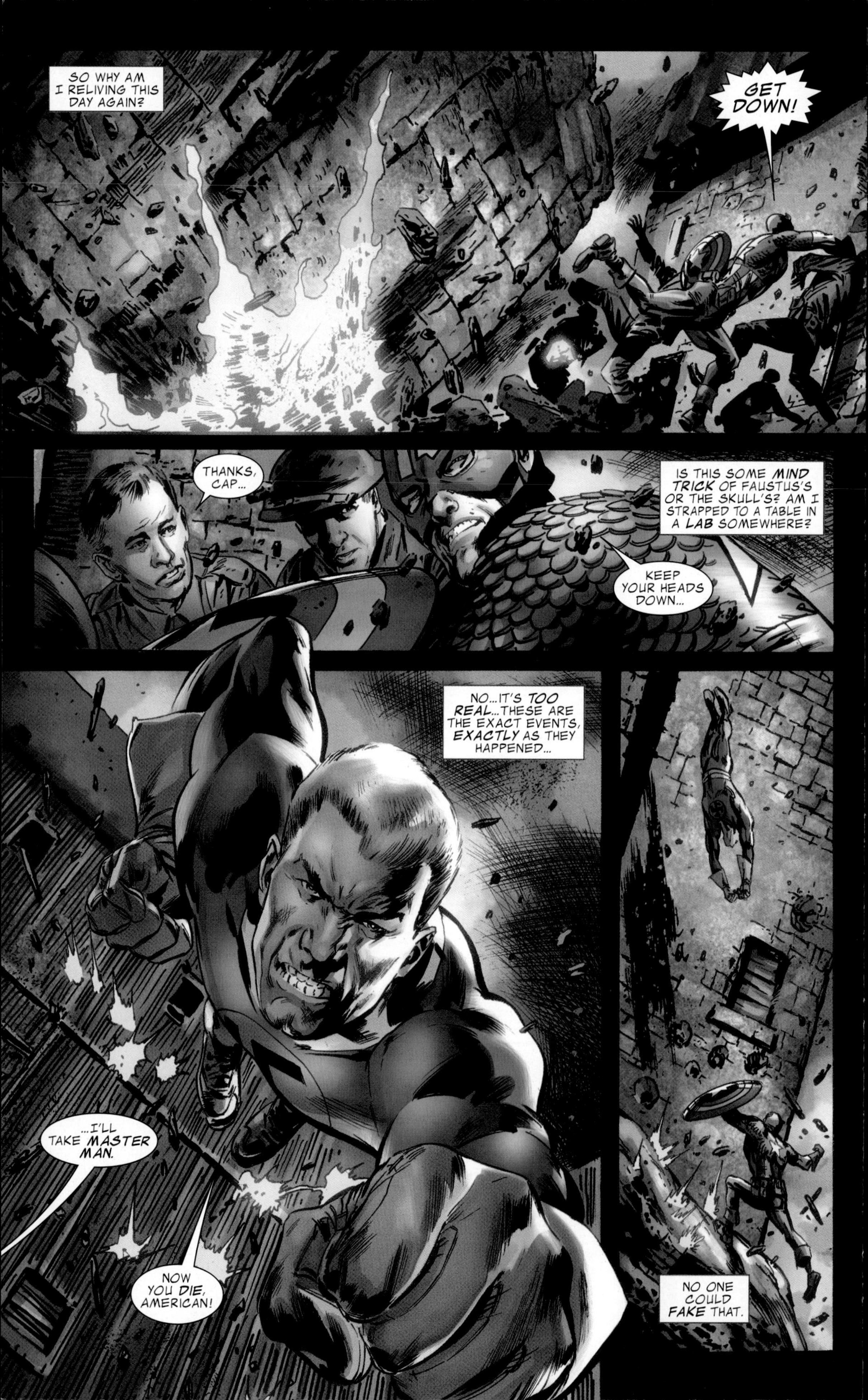
SO WHY AM I RELIVING THIS DAY AGAIN?
GET DOWN!
THANKS, CAP...
IS THIS SOME MIND TRICK OF FAUSTUS'S OR THE SKULL'S? AM I STRAPPED TO A TABLE IN A LAB SOMEWHERE?
KEEP YOUR HEADS DOWN...
NO...IT'S TOO REAL...THESE ARE THE EXACT EVENTS, EXACTLY AS THEY HAPPENED...
...I'LL TAKE MASTER MAN.
NOW YOU DIE, AMERICAN!
NO ONE COULD FAKE THAT.

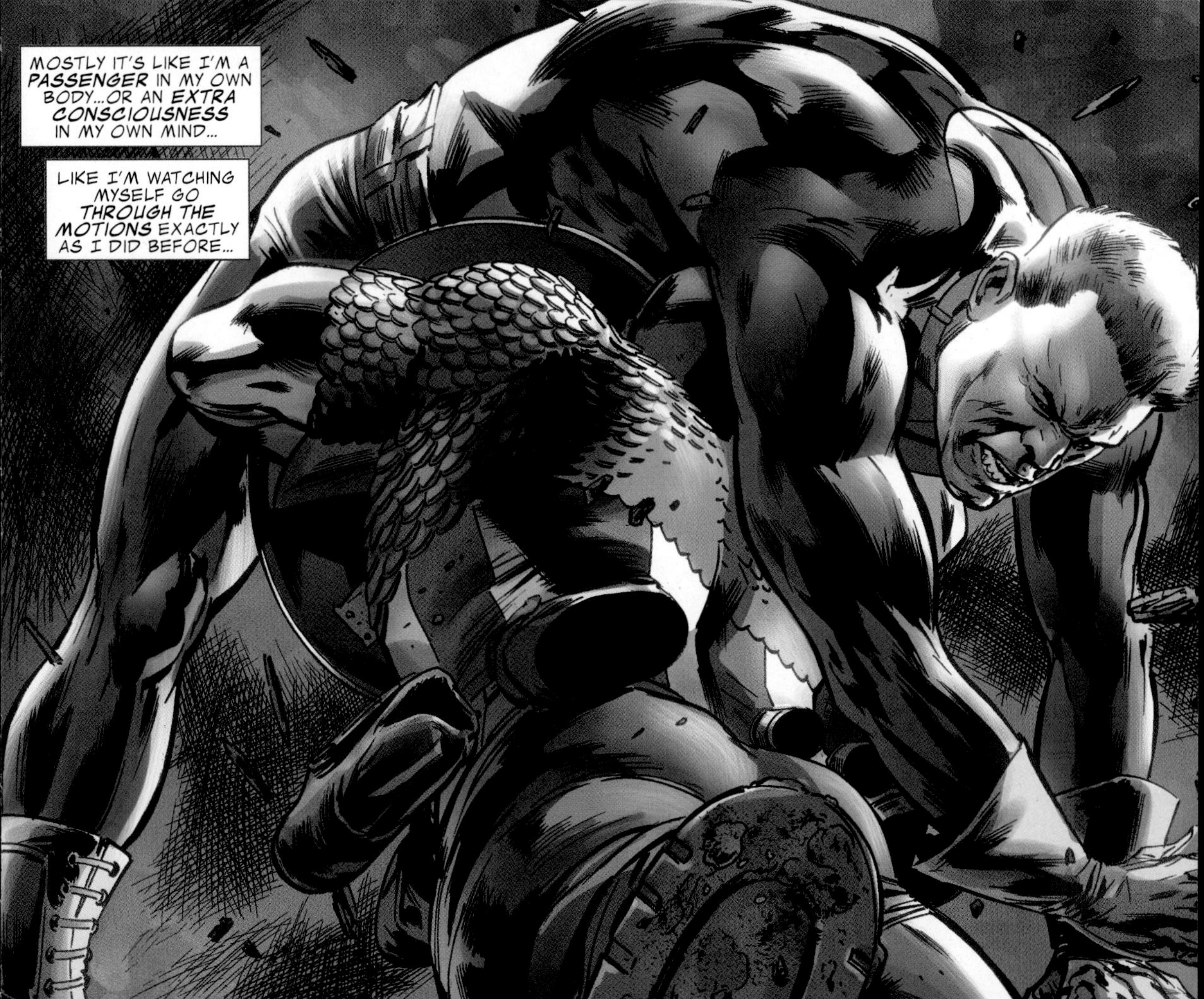
MOSTLY IT'S LIKE I'M A PASSENGER IN MY OWN BODY...OR AN EXTRA CONSCIOUSNESS IN MY OWN MIND...
LIKE I'M WATCHING MYSELF GO THROUGH THE MOTIONS EXACTLY AS I DID BEFORE...

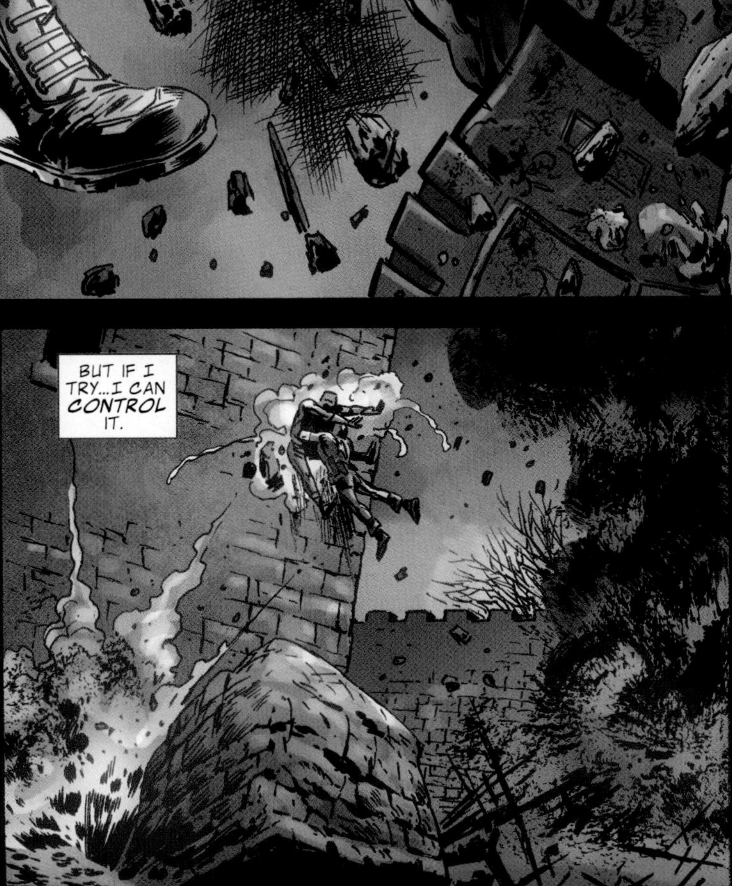
BUT IF I TRY...I CAN CONTROL IT.

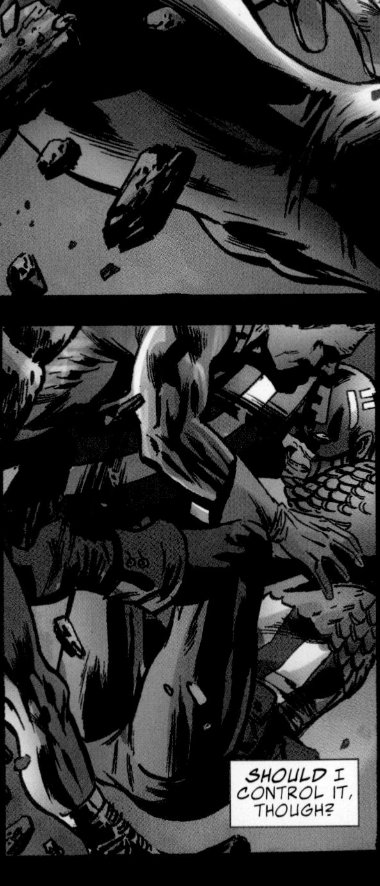
SHOULD I CONTROL IT, THOUGH?

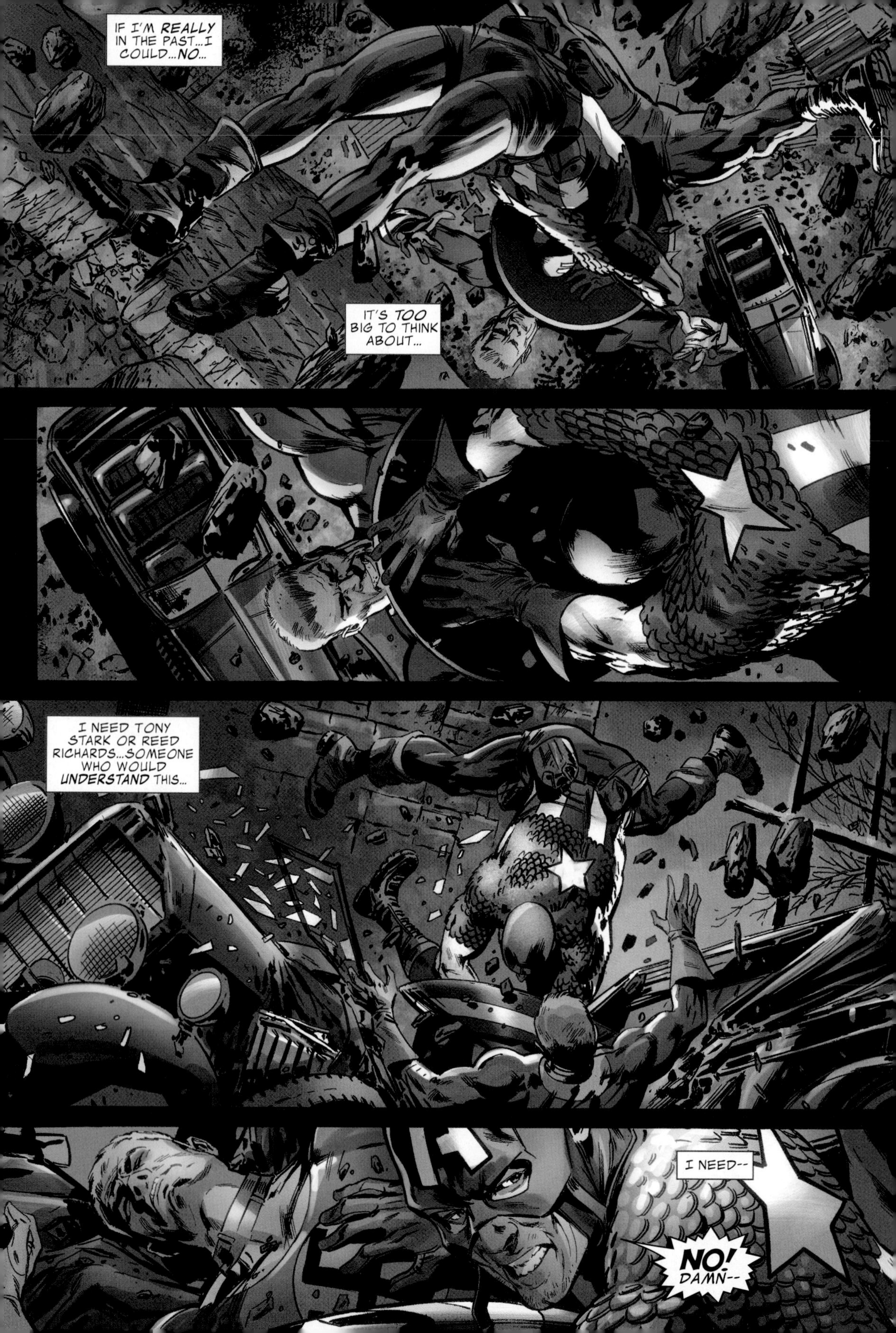

IF I'M REALLY IN THE PAST...I COULD...NO...
IT'S TOO BIG TO THINK ABOUT...
I NEED TONY STARK OR REED RICHARDS...SOMEONE WHO WOULD UNDERSTAND THIS...
I NEED--
NO! DAMN--

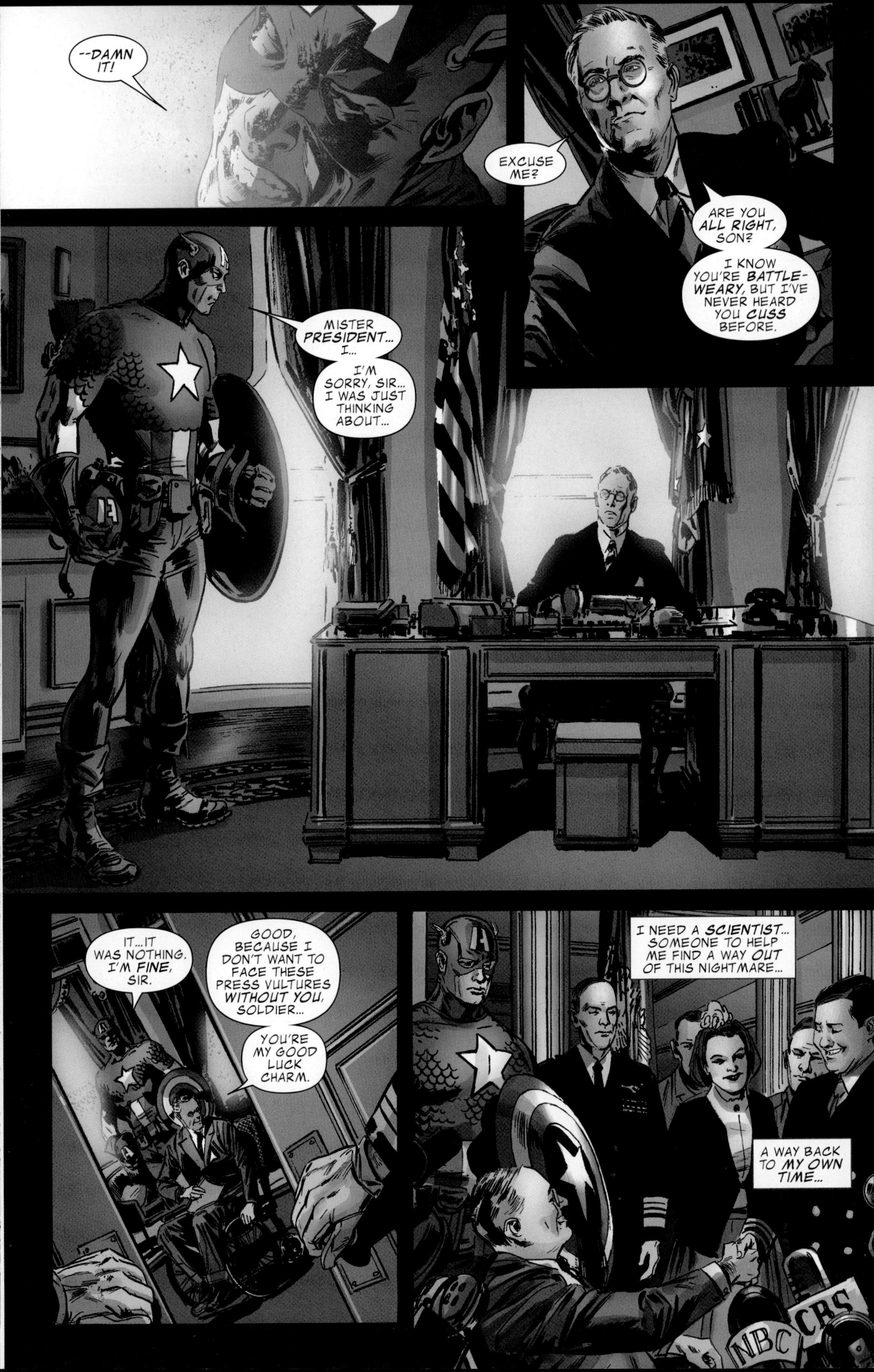
--DAMN IT!
EXCUSE ME?
ARE YOU ALL RIGHT, SON?
I KNOW YOU'RE BATTLE-WEARY, BUT I'VE NEVER HEARD YOU CUSS BEFORE.
MISTER PRESIDENT... I...
I'M SORRY, SIR... I WAS JUST THINKING ABOUT...
IT...IT WAS NOTHING. I'M FINE, SIR.
GOOD, BECAUSE I DON'T WANT TO FACE THESE PRESS VULTURES WITHOUT YOU, SOLDIER...
YOU'RE MY GOOD LUCK CHARM.
I NEED A SCIENTIST... SOMEONE TO HELP ME FIND A WAY OUT OF THIS NIGHTMARE...
A WAY BACK TO MY OWN TIME...
NBC
CBS

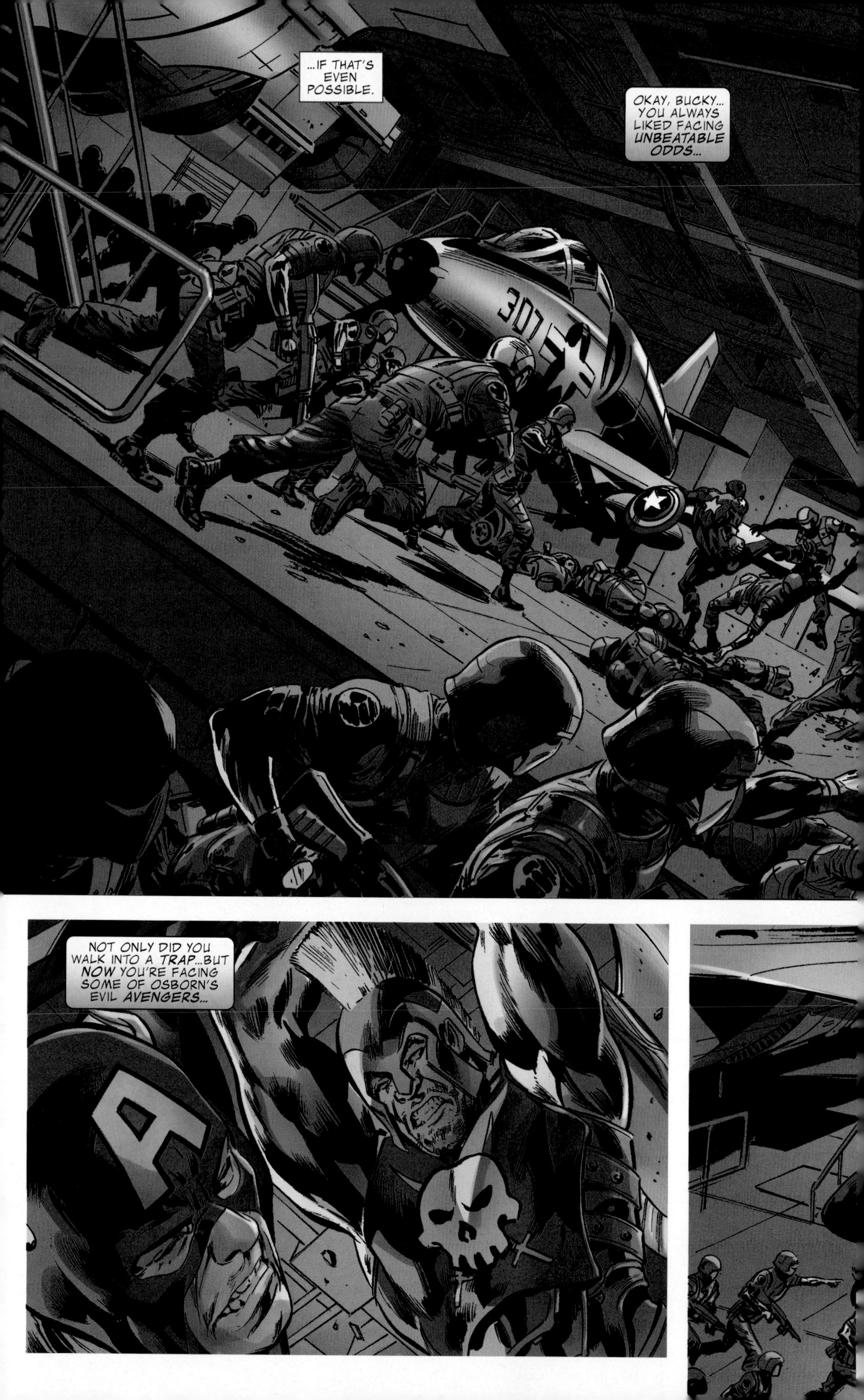
...IF THAT'S EVEN POSSIBLE.
OKAY, BUCKY... YOU ALWAYS LIKED FACING UNBEATABLE ODDS...
307
NOT ONLY DID YOU WALK INTO A TRAP...BUT NOW YOU'RE FACING SOME OF OSBORN'S EVIL AVENGERS...

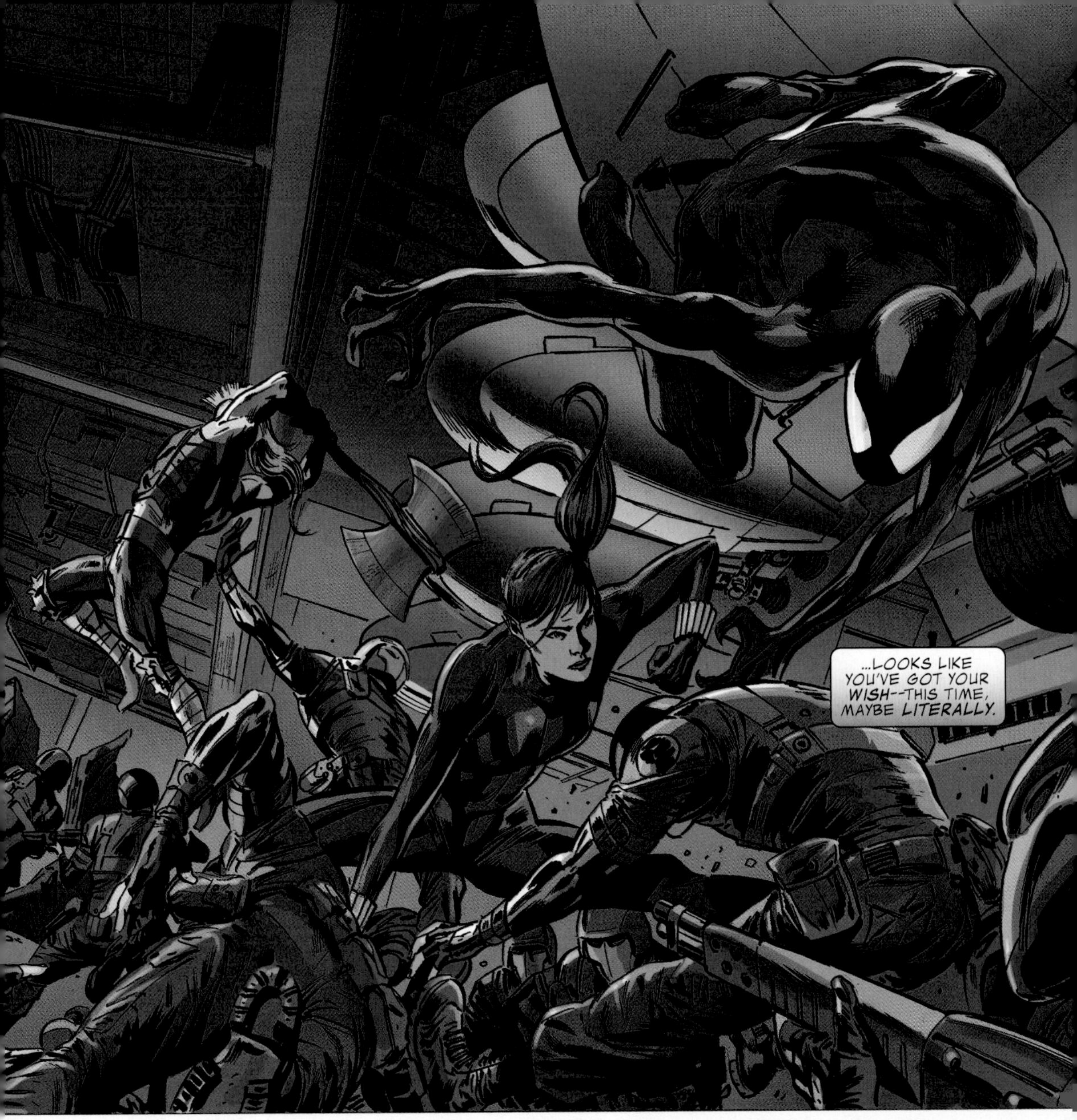
...LOOKS LIKE YOU'VE GOT YOUR *WISH*--THIS TIME, MAYBE *LITERALLY*.

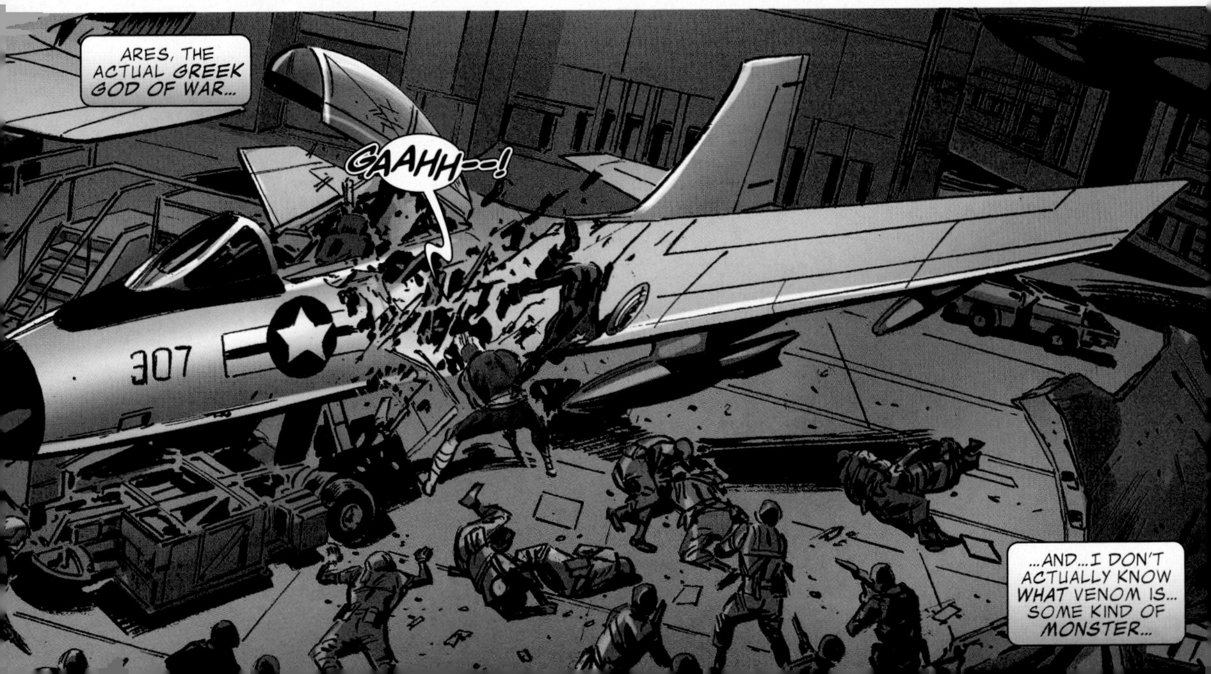
ARES, THE ACTUAL *GREEK GOD OF WAR*...
GAAHH--!
307
...AND...I DON'T ACTUALLY KNOW *WHAT* VENOM IS... SOME KIND OF *MONSTER*...

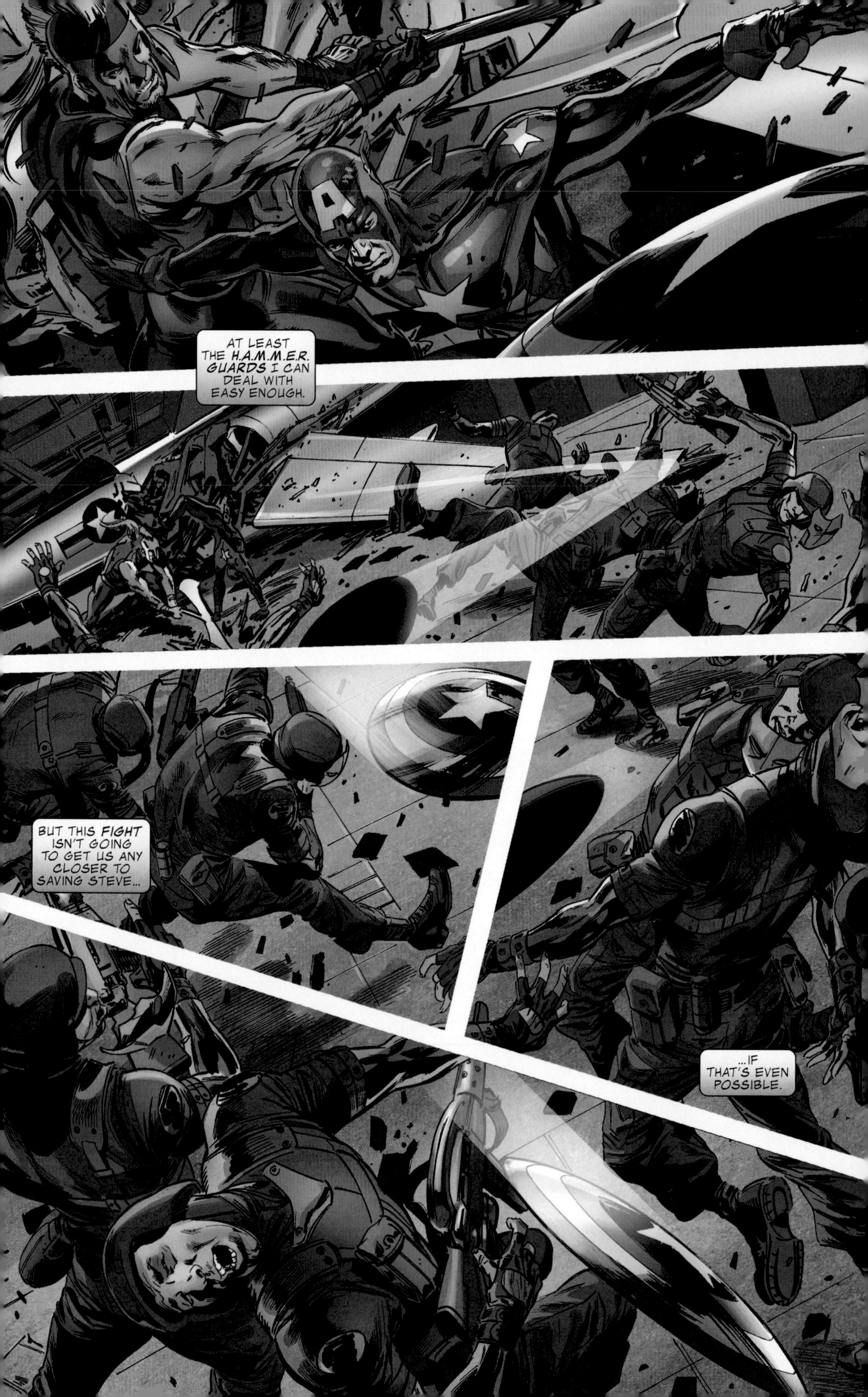
AT LEAST THE H.A.M.M.E.R. GUARDS I CAN DEAL WITH EASY ENOUGH.
BUT THIS FIGHT ISN'T GOING TO GET US ANY CLOSER TO SAVING STEVE...
...IF THAT'S EVEN POSSIBLE.

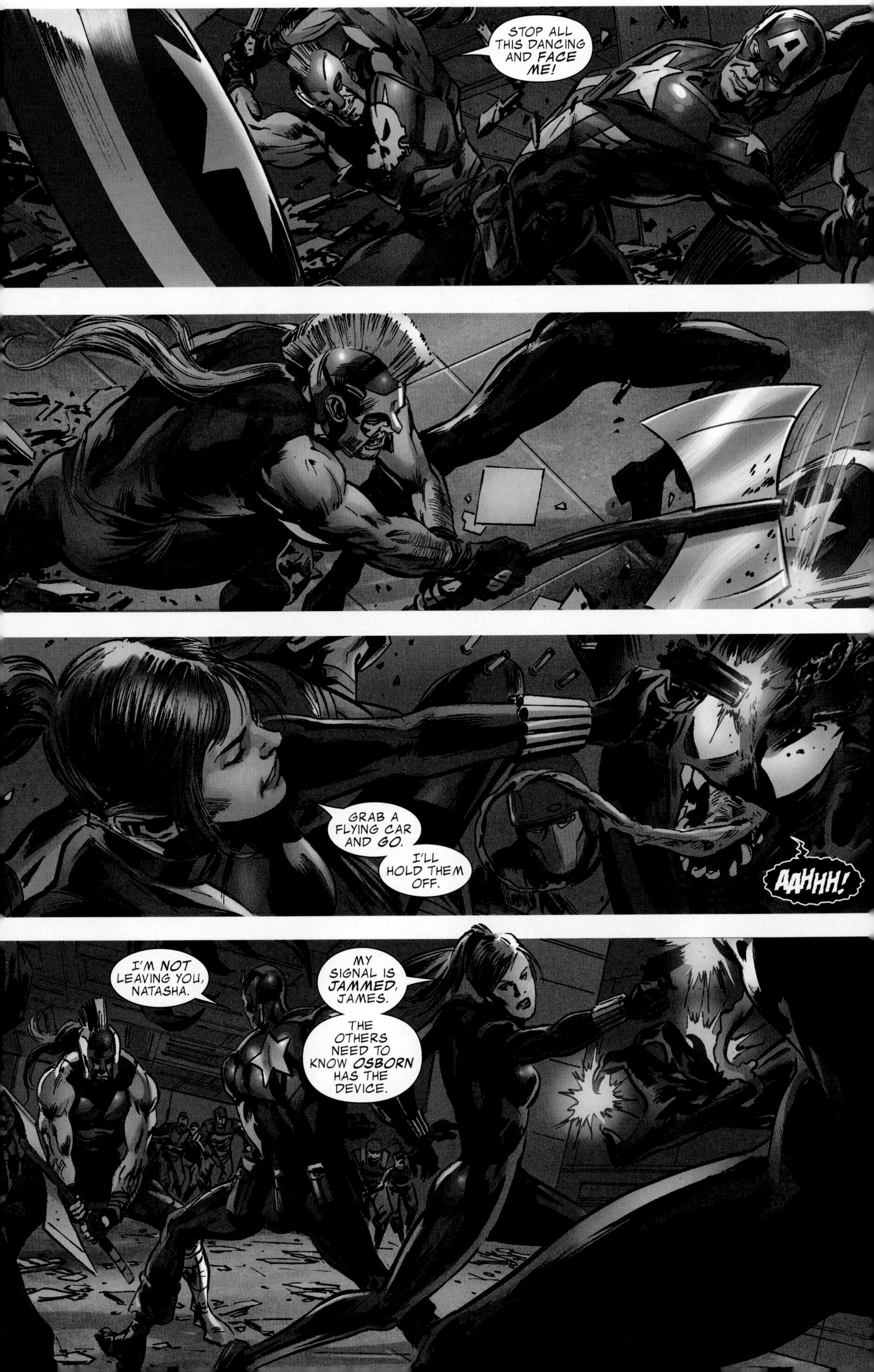
STOP ALL THIS DANCING AND FACE ME!
GRAB A FLYING CAR AND GO.
I'LL HOLD THEM OFF.
AAHHH!
I'M NOT LEAVING YOU, NATASHA.
MY SIGNAL IS JAMMED, JAMES.
THE OTHERS NEED TO KNOW OSBORN HAS THE DEVICE.

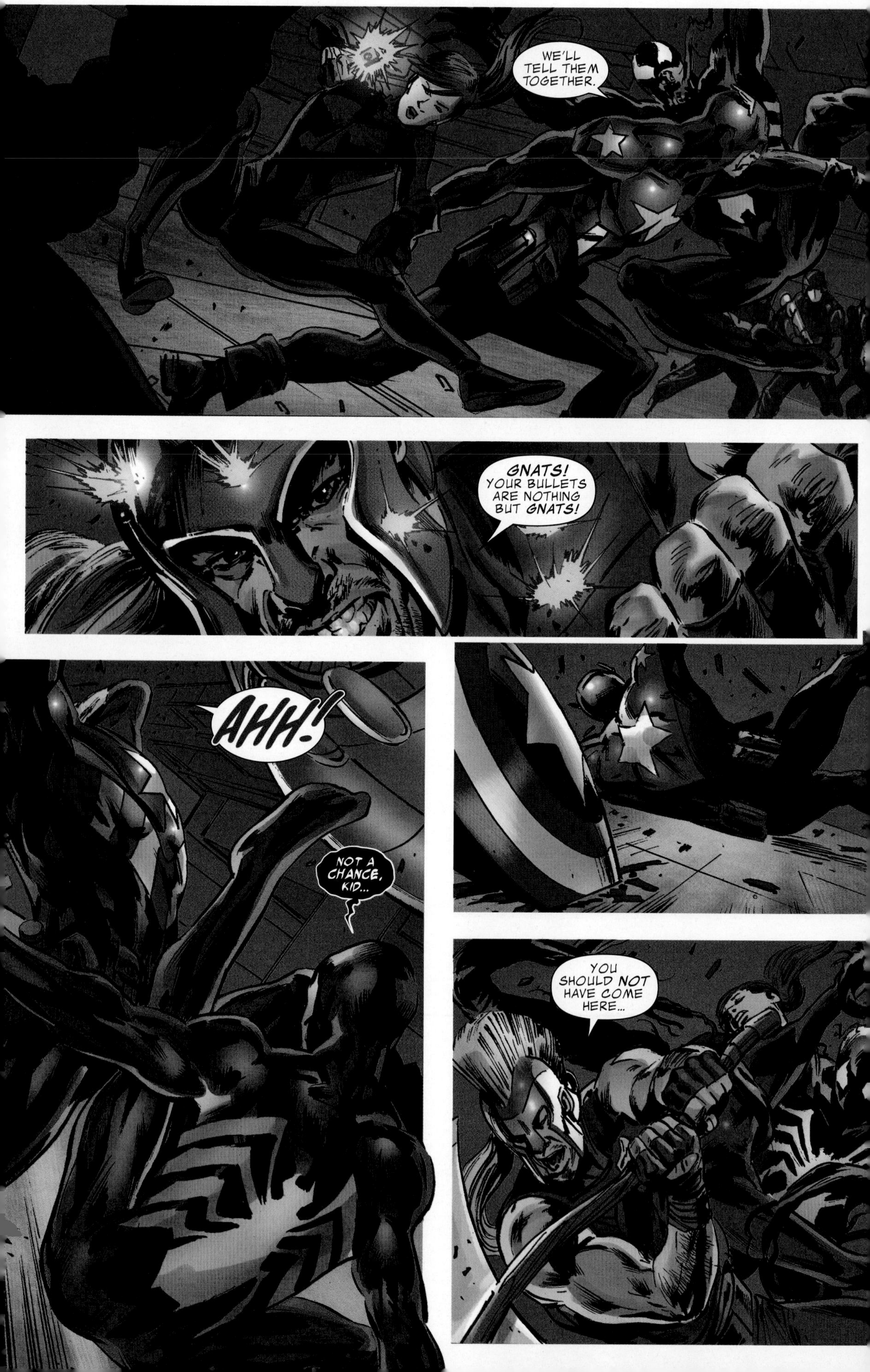
WE'LL TELL THEM TOGETHER.
GNATS! YOUR BULLETS ARE NOTHING BUT GNATS!
AHH!
NOT A CHANCE, KID...
YOU SHOULD NOT HAVE COME HERE...

WE AREN'T IN THE HABIT OF BEING *MERCIFUL*...

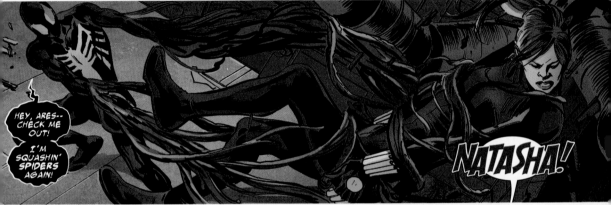

HEY, ARES-- CHECK ME OUT!

I'M SQUASHIN' *SPIDERS* AGAIN!

NATASHA!

UHHN!

BUT YOU TWO ARE IN *LUCK* THIS NIGHT...

...BECAUSE WE HAVE ORDERS TO BRING YOU IN *ALIVE*.

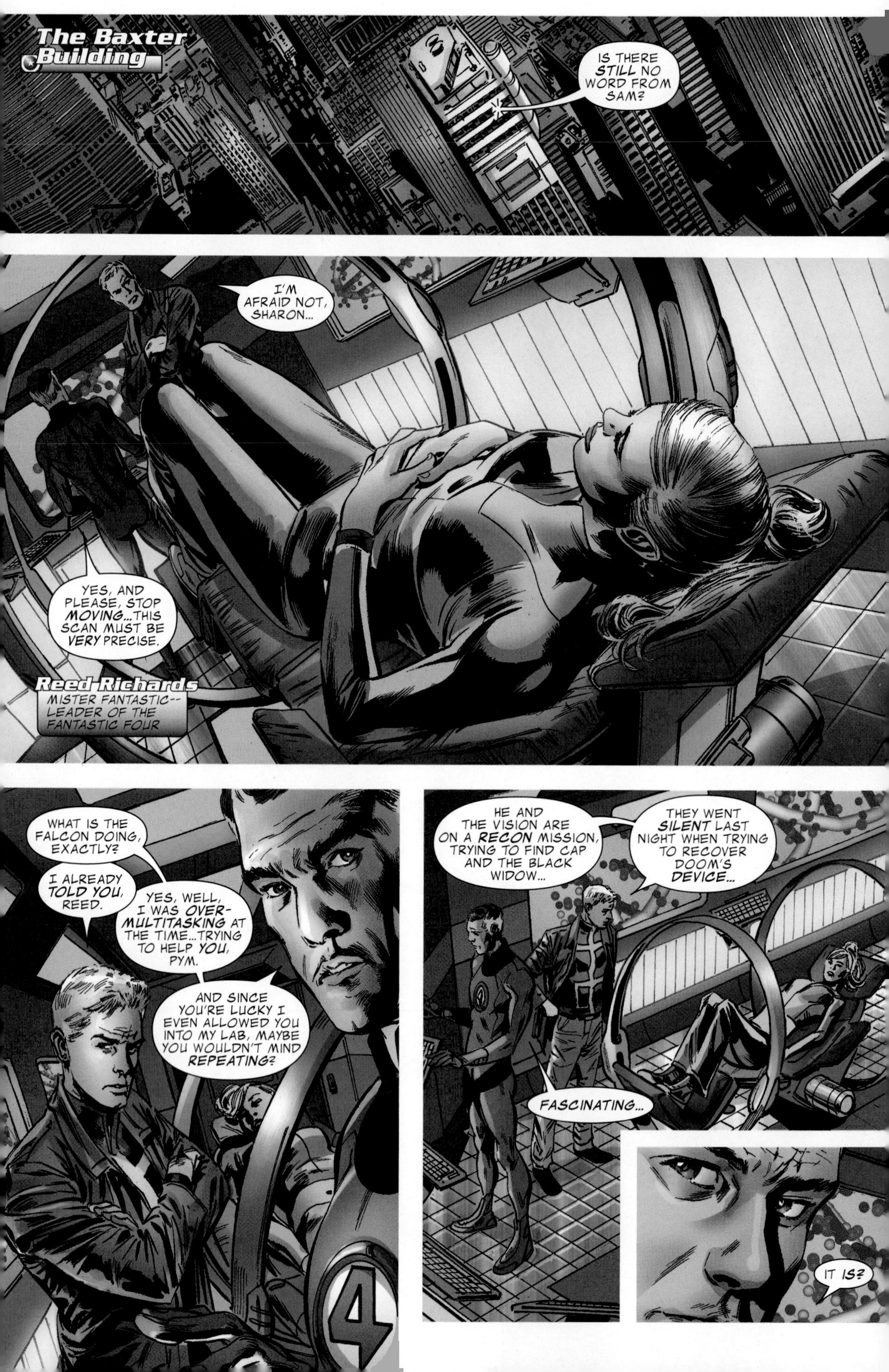
The Baxter Building
IS THERE STILL NO WORD FROM SAM?
I'M AFRAID NOT, SHARON...
YES, AND PLEASE, STOP MOVING...THIS SCAN MUST BE VERY PRECISE.
Reed Richards
MISTER FANTASTIC-- LEADER OF THE FANTASTIC FOUR
WHAT IS THE FALCON DOING, EXACTLY?
I ALREADY TOLD YOU, REED.
YES, WELL, I WAS OVER-MULTITASKING AT THE TIME...TRYING TO HELP YOU, PYM.
AND SINCE YOU'RE LUCKY I EVEN ALLOWED YOU INTO MY LAB, MAYBE YOU WOULDN'T MIND REPEATING?
HE AND THE VISION ARE ON A RECON MISSION, TRYING TO FIND CAP AND THE BLACK WIDOW...
THEY WENT SILENT LAST NIGHT WHEN TRYING TO RECOVER DOOM'S DEVICE...
FASCINATING...
IT IS?

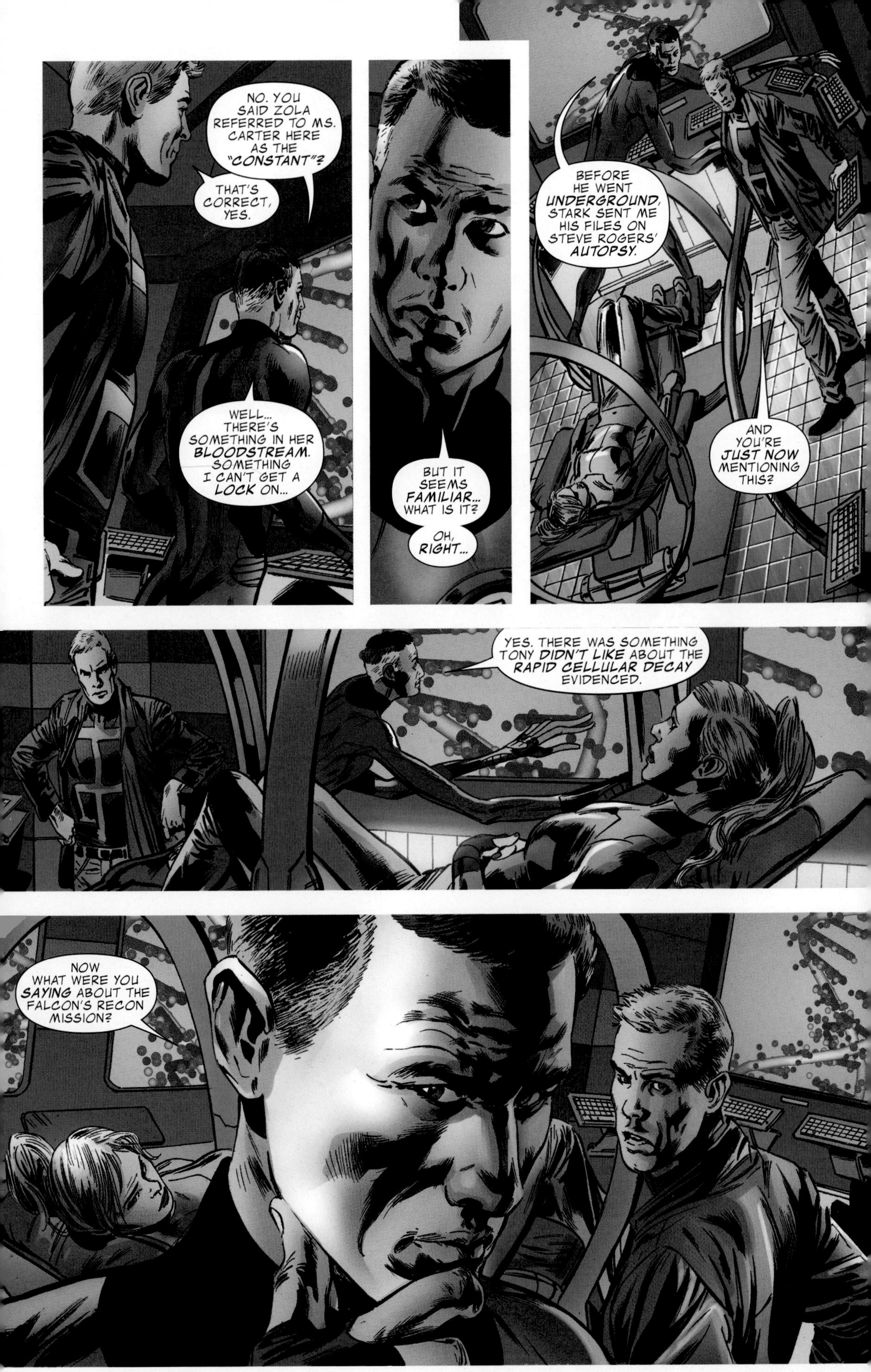
NO. YOU SAID ZOLA REFERRED TO MS. CARTER HERE AS THE "CONSTANT"?
THAT'S CORRECT, YES.
WELL... THERE'S SOMETHING IN HER BLOODSTREAM. SOMETHING I CAN'T GET A LOCK ON...
BUT IT SEEMS FAMILIAR... WHAT IS IT?
OH, RIGHT...
BEFORE HE WENT UNDERGROUND, STARK SENT ME HIS FILES ON STEVE ROGERS' AUTOPSY.
AND YOU'RE JUST NOW MENTIONING THIS?
YES. THERE WAS SOMETHING TONY DIDN'T LIKE ABOUT THE RAPID CELLULAR DECAY EVIDENCED.
NOW WHAT WERE YOU SAYING ABOUT THE FALCON'S RECON MISSION?

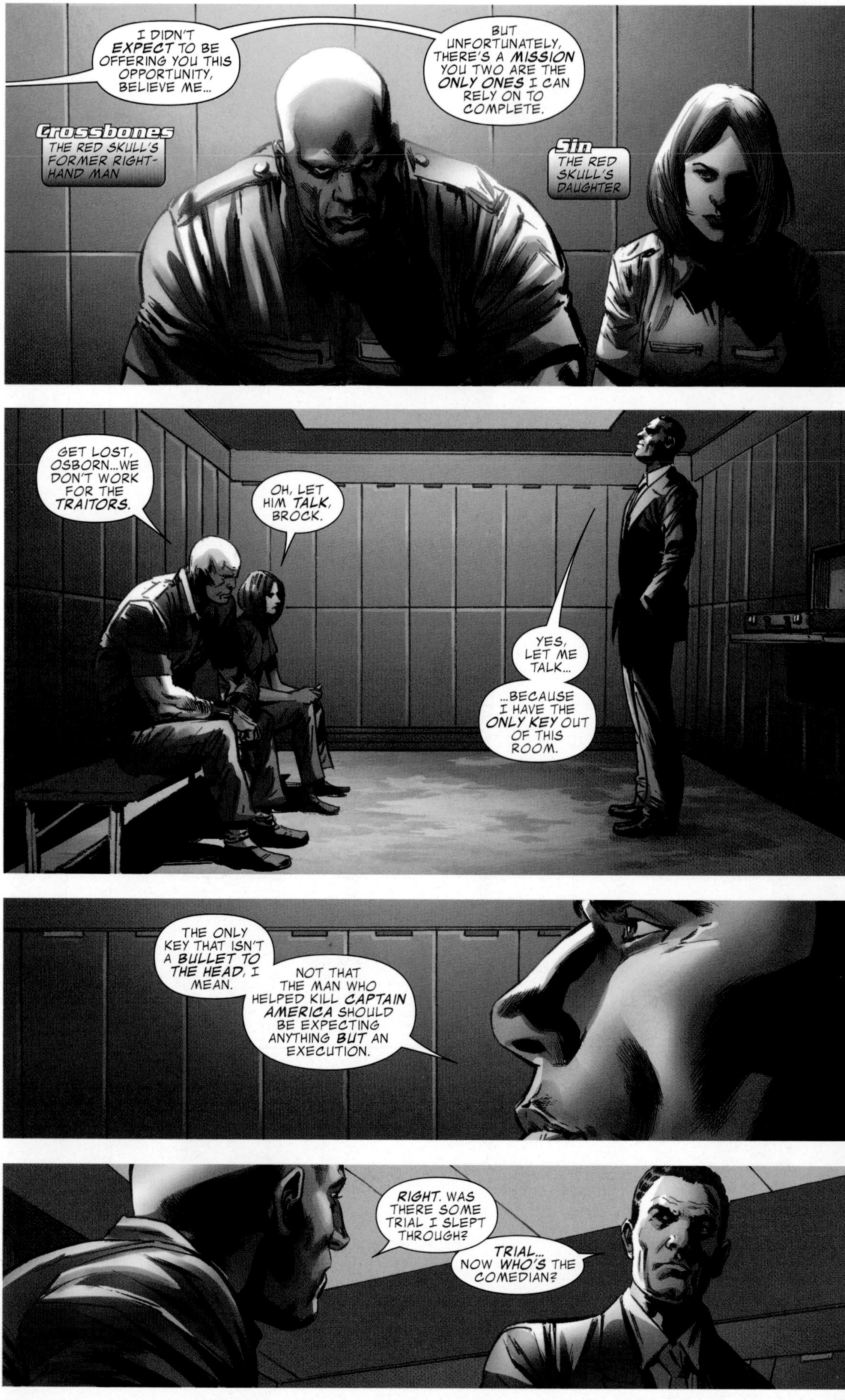
I DIDN'T EXPECT TO BE OFFERING YOU THIS OPPORTUNITY, BELIEVE ME...
BUT UNFORTUNATELY, THERE'S A MISSION YOU TWO ARE THE ONLY ONES I CAN RELY ON TO COMPLETE.
Crossbones
THE RED SKULL'S FORMER RIGHT-HAND MAN
Sin
THE RED SKULL'S DAUGHTER
GET LOST, OSBORN...WE DON'T WORK FOR THE TRAITORS.
OH, LET HIM TALK, BROCK.
YES, LET ME TALK...
...BECAUSE I HAVE THE ONLY KEY OUT OF THIS ROOM.
THE ONLY KEY THAT ISN'T A BULLET TO THE HEAD, I MEAN.
NOT THAT THE MAN WHO HELPED KILL CAPTAIN AMERICA SHOULD BE EXPECTING ANYTHING BUT AN EXECUTION.
RIGHT. WAS THERE SOME TRIAL I SLEPT THROUGH?
TRIAL... NOW WHO'S THE COMEDIAN?

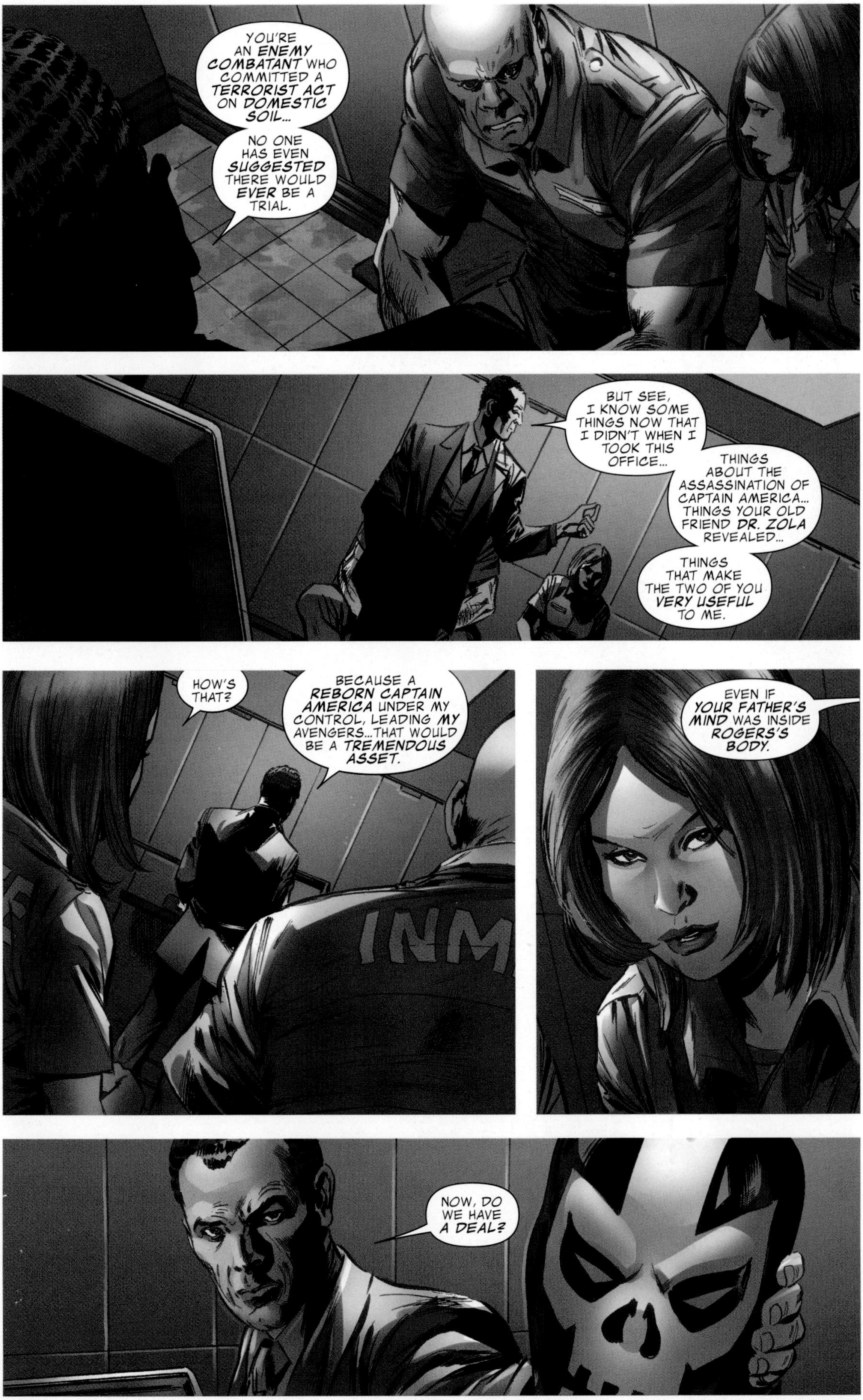
YOU'RE AN ENEMY COMBATANT WHO COMMITTED A TERRORIST ACT ON DOMESTIC SOIL...
NO ONE HAS EVEN SUGGESTED THERE WOULD EVER BE A TRIAL.
BUT SEE, I KNOW SOME THINGS NOW THAT I DIDN'T WHEN I TOOK THIS OFFICE...
THINGS ABOUT THE ASSASSINATION OF CAPTAIN AMERICA... THINGS YOUR OLD FRIEND DR. ZOLA REVEALED...
THINGS THAT MAKE THE TWO OF YOU VERY USEFUL TO ME.
HOW'S THAT?
BECAUSE A REBORN CAPTAIN AMERICA UNDER MY CONTROL, LEADING MY AVENGERS...THAT WOULD BE A TREMENDOUS ASSET.
INM
EVEN IF YOUR FATHER'S MIND WAS INSIDE ROGERS'S BODY.
NOW, DO WE HAVE A DEAL?

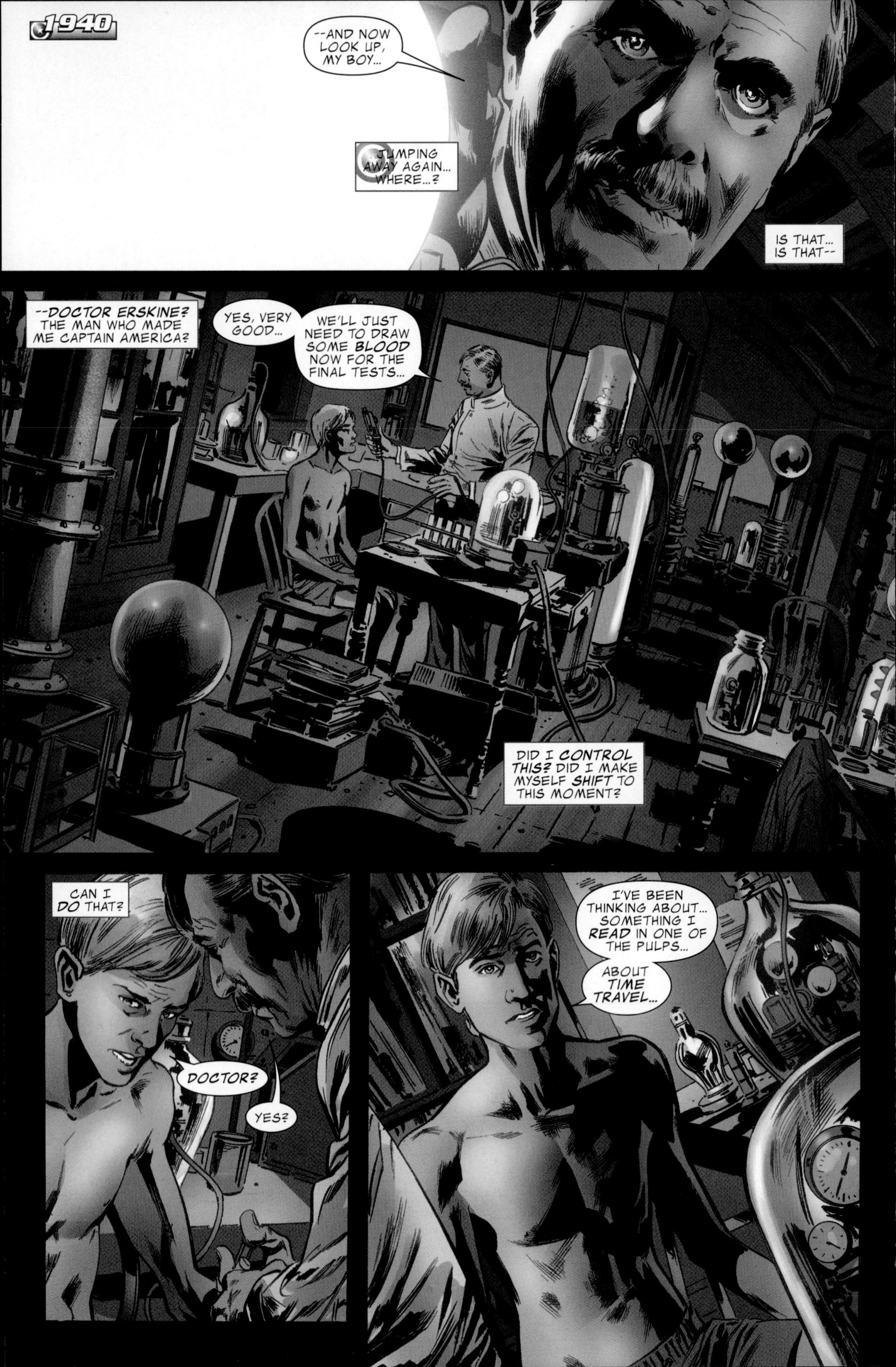
1940
--AND NOW LOOK UP, MY BOY...
JUMPING AWAY AGAIN... WHERE...?
IS THAT... IS THAT--
--DOCTOR ERSKINE? THE MAN WHO MADE ME CAPTAIN AMERICA?
YES, VERY GOOD...
WE'LL JUST NEED TO DRAW SOME BLOOD NOW FOR THE FINAL TESTS...
DID I CONTROL THIS? DID I MAKE MYSELF SHIFT TO THIS MOMENT?
CAN I DO THAT?
DOCTOR?
YES?
I'VE BEEN THINKING ABOUT... SOMETHING I READ IN ONE OF THE PULPS...
ABOUT TIME TRAVEL...

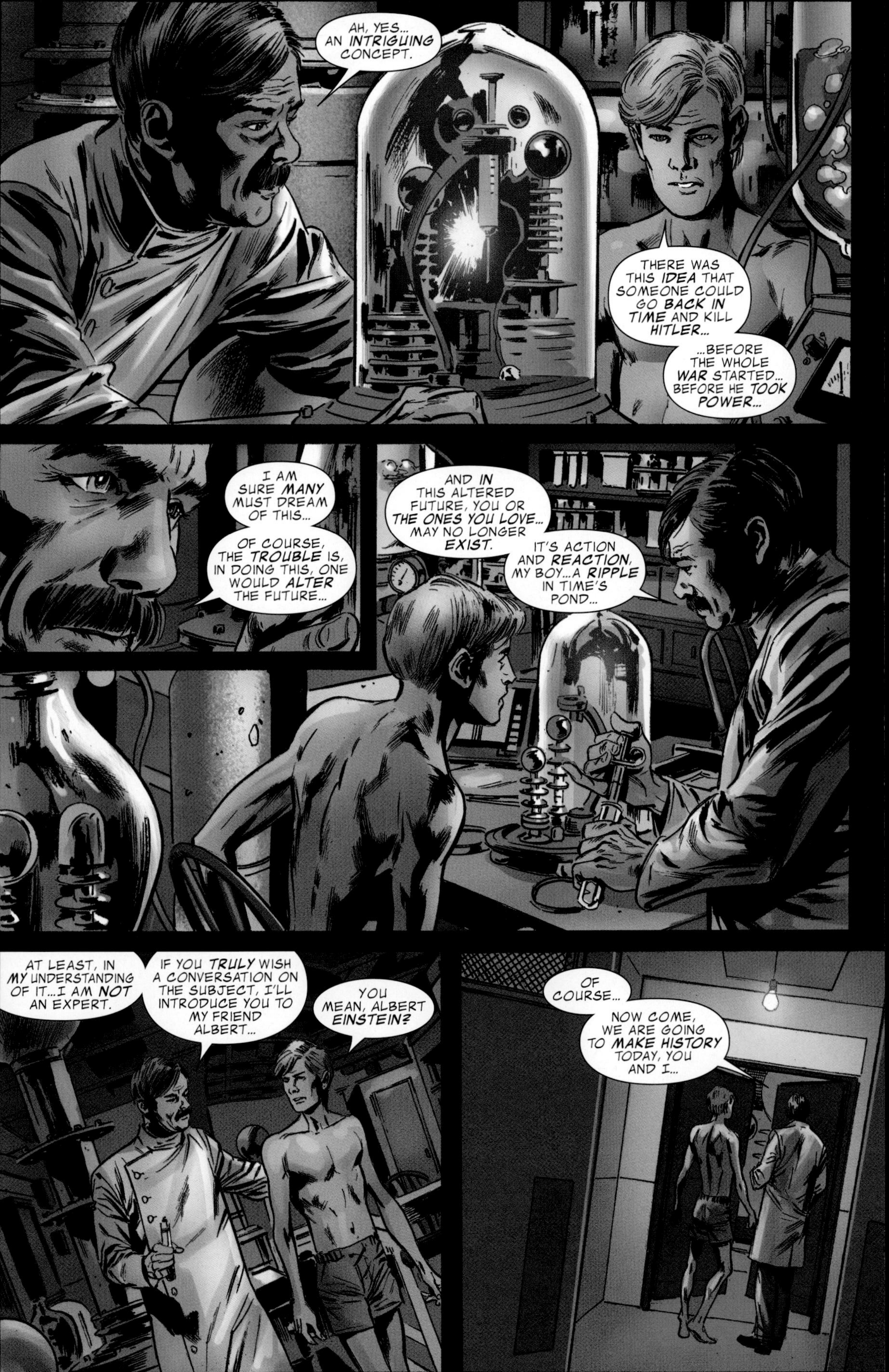
AH, YES... AN INTRIGUING CONCEPT.
THERE WAS THIS IDEA THAT SOMEONE COULD GO BACK IN TIME AND KILL HITLER...
...BEFORE THE WHOLE WAR STARTED... BEFORE HE TOOK POWER...
I AM SURE MANY MUST DREAM OF THIS...
OF COURSE, THE TROUBLE IS, IN DOING THIS, ONE WOULD ALTER THE FUTURE...
AND IN THIS ALTERED FUTURE, YOU OR THE ONES YOU LOVE... MAY NO LONGER EXIST.
IT'S ACTION AND REACTION, MY BOY...A RIPPLE IN TIME'S POND...
AT LEAST, IN MY UNDERSTANDING OF IT...I AM NOT AN EXPERT.
IF YOU TRULY WISH A CONVERSATION ON THE SUBJECT, I'LL INTRODUCE YOU TO MY FRIEND ALBERT...
YOU MEAN, ALBERT EINSTEIN?
OF COURSE...
NOW COME, WE ARE GOING TO MAKE HISTORY TODAY, YOU AND I...

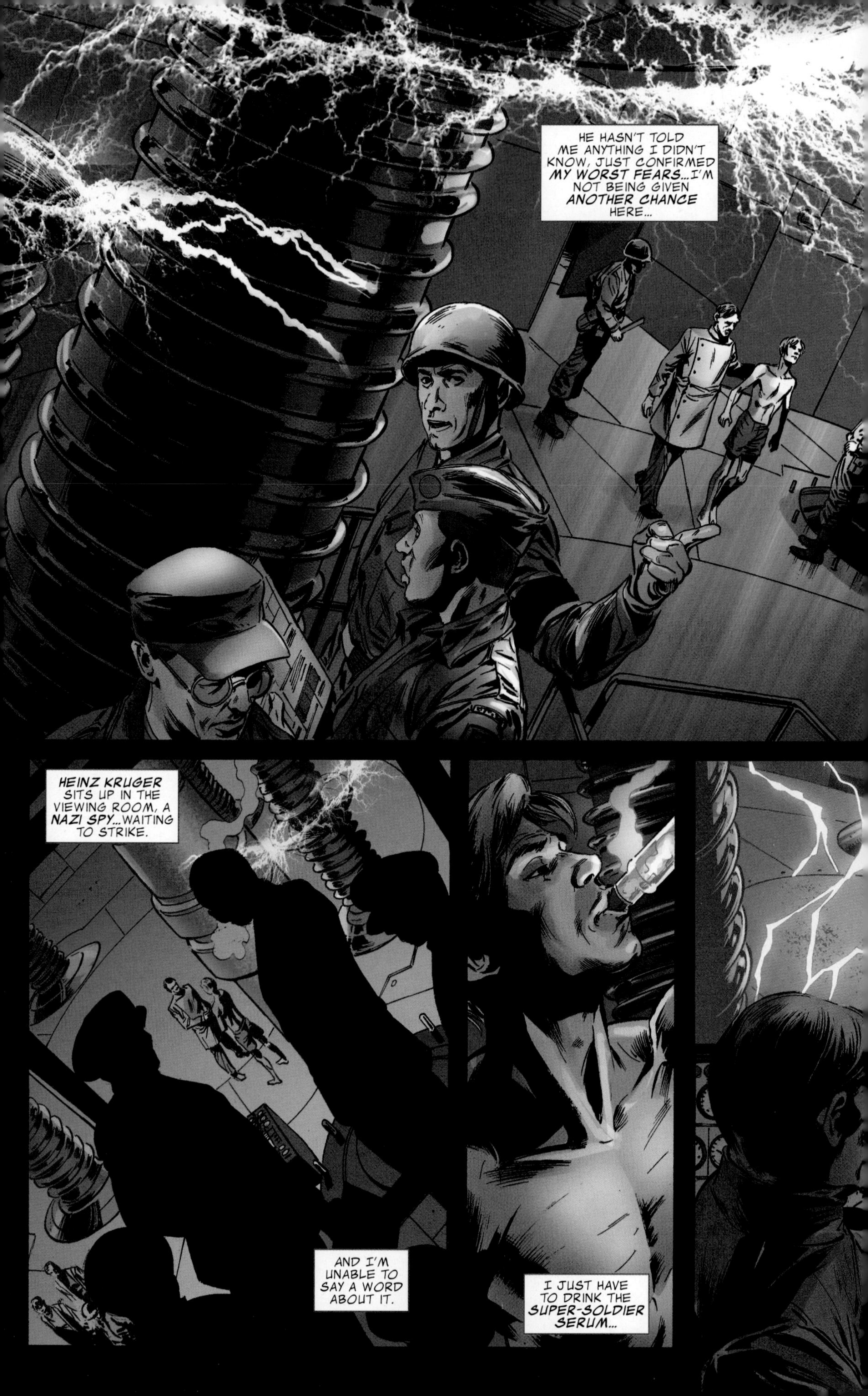
HE HASN'T TOLD ME ANYTHING I DIDN'T KNOW, JUST CONFIRMED MY WORST FEARS... I'M NOT BEING GIVEN ANOTHER CHANCE HERE...
HEINZ KRUGER SITS UP IN THE VIEWING ROOM, A NAZI SPY... WAITING TO STRIKE.
AND I'M UNABLE TO SAY A WORD ABOUT IT.
I JUST HAVE TO DRINK THE SUPER-SOLDIER SERUM...

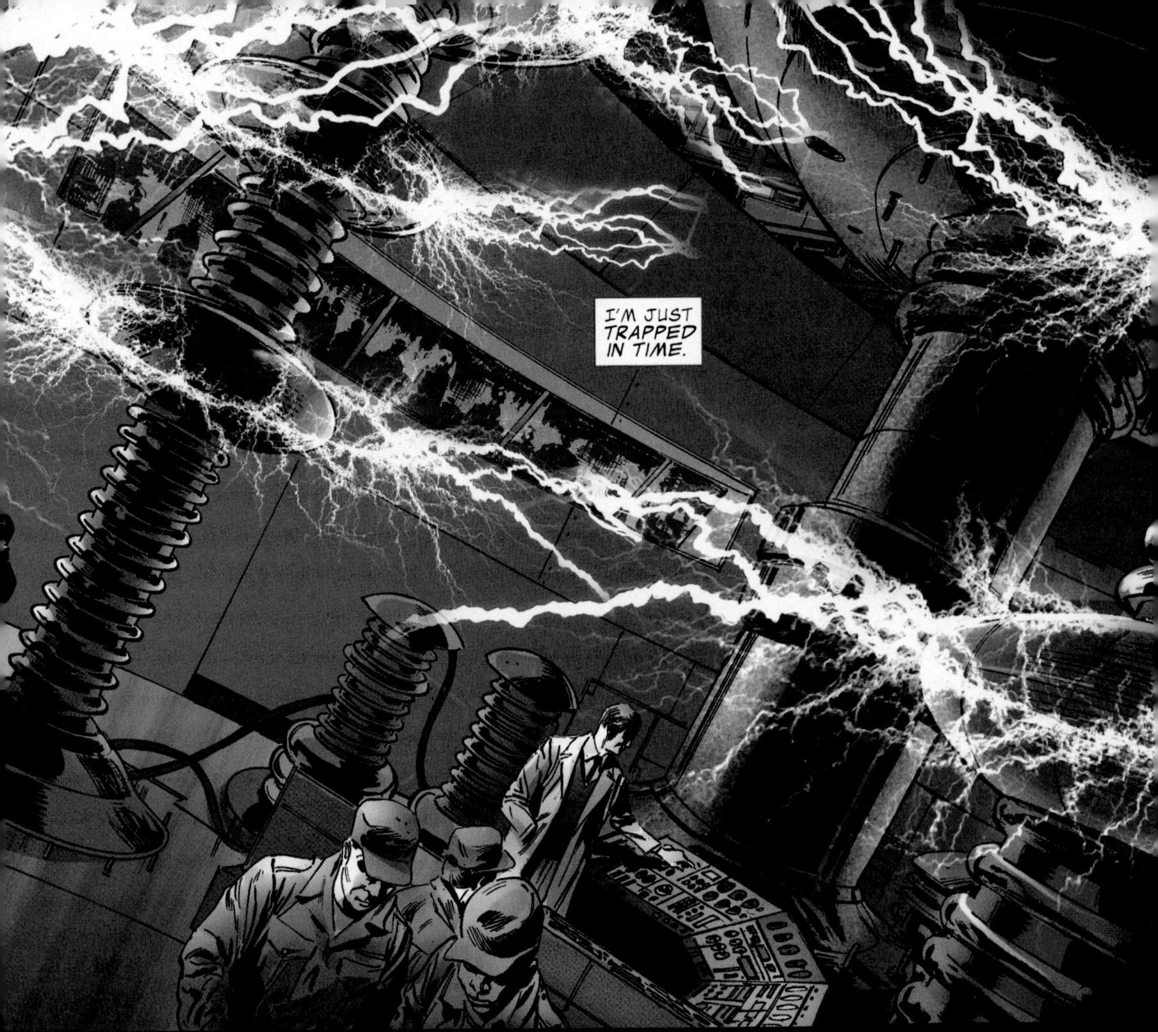
I'M JUST TRAPPED IN TIME.

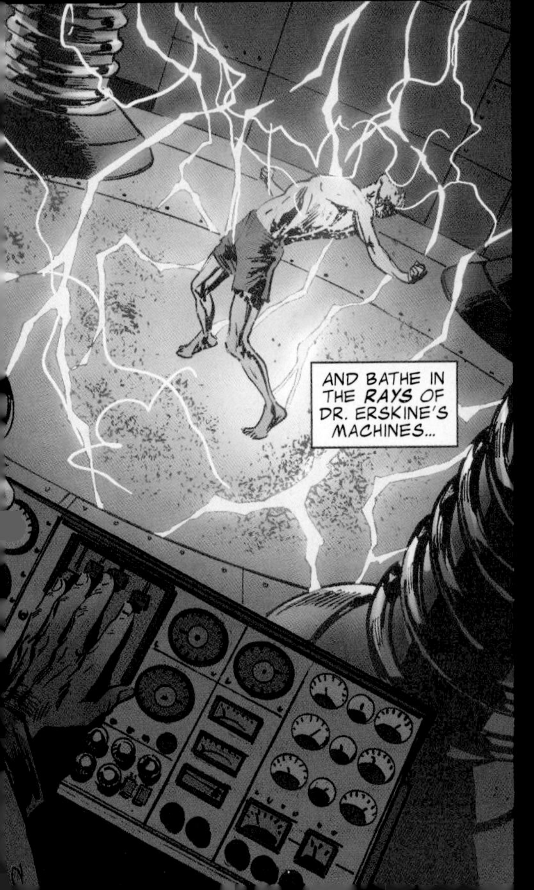
AND BATHE IN THE RAYS OF DR. ERSKINE'S MACHINES...

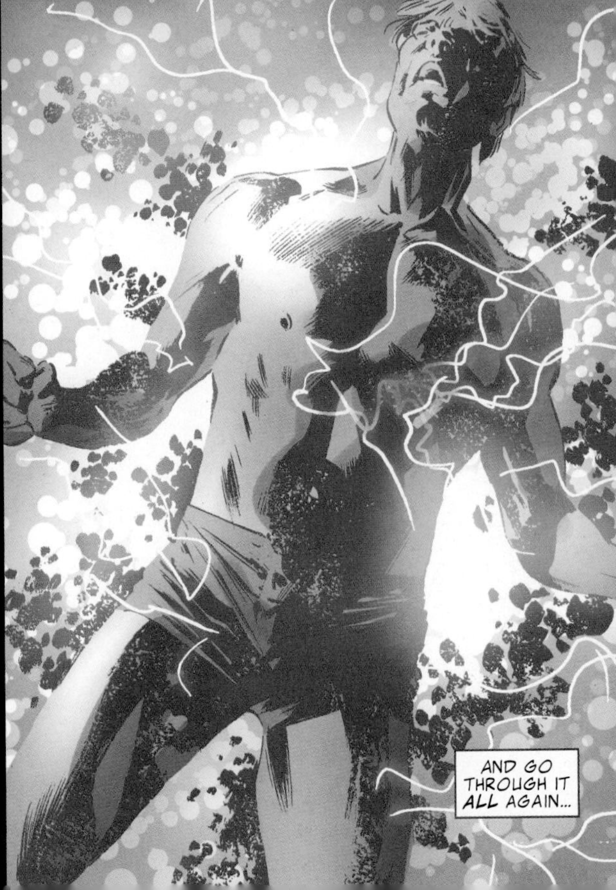
AND GO THROUGH IT ALL AGAIN...

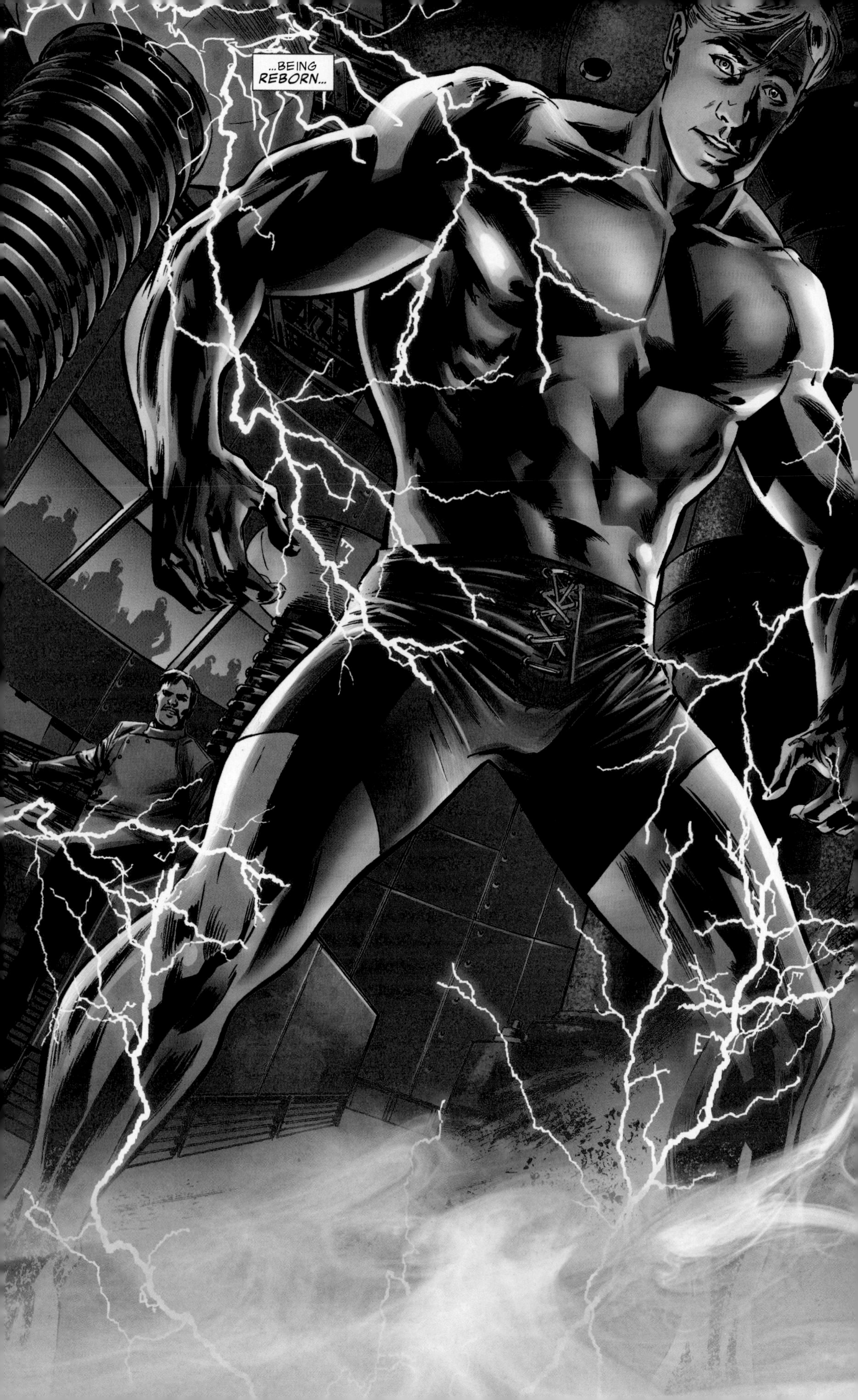
...BEING REBORN...

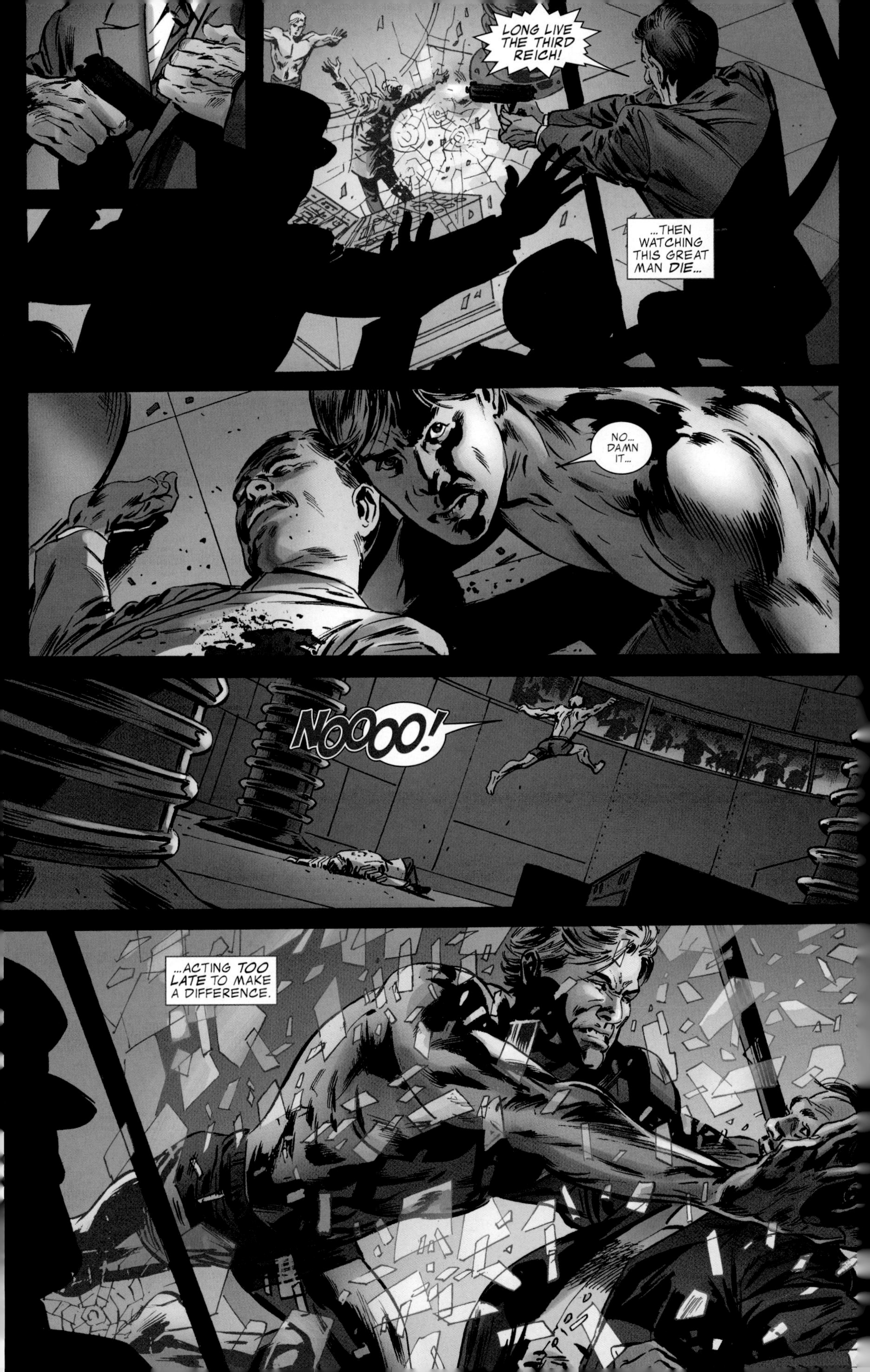
LONG LIVE THE THIRD REICH!
...THEN WATCHING THIS GREAT MAN DIE...
NO... DAMN IT...
NOOOO!
...ACTING TOO LATE TO MAKE A DIFFERENCE.

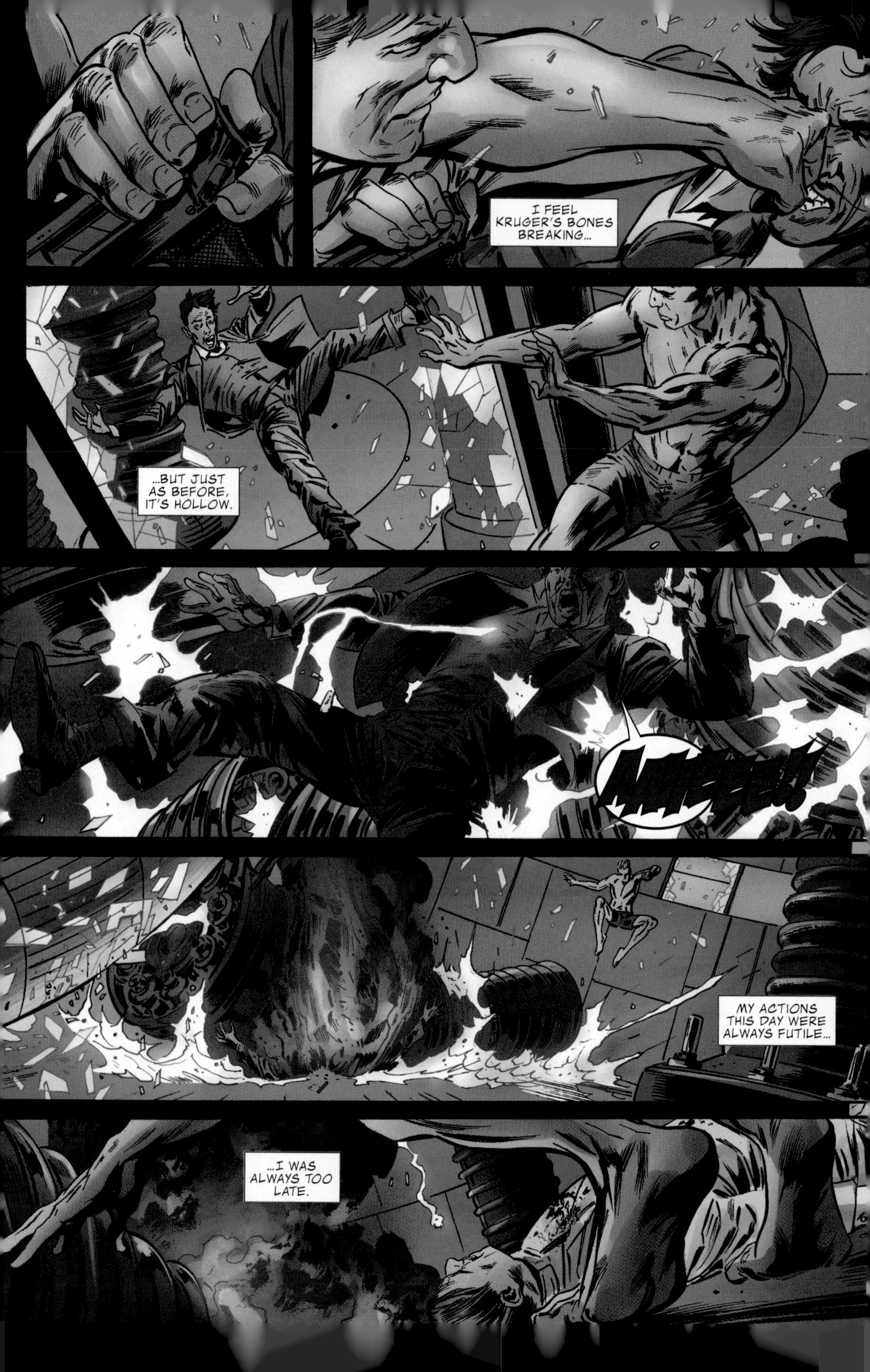
I FEEL KRUGER'S BONES BREAKING...
...BUT JUST AS BEFORE, IT'S HOLLOW.
MY ACTIONS THIS DAY WERE ALWAYS FUTILE...
...I WAS ALWAYS TOO LATE.

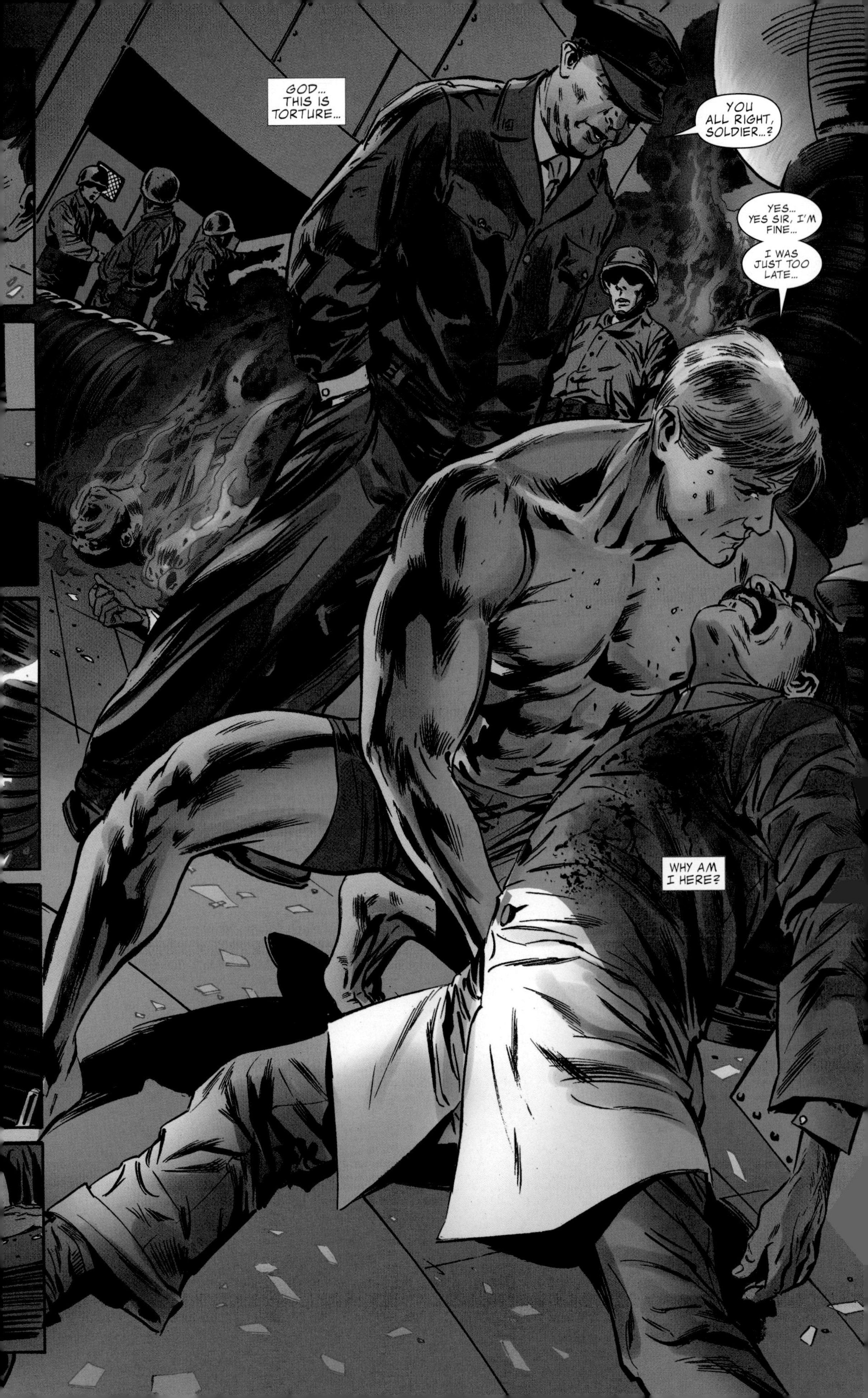
GOD... THIS IS TORTURE...
YOU ALL RIGHT, SOLDIER...?
YES... YES SIR, I'M FINE...
I WAS JUST TOO LATE...
WHY AM I HERE?

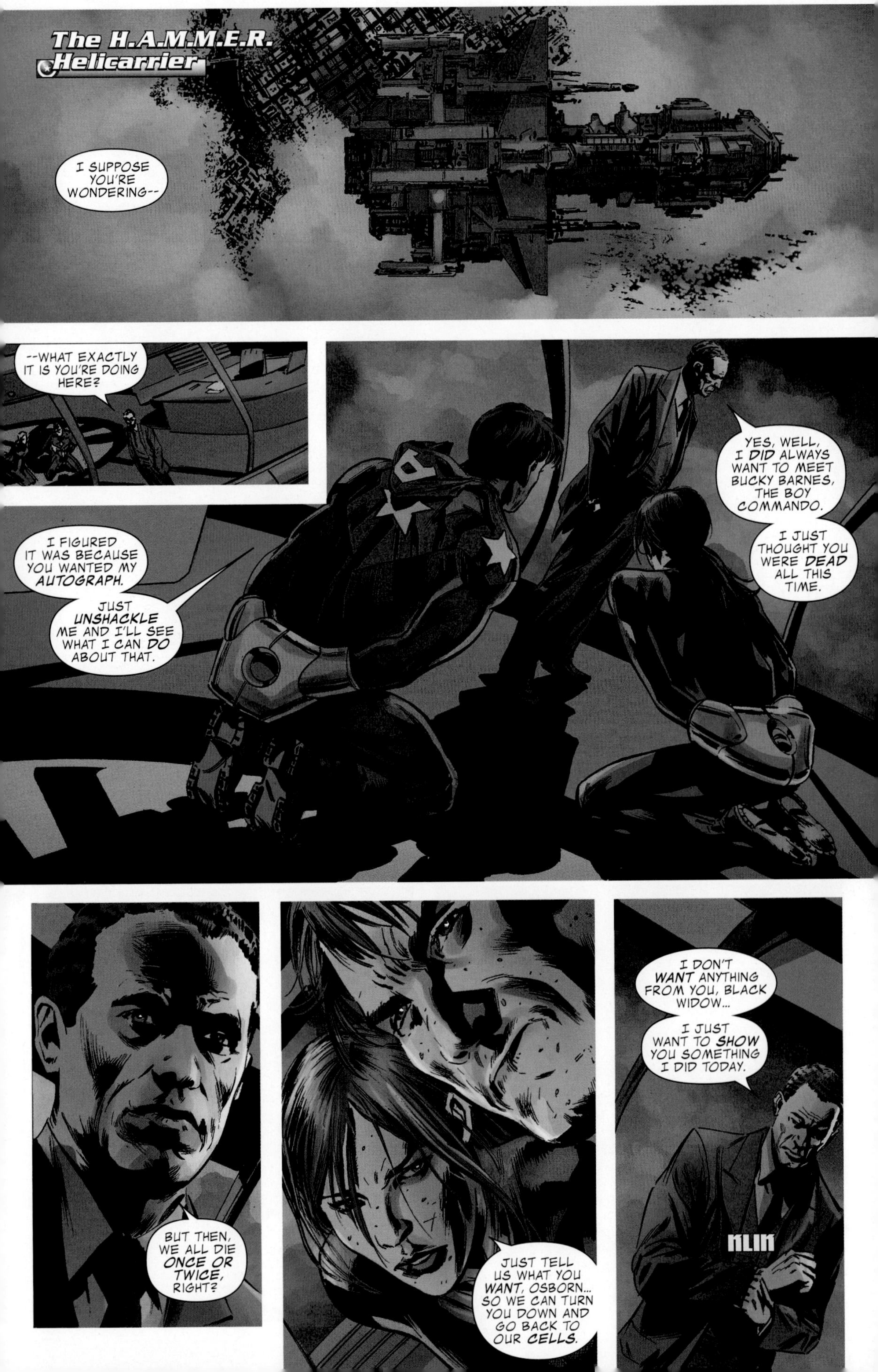
The H.A.M.M.E.R. Helicarrier
I SUPPOSE YOU'RE WONDERING--
--WHAT EXACTLY IT IS YOU'RE DOING HERE?
YES, WELL, I DID ALWAYS WANT TO MEET BUCKY BARNES, THE BOY COMMANDO.
I JUST THOUGHT YOU WERE DEAD ALL THIS TIME.
I FIGURED IT WAS BECAUSE YOU WANTED MY AUTOGRAPH.
JUST UNSHACKLE ME AND I'LL SEE WHAT I CAN DO ABOUT THAT.
BUT THEN, WE ALL DIE ONCE OR TWICE, RIGHT?
JUST TELL US WHAT YOU WANT, OSBORN... SO WE CAN TURN YOU DOWN AND GO BACK TO OUR CELLS.
I DON'T WANT ANYTHING FROM YOU, BLACK WIDOW...
I JUST WANT TO SHOW YOU SOMETHING I DID TODAY.
KLIK

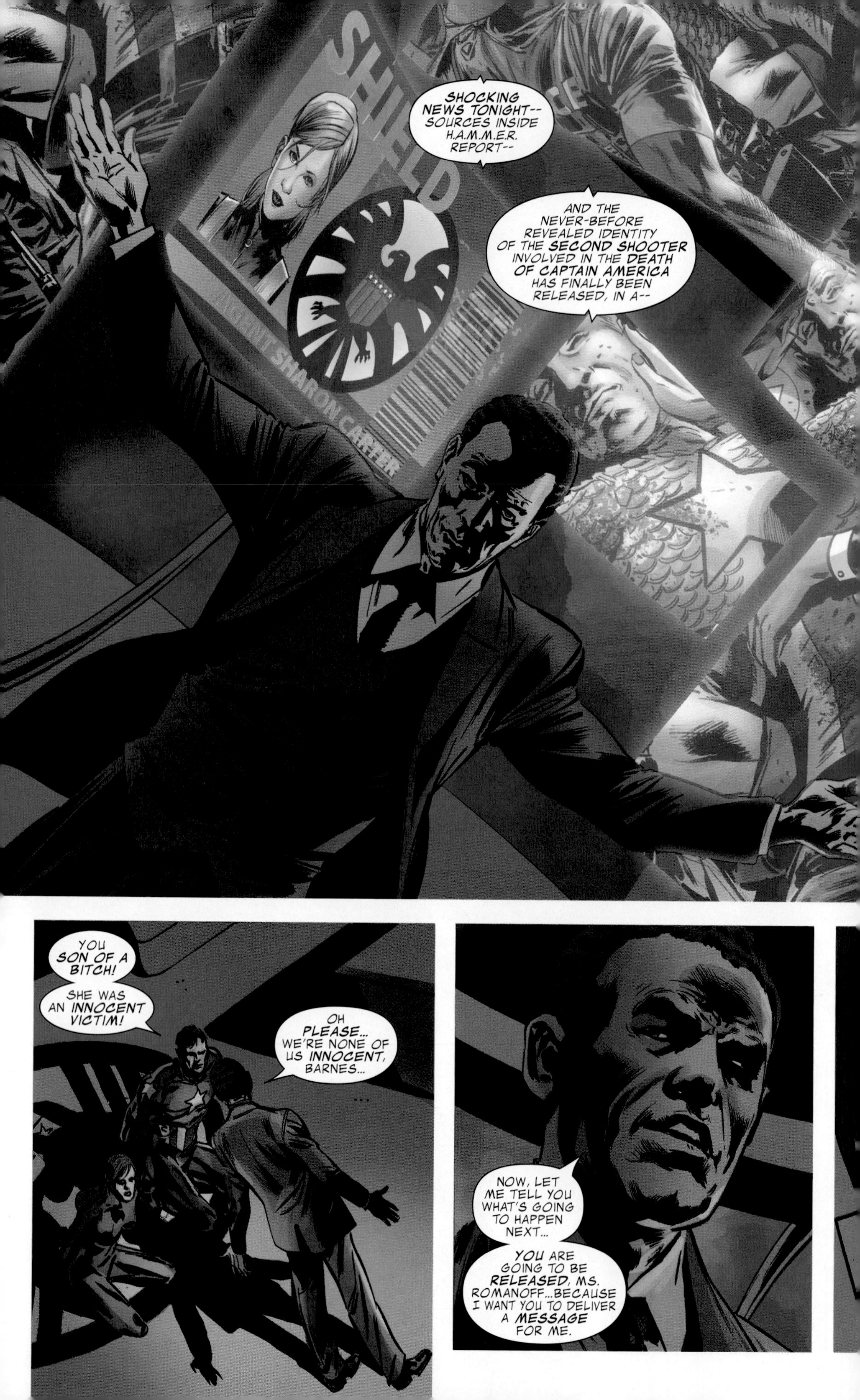
SHIELD
AGENT SHARON CARTER
SHOCKING NEWS TONIGHT-- SOURCES INSIDE H.A.M.M.E.R. REPORT--
AND THE NEVER-BEFORE REVEALED IDENTITY OF THE SECOND SHOOTER INVOLVED IN THE DEATH OF CAPTAIN AMERICA HAS FINALLY BEEN RELEASED, IN A--
YOU SON OF A BITCH!
SHE WAS AN INNOCENT VICTIM!
OH PLEASE... WE'RE NONE OF US INNOCENT, BARNES...
NOW, LET ME TELL YOU WHAT'S GOING TO HAPPEN NEXT...
YOU ARE GOING TO BE RELEASED, MS. ROMANOFF...BECAUSE I WANT YOU TO DELIVER A MESSAGE FOR ME.

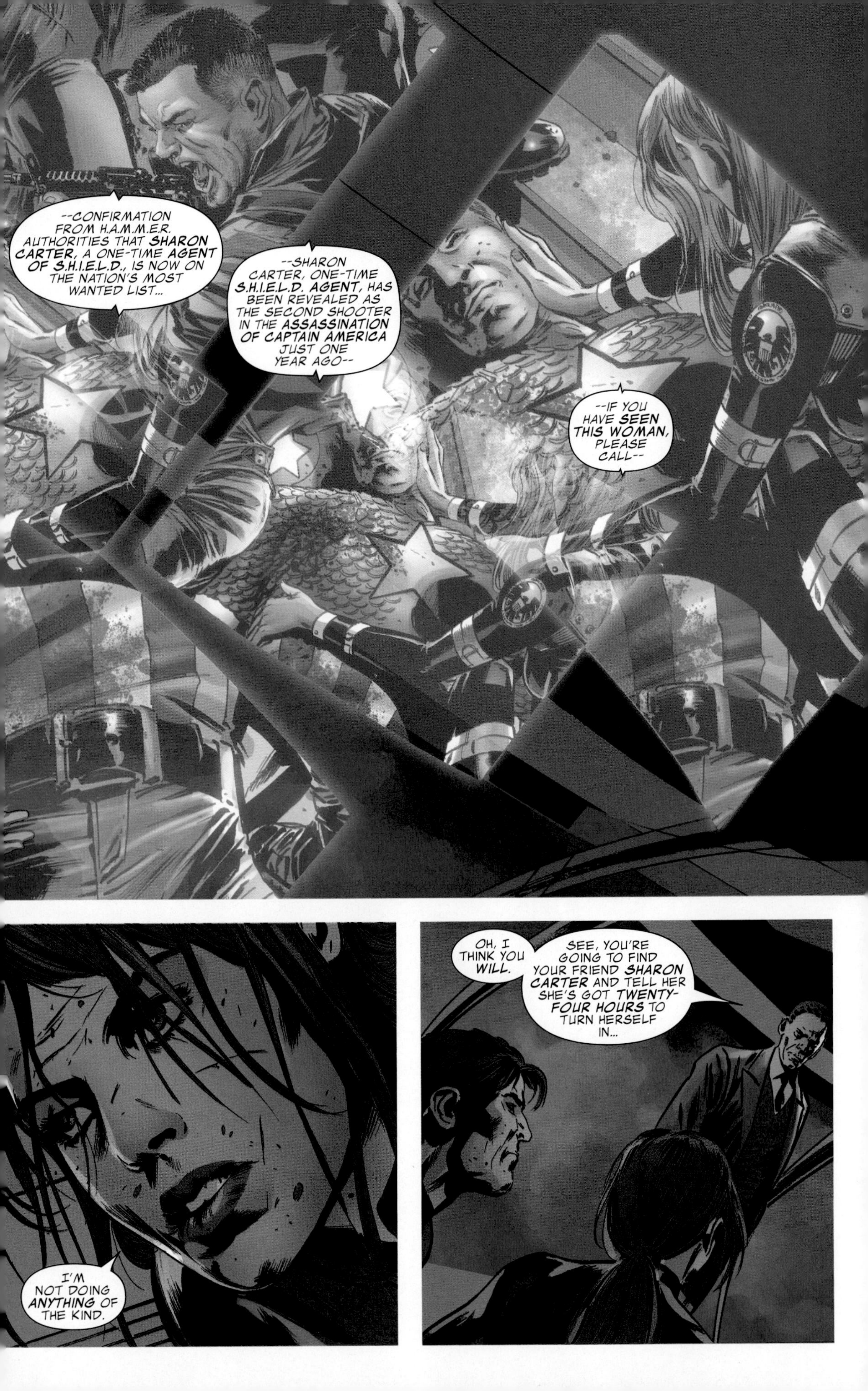
--CONFIRMATION FROM H.A.M.M.E.R. AUTHORITIES THAT SHARON CARTER, A ONE-TIME AGENT OF S.H.I.E.L.D., IS NOW ON THE NATION'S MOST WANTED LIST...
--SHARON CARTER, ONE-TIME S.H.I.E.L.D. AGENT, HAS BEEN REVEALED AS THE SECOND SHOOTER IN THE ASSASSINATION OF CAPTAIN AMERICA JUST ONE YEAR AGO--
--IF YOU HAVE SEEN THIS WOMAN, PLEASE CALL--
I'M NOT DOING ANYTHING OF THE KIND.
OH, I THINK YOU WILL.
SEE, YOU'RE GOING TO FIND YOUR FRIEND SHARON CARTER AND TELL HER SHE'S GOT TWENTY-FOUR HOURS TO TURN HERSELF IN...

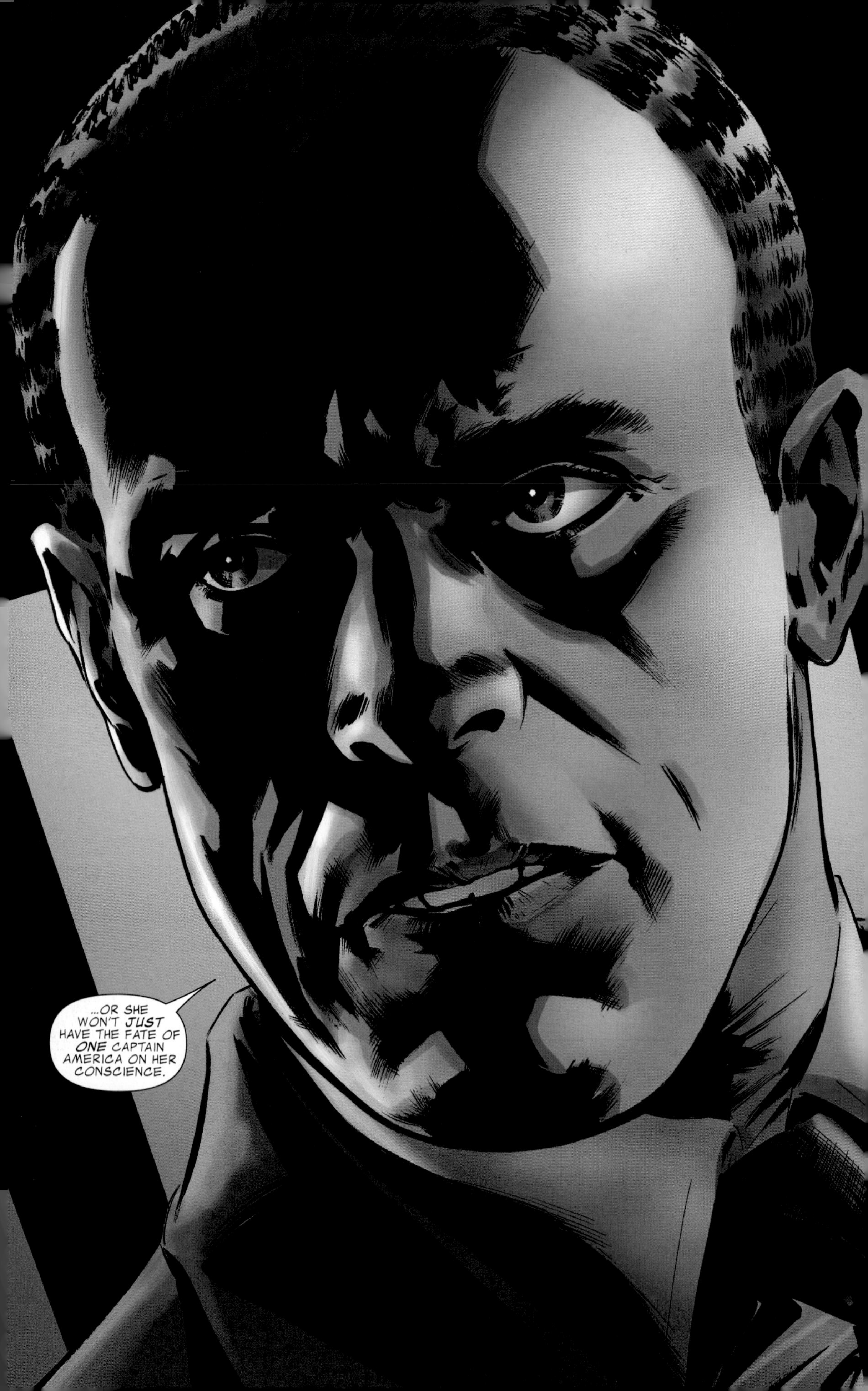
...OR SHE WON'T *JUST* HAVE THE FATE OF *ONE* CAPTAIN AMERICA ON HER CONSCIENCE.

"The tree of liberty must be refreshed
from time to time with the blood of patriots"

– *Jefferson*

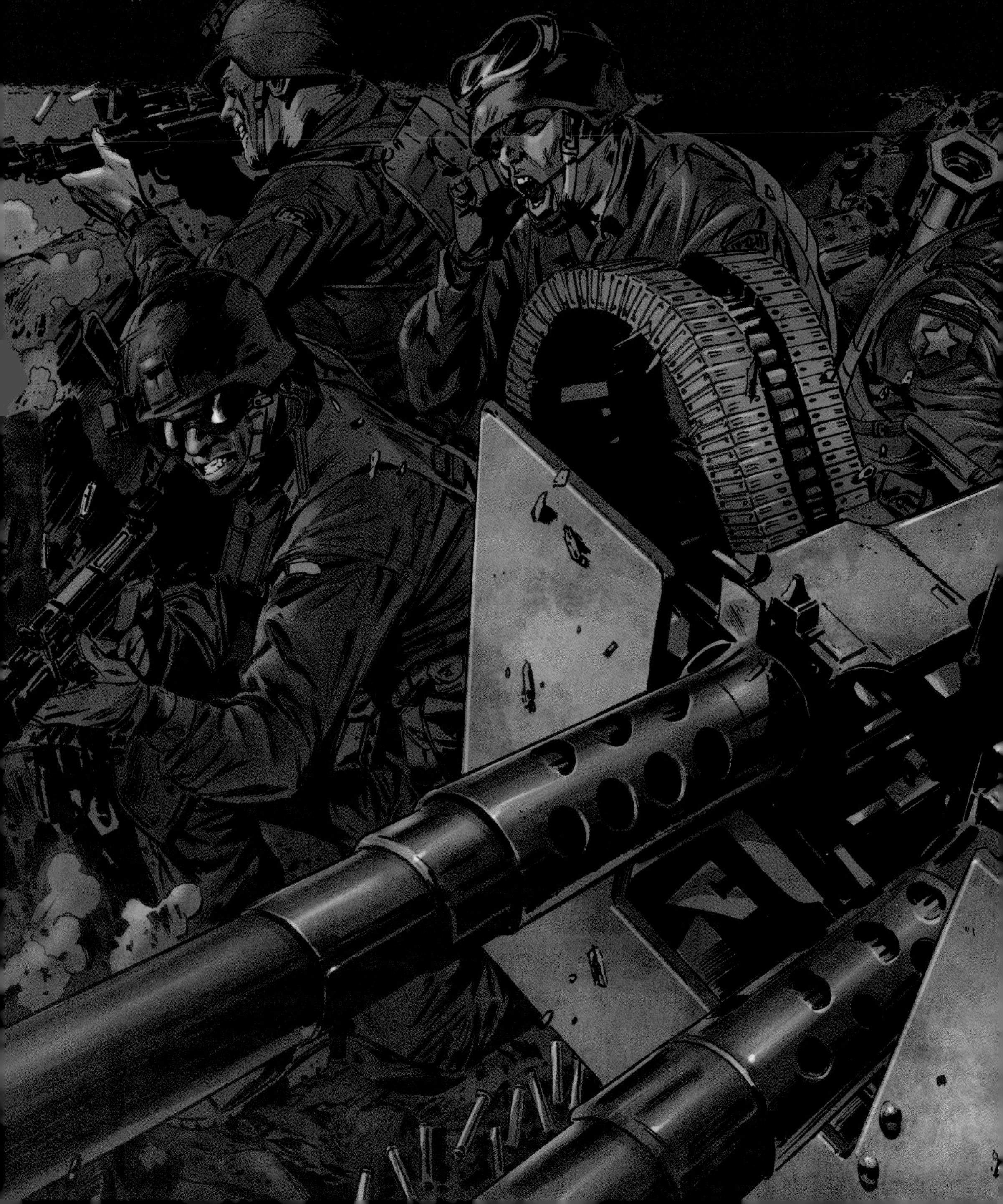

3

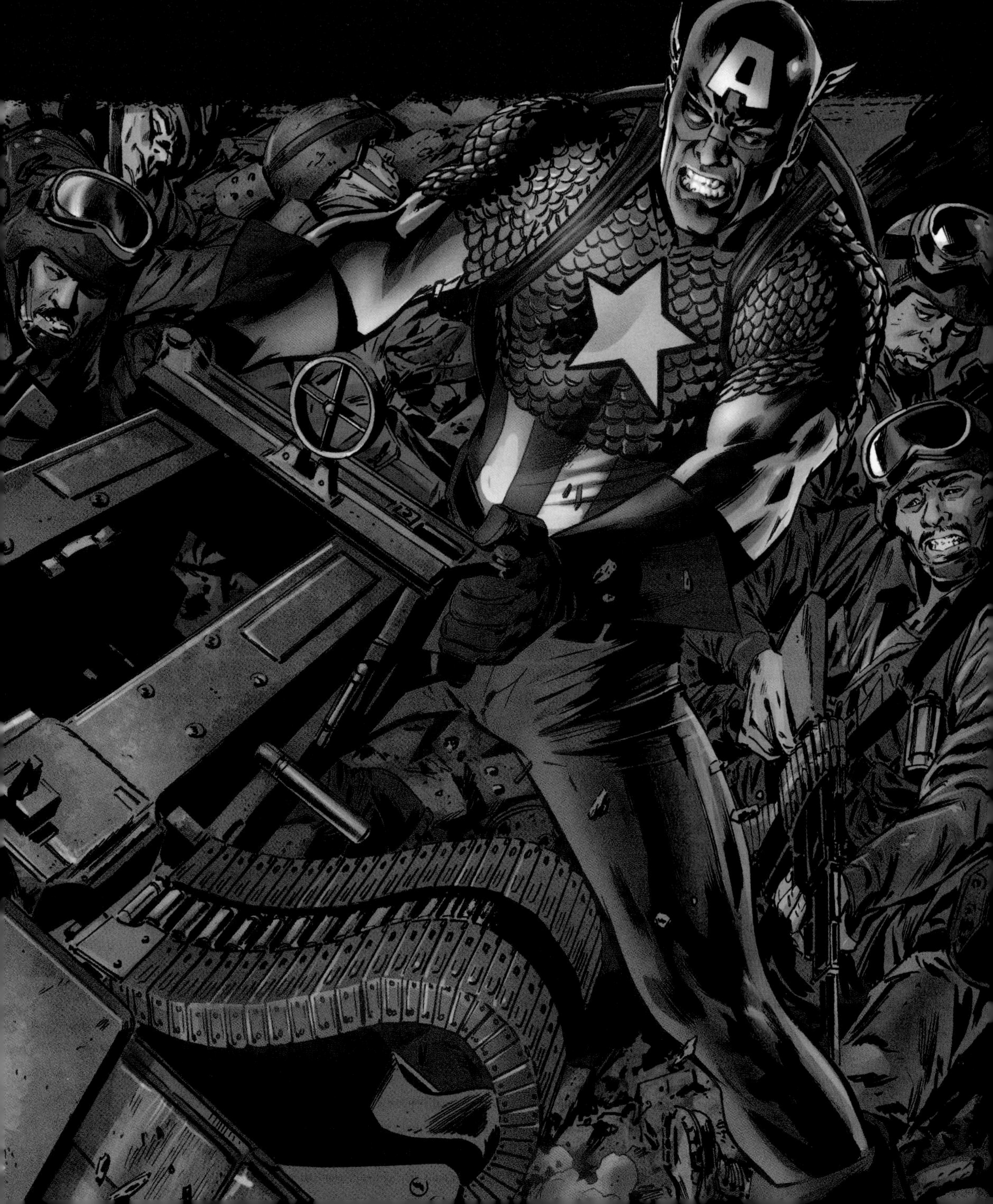

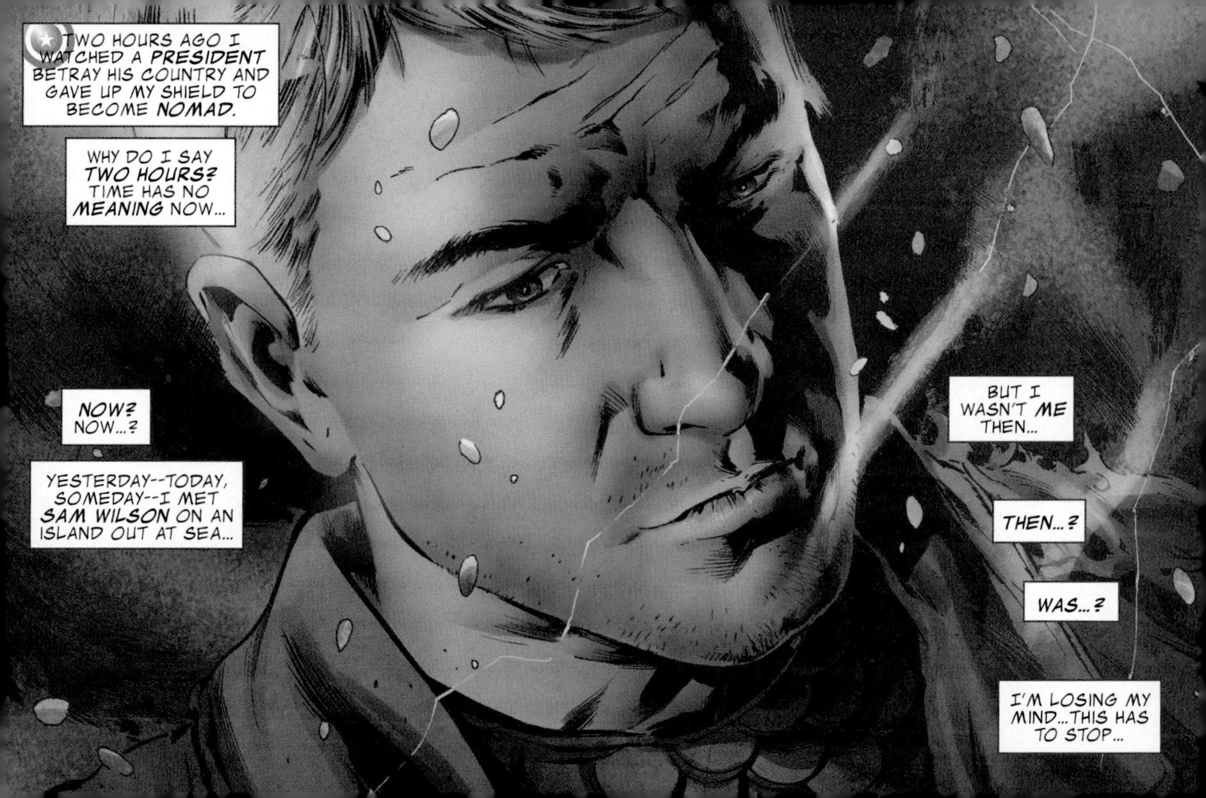
TWO HOURS AGO I WATCHED A PRESIDENT BETRAY HIS COUNTRY AND GAVE UP MY SHIELD TO BECOME NOMAD.
WHY DO I SAY TWO HOURS? TIME HAS NO MEANING NOW...
NOW? NOW...?
YESTERDAY--TODAY, SOMEDAY--I MET SAM WILSON ON AN ISLAND OUT AT SEA...
BUT I WASN'T ME THEN...
THEN...?
WAS...?
I'M LOSING MY MIND...THIS HAS TO STOP...

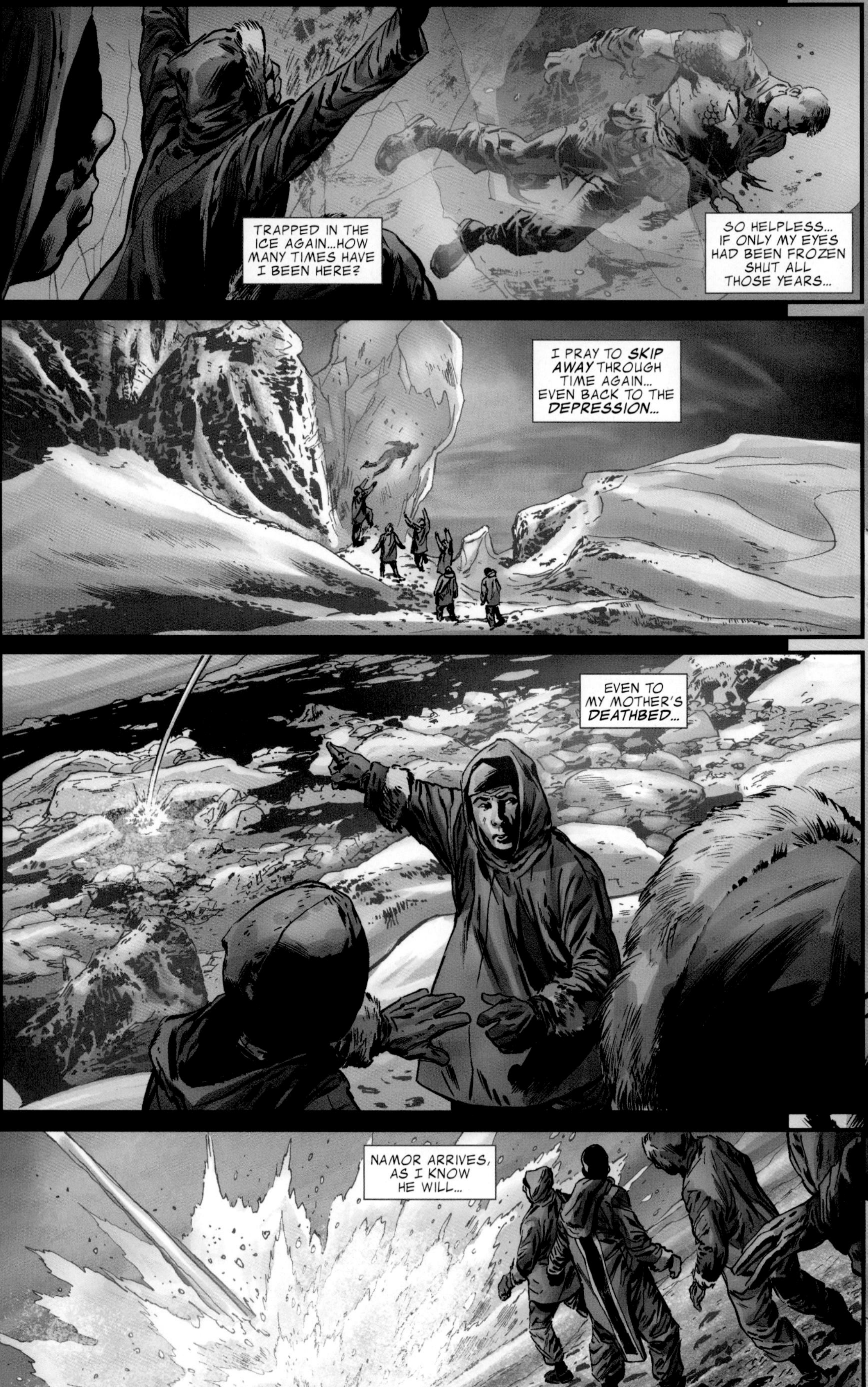
TRAPPED IN THE ICE AGAIN...HOW MANY TIMES HAVE I BEEN HERE?
SO HELPLESS... IF ONLY MY EYES HAD BEEN FROZEN SHUT ALL THOSE YEARS...
I PRAY TO **SKIP AWAY** THROUGH TIME AGAIN... EVEN BACK TO THE ***DEPRESSION***...
EVEN TO MY MOTHER'S ***DEATHBED***...
NAMOR ARRIVES, AS I KNOW HE WILL...

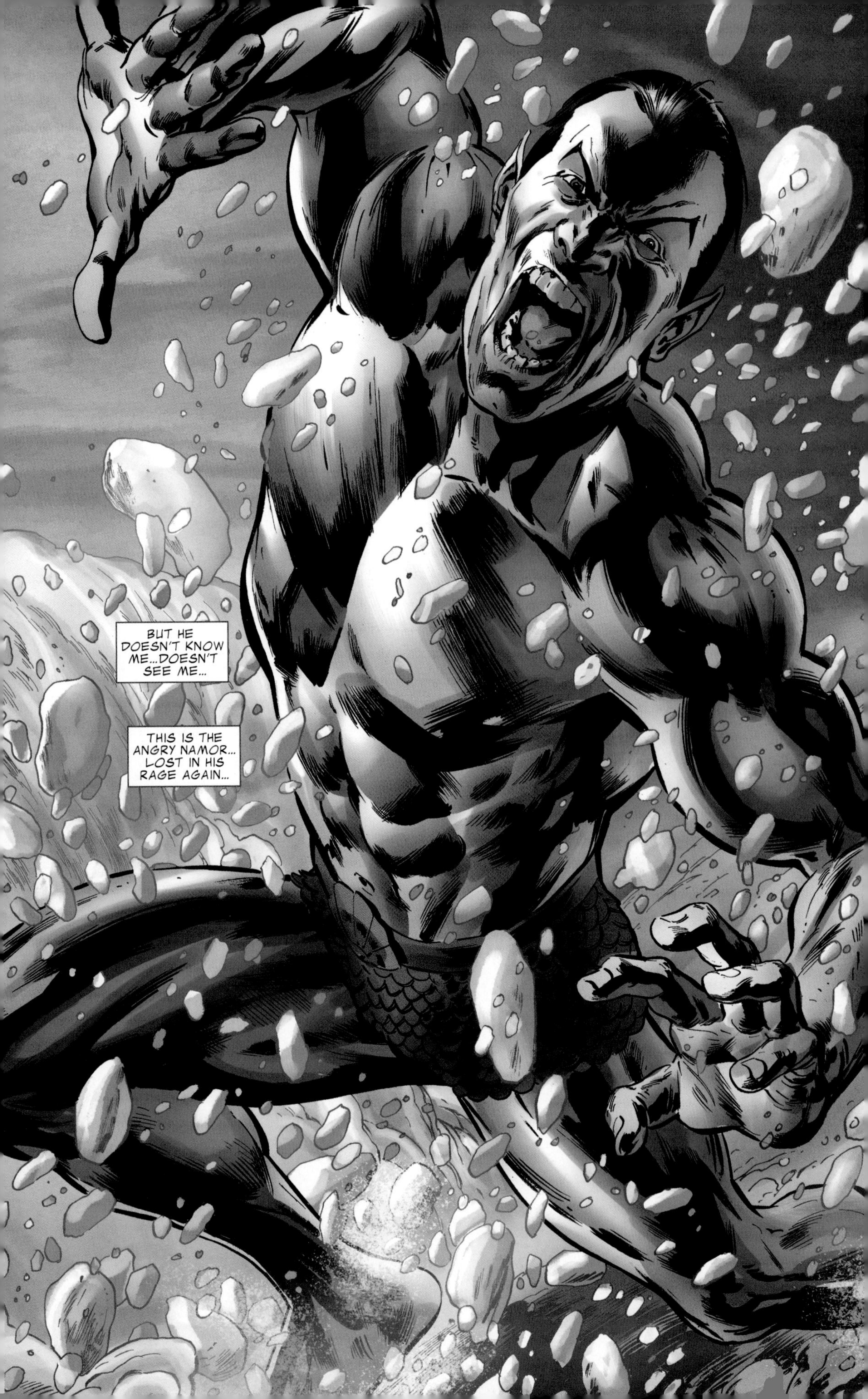
BUT HE DOESN'T KNOW ME...DOESN'T SEE ME...
THIS IS THE ANGRY NAMOR... LOST IN HIS RAGE AGAIN...

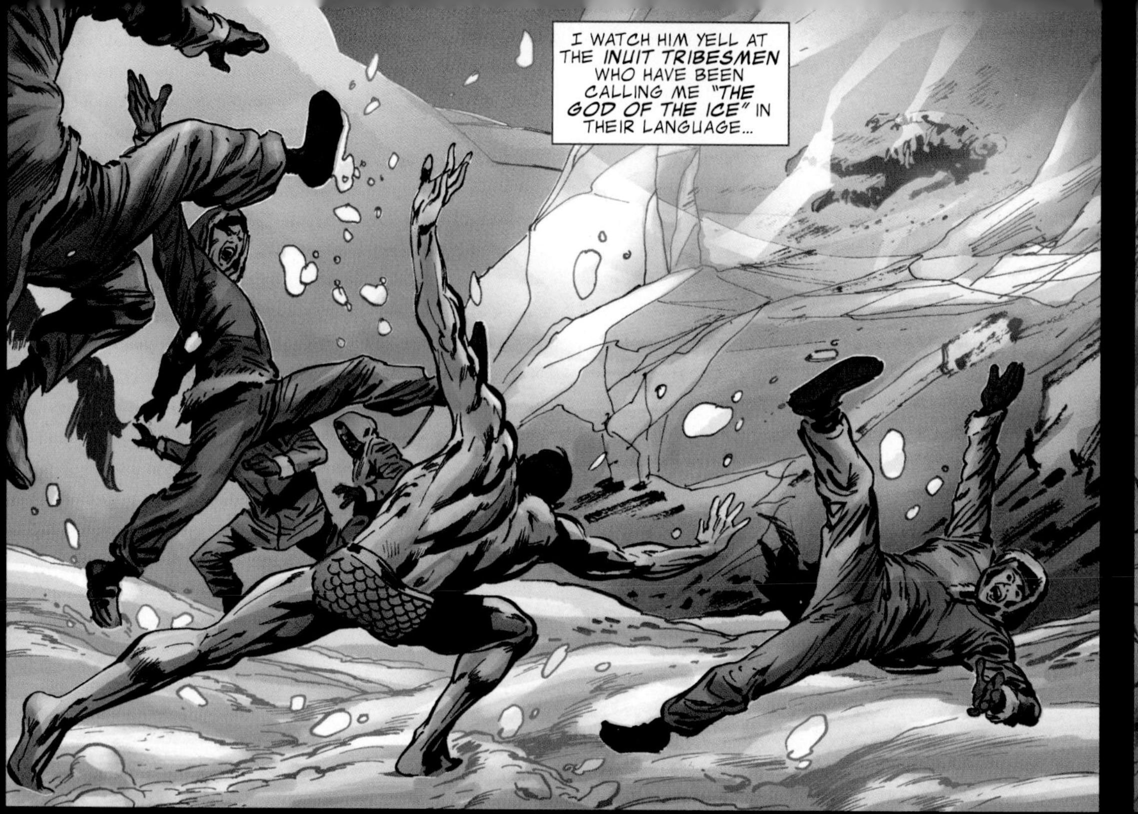
I WATCH HIM YELL AT THE *INUIT TRIBESMEN* WHO HAVE BEEN CALLING ME *"THE GOD OF THE ICE"* IN THEIR LANGUAGE...

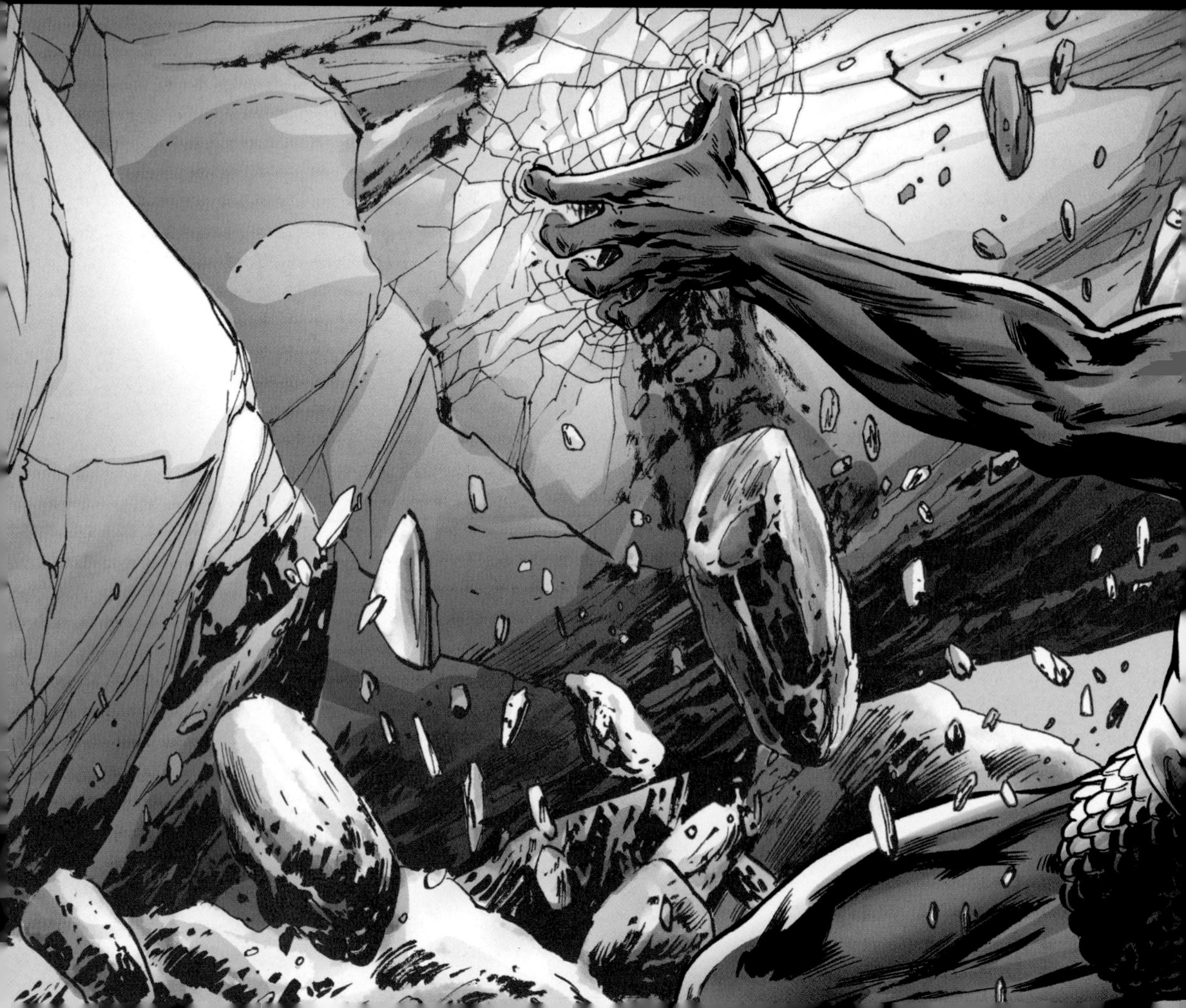

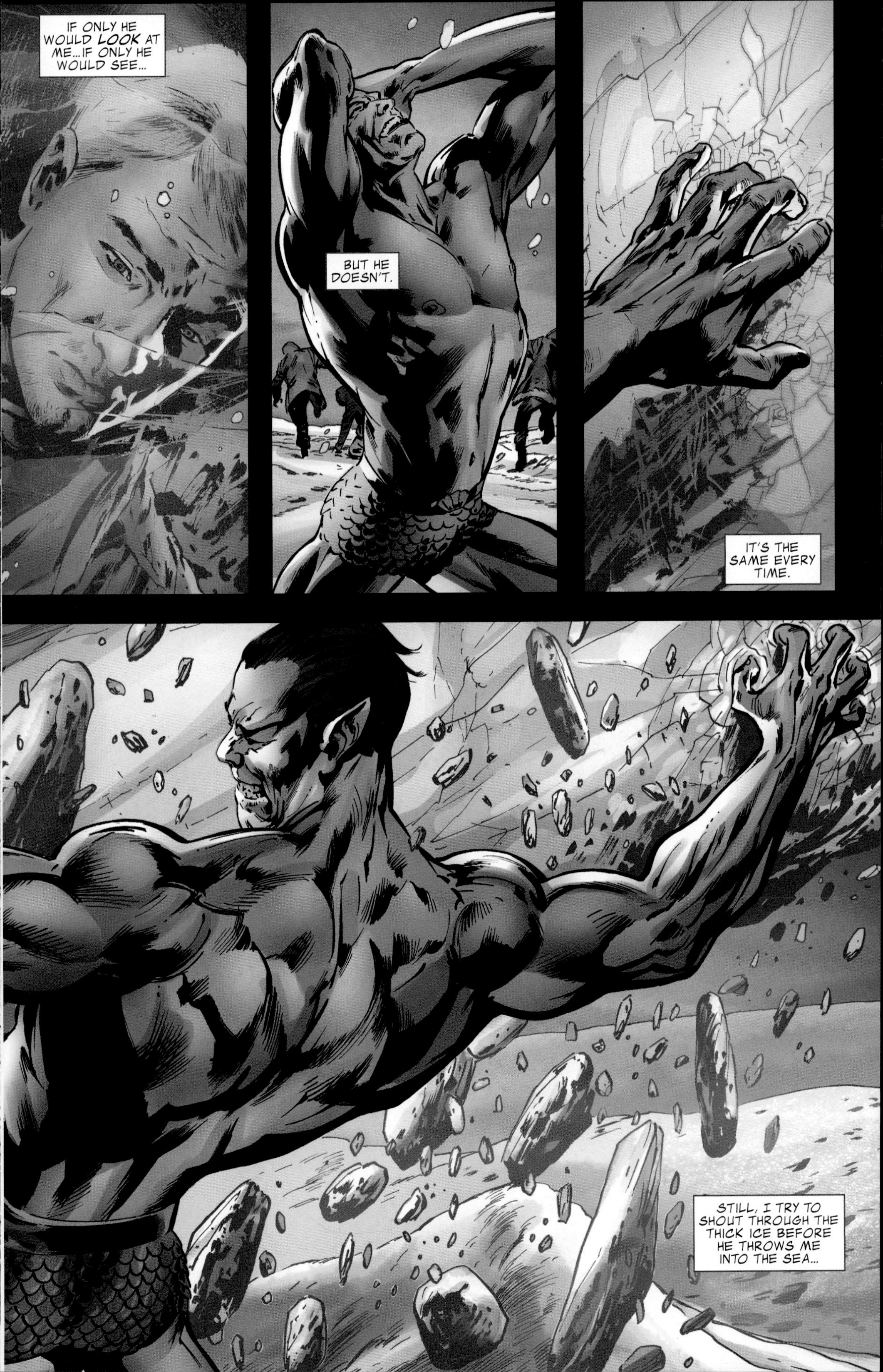
IF ONLY HE WOULD LOOK AT ME...IF ONLY HE WOULD SEE...
BUT HE DOESN'T.
IT'S THE SAME EVERY TIME.
STILL, I TRY TO SHOUT THROUGH THE THICK ICE BEFORE HE THROWS ME INTO THE SEA...

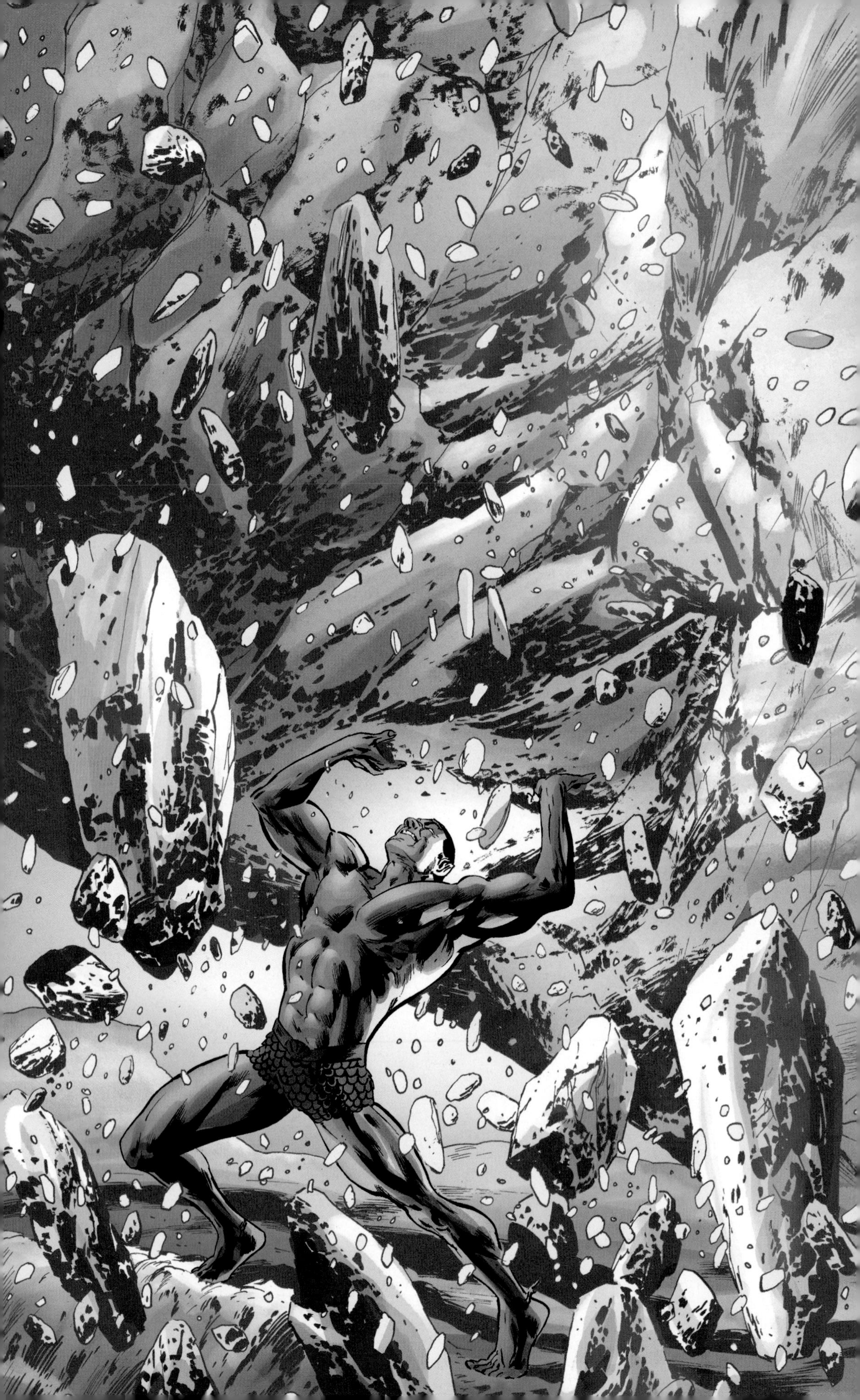

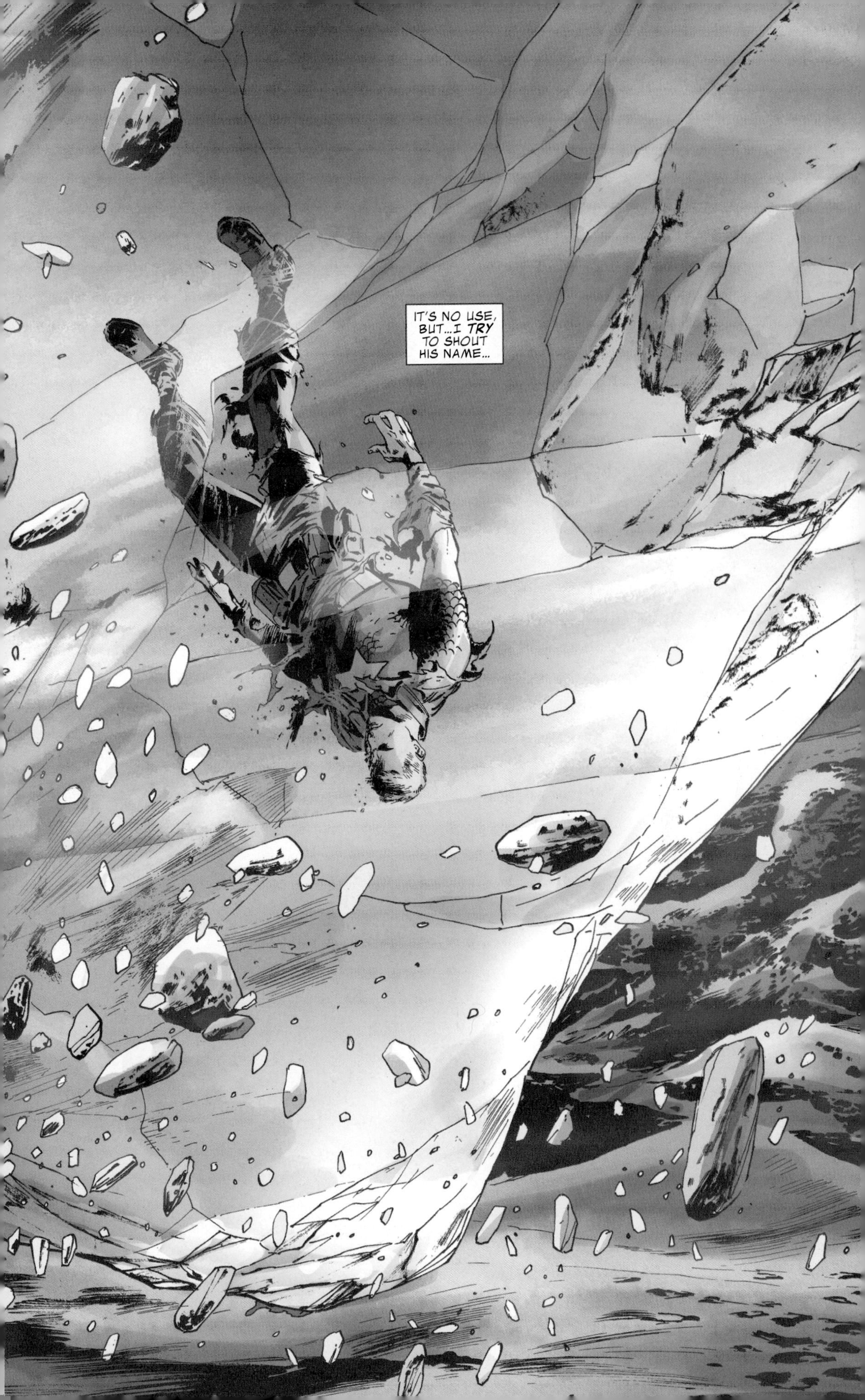
IT'S NO USE, BUT...I TRY TO SHOUT HIS NAME...

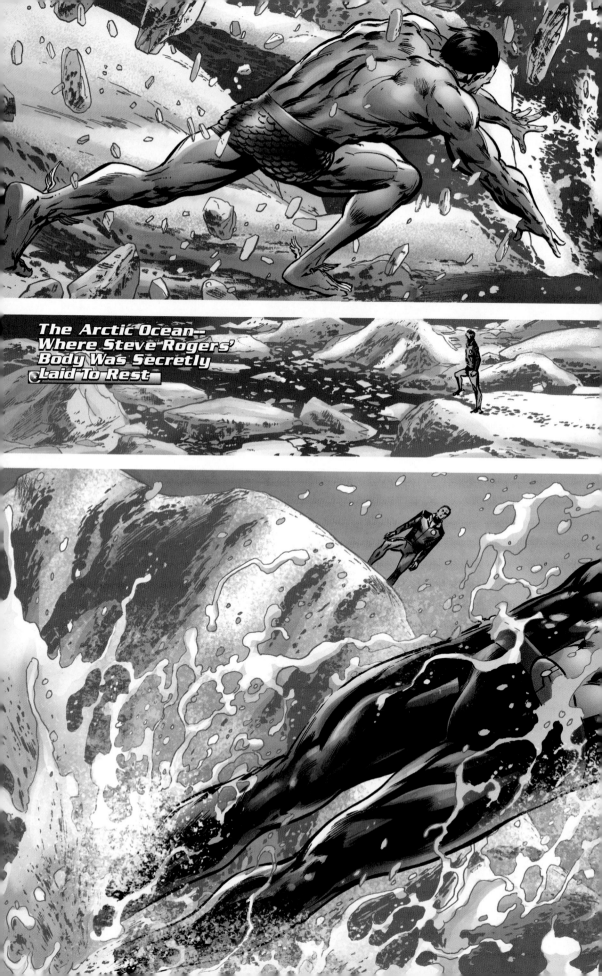

The Arctic Ocean—
Where Steve Rogers'
Body Was Secretly
Laid To Rest

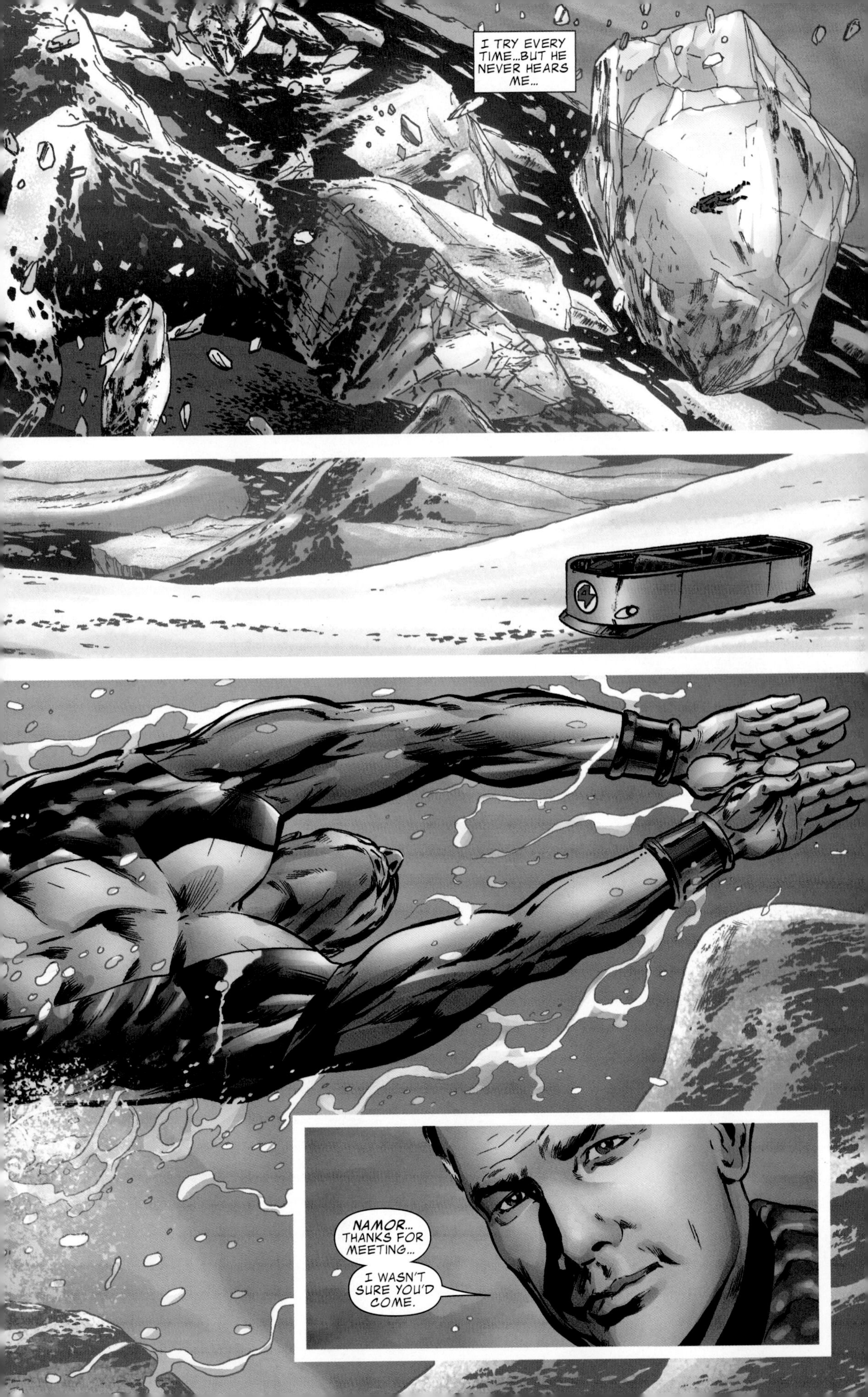
I TRY EVERY TIME...BUT HE NEVER HEARS ME...
NAMOR... THANKS FOR MEETING...
I WASN'T SURE YOU'D COME.

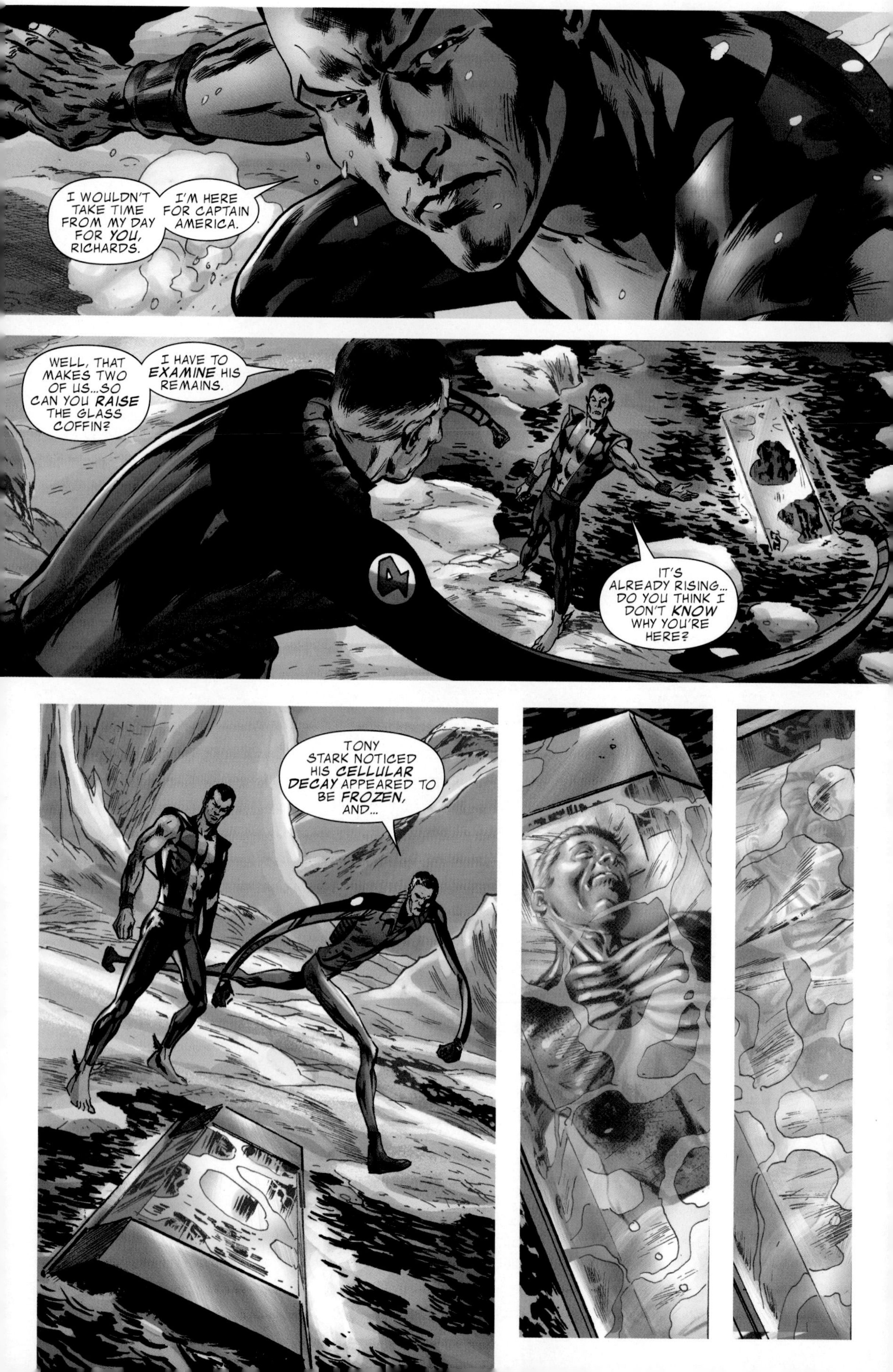

I WOULDN'T TAKE TIME FROM MY DAY FOR *YOU*, RICHARDS.
I'M HERE FOR CAPTAIN AMERICA.
WELL, THAT MAKES TWO OF US...SO CAN YOU *RAISE* THE GLASS COFFIN?
I HAVE TO *EXAMINE* HIS REMAINS.
IT'S ALREADY RISING... DO YOU THINK I DON'T *KNOW* WHY YOU'RE HERE?
TONY STARK NOTICED HIS *CELLULAR DECAY* APPEARED TO BE *FROZEN*, AND...

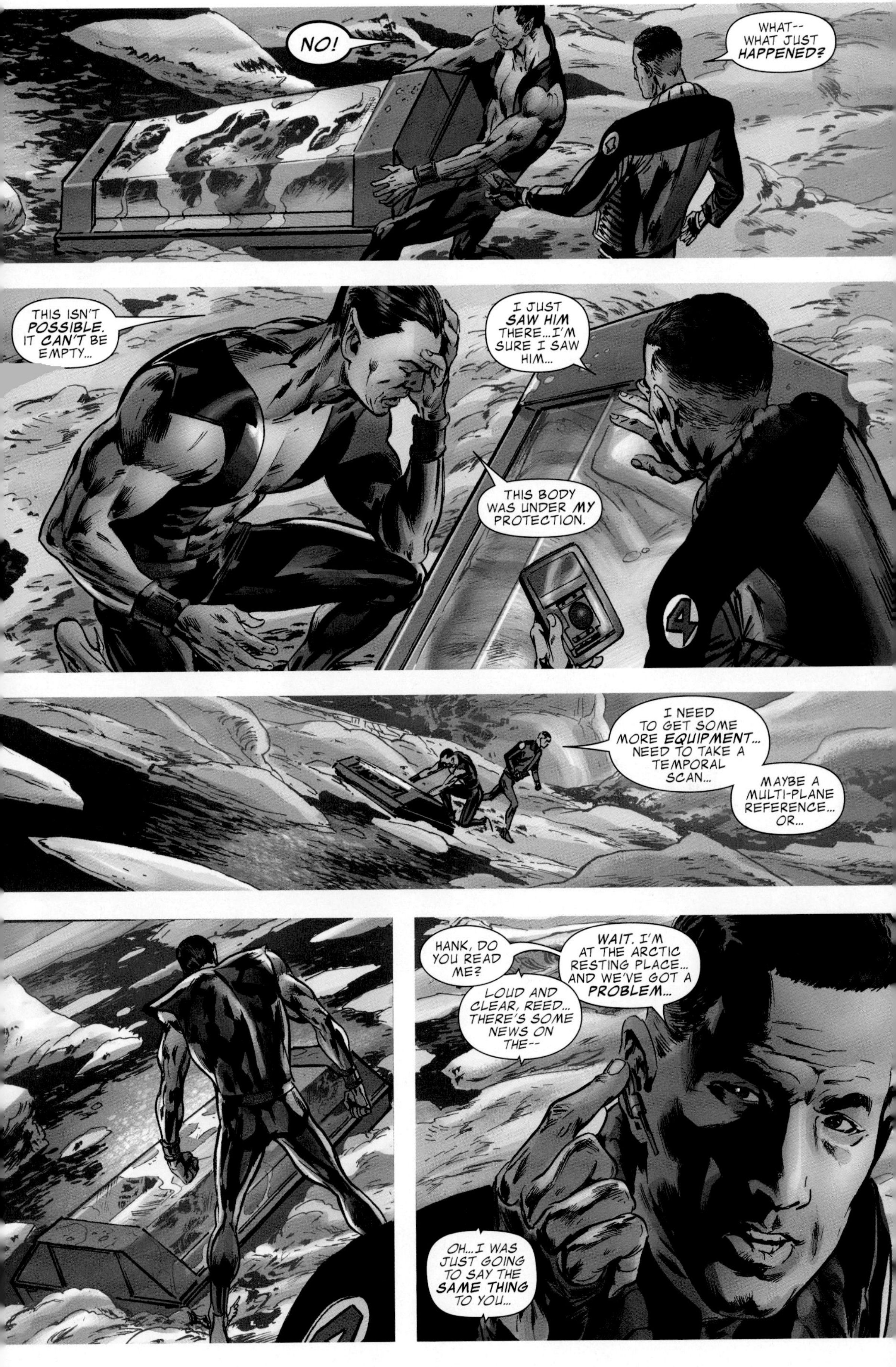
NO!
WHAT-- WHAT JUST HAPPENED?
THIS ISN'T POSSIBLE. IT CAN'T BE EMPTY...
I JUST SAW HIM THERE...I'M SURE I SAW HIM...
THIS BODY WAS UNDER MY PROTECTION.
I NEED TO GET SOME MORE EQUIPMENT... NEED TO TAKE A TEMPORAL SCAN...
MAYBE A MULTI-PLANE REFERENCE... OR...
HANK, DO YOU READ ME?
WAIT. I'M AT THE ARCTIC RESTING PLACE... AND WE'VE GOT A PROBLEM...
LOUD AND CLEAR, REED... THERE'S SOME NEWS ON THE--
OH...I WAS JUST GOING TO SAY THE SAME THING TO YOU...

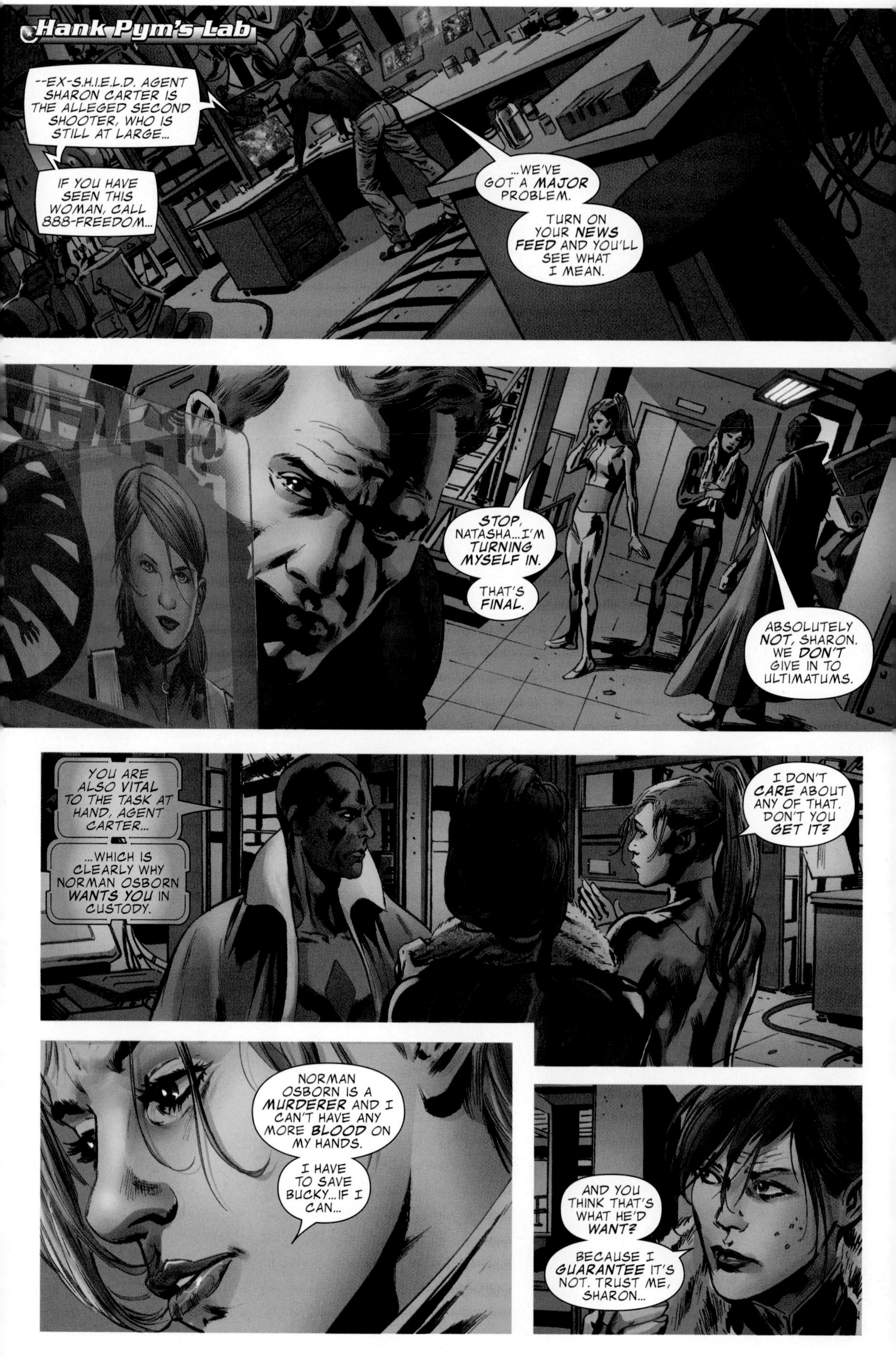
Hank Pym's Lab
--EX-S.H.I.E.L.D. AGENT SHARON CARTER IS THE ALLEGED SECOND SHOOTER, WHO IS STILL AT LARGE...
IF YOU HAVE SEEN THIS WOMAN, CALL 888-FREEDOM...
...WE'VE GOT A MAJOR PROBLEM.
TURN ON YOUR NEWS FEED AND YOU'LL SEE WHAT I MEAN.
STOP, NATASHA...I'M TURNING MYSELF IN.
THAT'S FINAL.
ABSOLUTELY NOT, SHARON. WE DON'T GIVE IN TO ULTIMATUMS.
YOU ARE ALSO VITAL TO THE TASK AT HAND, AGENT CARTER...
...WHICH IS CLEARLY WHY NORMAN OSBORN WANTS YOU IN CUSTODY.
I DON'T CARE ABOUT ANY OF THAT. DON'T YOU GET IT?
NORMAN OSBORN IS A MURDERER AND I CAN'T HAVE ANY MORE BLOOD ON MY HANDS.
I HAVE TO SAVE BUCKY...IF I CAN...
AND YOU THINK THAT'S WHAT HE'D WANT?
BECAUSE I GUARANTEE IT'S NOT. TRUST ME, SHARON...

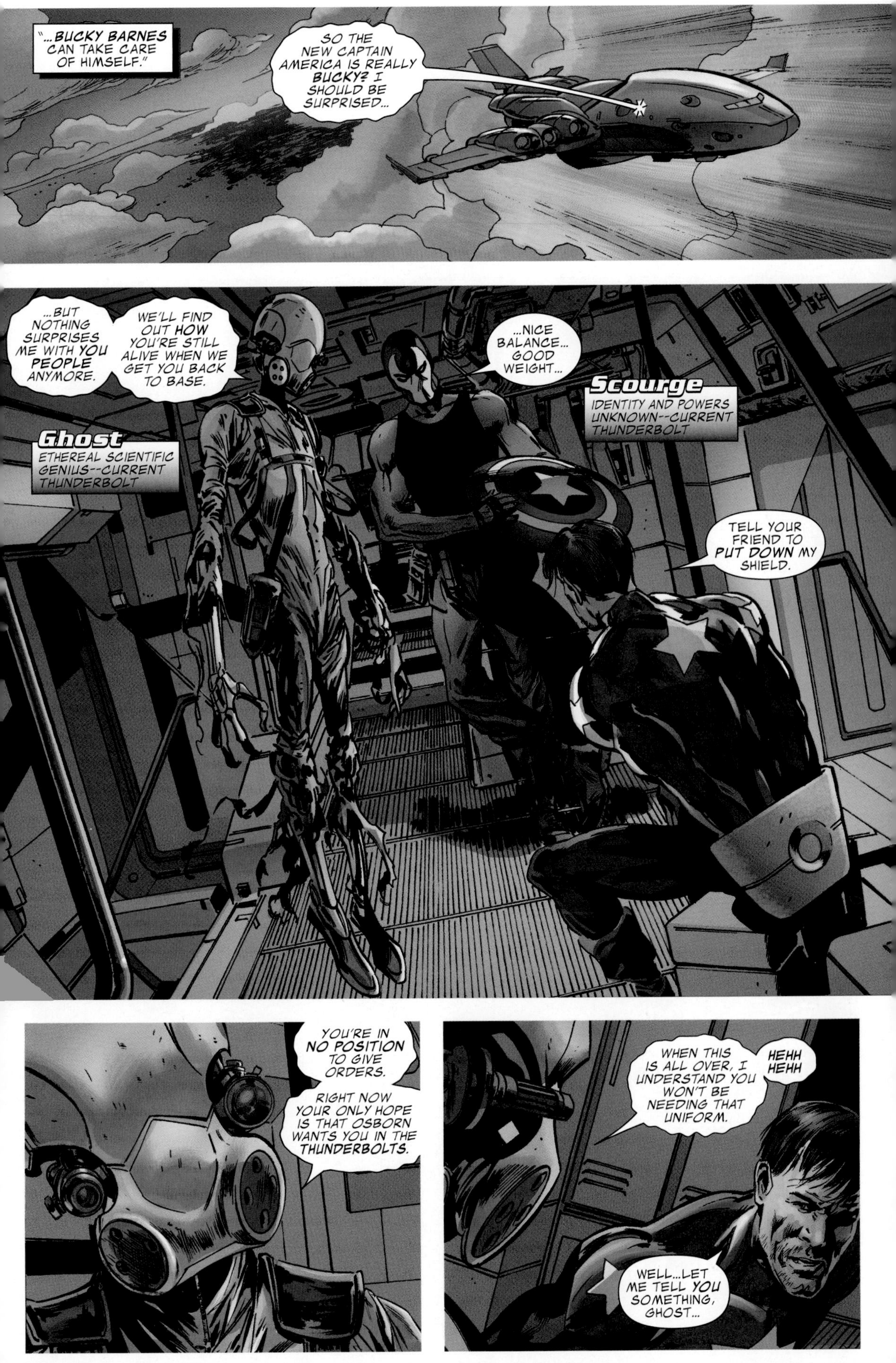
"...BUCKY BARNES CAN TAKE CARE OF HIMSELF."
SO THE NEW CAPTAIN AMERICA IS REALLY BUCKY? I SHOULD BE SURPRISED...
...BUT NOTHING SURPRISES ME WITH YOU PEOPLE ANYMORE.
WE'LL FIND OUT HOW YOU'RE STILL ALIVE WHEN WE GET YOU BACK TO BASE.
...NICE BALANCE... GOOD WEIGHT...
Scourge
IDENTITY AND POWERS UNKNOWN--CURRENT THUNDERBOLT
Ghost
ETHEREAL SCIENTIFIC GENIUS--CURRENT THUNDERBOLT
TELL YOUR FRIEND TO PUT DOWN MY SHIELD.
YOU'RE IN NO POSITION TO GIVE ORDERS.
RIGHT NOW YOUR ONLY HOPE IS THAT OSBORN WANTS YOU IN THE THUNDERBOLTS.
WHEN THIS IS ALL OVER, I UNDERSTAND YOU WON'T BE NEEDING THAT UNIFORM.
HEHH HEHH
WELL...LET ME TELL YOU SOMETHING, GHOST...

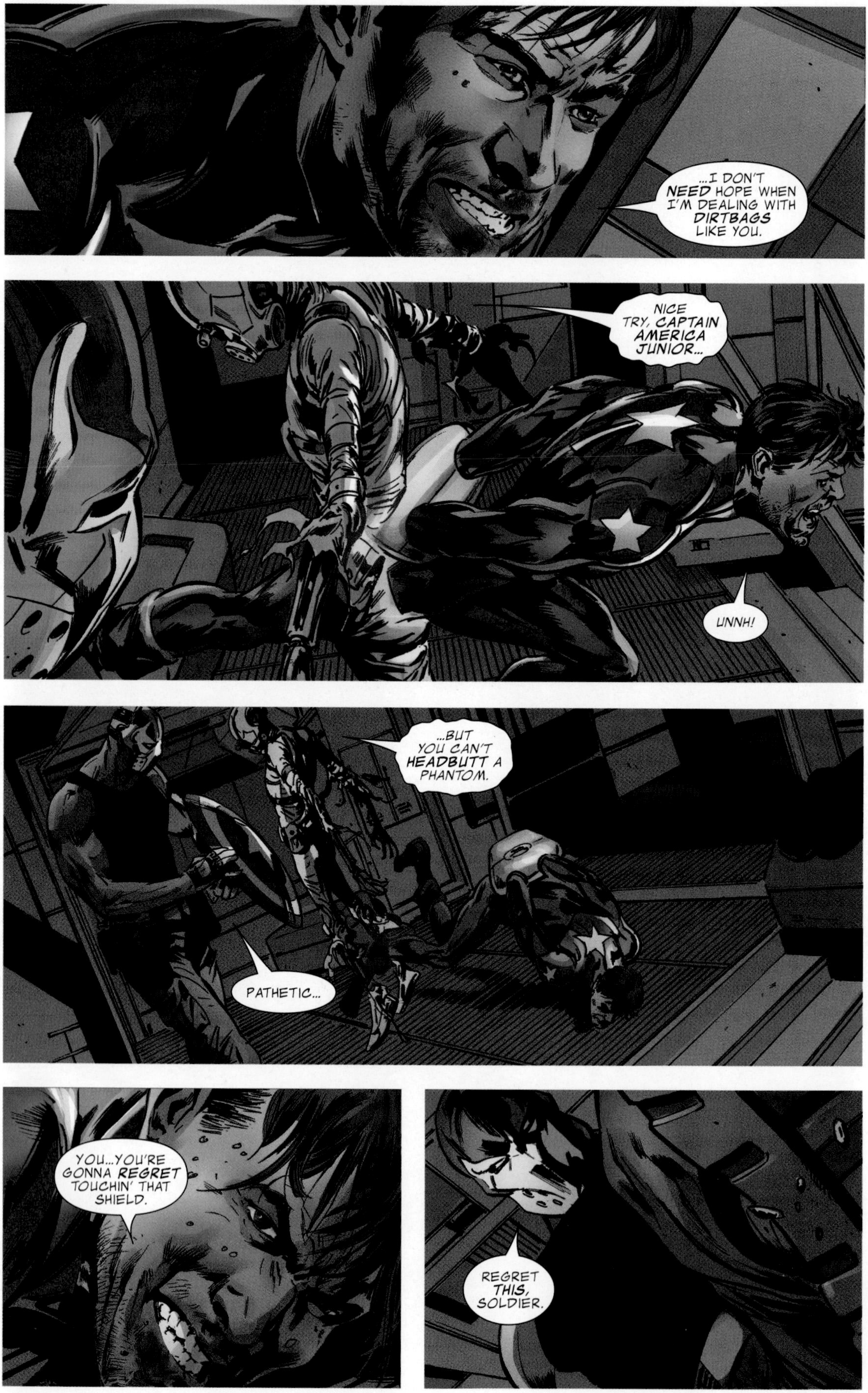
...I DON'T NEED HOPE WHEN I'M DEALING WITH DIRTBAGS LIKE YOU.
NICE TRY, CAPTAIN AMERICA JUNIOR...
UNNH!
...BUT YOU CAN'T HEADBUTT A PHANTOM.
PATHETIC...
YOU...YOU'RE GONNA REGRET TOUCHIN' THAT SHIELD.
REGRET THIS, SOLDIER.

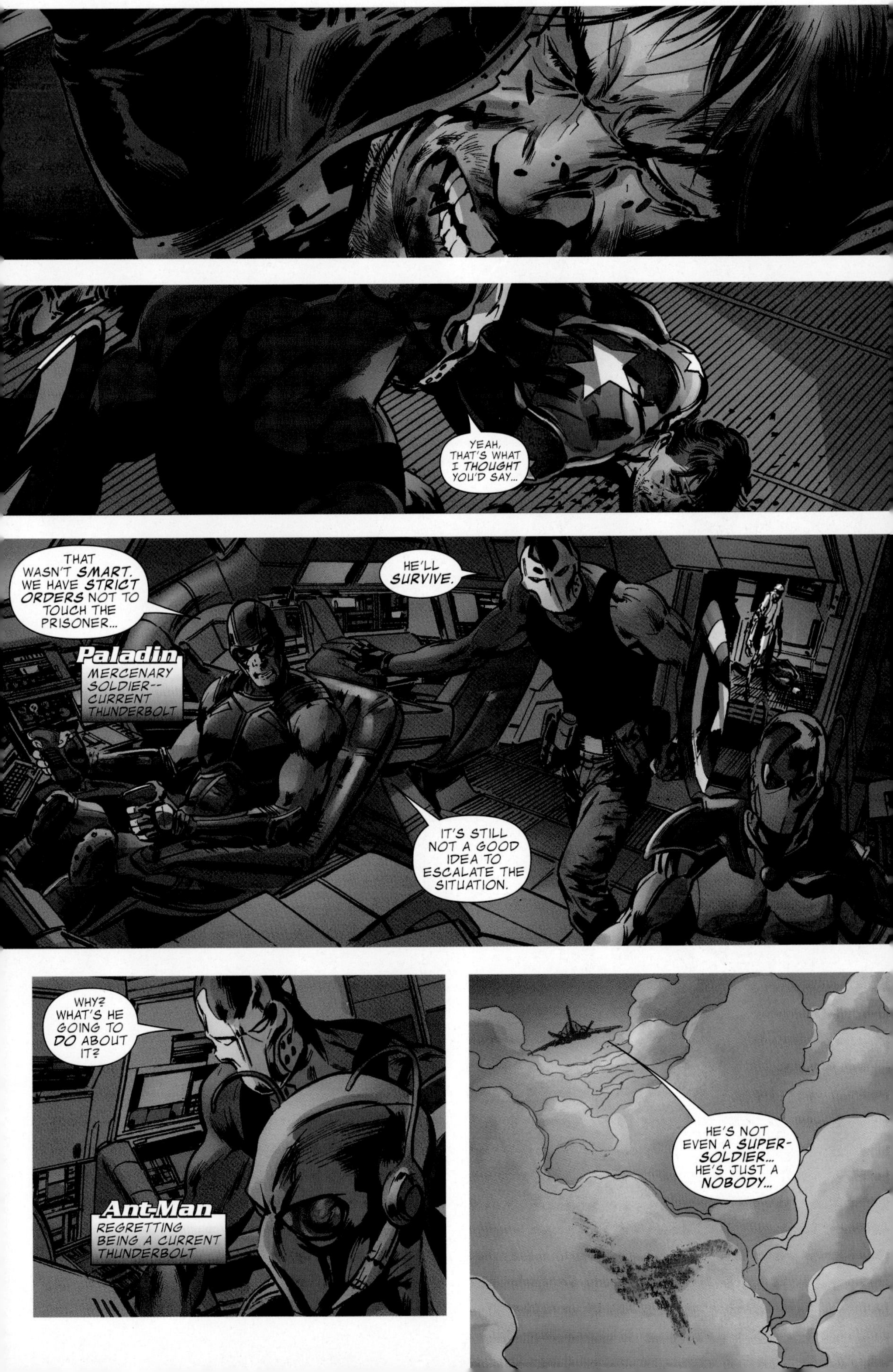
YEAH, THAT'S WHAT I *THOUGHT* YOU'D SAY...
THAT WASN'T **SMART**. WE HAVE **STRICT ORDERS** NOT TO TOUCH THE PRISONER...
Paladin
MERCENARY SOLDIER-- CURRENT THUNDERBOLT
HE'LL **SURVIVE**.
IT'S STILL NOT A GOOD IDEA TO ESCALATE THE SITUATION.
WHY? WHAT'S HE GOING TO **DO** ABOUT IT?
Ant-Man
REGRETTING BEING A CURRENT THUNDERBOLT
HE'S NOT EVEN A **SUPER-SOLDIER**... HE'S JUST A **NOBODY**...

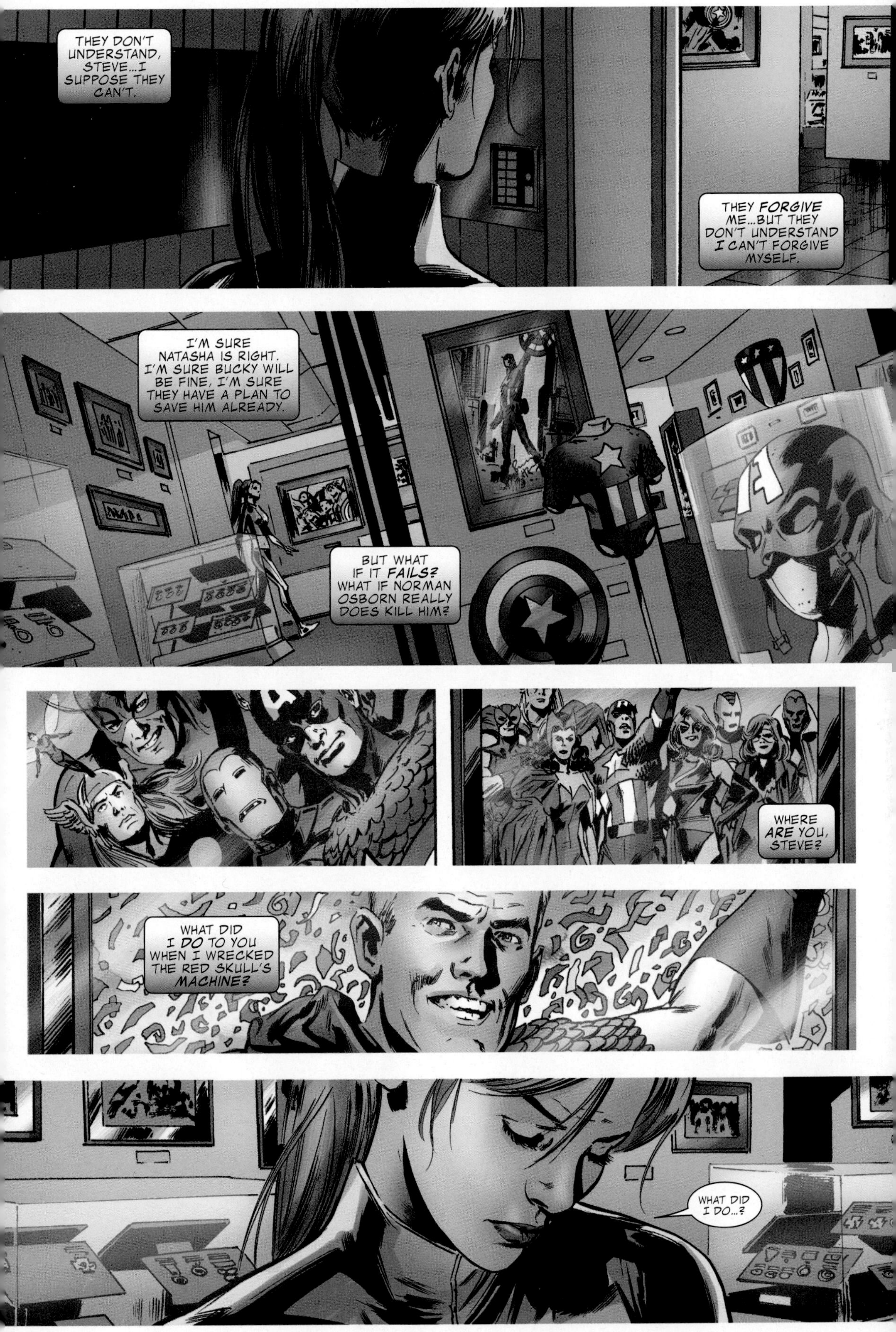
THEY DON'T UNDERSTAND, STEVE...I SUPPOSE THEY CAN'T.
THEY FORGIVE ME...BUT THEY DON'T UNDERSTAND I CAN'T FORGIVE MYSELF.
I'M SURE NATASHA IS RIGHT. I'M SURE BUCKY WILL BE FINE, I'M SURE THEY HAVE A PLAN TO SAVE HIM ALREADY.
BUT WHAT IF IT FAILS? WHAT IF NORMAN OSBORN REALLY DOES KILL HIM?
WHERE ARE YOU, STEVE?
WHAT DID I DO TO YOU WHEN I WRECKED THE RED SKULL'S MACHINE?
WHAT DID I DO...?

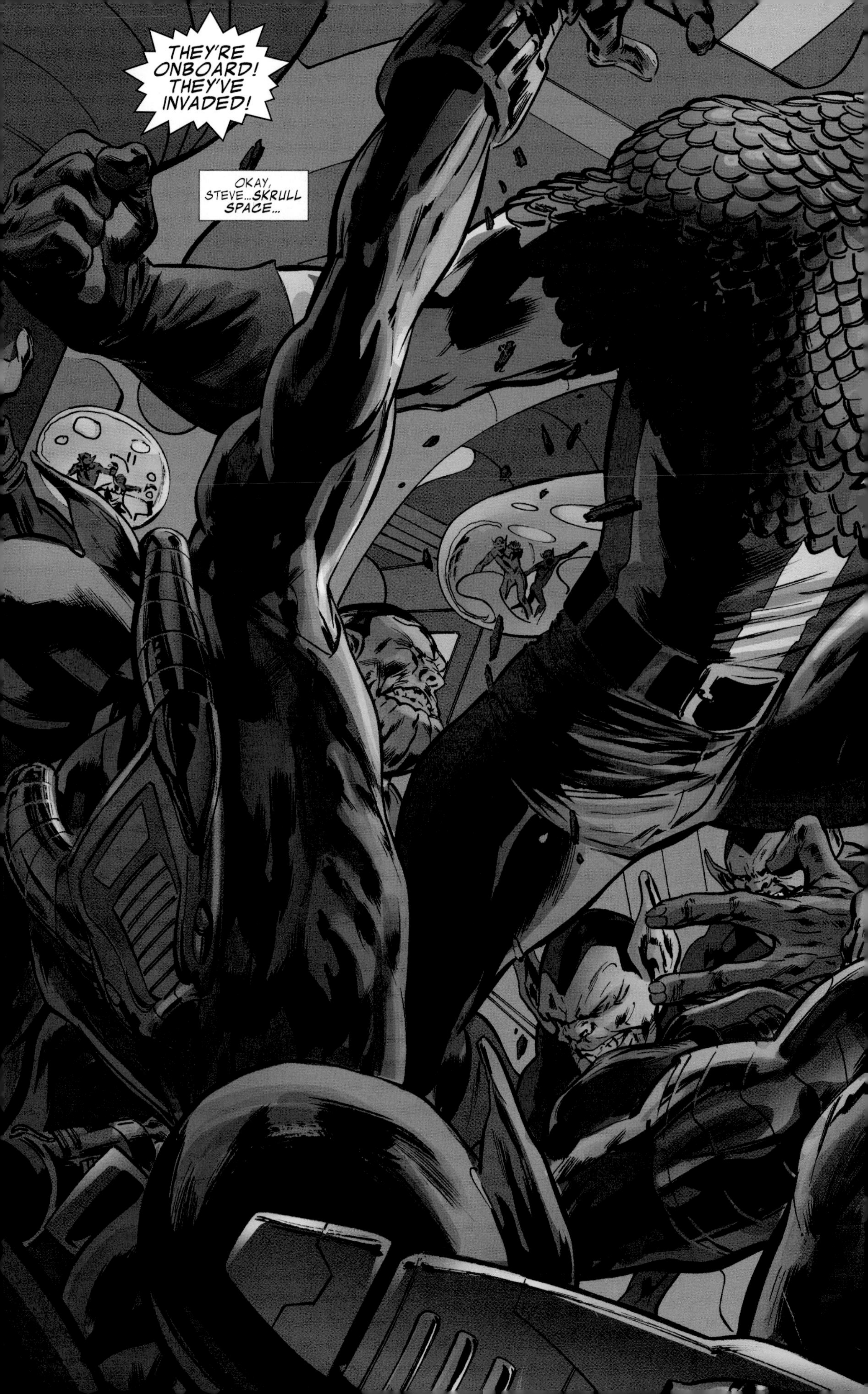
THEY'RE ONBOARD! THEY'VE INVADED!
OKAY, STEVE...SKRULL SPACE...

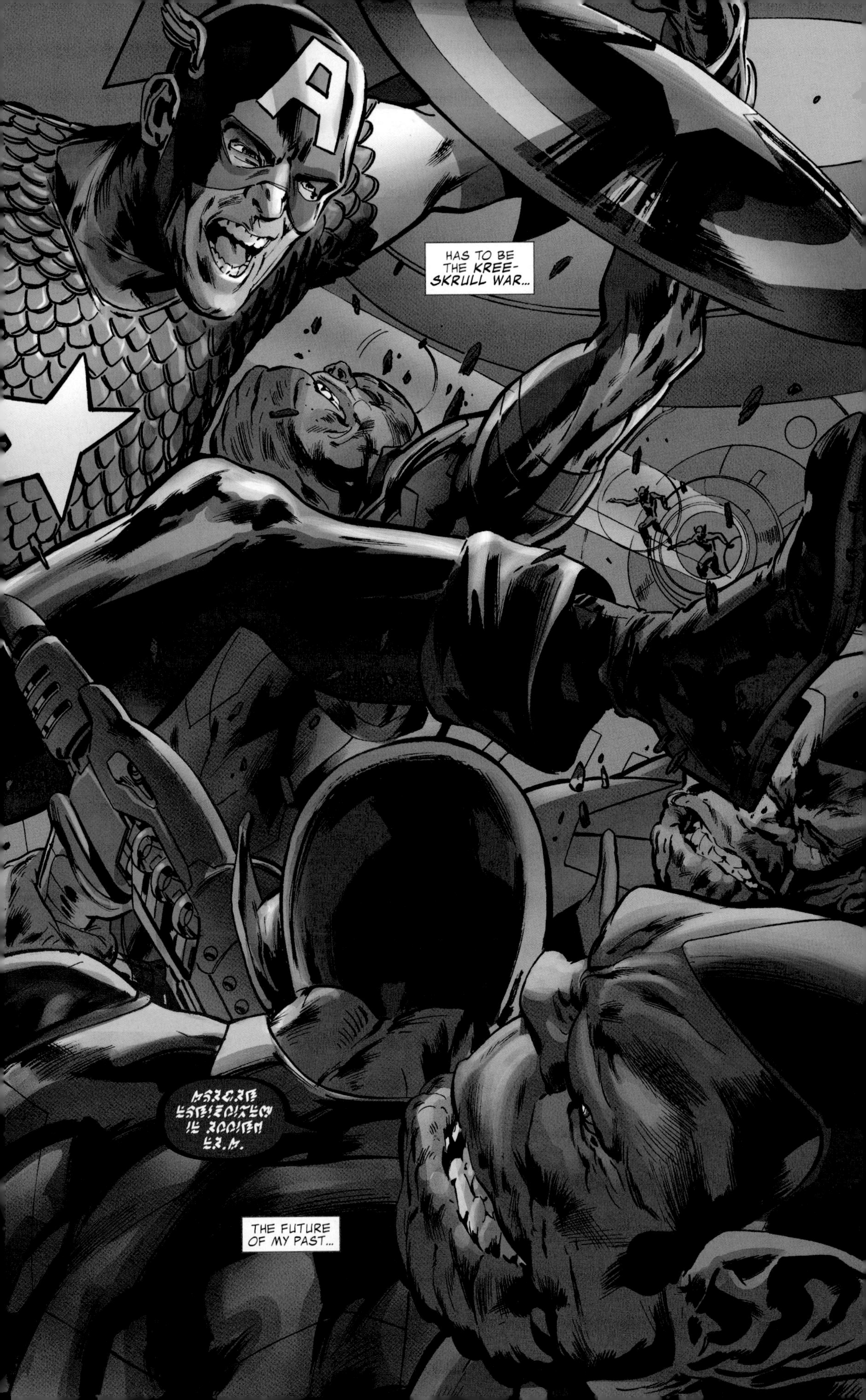
HAS TO BE THE KREE-SKRULL WAR...
THE FUTURE OF MY PAST...

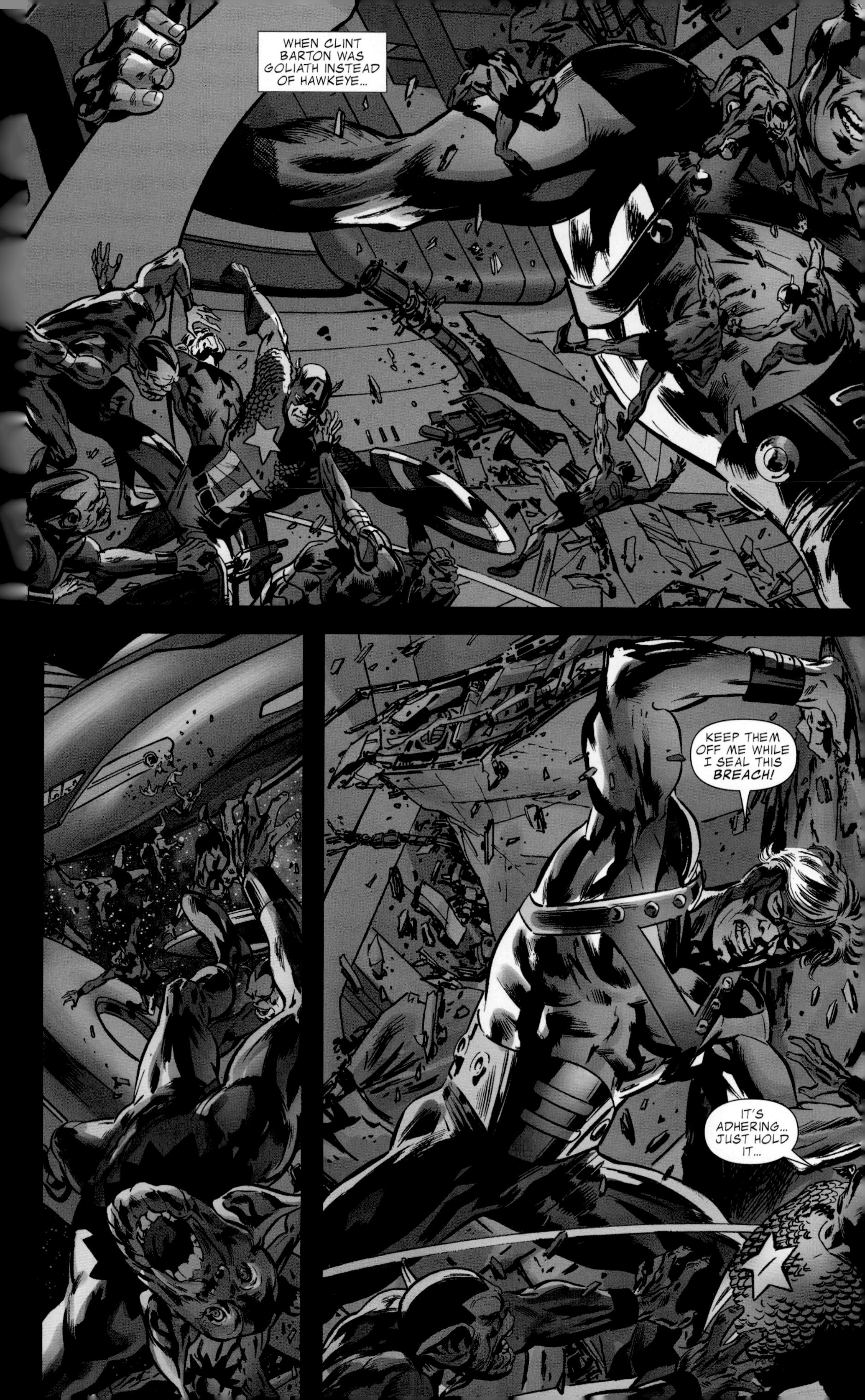
WHEN CLINT BARTON WAS GOLIATH INSTEAD OF HAWKEYE...
KEEP THEM OFF ME WHILE I SEAL THIS BREACH!
IT'S ADHERING... JUST HOLD IT...

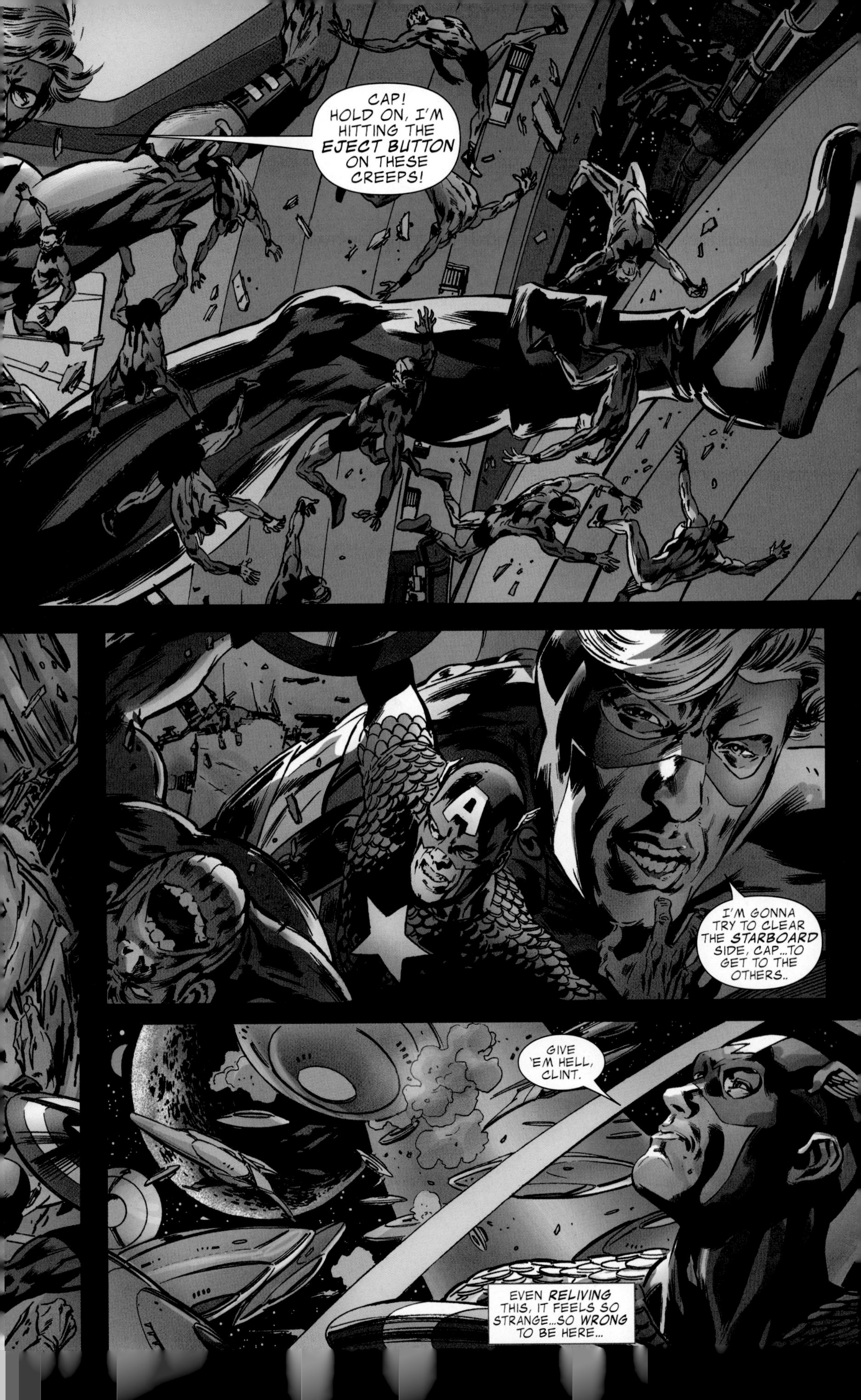
CAP! HOLD ON, I'M HITTING THE EJECT BUTTON ON THESE CREEPS!
I'M GONNA TRY TO CLEAR THE STARBOARD SIDE, CAP...TO GET TO THE OTHERS..
GIVE 'EM HELL, CLINT.
EVEN RELIVING THIS, IT FEELS SO STRANGE...SO WRONG TO BE HERE...

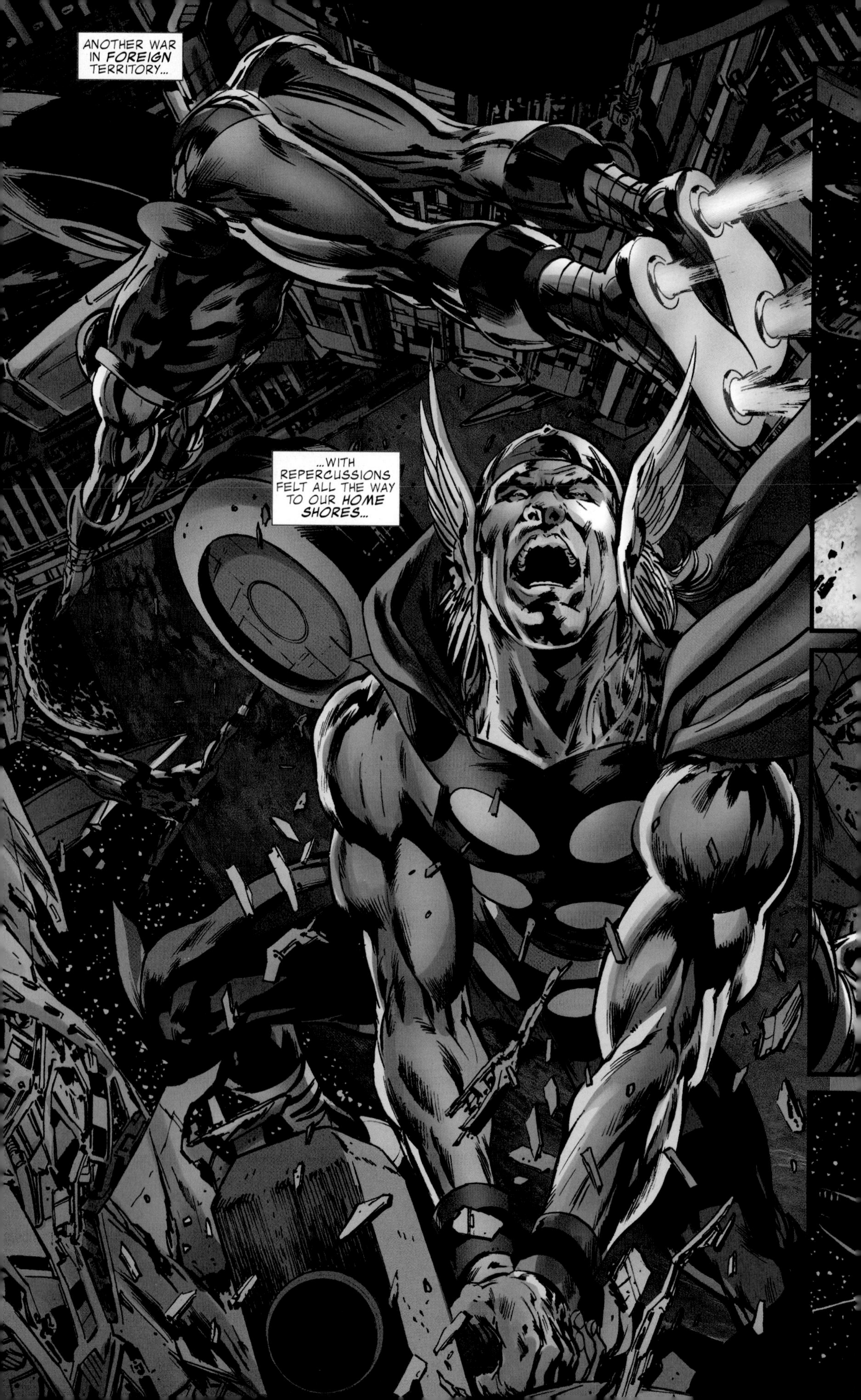
ANOTHER WAR IN FOREIGN TERRITORY...
...WITH REPERCUSSIONS FELT ALL THE WAY TO OUR HOME SHORES...

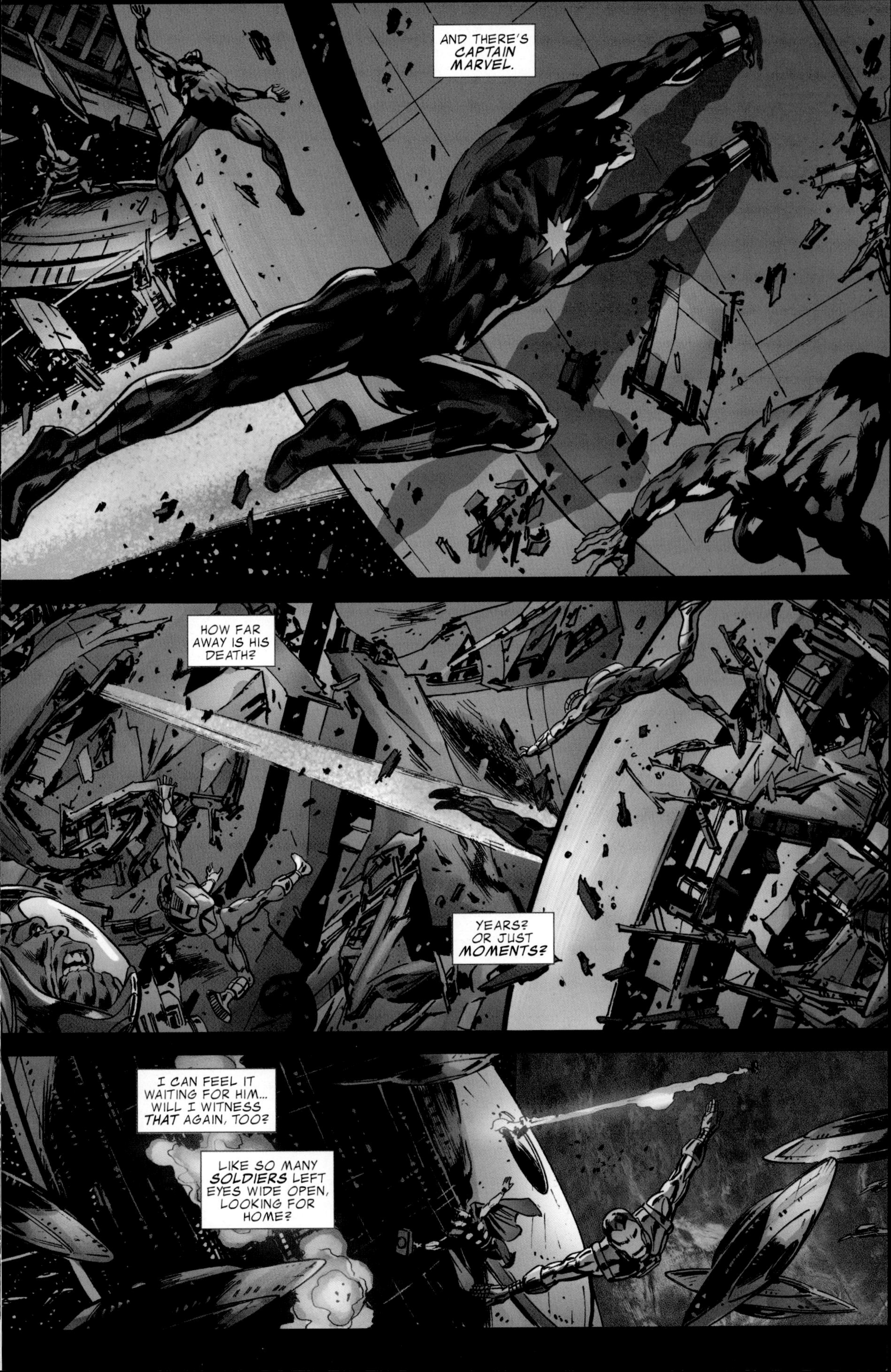
AND THERE'S *CAPTAIN MARVEL.*
HOW FAR AWAY IS HIS DEATH?
YEARS? OR JUST **MOMENTS?**
I CAN FEEL IT WAITING FOR HIM... WILL I WITNESS ***THAT*** AGAIN, TOO?
LIKE SO MANY ***SOLDIERS*** LEFT EYES WIDE OPEN, LOOKING FOR HOME?

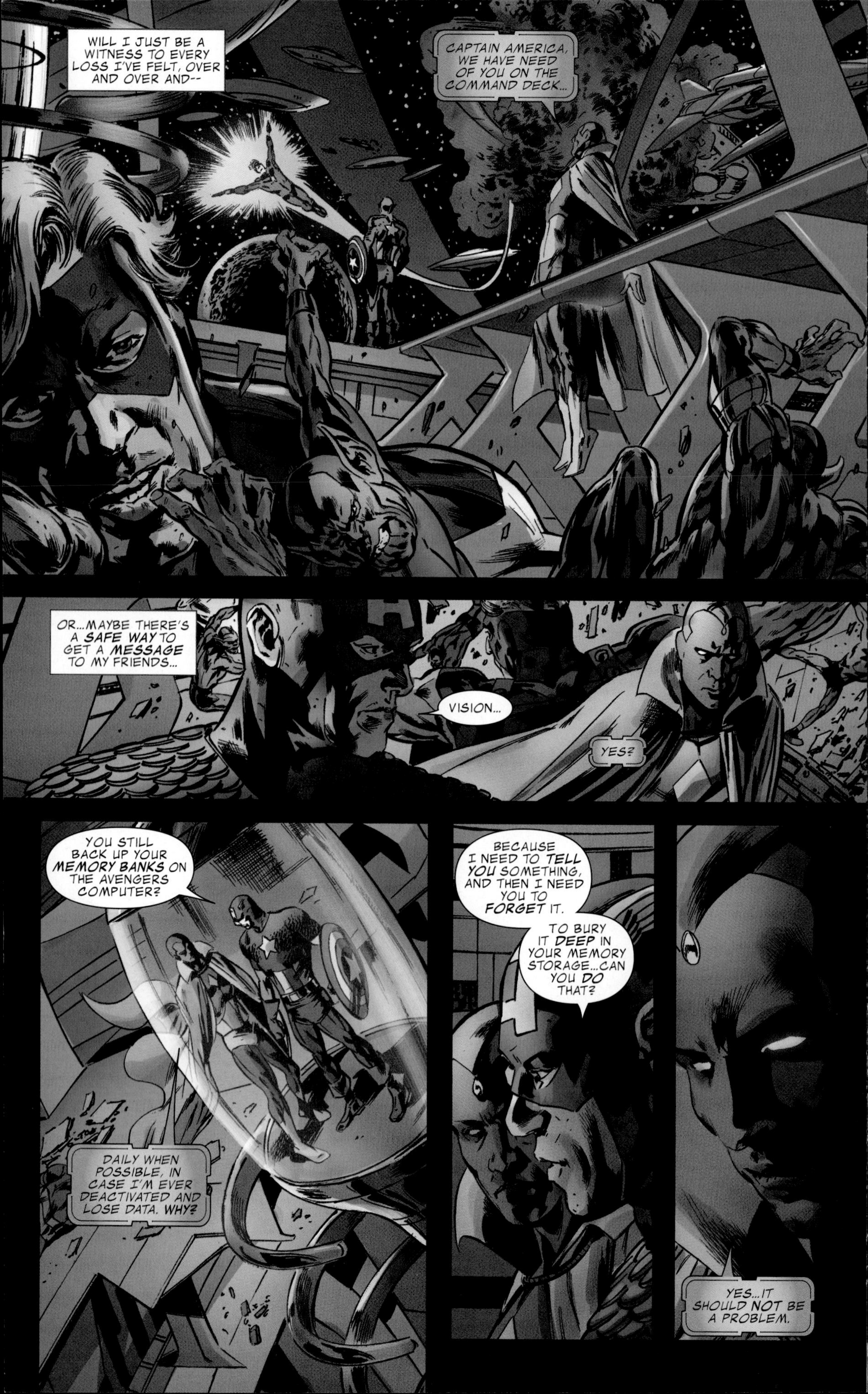

WILL I JUST BE A WITNESS TO EVERY LOSS I'VE FELT, OVER AND OVER AND--
CAPTAIN AMERICA, WE HAVE NEED OF YOU ON THE COMMAND DECK...
OR...MAYBE THERE'S A SAFE WAY TO GET A MESSAGE TO MY FRIENDS...
VISION...
YES?
YOU STILL BACK UP YOUR MEMORY BANKS ON THE AVENGERS COMPUTER?
DAILY WHEN POSSIBLE, IN CASE I'M EVER DEACTIVATED AND LOSE DATA. WHY?
BECAUSE I NEED TO TELL YOU SOMETHING, AND THEN I NEED YOU TO FORGET IT.
TO BURY IT DEEP IN YOUR MEMORY STORAGE...CAN YOU DO THAT?
YES...IT SHOULD NOT BE A PROBLEM.

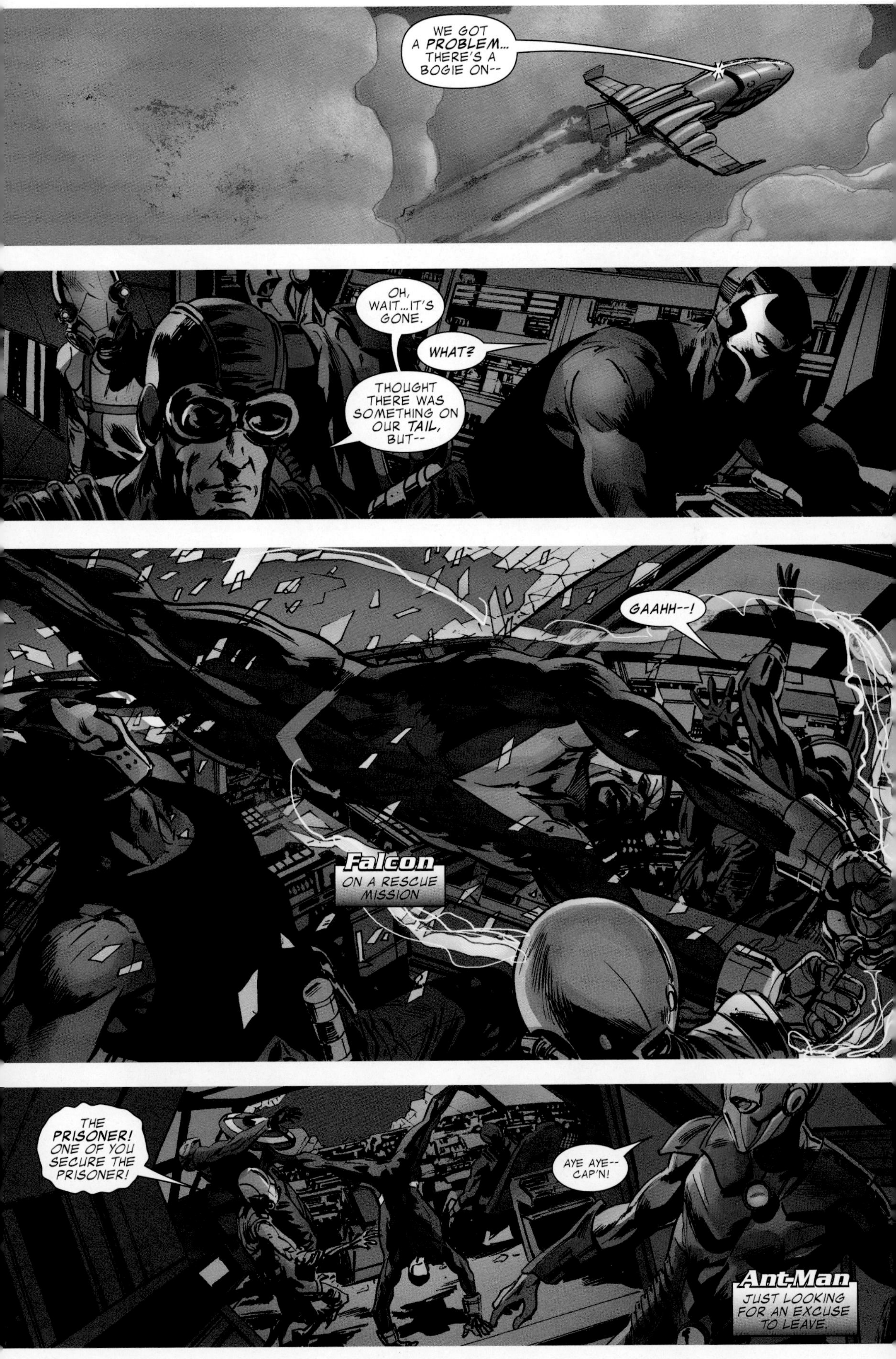
WE GOT A PROBLEM... THERE'S A BOGIE ON--
OH, WAIT...IT'S GONE.
WHAT?
THOUGHT THERE WAS SOMETHING ON OUR TAIL, BUT--
GAAHH--!
Falcon
ON A RESCUE MISSION
THE PRISONER! ONE OF YOU SECURE THE PRISONER!
AYE AYE-- CAP'N!
Ant-Man
JUST LOOKING FOR AN EXCUSE TO LEAVE.

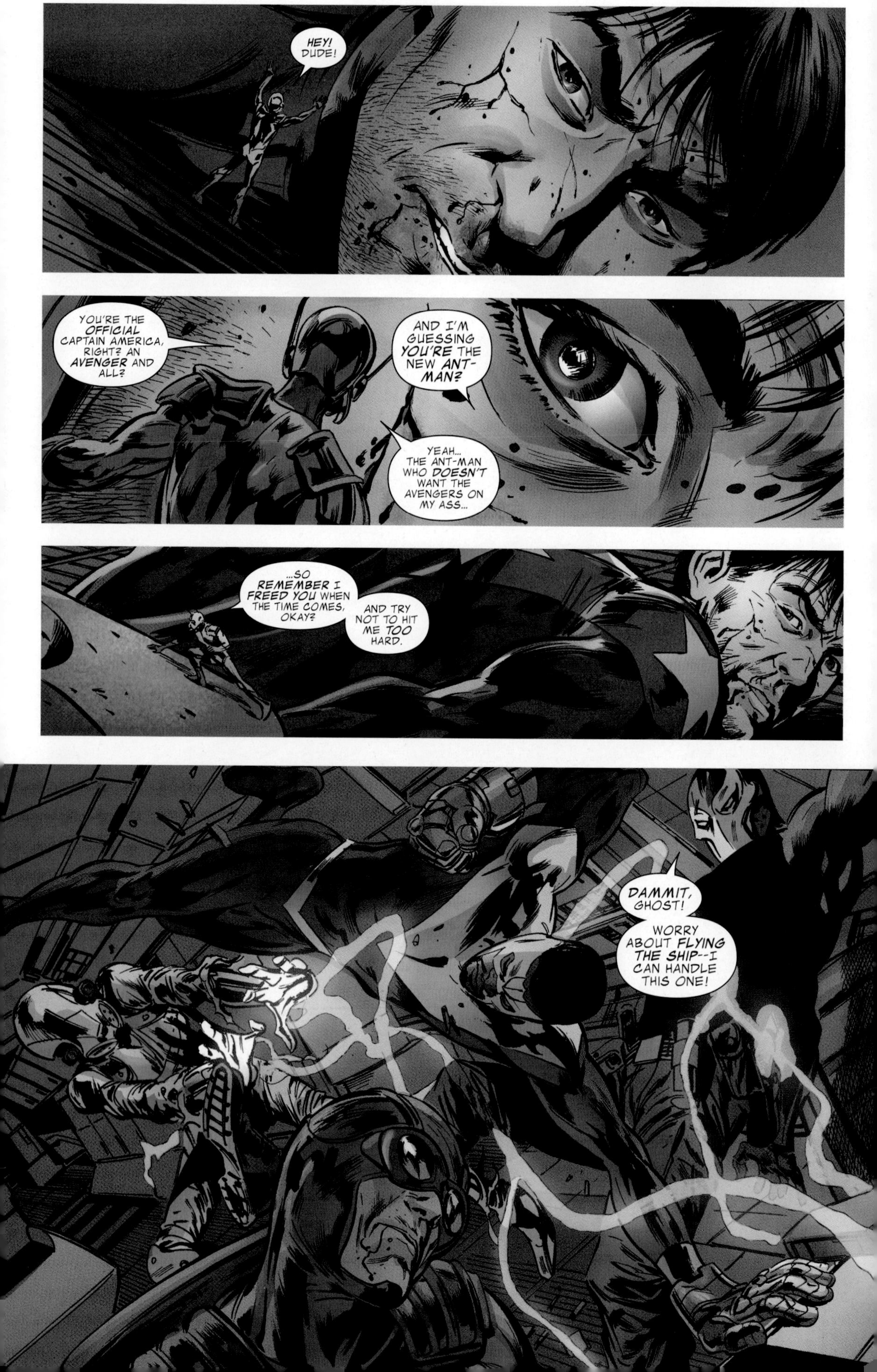
HEY! DUDE!
YOU'RE THE OFFICIAL CAPTAIN AMERICA, RIGHT? AN AVENGER AND ALL?
AND I'M GUESSING YOU'RE THE NEW ANT-MAN?
YEAH... THE ANT-MAN WHO DOESN'T WANT THE AVENGERS ON MY ASS...
...SO REMEMBER I FREED YOU WHEN THE TIME COMES, OKAY?
AND TRY NOT TO HIT ME TOO HARD.
DAMMIT, GHOST!
WORRY ABOUT FLYING THE SHIP--I CAN HANDLE THIS ONE!

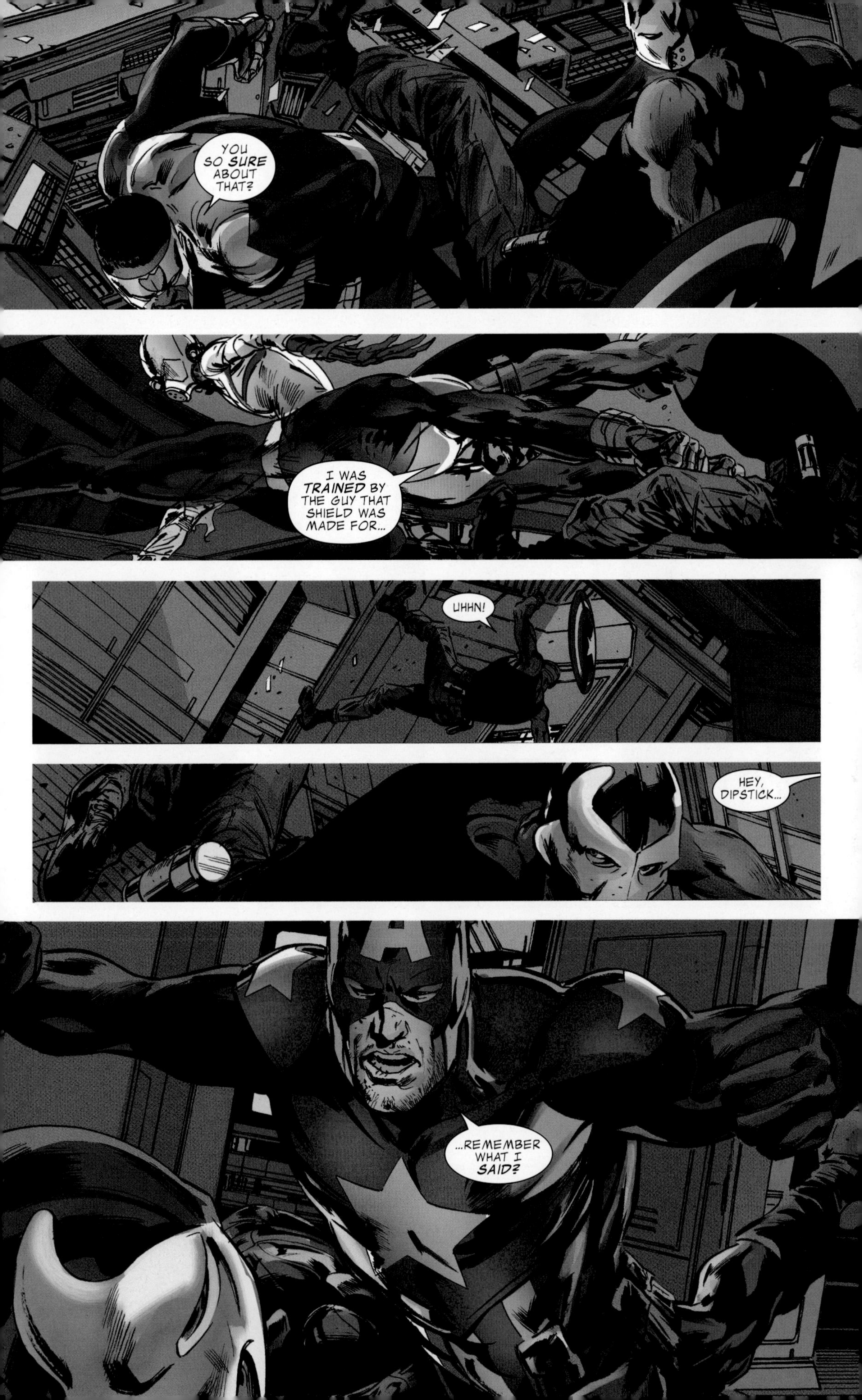
YOU SO SURE ABOUT THAT?
I WAS TRAINED BY THE GUY THAT SHIELD WAS MADE FOR...
UHHN!
HEY, DIPSTICK...
...REMEMBER WHAT I SAID?

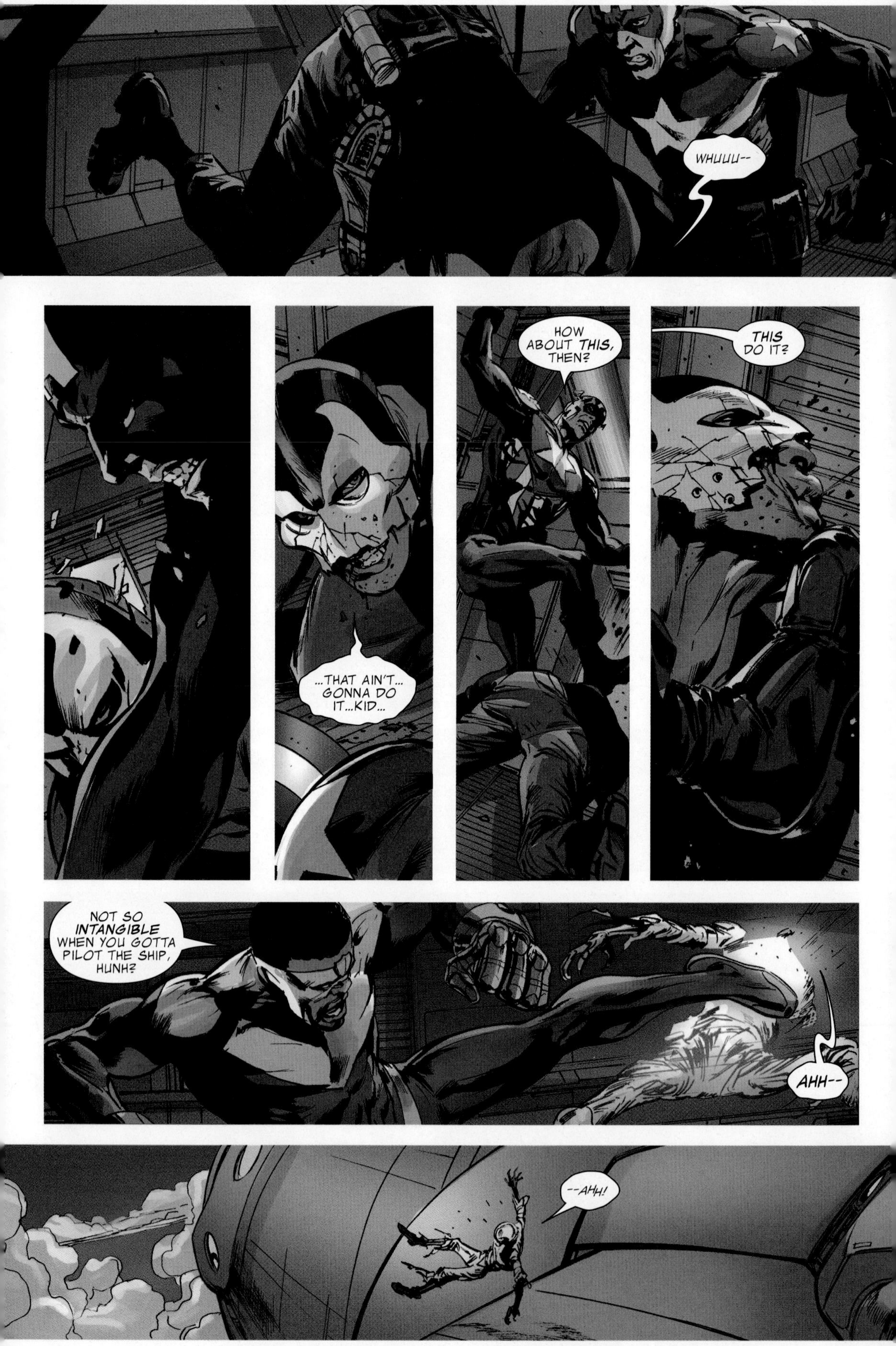
WHUUU--
...THAT AIN'T... GONNA DO IT...KID...
HOW ABOUT THIS, THEN?
THIS DO IT?
NOT SO INTANGIBLE WHEN YOU GOTTA PILOT THE SHIP, HUNH?
AHH--
--AHH!

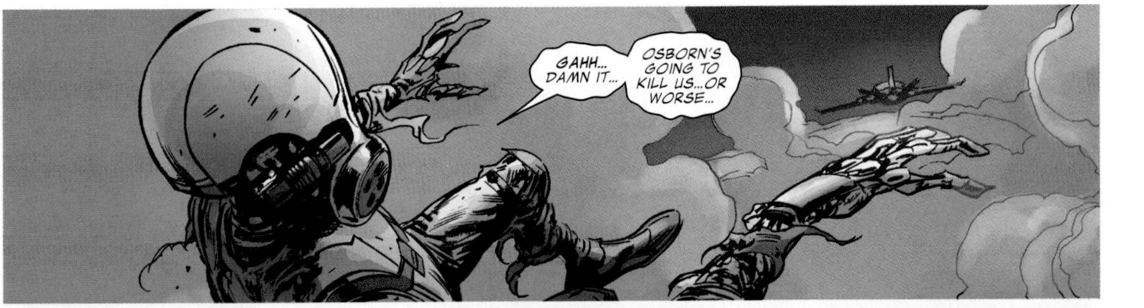
GAHH... DAMN IT...
OSBORN'S GOING TO KILL US...OR WORSE...

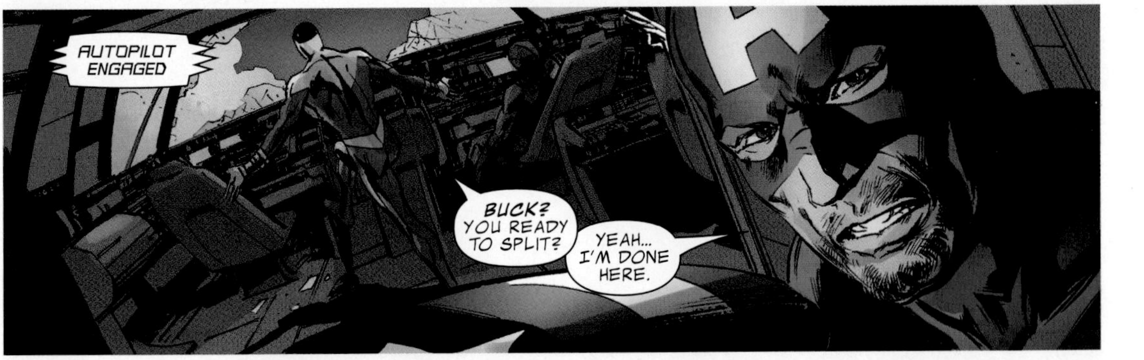
AUTOPILOT ENGAGED
BUCK? YOU READY TO SPLIT?
YEAH... I'M DONE HERE.

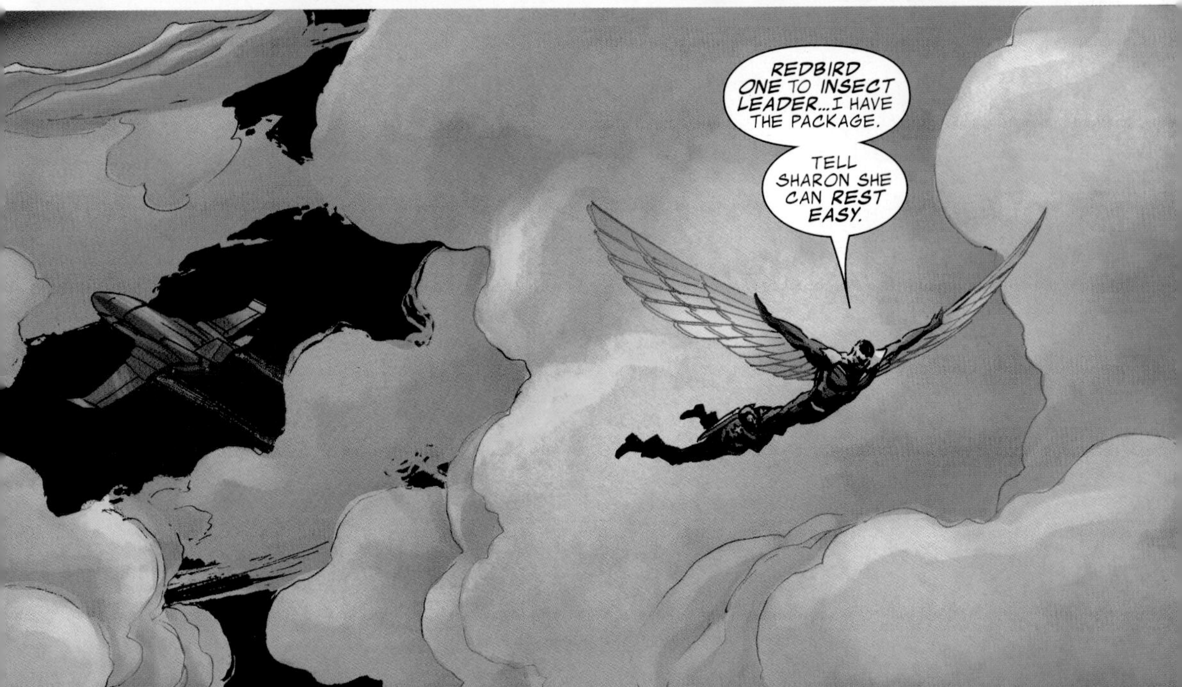
REDBIRD ONE TO INSECT LEADER...I HAVE THE PACKAGE.
TELL SHARON SHE CAN REST EASY.

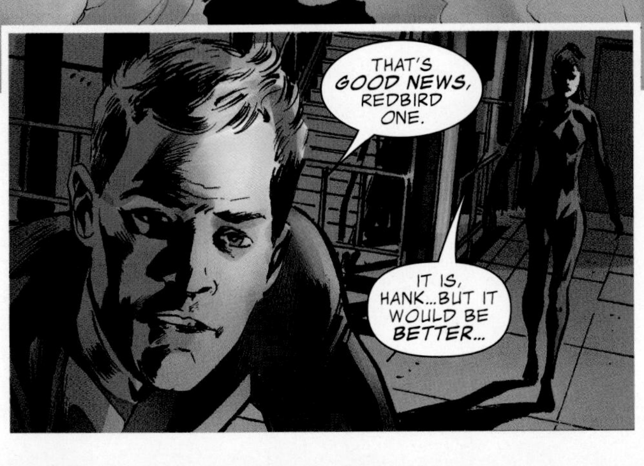
THAT'S GOOD NEWS, REDBIRD ONE.
IT IS, HANK...BUT IT WOULD BE BETTER...

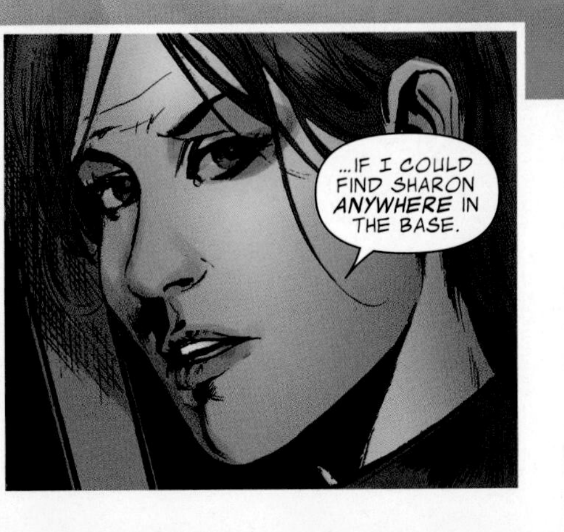
...IF I COULD FIND SHARON ANYWHERE IN THE BASE.

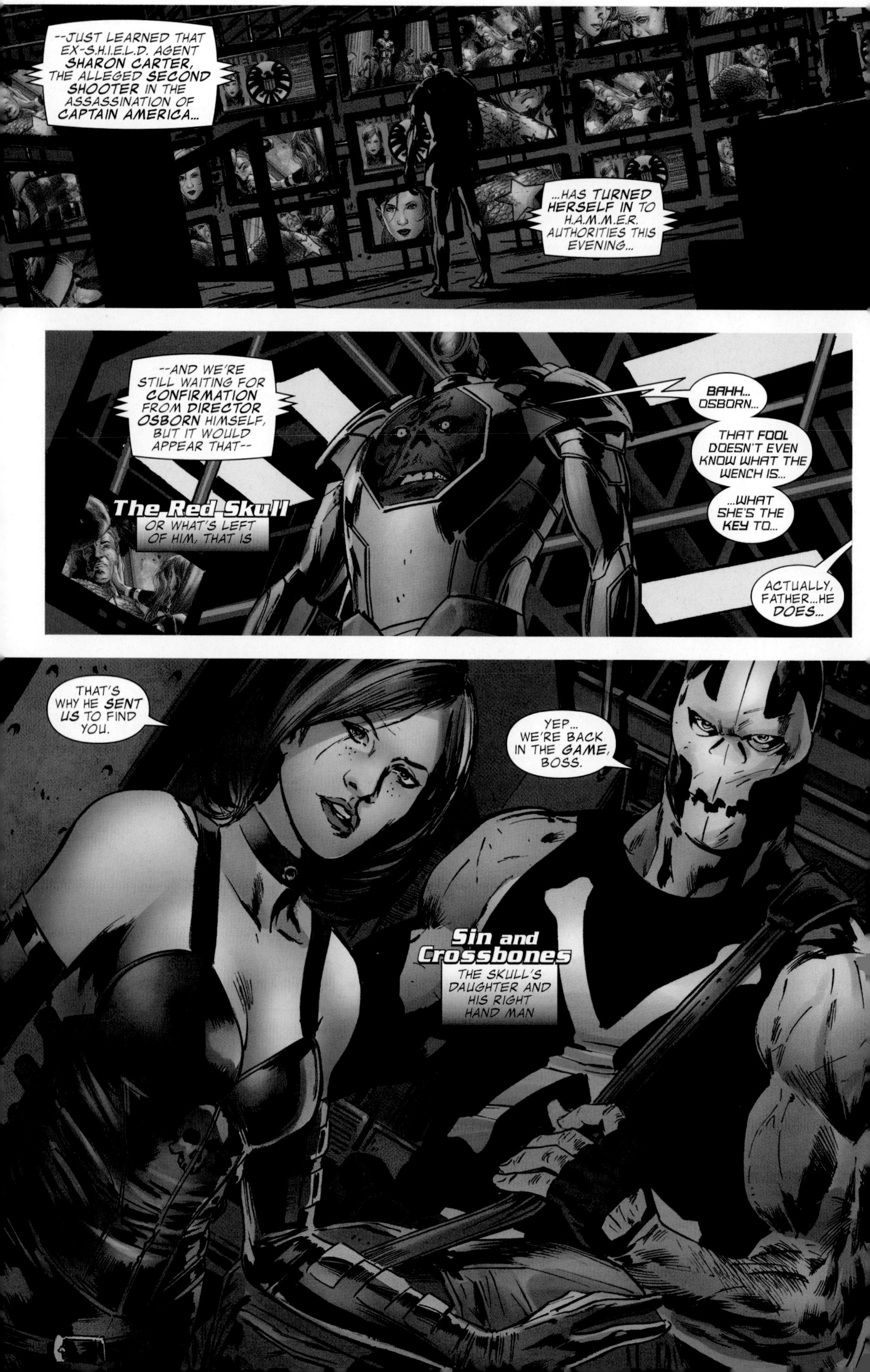
--JUST LEARNED THAT EX-S.H.I.E.L.D. AGENT SHARON CARTER, THE ALLEGED SECOND SHOOTER IN THE ASSASSINATION OF CAPTAIN AMERICA...
...HAS TURNED HERSELF IN TO H.A.M.M.E.R. AUTHORITIES THIS EVENING...
--AND WE'RE STILL WAITING FOR CONFIRMATION FROM DIRECTOR OSBORN HIMSELF, BUT IT WOULD APPEAR THAT--
The Red Skull
OR WHAT'S LEFT OF HIM, THAT IS
BAHH... OSBORN...
THAT FOOL DOESN'T EVEN KNOW WHAT THE WENCH IS...
...WHAT SHE'S THE KEY TO...
ACTUALLY, FATHER...HE DOES...
THAT'S WHY HE SENT US TO FIND YOU.
YEP... WE'RE BACK IN THE GAME, BOSS.
Sin and Crossbones
THE SKULL'S DAUGHTER AND HIS RIGHT HAND MAN

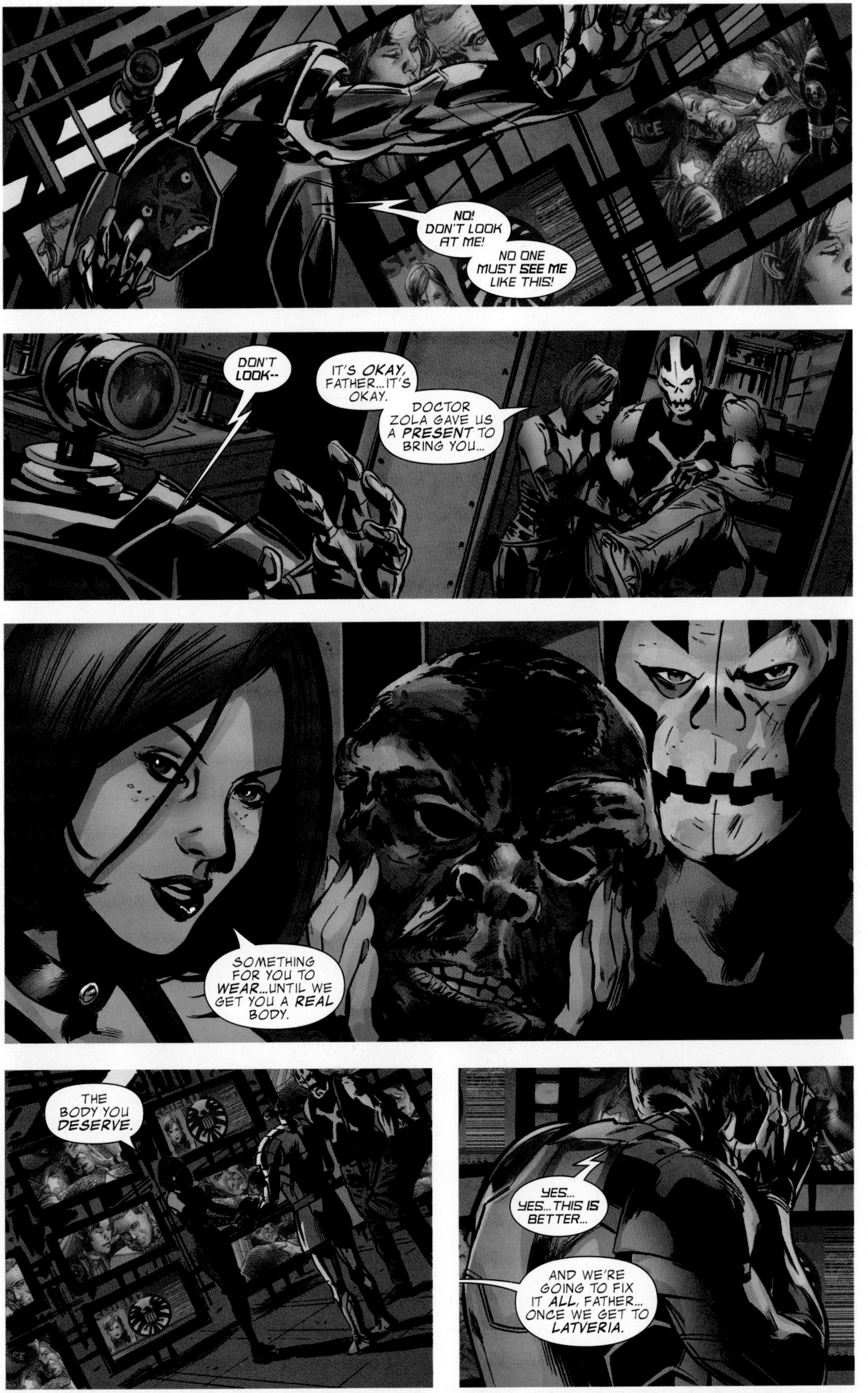
NO! DON'T LOOK AT ME!
NO ONE MUST SEE ME LIKE THIS!
DON'T LOOK--
IT'S OKAY, FATHER...IT'S OKAY.
DOCTOR ZOLA GAVE US A PRESENT TO BRING YOU...
SOMETHING FOR YOU TO WEAR...UNTIL WE GET YOU A REAL BODY.
THE BODY YOU DESERVE.
YES... YES...THIS IS BETTER...
AND WE'RE GOING TO FIX IT ALL, FATHER... ONCE WE GET TO LATVERIA.

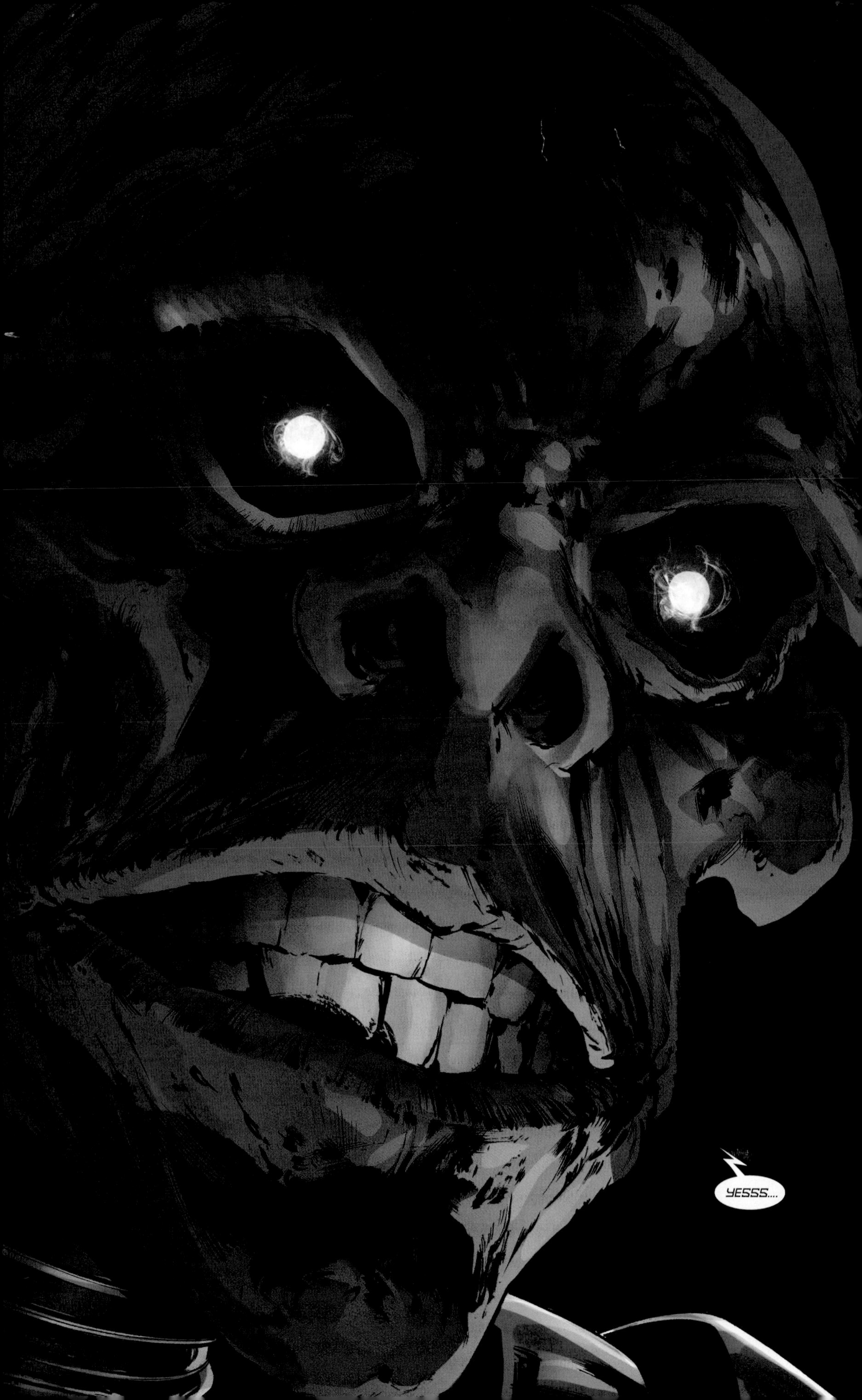
YESSS....

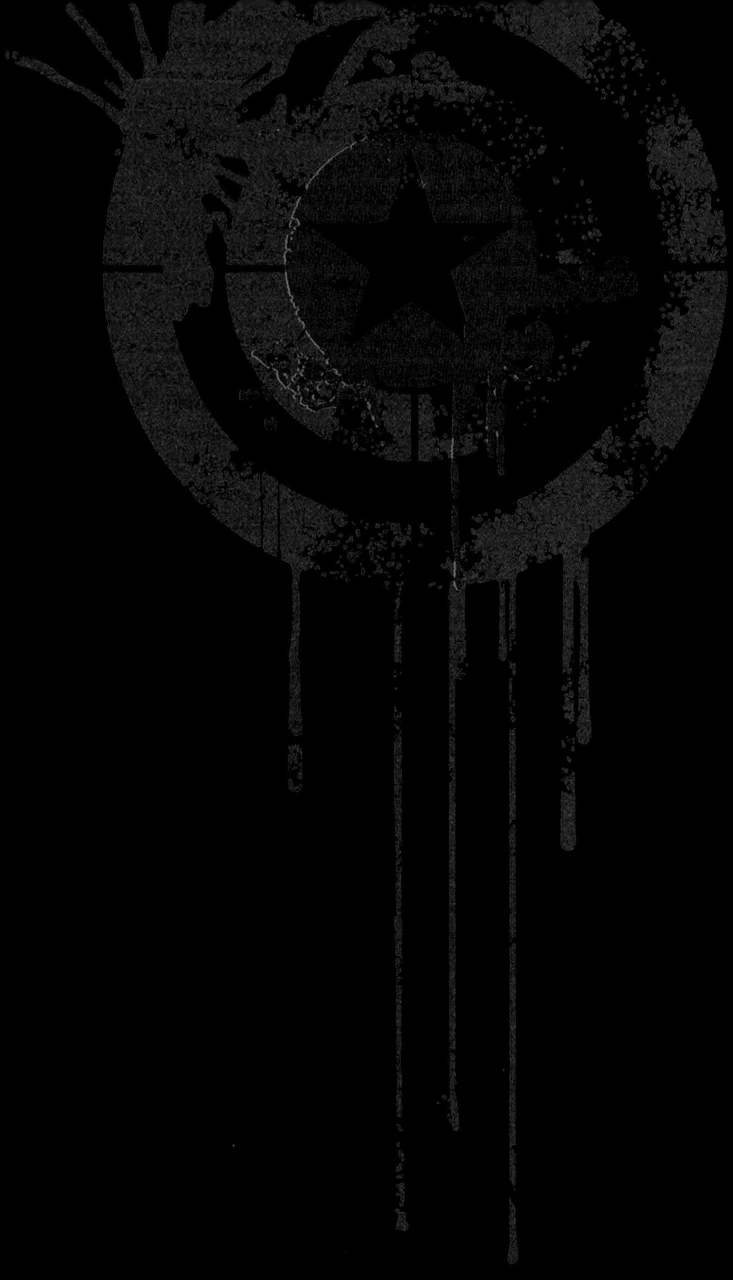

"He that would keep liberty secure
must guard even his enemy"

- Thomas Paine

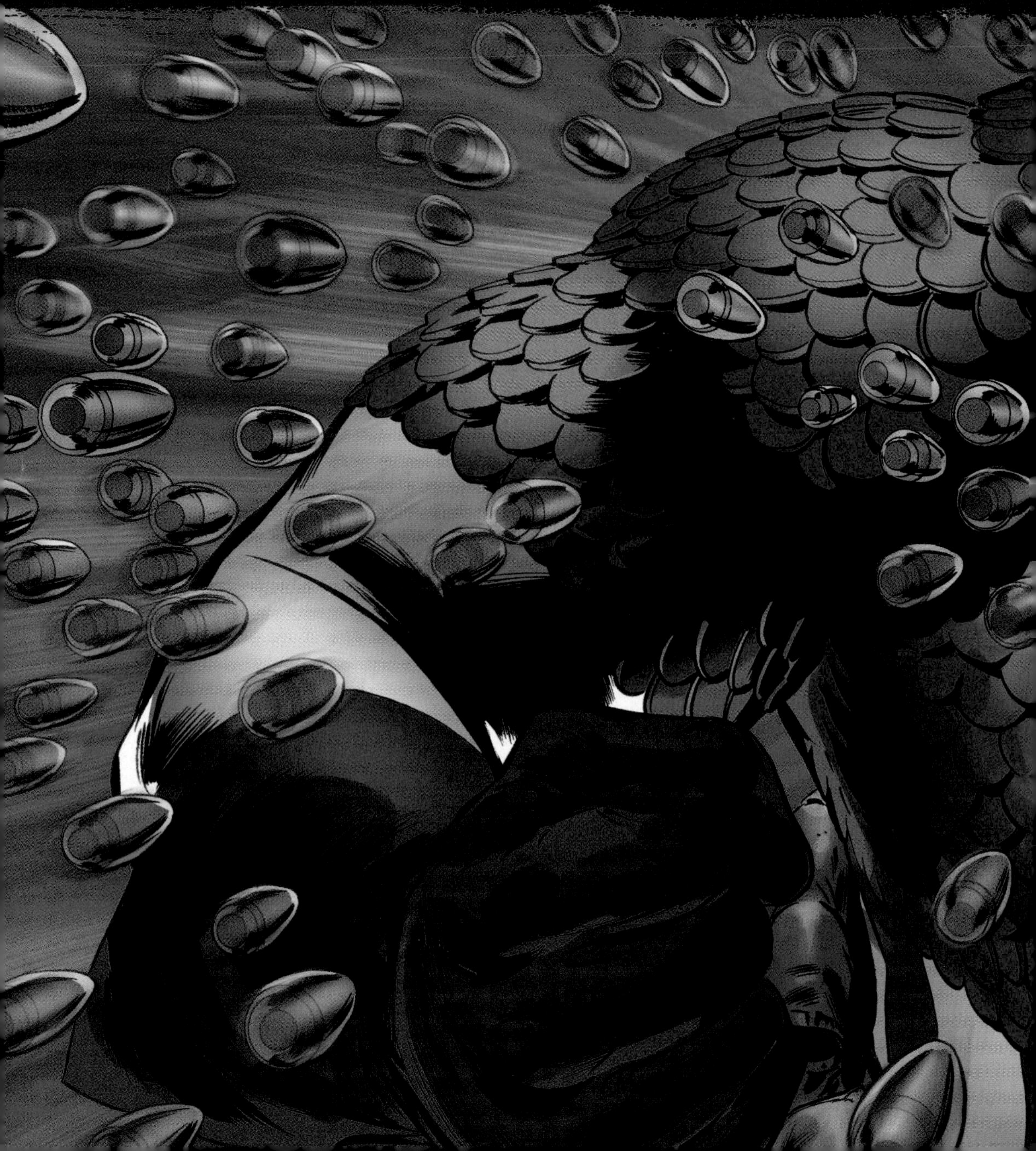

4

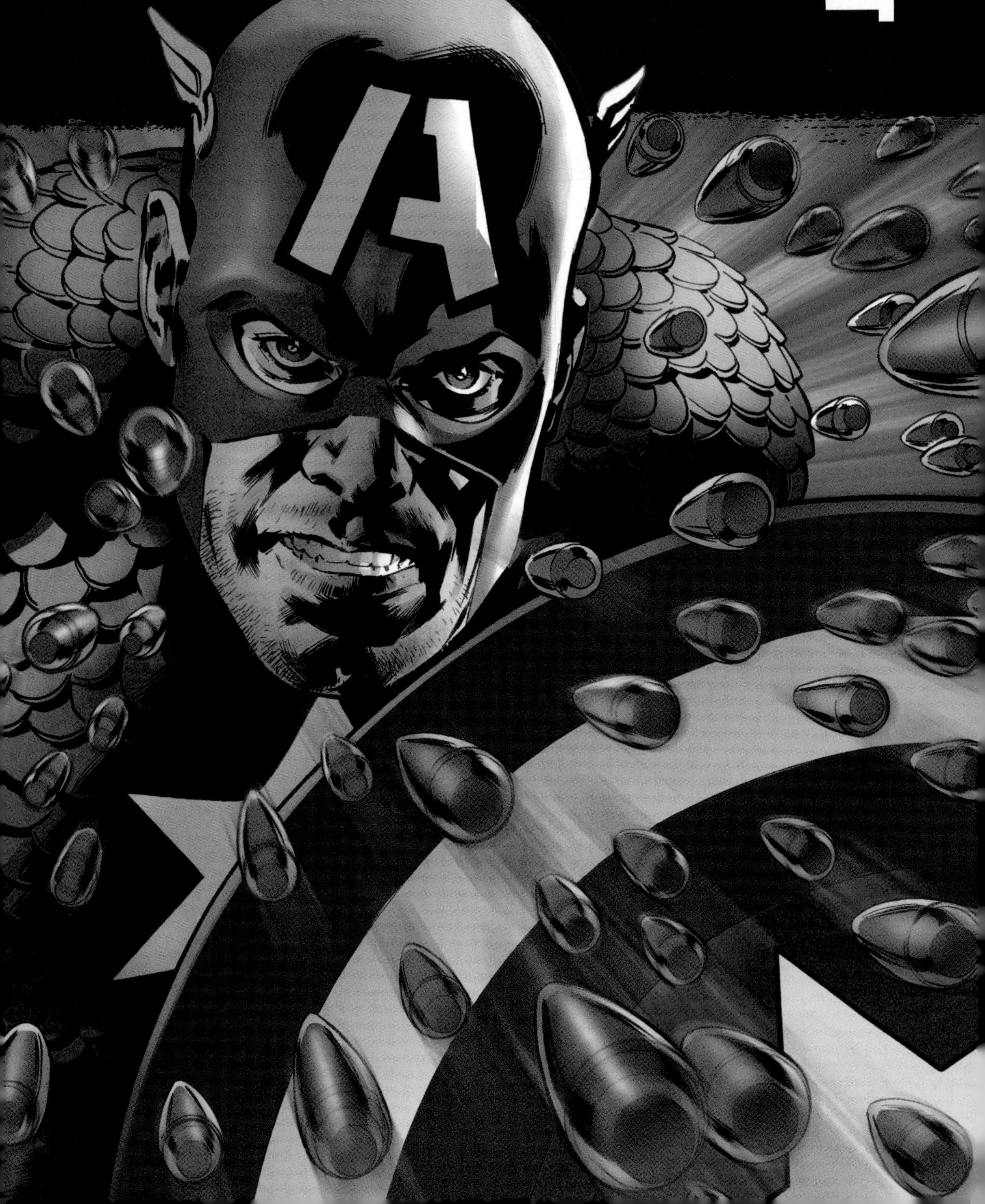

Latveria--
Present
Day

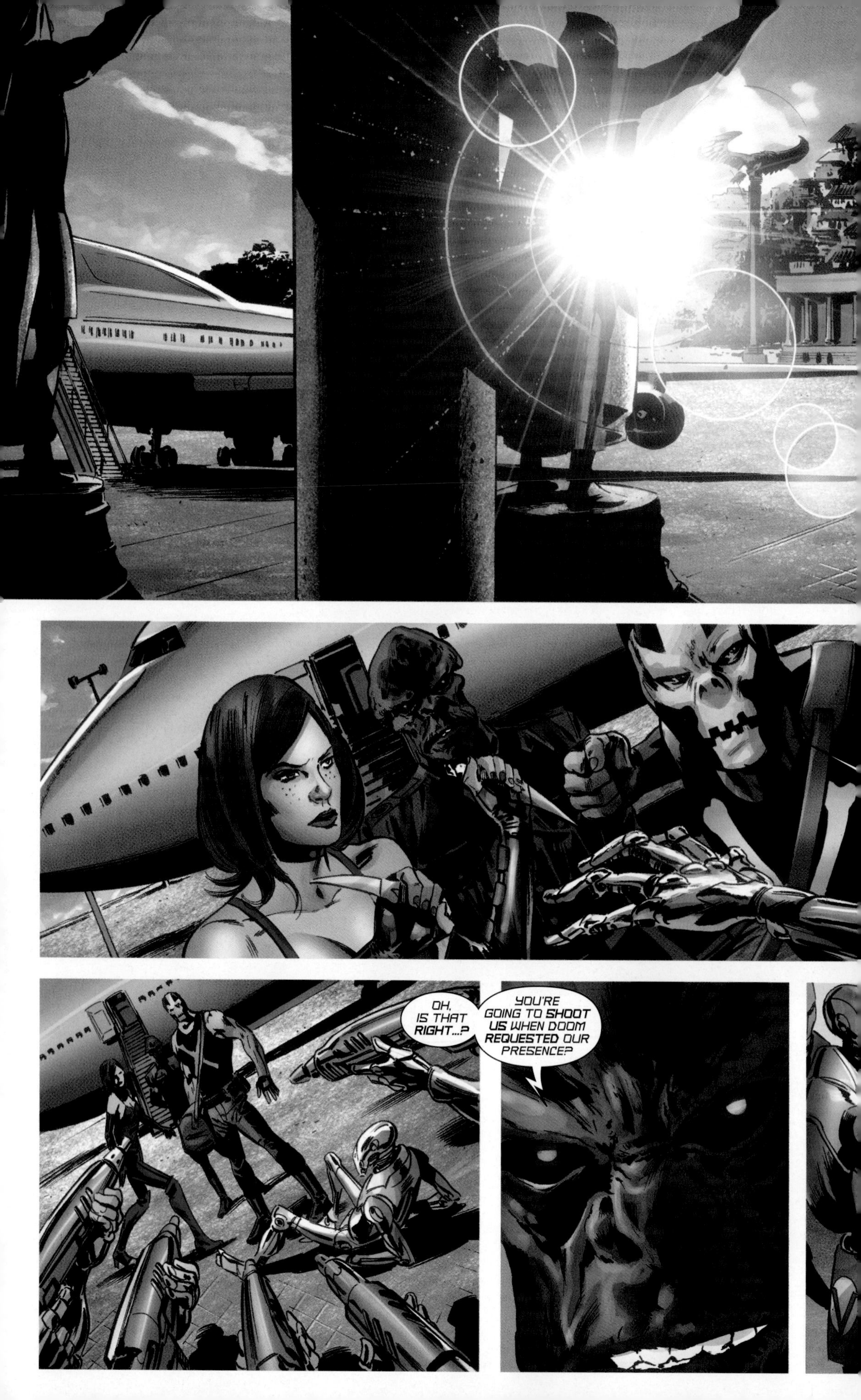
OH, IS THAT RIGHT...?
YOU'RE GOING TO SHOOT US WHEN DOOM REQUESTED OUR PRESENCE?

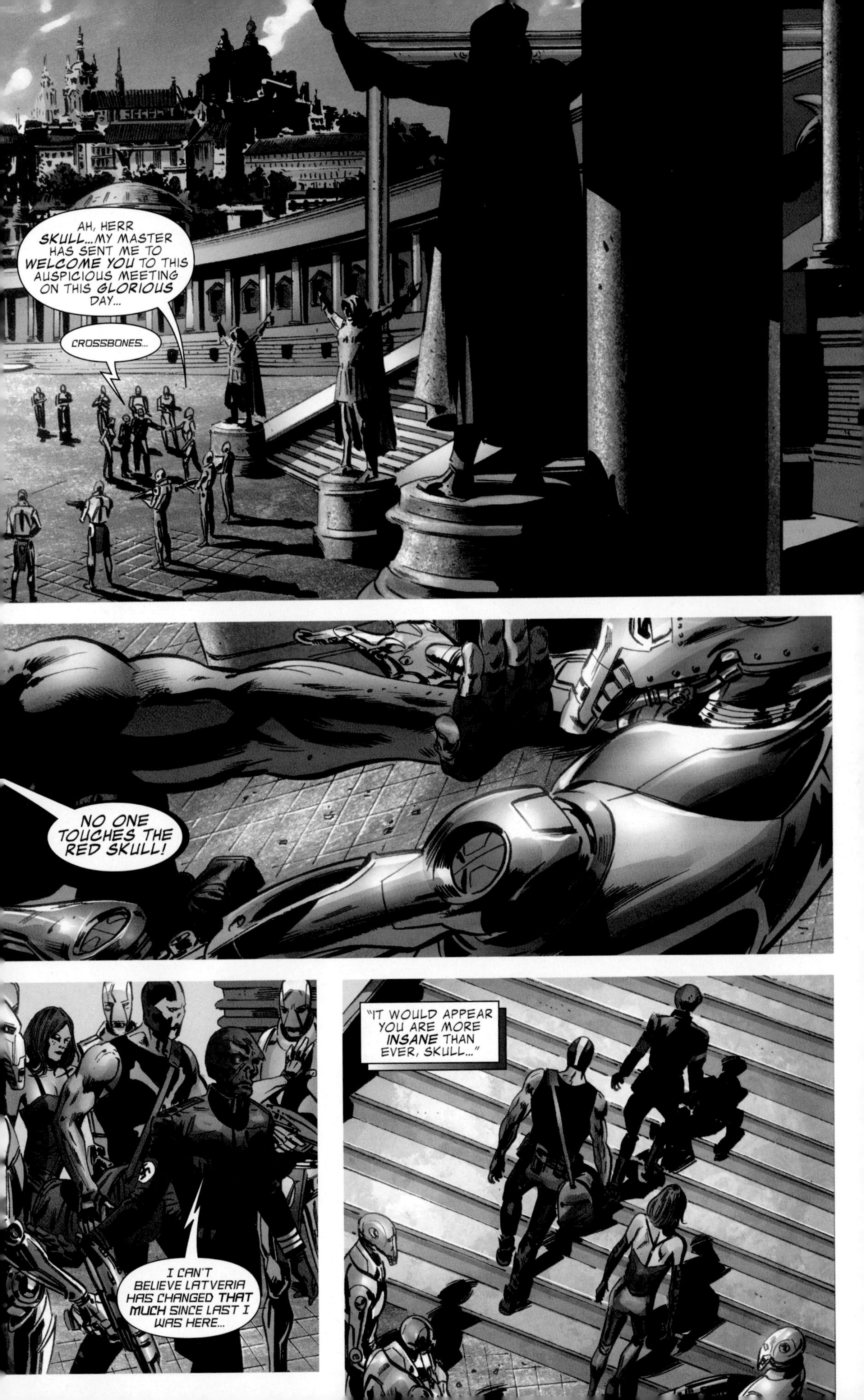
AH, HERR SKULL...MY MASTER HAS SENT ME TO WELCOME YOU TO THIS AUSPICIOUS MEETING ON THIS GLORIOUS DAY...
CROSSBONES...
NO ONE TOUCHES THE RED SKULL!
I CAN'T BELIEVE LATVERIA HAS CHANGED THAT MUCH SINCE LAST I WAS HERE...
"IT WOULD APPEAR YOU ARE MORE INSANE THAN EVER, SKULL..."

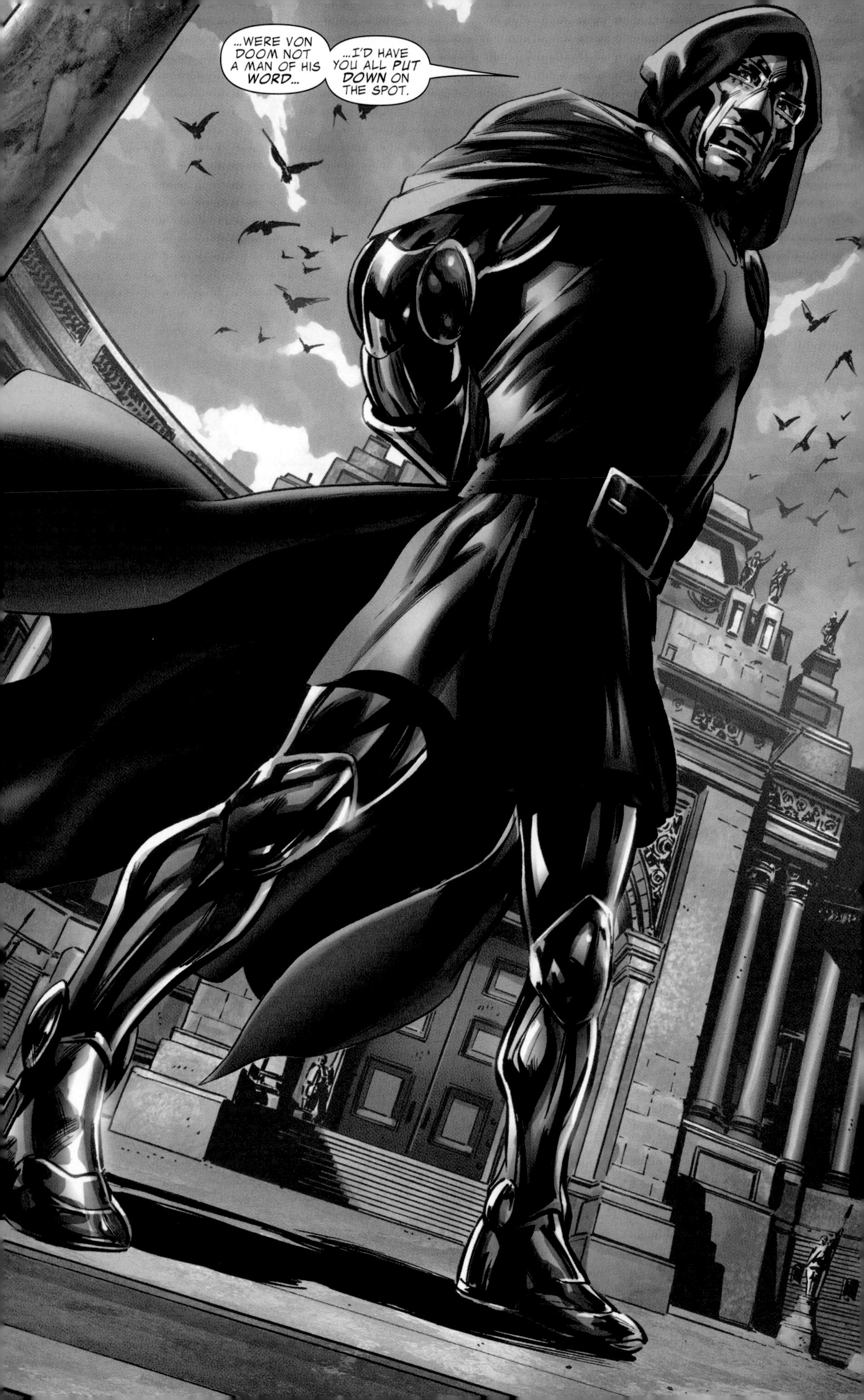
...WERE VON DOOM NOT A MAN OF HIS WORD...
...I'D HAVE YOU ALL PUT DOWN ON THE SPOT.

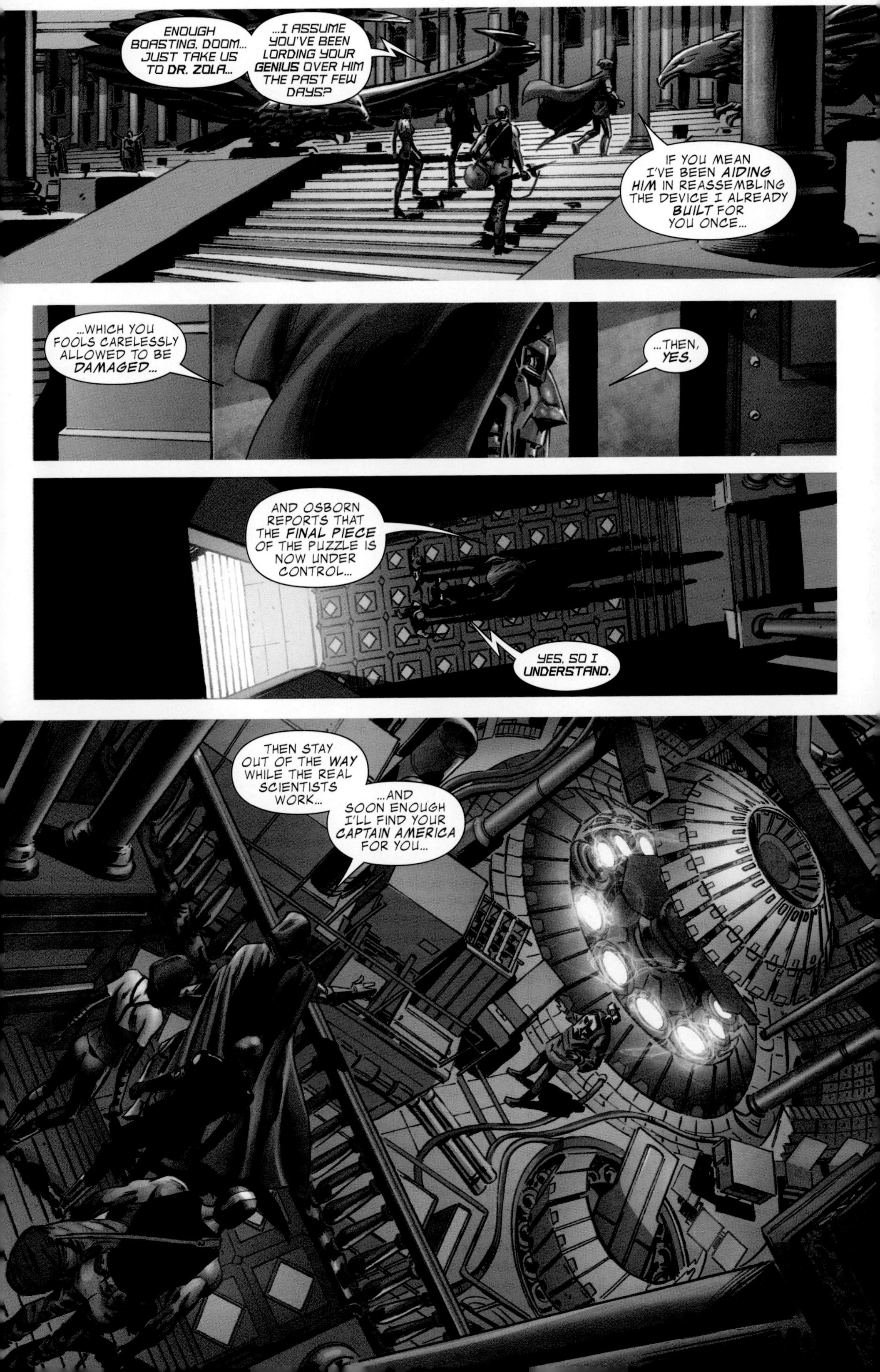

ENOUGH BOASTING, DOOM... JUST TAKE US TO DR. ZOLA...
...I ASSUME YOU'VE BEEN LORDING YOUR GENIUS OVER HIM THE PAST FEW DAYS?
IF YOU MEAN I'VE BEEN AIDING HIM IN REASSEMBLING THE DEVICE I ALREADY BUILT FOR YOU ONCE...
...WHICH YOU FOOLS CARELESSLY ALLOWED TO BE DAMAGED...
...THEN, YES.
AND OSBORN REPORTS THAT THE FINAL PIECE OF THE PUZZLE IS NOW UNDER CONTROL...
YES, SO I UNDERSTAND.
THEN STAY OUT OF THE WAY WHILE THE REAL SCIENTISTS WORK...
...AND SOON ENOUGH I'LL FIND YOUR CAPTAIN AMERICA FOR YOU...

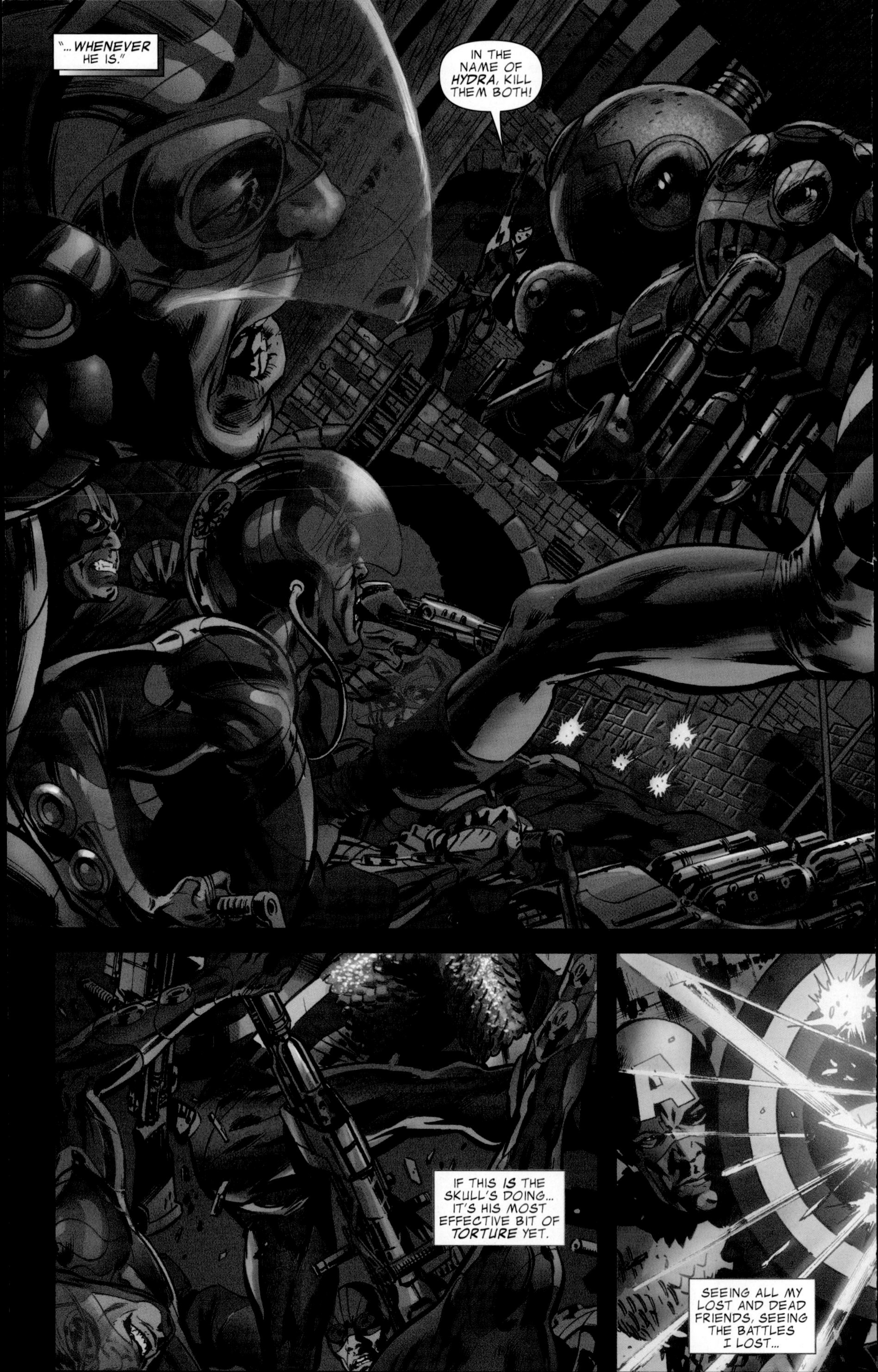
"...WHENEVER HE IS."
IN THE NAME OF HYDRA, KILL THEM BOTH!
IF THIS IS THE SKULL'S DOING... IT'S HIS MOST EFFECTIVE BIT OF TORTURE YET.
SEEING ALL MY LOST AND DEAD FRIENDS, SEEING THE BATTLES I LOST...

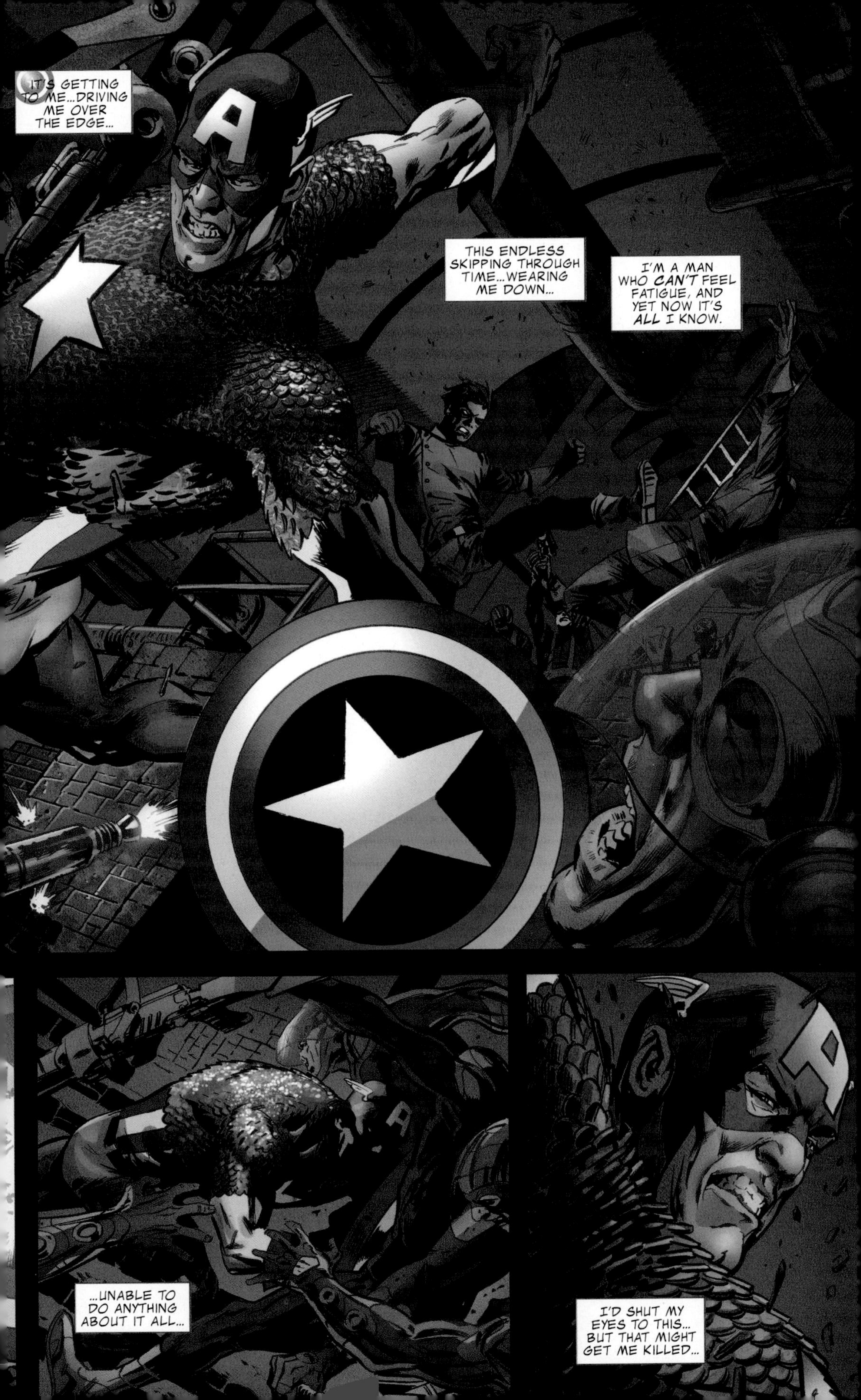

IT'S GETTING TO ME...DRIVING ME OVER THE EDGE...
THIS ENDLESS SKIPPING THROUGH TIME...WEARING ME DOWN...
I'M A MAN WHO CAN'T FEEL FATIGUE, AND YET NOW IT'S ALL I KNOW.
...UNABLE TO DO ANYTHING ABOUT IT ALL...
I'D SHUT MY EYES TO THIS... BUT THAT MIGHT GET ME KILLED...

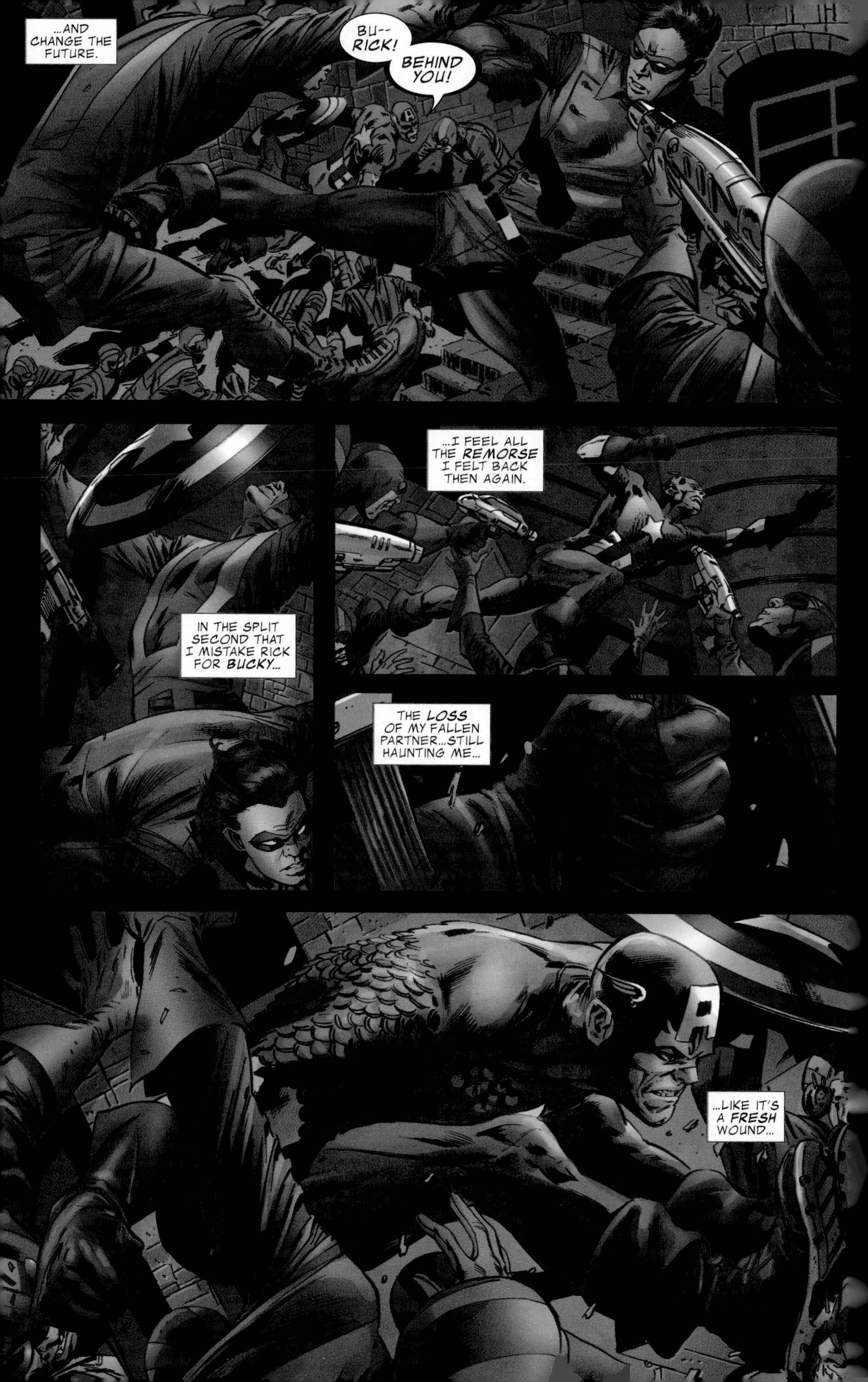
...AND CHANGE THE FUTURE.
BU-- RICK!
BEHIND YOU!
IN THE SPLIT SECOND THAT I MISTAKE RICK FOR BUCKY...
...I FEEL ALL THE REMORSE I FELT BACK THEN AGAIN.
THE LOSS OF MY FALLEN PARTNER...STILL HAUNTING ME...
...LIKE IT'S A FRESH WOUND...

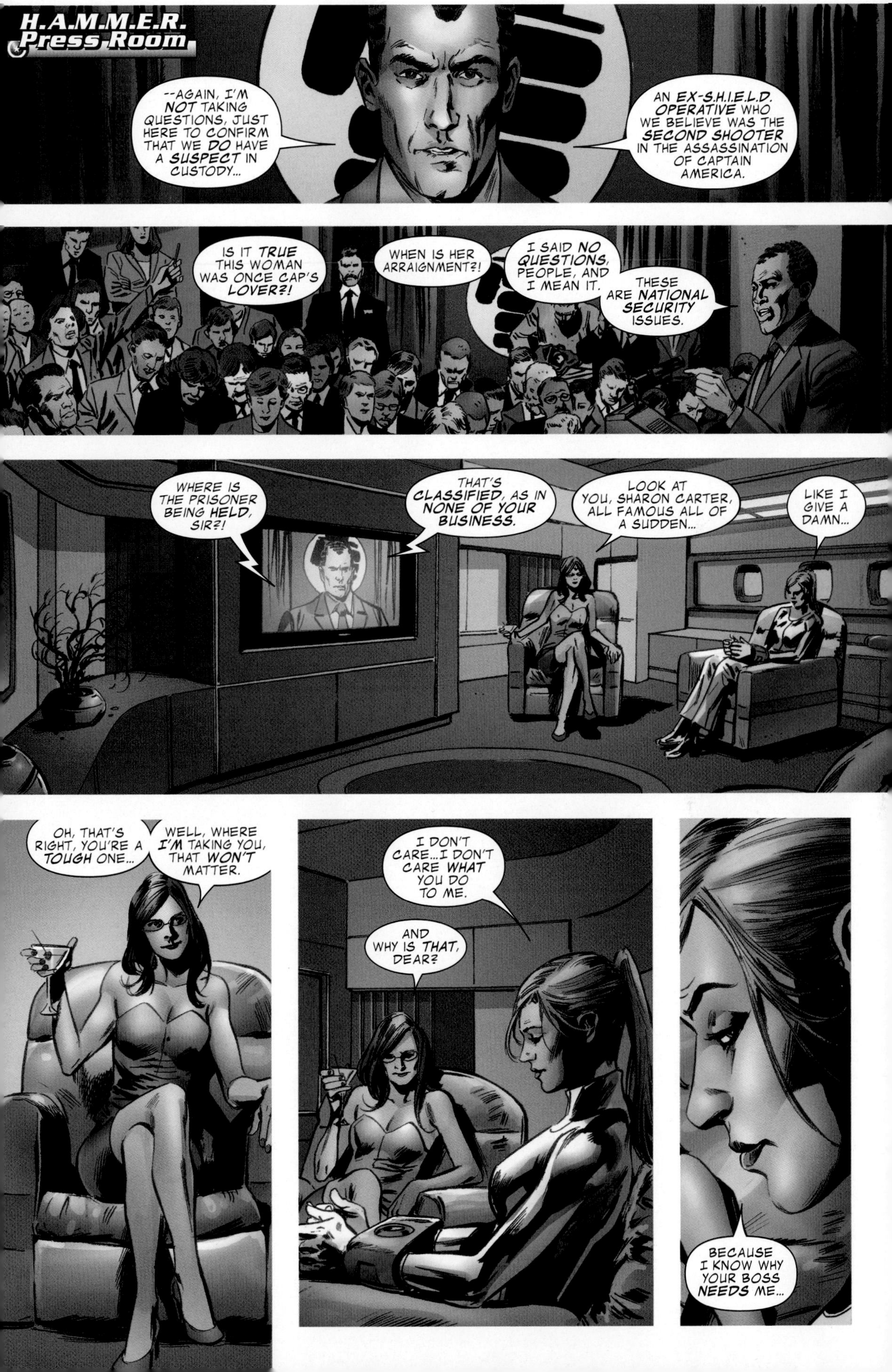
H.A.M.M.E.R. Press Room
--AGAIN, I'M NOT TAKING QUESTIONS, JUST HERE TO CONFIRM THAT WE DO HAVE A SUSPECT IN CUSTODY...
AN EX-S.H.I.E.L.D. OPERATIVE WHO WE BELIEVE WAS THE SECOND SHOOTER IN THE ASSASSINATION OF CAPTAIN AMERICA.
IS IT TRUE THIS WOMAN WAS ONCE CAP'S LOVER?!
WHEN IS HER ARRAIGNMENT?!
I SAID NO QUESTIONS, PEOPLE, AND I MEAN IT.
THESE ARE NATIONAL SECURITY ISSUES.
WHERE IS THE PRISONER BEING HELD, SIR?!
THAT'S CLASSIFIED, AS IN NONE OF YOUR BUSINESS.
LOOK AT YOU, SHARON CARTER, ALL FAMOUS ALL OF A SUDDEN...
LIKE I GIVE A DAMN...
OH, THAT'S RIGHT, YOU'RE A TOUGH ONE...
WELL, WHERE I'M TAKING YOU, THAT WON'T MATTER.
I DON'T CARE...I DON'T CARE WHAT YOU DO TO ME.
AND WHY IS THAT, DEAR?
BECAUSE I KNOW WHY YOUR BOSS NEEDS ME...

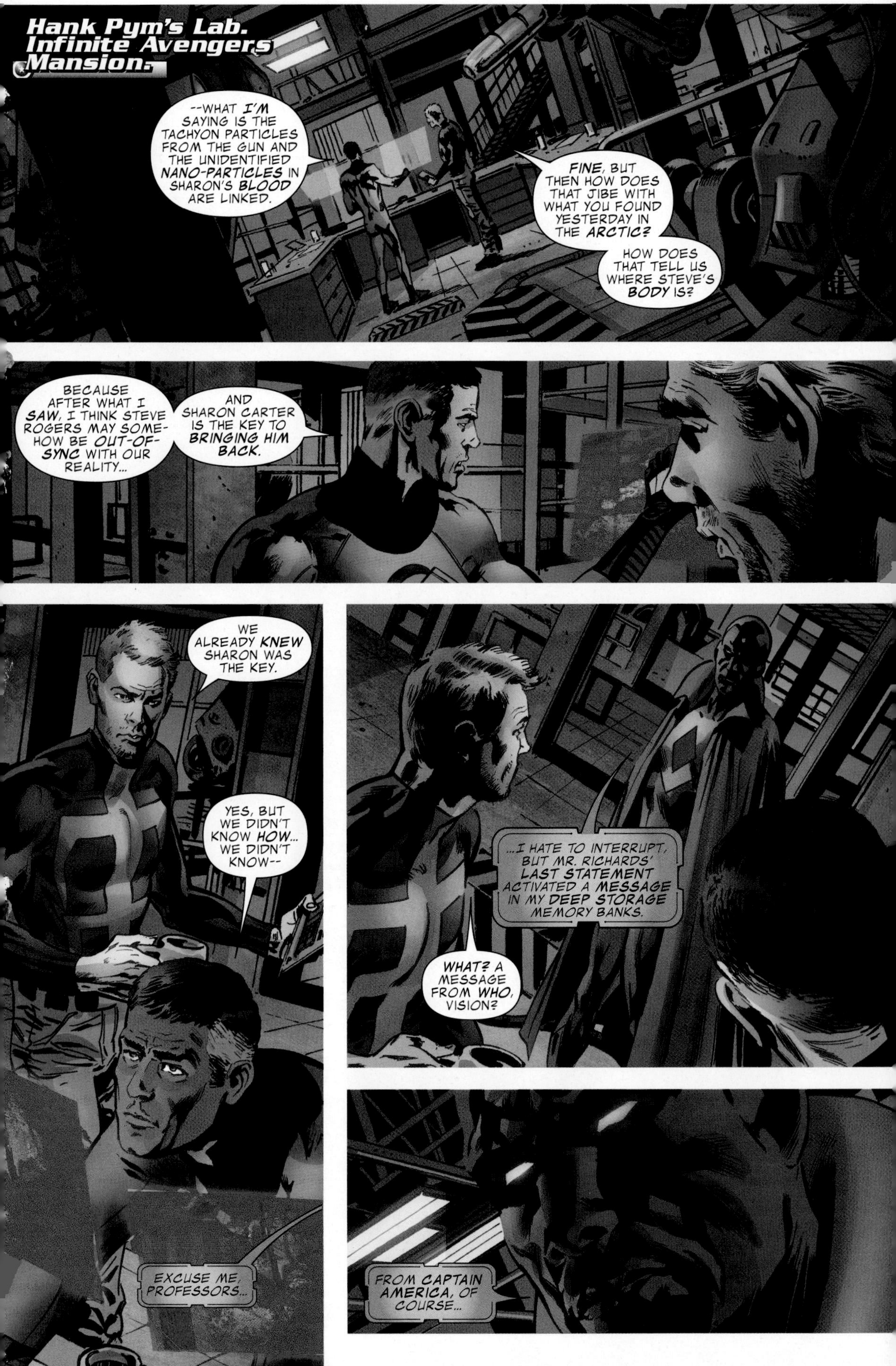
Hank Pym's Lab. Infinite Avengers Mansion.
--WHAT I'M SAYING IS THE TACHYON PARTICLES FROM THE GUN AND THE UNIDENTIFIED NANO-PARTICLES IN SHARON'S BLOOD ARE LINKED.
FINE, BUT THEN HOW DOES THAT JIBE WITH WHAT YOU FOUND YESTERDAY IN THE ARCTIC?
HOW DOES THAT TELL US WHERE STEVE'S BODY IS?
BECAUSE AFTER WHAT I SAW, I THINK STEVE ROGERS MAY SOMEHOW BE OUT-OF-SYNC WITH OUR REALITY...
AND SHARON CARTER IS THE KEY TO BRINGING HIM BACK.
WE ALREADY KNEW SHARON WAS THE KEY.
YES, BUT WE DIDN'T KNOW HOW... WE DIDN'T KNOW--
EXCUSE ME, PROFESSORS...
...I HATE TO INTERRUPT, BUT MR. RICHARDS' LAST STATEMENT ACTIVATED A MESSAGE IN MY DEEP STORAGE MEMORY BANKS.
WHAT? A MESSAGE FROM WHO, VISION?
FROM CAPTAIN AMERICA, OF COURSE...

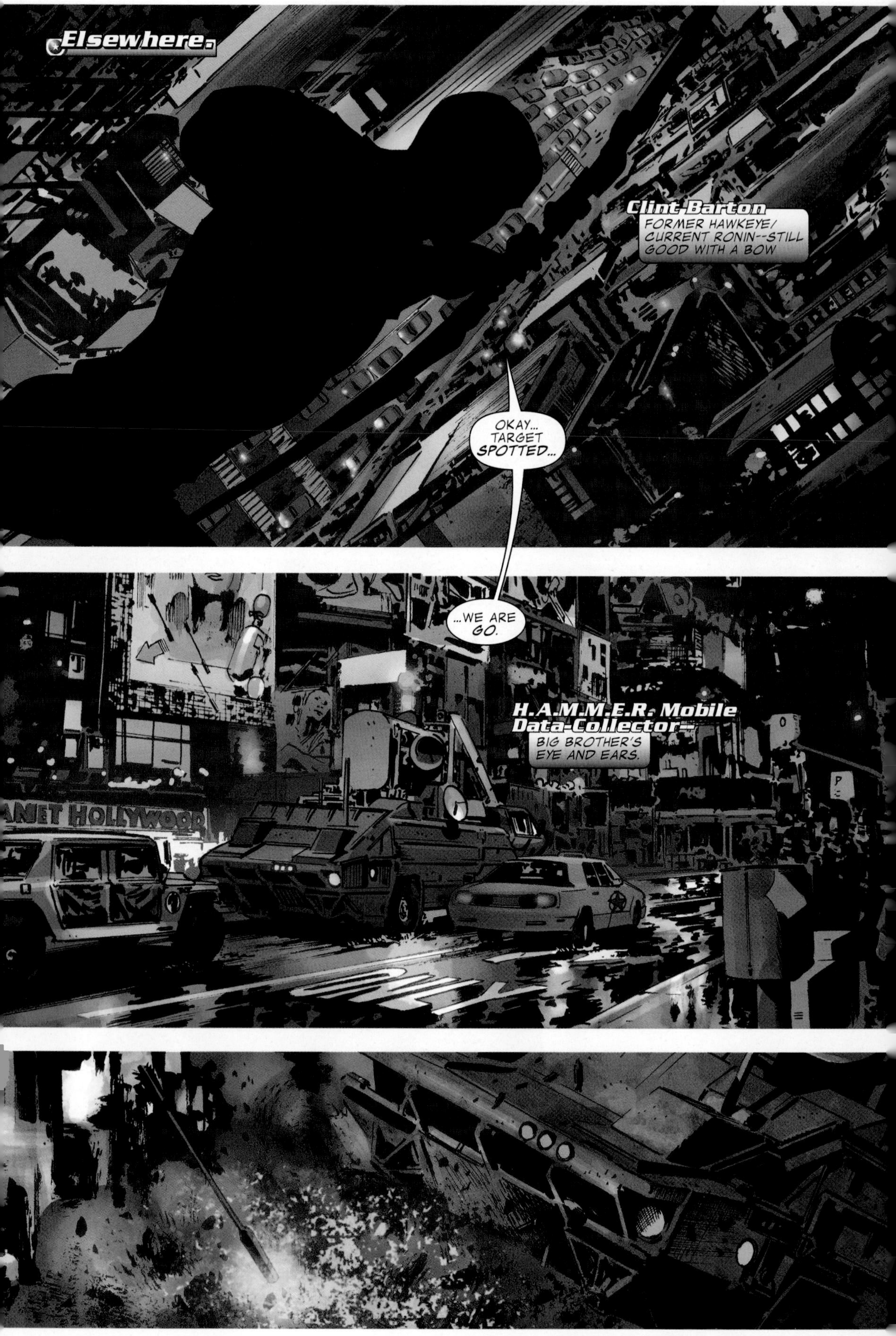
Elsewhere.
Clint Barton
FORMER HAWKEYE/ CURRENT RONIN--STILL GOOD WITH A BOW
OKAY... TARGET SPOTTED...
...WE ARE GO.
H.A.M.M.E.R. Mobile Data-Collector--
BIG BROTHER'S EYE AND EARS.
ANET HOLLYWOOD

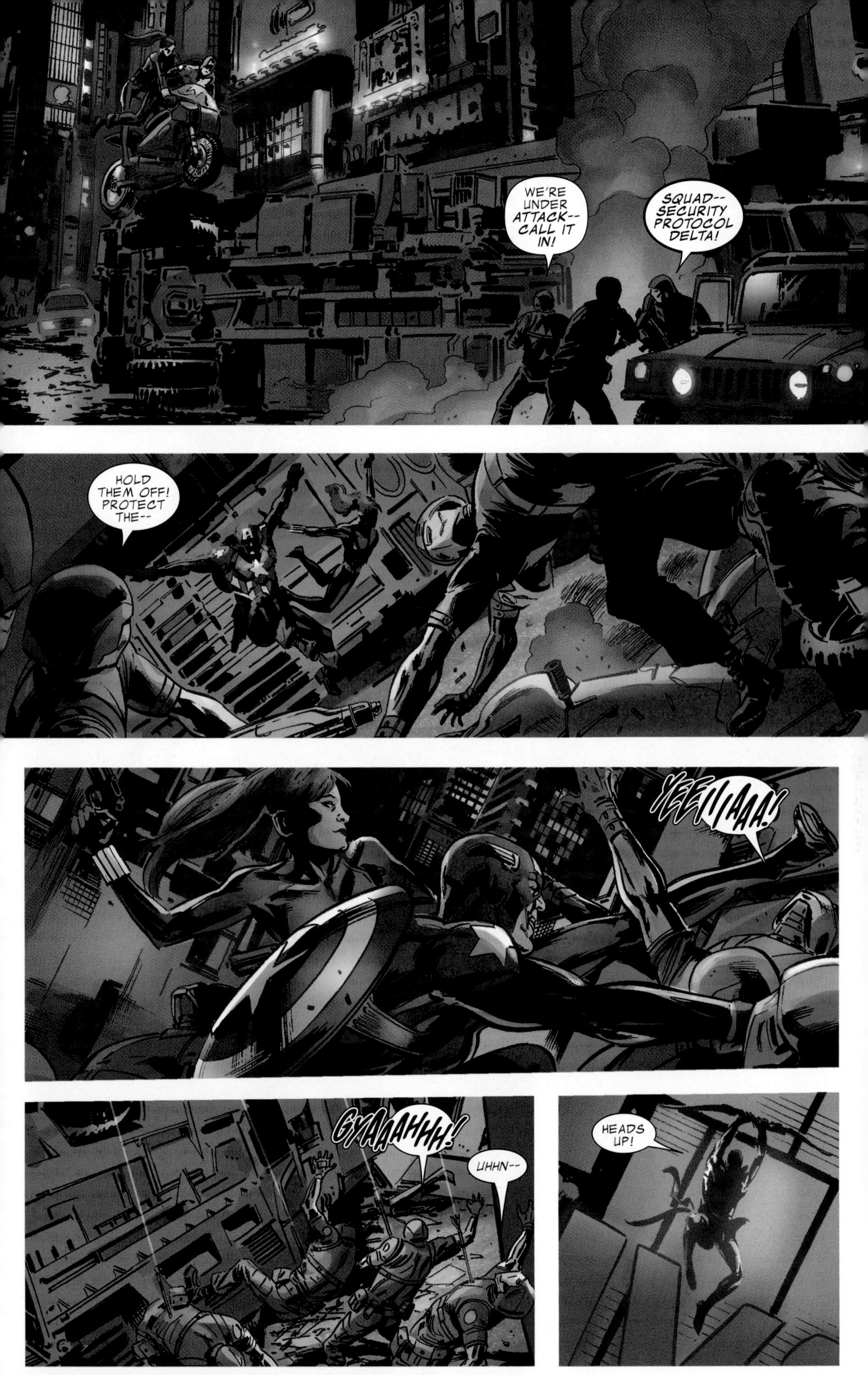
WE'RE UNDER ATTACK-- CALL IT IN!
SQUAD-- SECURITY PROTOCOL DELTA!
HOLD THEM OFF! PROTECT THE--
YEEIIAAA!
GYAAAHHH!
UHHN--
HEADS UP!

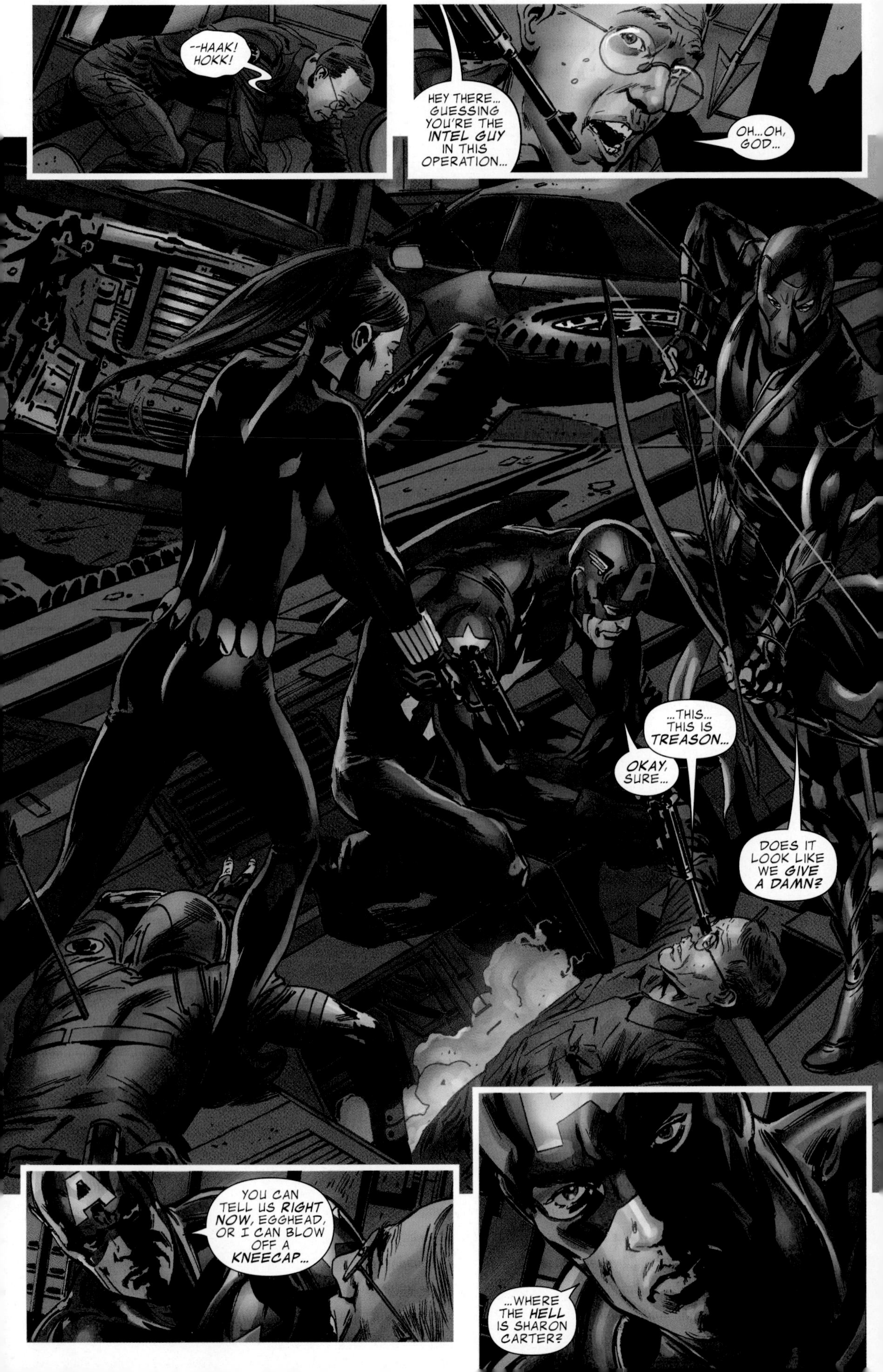
--HAAK! HOKK!
HEY THERE... GUESSING YOU'RE THE INTEL GUY IN THIS OPERATION...
OH...OH, GOD...
...THIS... THIS IS TREASON...
OKAY, SURE...
DOES IT LOOK LIKE WE GIVE A DAMN?
YOU CAN TELL US RIGHT NOW, EGGHEAD, OR I CAN BLOW OFF A KNEECAP...
...WHERE THE HELL IS SHARON CARTER?

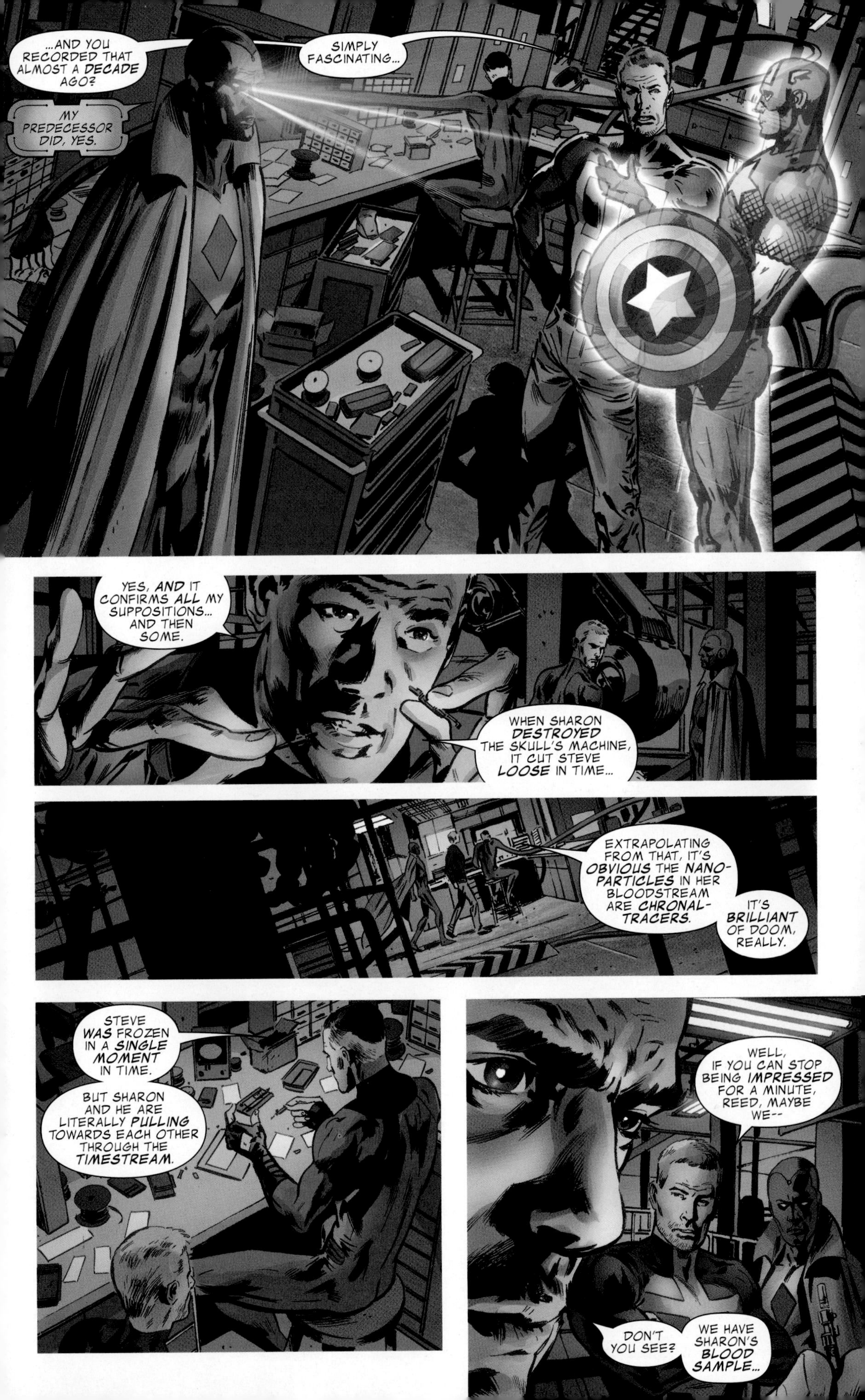
...AND YOU RECORDED THAT ALMOST A DECADE AGO?
MY PREDECESSOR DID, YES.
SIMPLY FASCINATING...
YES, AND IT CONFIRMS ALL MY SUPPOSITIONS... AND THEN SOME.
WHEN SHARON DESTROYED THE SKULL'S MACHINE, IT CUT STEVE LOOSE IN TIME...
EXTRAPOLATING FROM THAT, IT'S OBVIOUS THE NANO-PARTICLES IN HER BLOODSTREAM ARE CHRONAL-TRACERS.
IT'S BRILLIANT OF DOOM, REALLY.
STEVE WAS FROZEN IN A SINGLE MOMENT IN TIME.
BUT SHARON AND HE ARE LITERALLY PULLING TOWARDS EACH OTHER THROUGH THE TIMESTREAM.
WELL, IF YOU CAN STOP BEING IMPRESSED FOR A MINUTE, REED, MAYBE WE--
DON'T YOU SEE?
WE HAVE SHARON'S BLOOD SAMPLE...

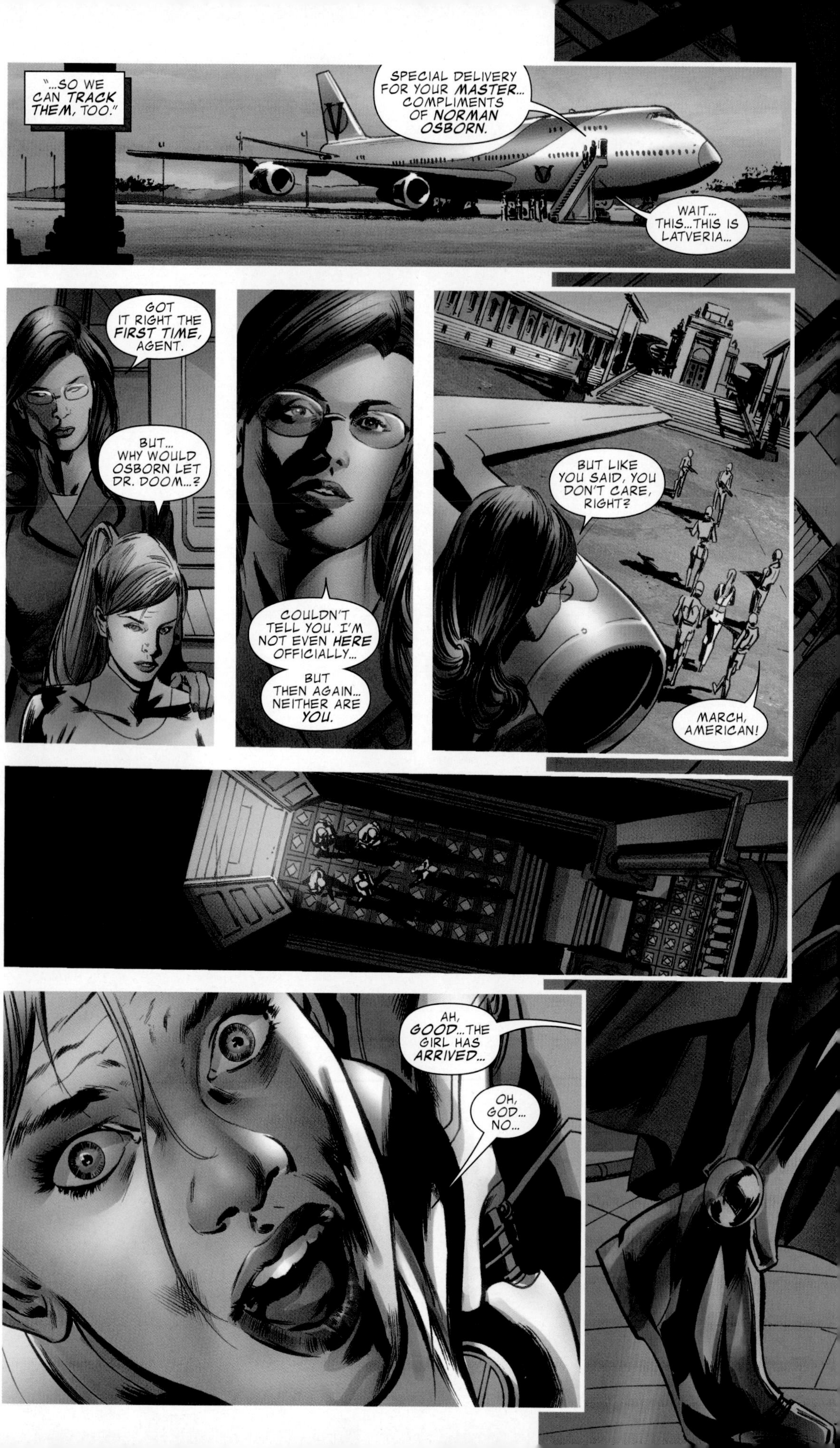
"...SO WE CAN TRACK THEM, TOO."
SPECIAL DELIVERY FOR YOUR MASTER... COMPLIMENTS OF NORMAN OSBORN.
WAIT... THIS...THIS IS LATVERIA...
GOT IT RIGHT THE FIRST TIME, AGENT.
BUT... WHY WOULD OSBORN LET DR. DOOM...?
COULDN'T TELL YOU. I'M NOT EVEN HERE OFFICIALLY...
BUT THEN AGAIN... NEITHER ARE YOU.
BUT LIKE YOU SAID, YOU DON'T CARE, RIGHT?
MARCH, AMERICAN!
AH, GOOD...THE GIRL HAS ARRIVED...
OH, GOD... NO...

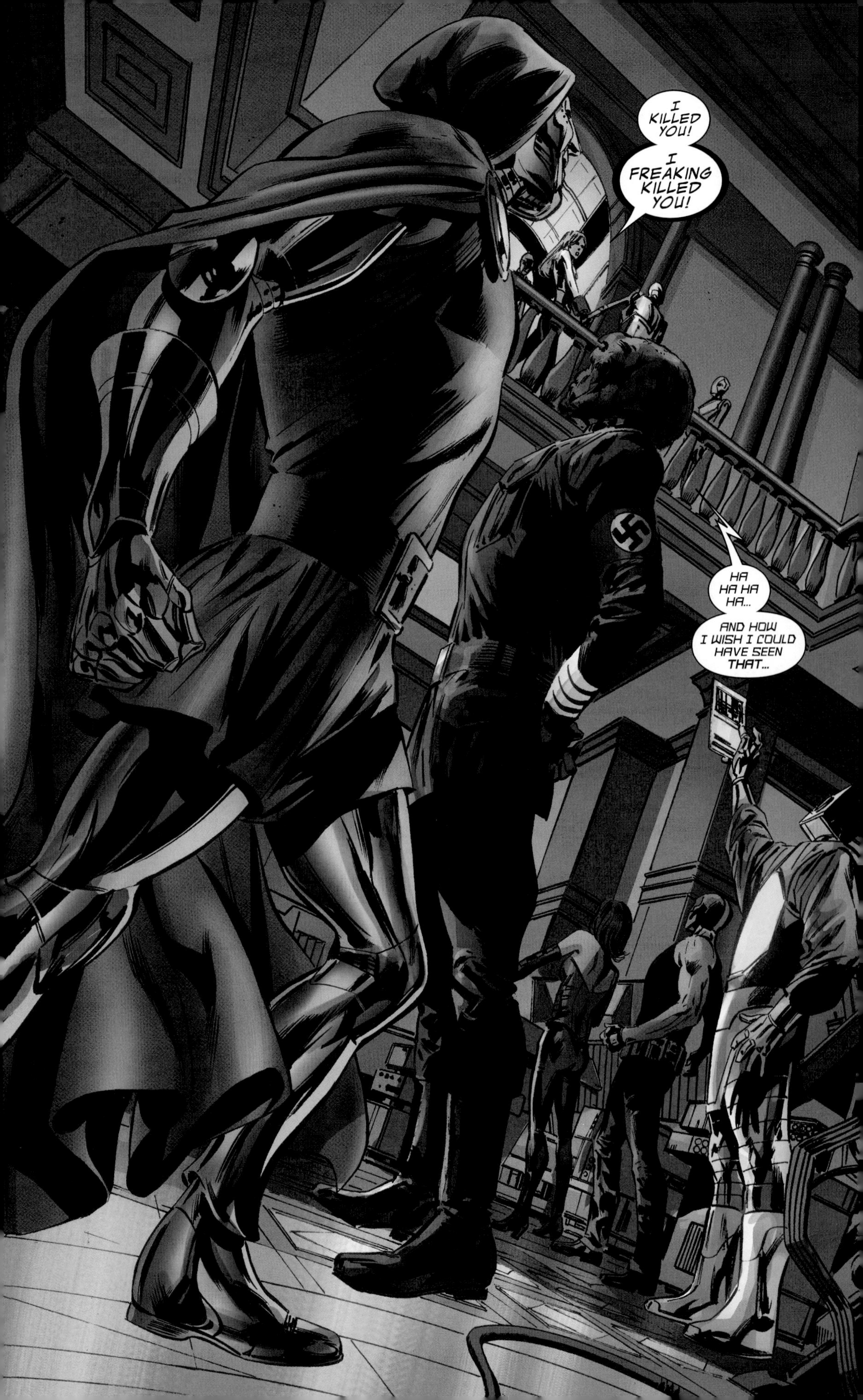
I KILLED YOU!
I FREAKING KILLED YOU!
HA HA HA HA...
AND HOW I WISH I COULD HAVE SEEN THAT...

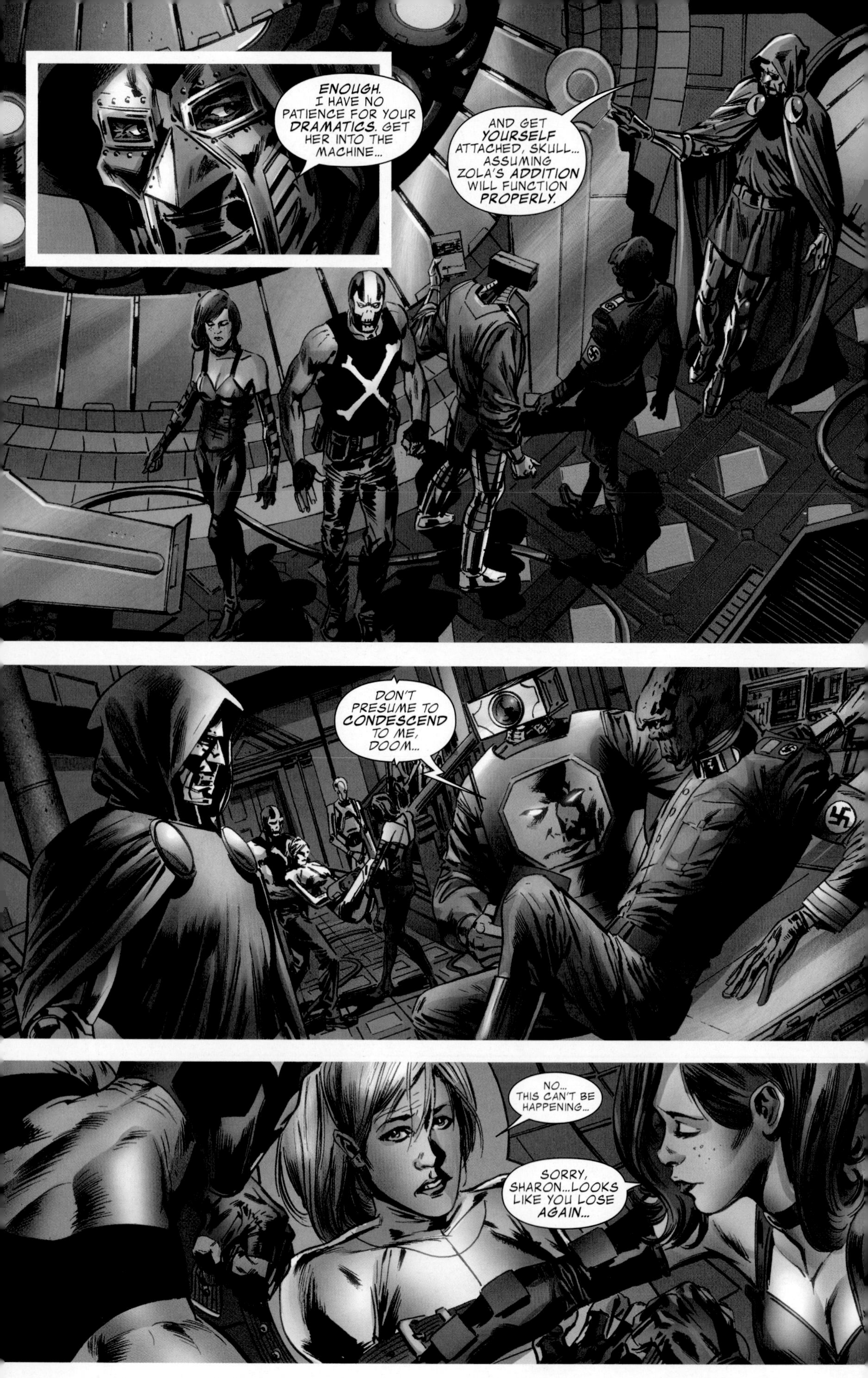
ENOUGH. I HAVE NO PATIENCE FOR YOUR DRAMATICS. GET HER INTO THE MACHINE...
AND GET YOURSELF ATTACHED, SKULL... ASSUMING ZOLA'S ADDITION WILL FUNCTION PROPERLY.
DON'T PRESUME TO CONDESCEND TO ME, DOOM...
NO... THIS CAN'T BE HAPPENING...
SORRY, SHARON...LOOKS LIKE YOU LOSE AGAIN...

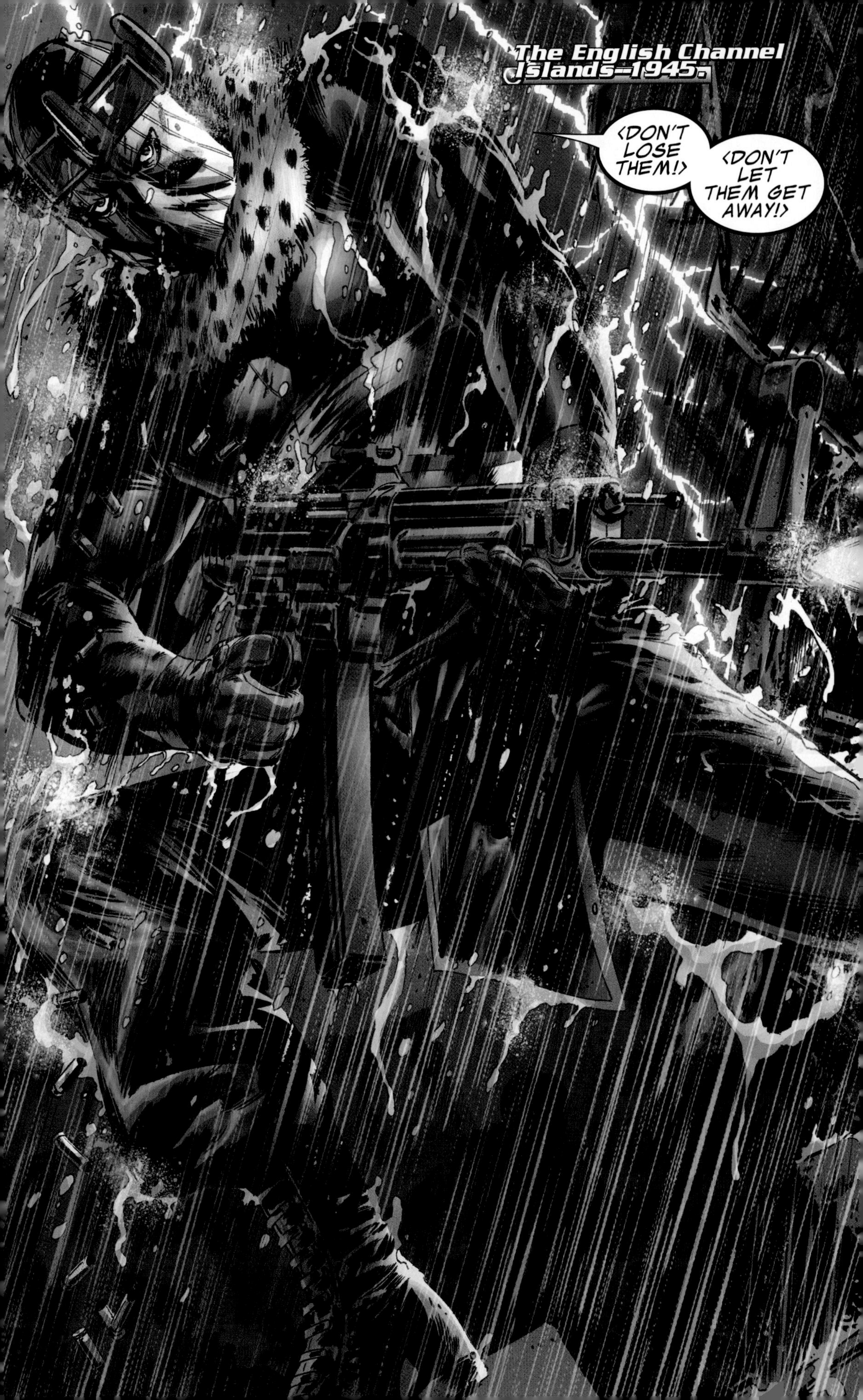
The English Channel Islands--1945.
‹DON'T LOSE THEM!›
‹DON'T LET THEM GET AWAY!›

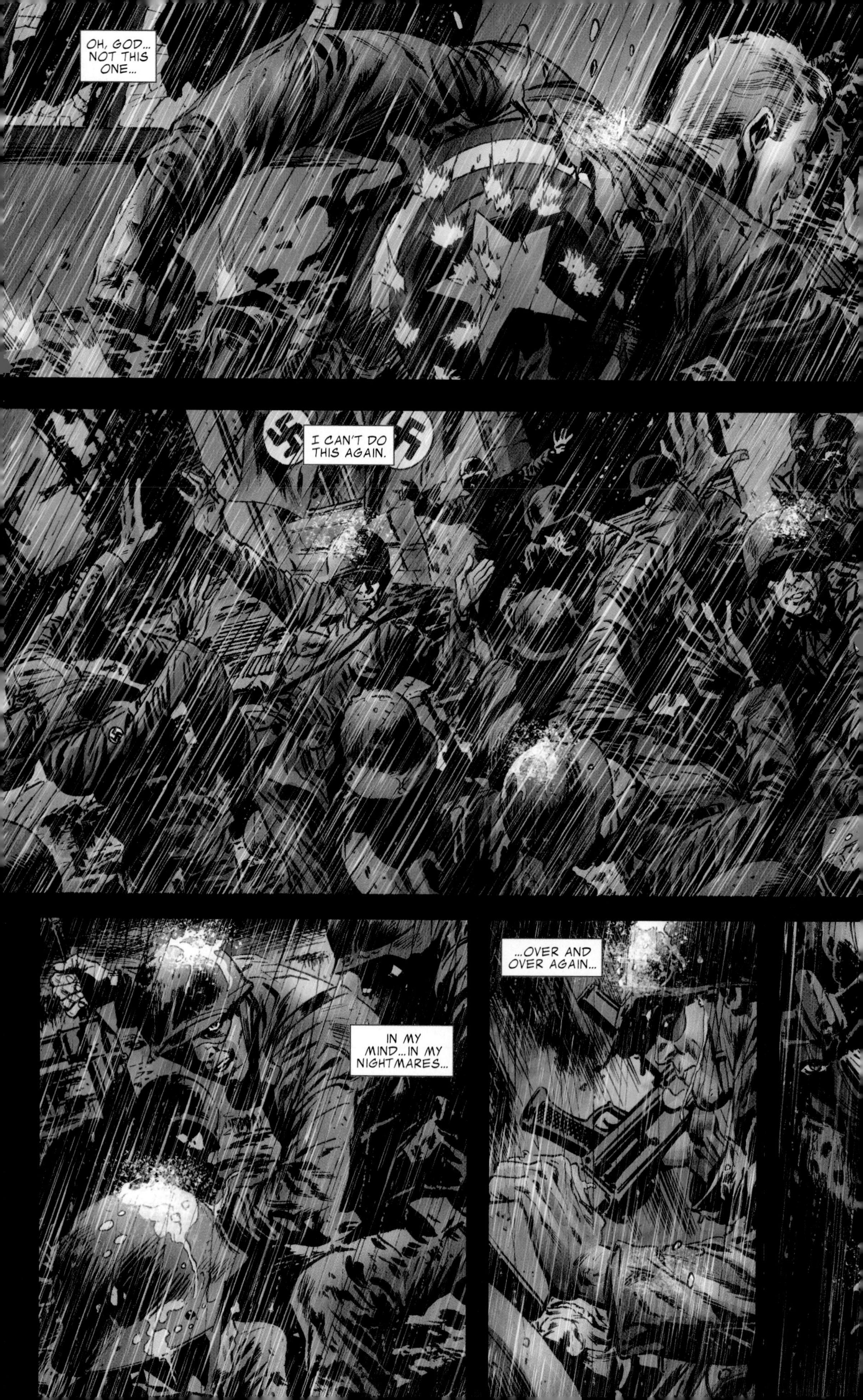
OH, GOD... NOT THIS ONE...
I CAN'T DO THIS AGAIN.
IN MY MIND...IN MY NIGHTMARES...
...OVER AND OVER AGAIN...

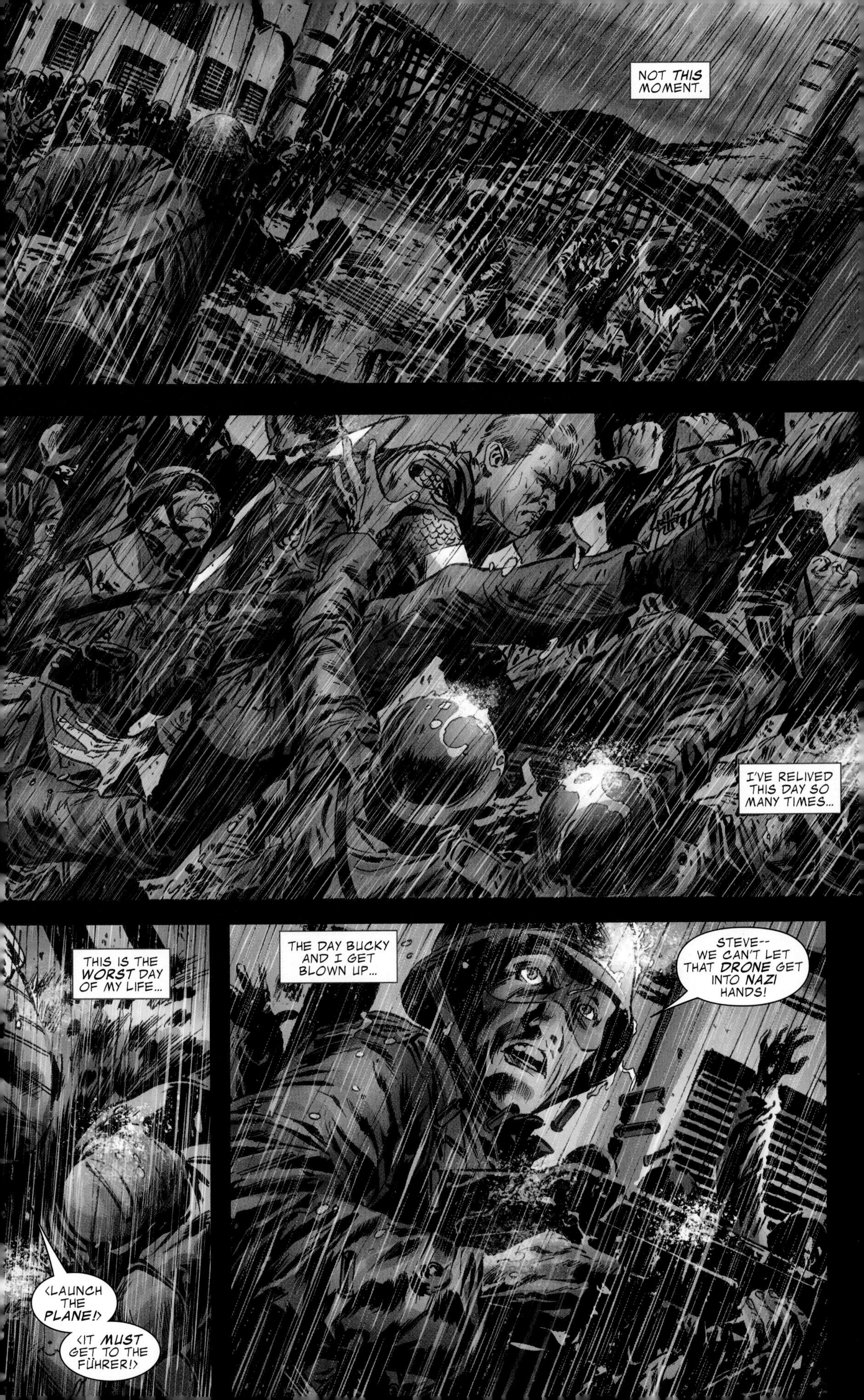
NOT THIS MOMENT.
I'VE RELIVED THIS DAY SO MANY TIMES...
THIS IS THE WORST DAY OF MY LIFE...
<LAUNCH THE PLANE!>
<IT MUST GET TO THE FÜHRER!>
THE DAY BUCKY AND I GET BLOWN UP...
STEVE-- WE CAN'T LET THAT DRONE GET INTO NAZI HANDS!

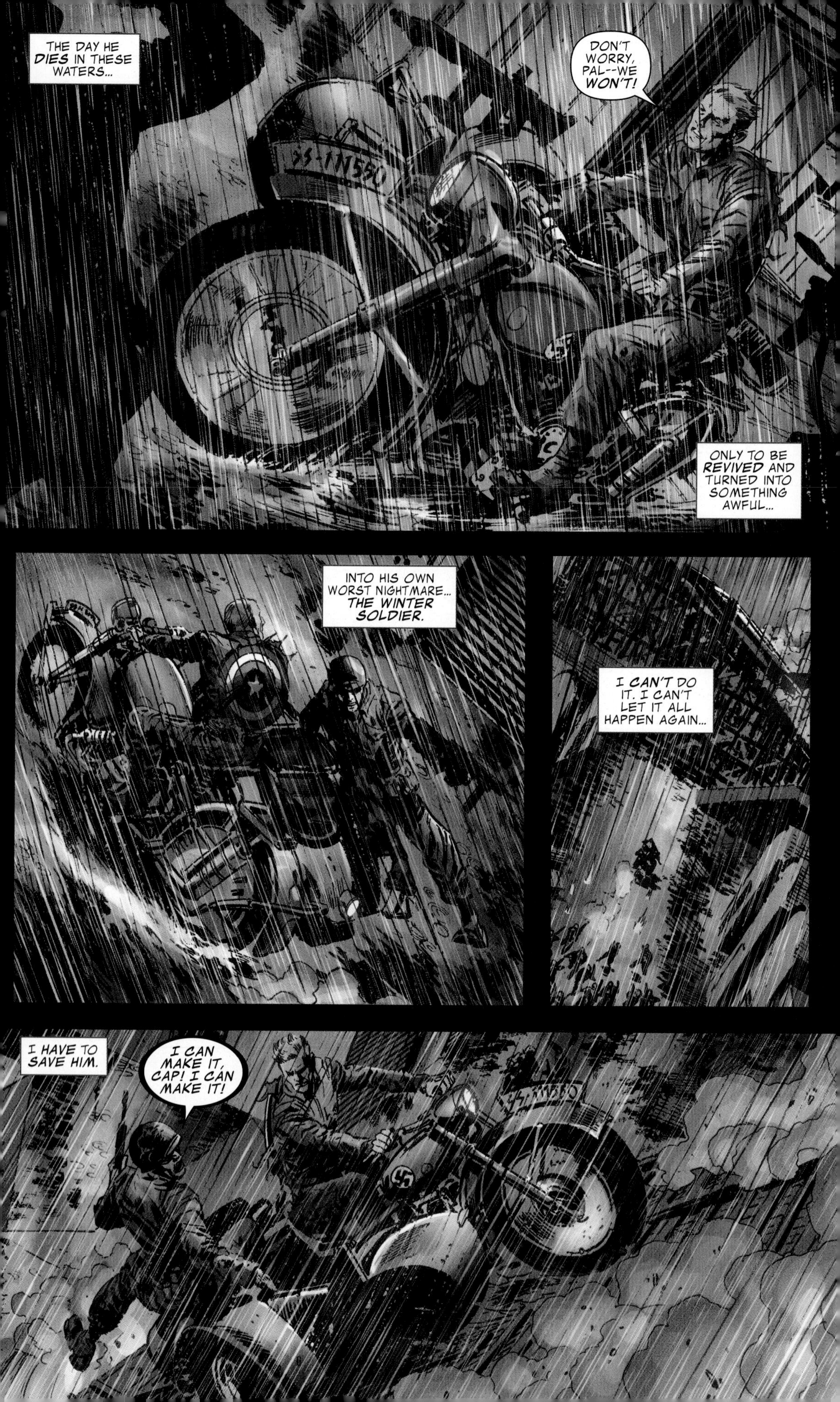

THE DAY HE DIES IN THESE WATERS...
DON'T WORRY, PAL--WE WON'T!
ONLY TO BE REVIVED AND TURNED INTO SOMETHING AWFUL...
INTO HIS OWN WORST NIGHTMARE... THE WINTER SOLDIER.
I CAN'T DO IT. I CAN'T LET IT ALL HAPPEN AGAIN...
I HAVE TO SAVE HIM.
I CAN MAKE IT, CAP! I CAN MAKE IT!

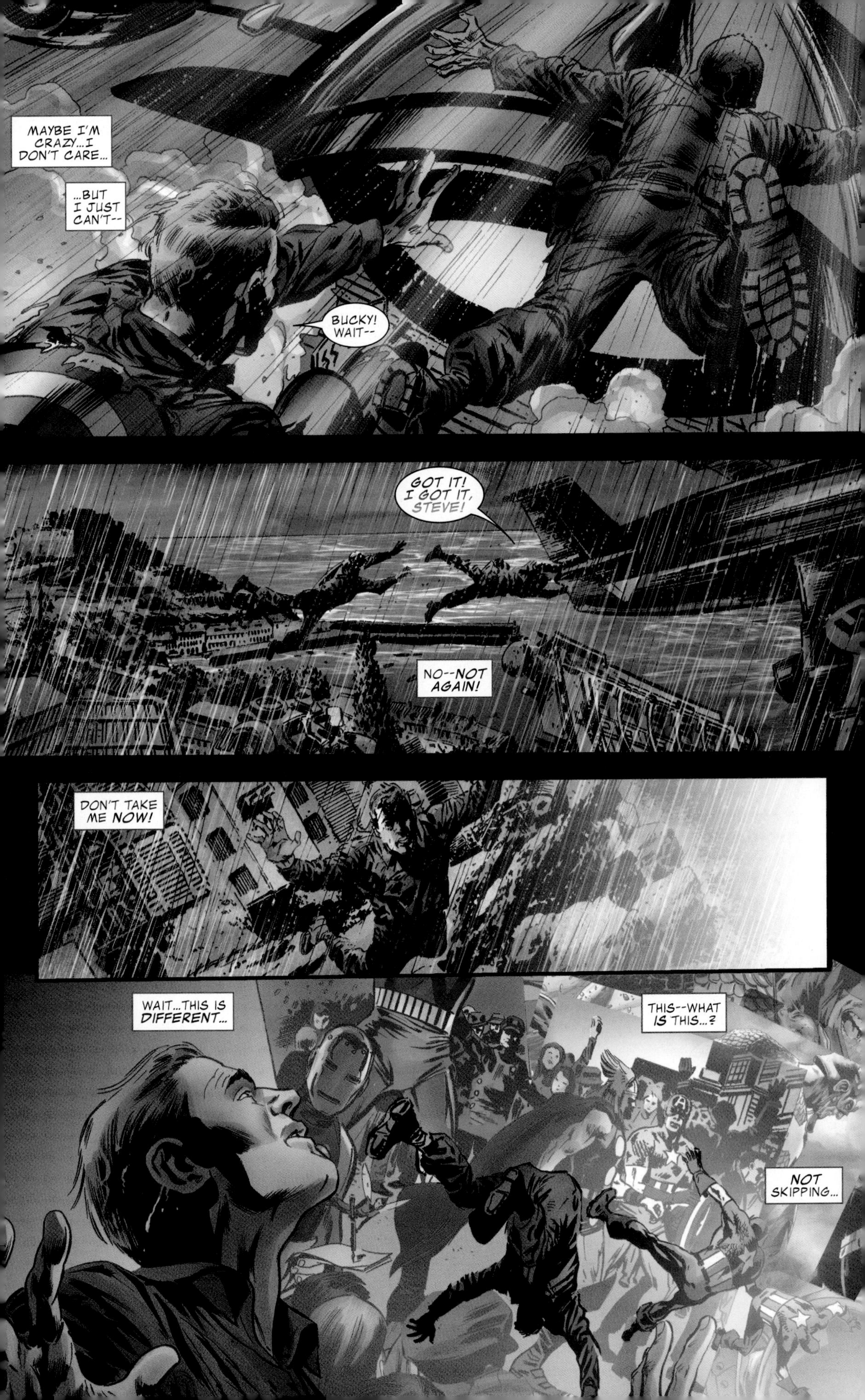
MAYBE I'M CRAZY...I DON'T CARE...
...BUT I JUST CAN'T--
BUCKY! WAIT--
GOT IT! I GOT IT, STEVE!
NO--NOT AGAIN!
DON'T TAKE ME NOW!
WAIT...THIS IS DIFFERENT...
THIS--WHAT IS THIS...?
NOT SKIPPING...

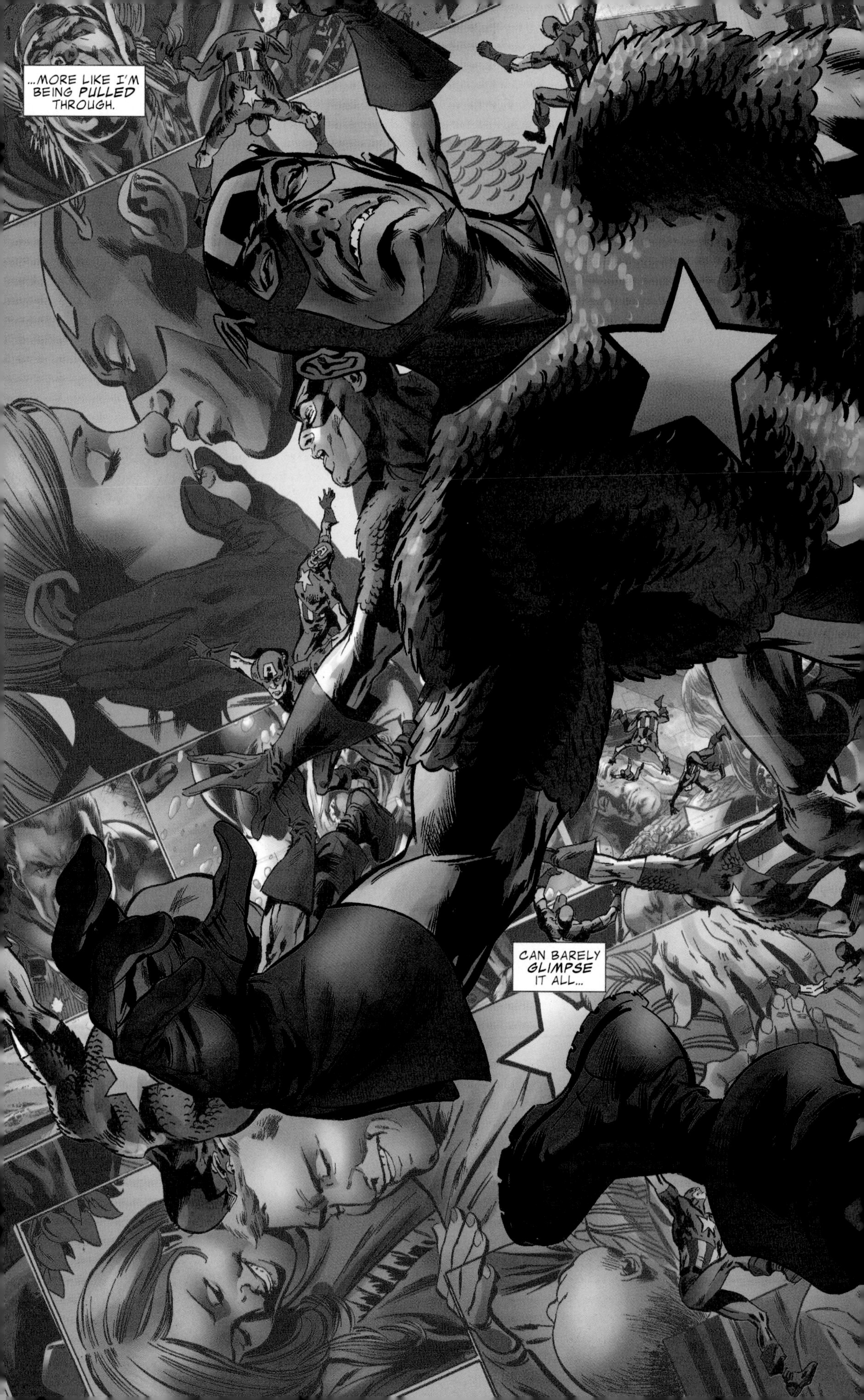
...MORE LIKE I'M BEING PULLED THROUGH.
CAN BARELY GLIMPSE IT ALL...

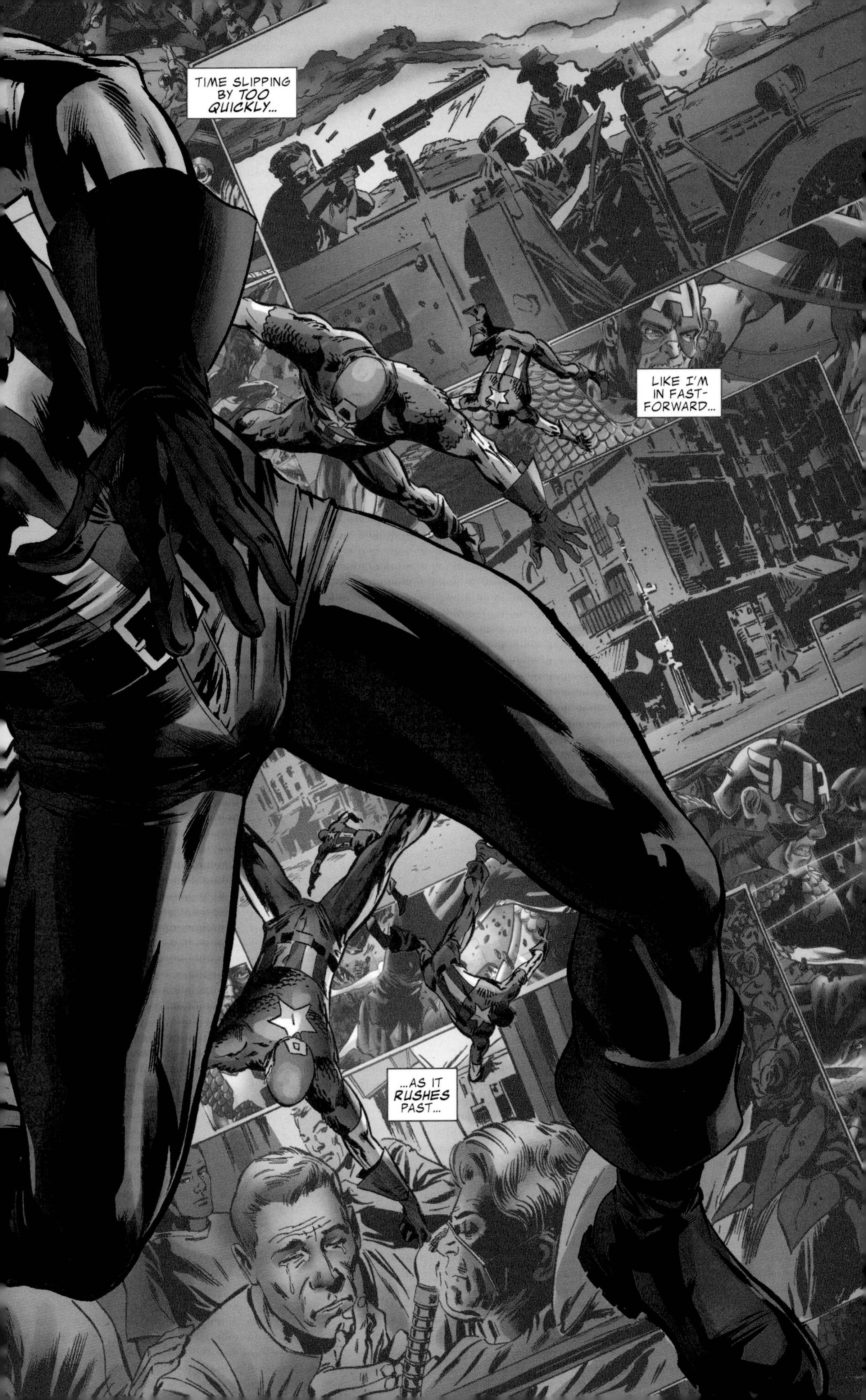
TIME SLIPPING BY TOO QUICKLY...
LIKE I'M IN FAST-FORWARD...
...AS IT RUSHES PAST...

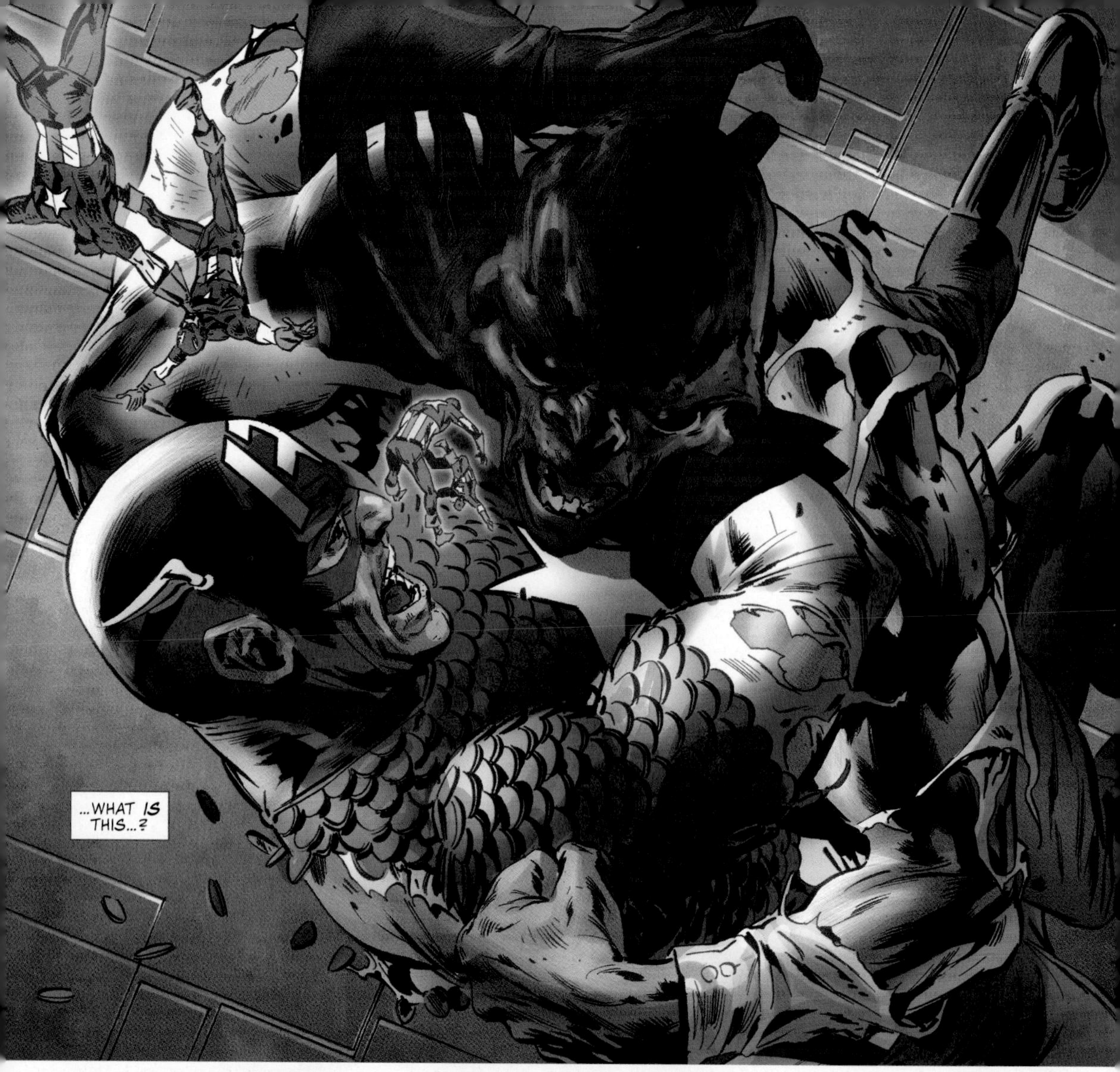
...WHAT IS THIS...?
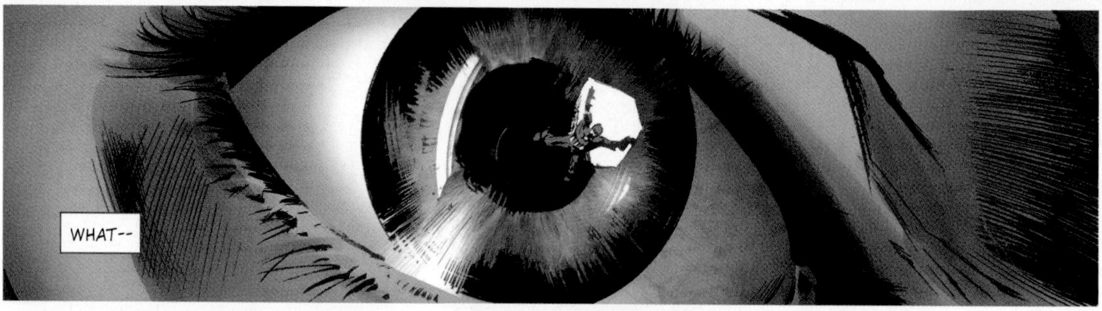
WHAT--
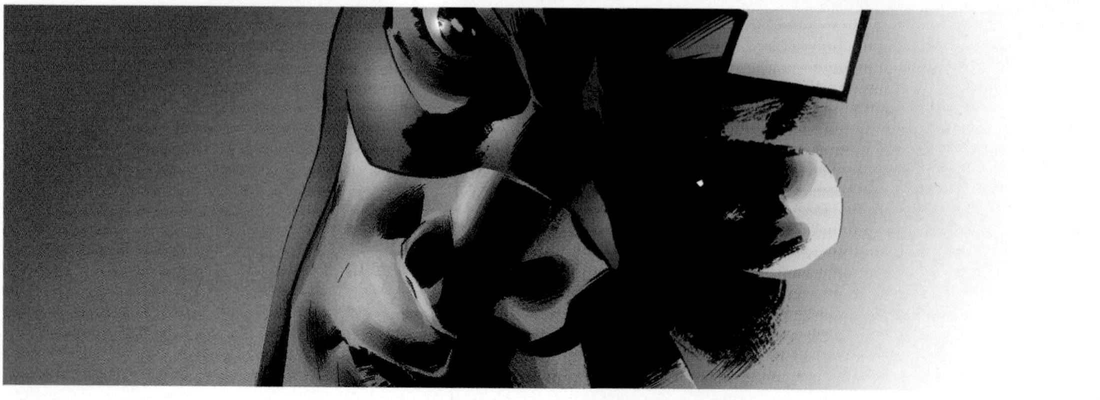

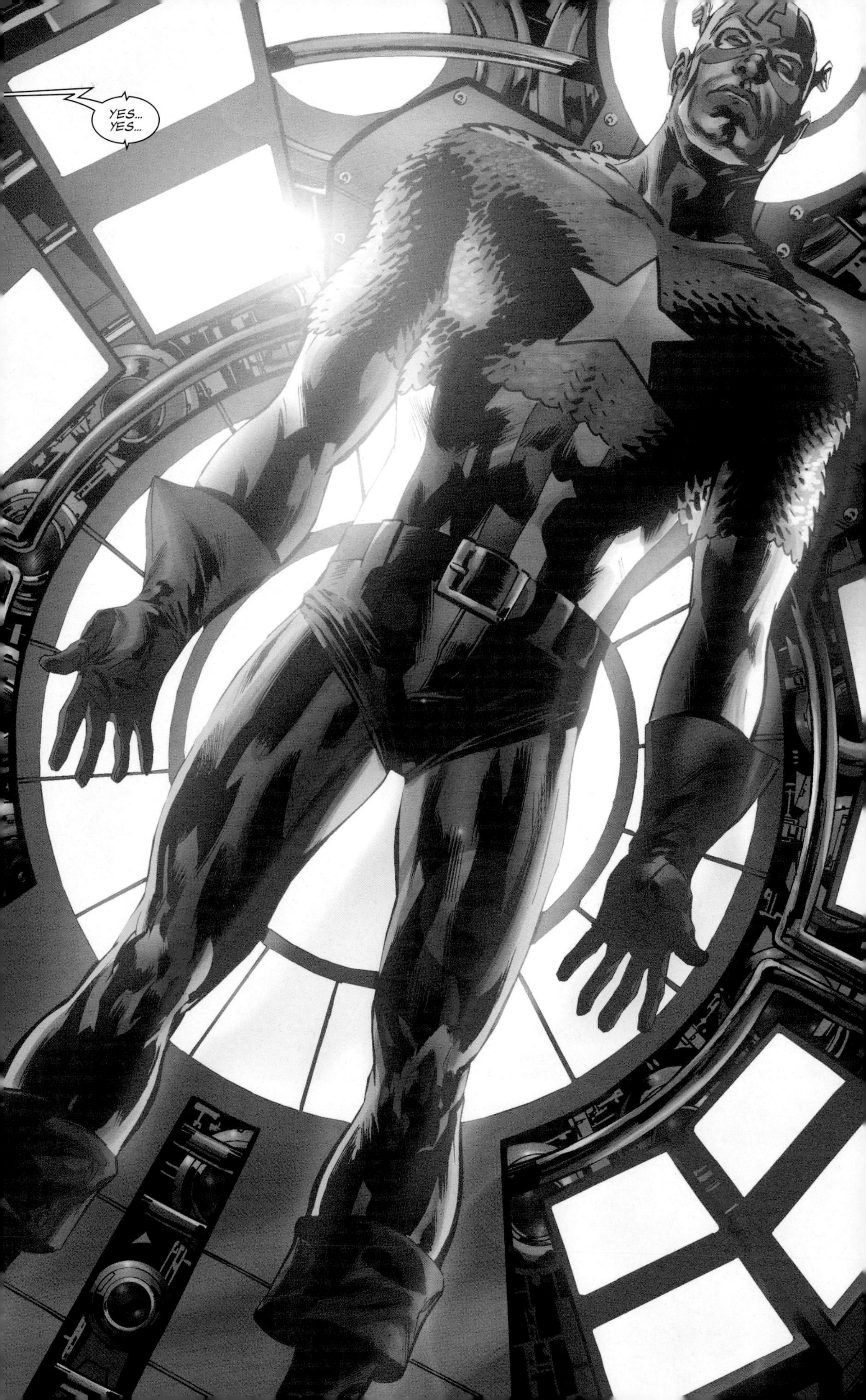
YES... YES...

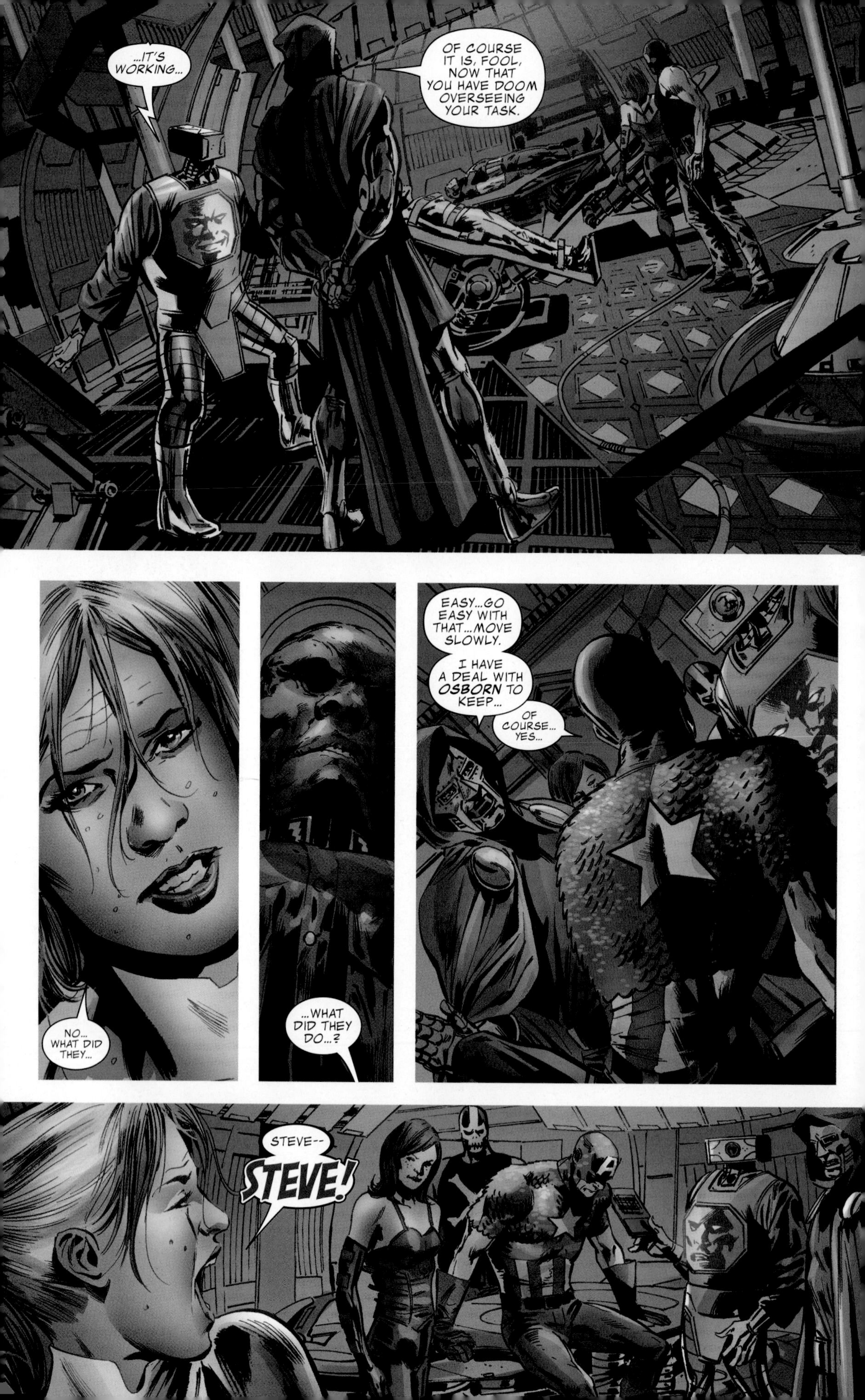
...IT'S WORKING...
OF COURSE IT IS, FOOL, NOW THAT YOU HAVE DOOM OVERSEEING YOUR TASK.
NO... WHAT DID THEY...
...WHAT DID THEY DO...?
EASY...GO EASY WITH THAT...MOVE SLOWLY.
I HAVE A DEAL WITH OSBORN TO KEEP...
OF COURSE... YES...
STEVE--
STEVE!

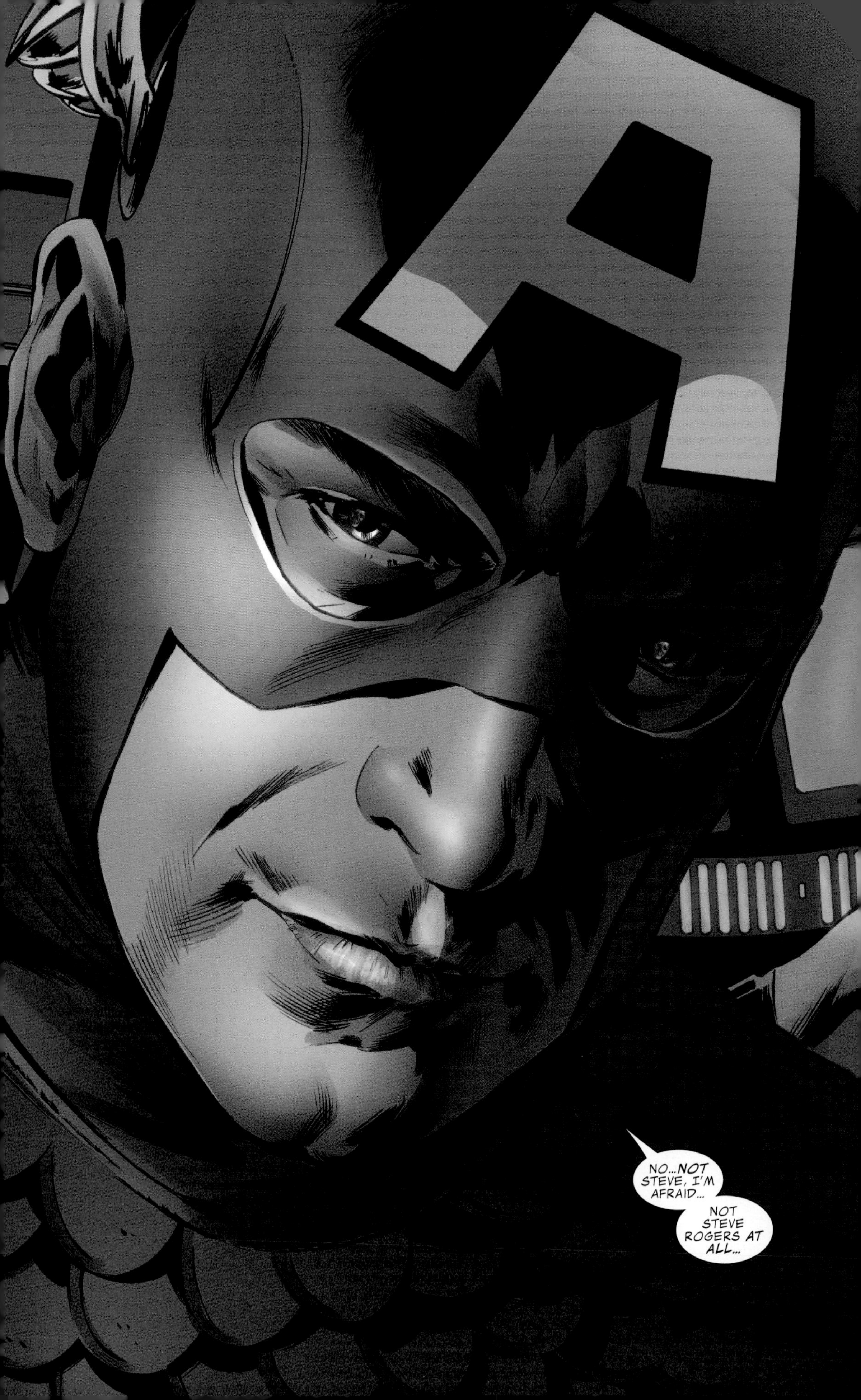
NO...NOT STEVE, I'M AFRAID...
NOT STEVE ROGERS AT ALL...

"Patriotism is the virtue of the vicious."

– *Wilde*

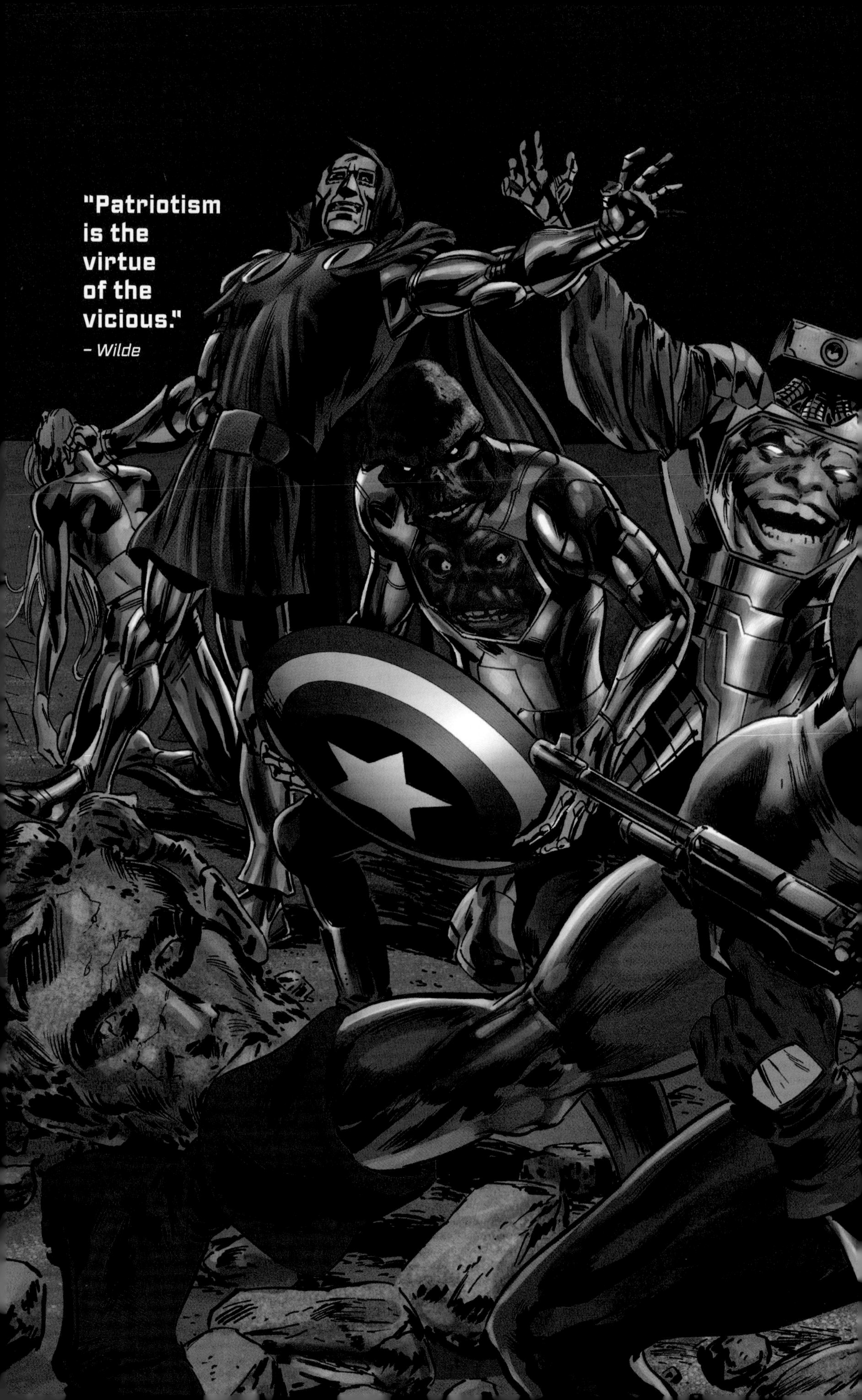

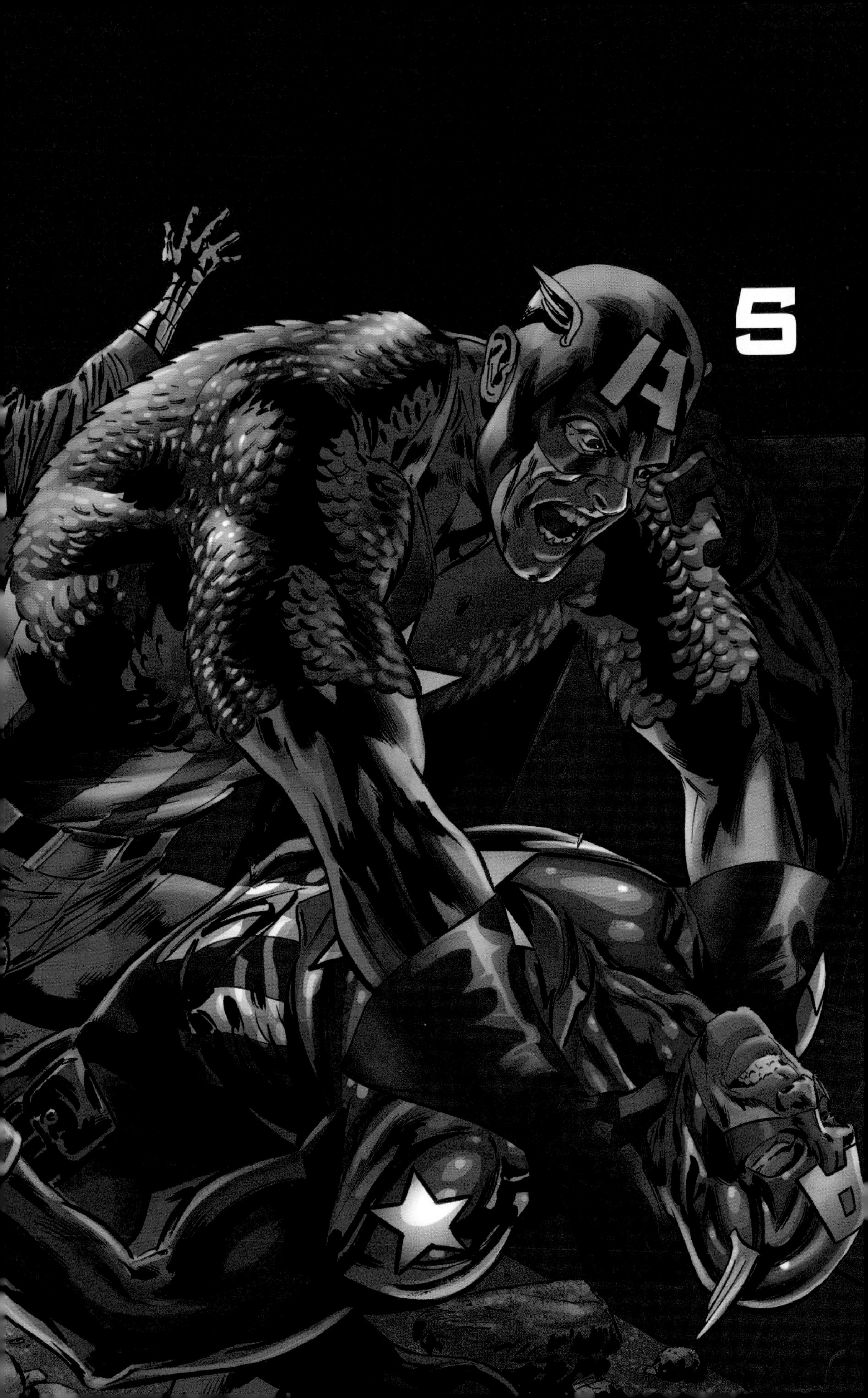
5

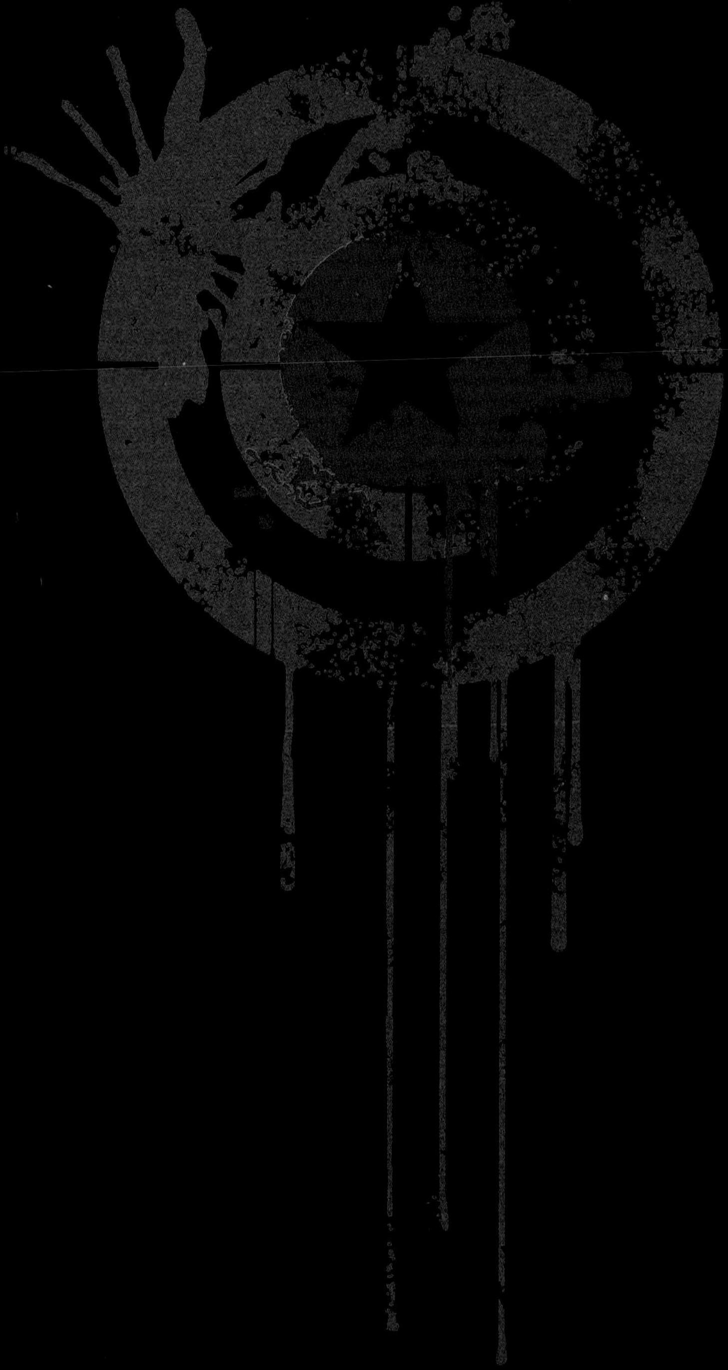

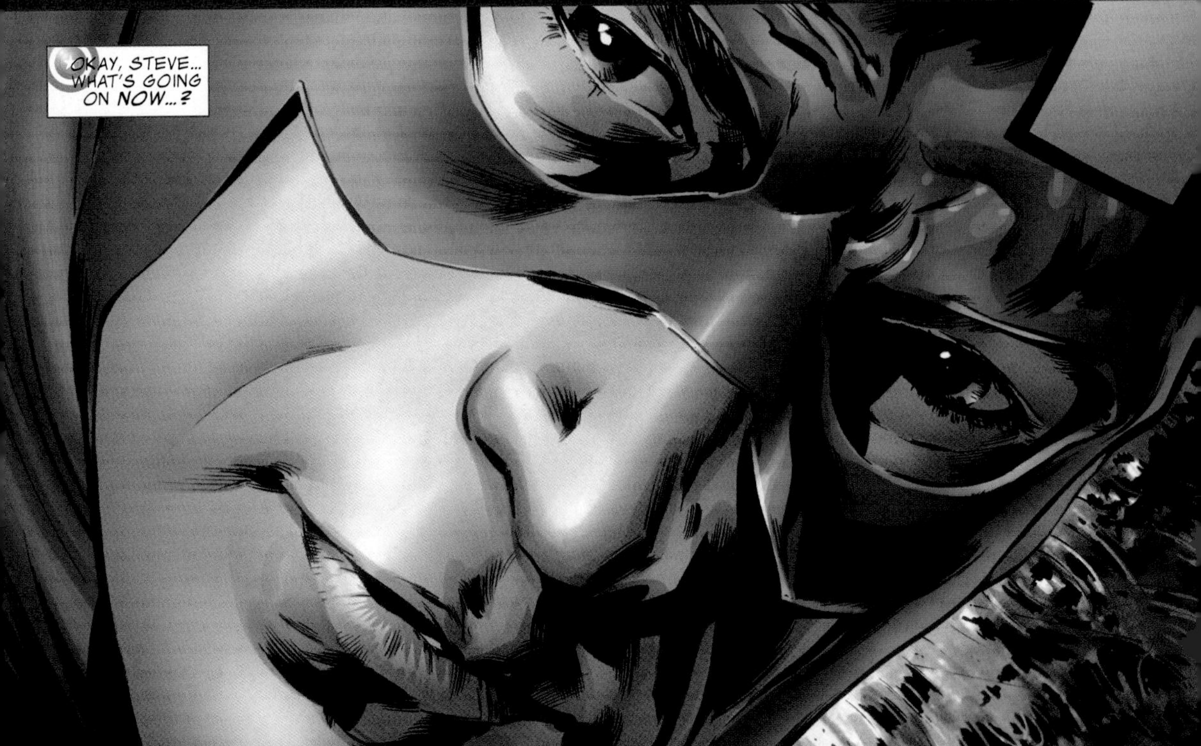
OKAY, STEVE... WHAT'S GOING ON NOW...?

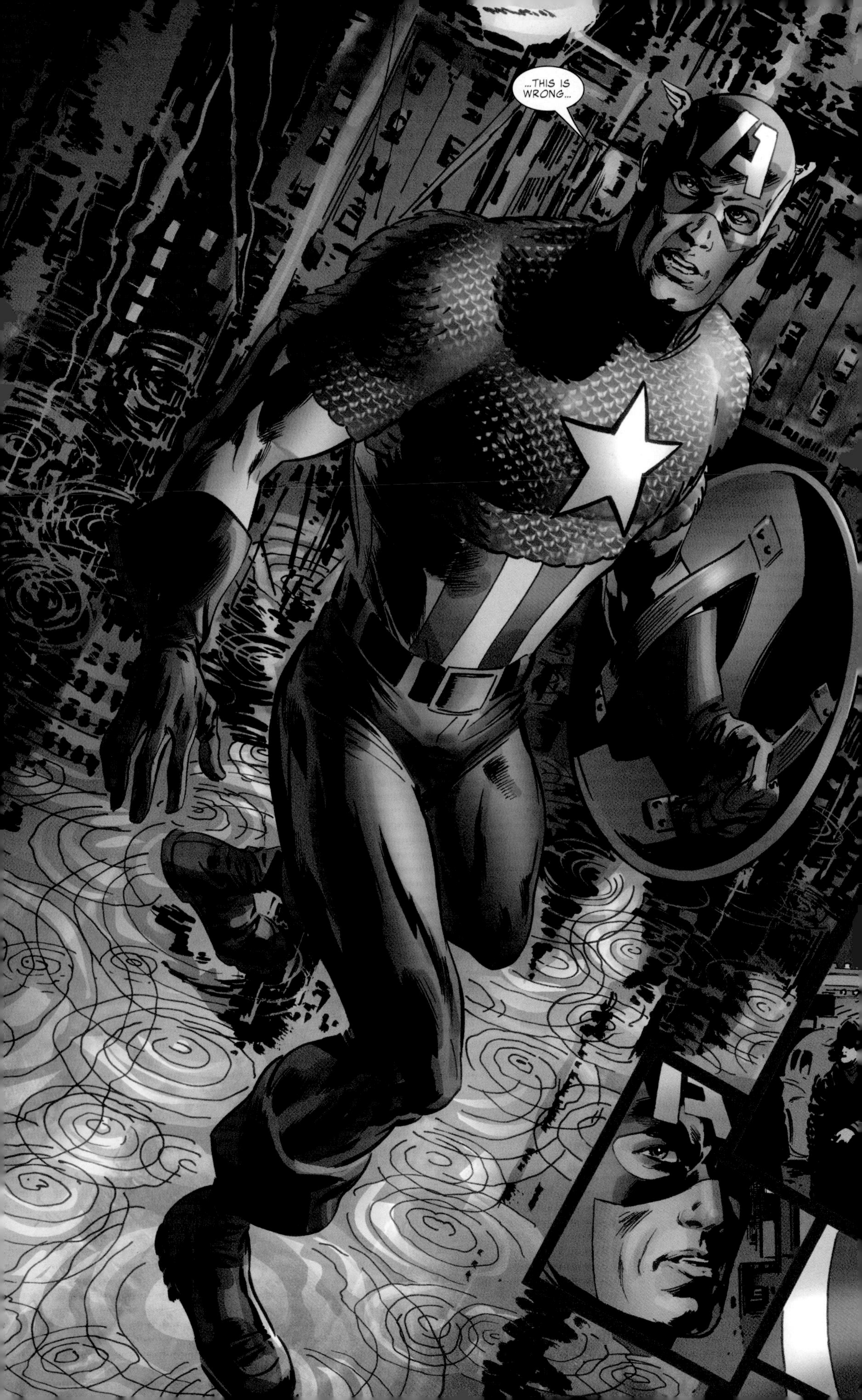
...THIS IS WRONG...

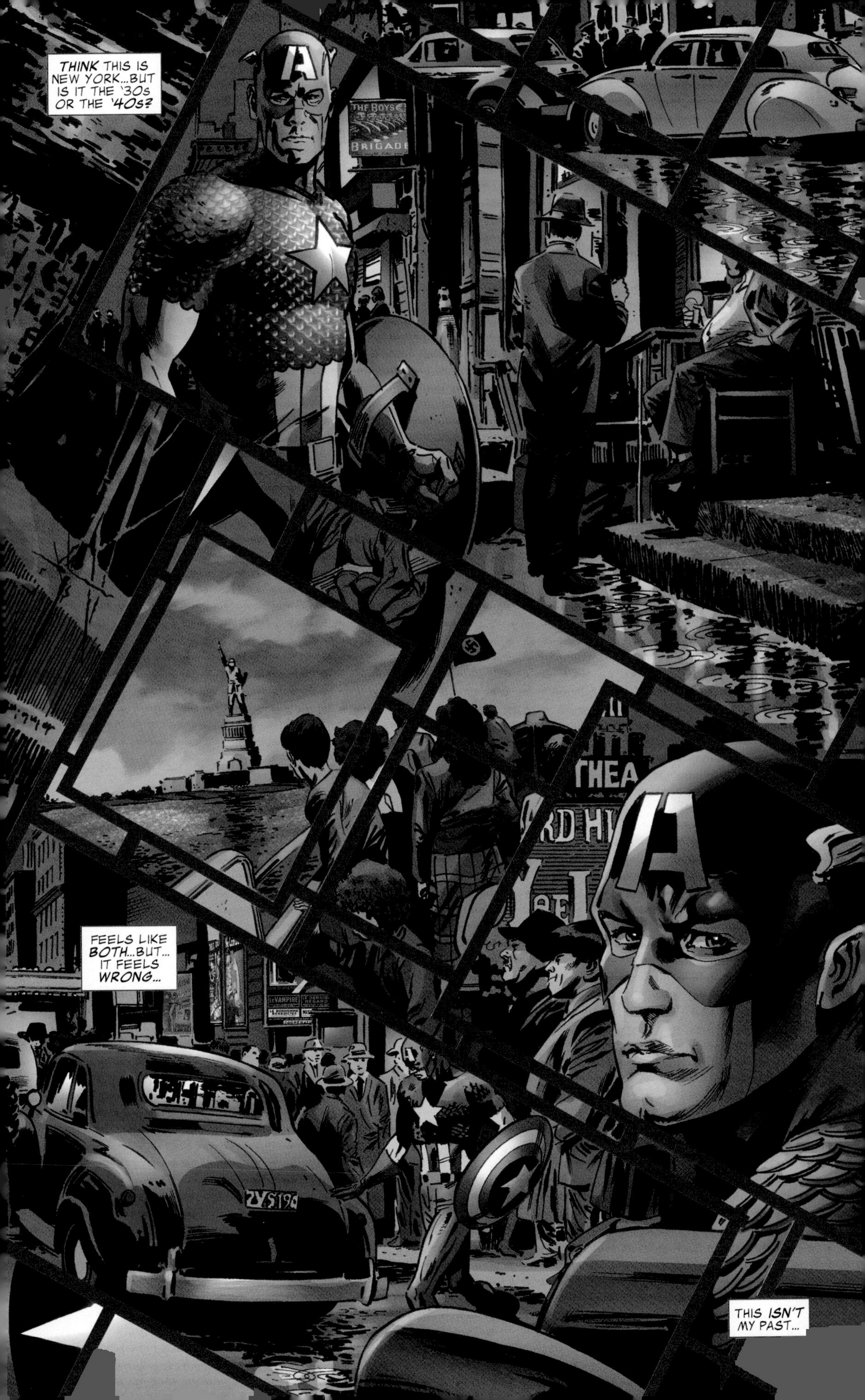
THINK THIS IS NEW YORK...BUT IS IT THE '30s OR THE '40s?
THE BOYS
BRIGADE
THEA
FEELS LIKE BOTH...BUT... IT FEELS WRONG...
THIS ISN'T MY PAST...

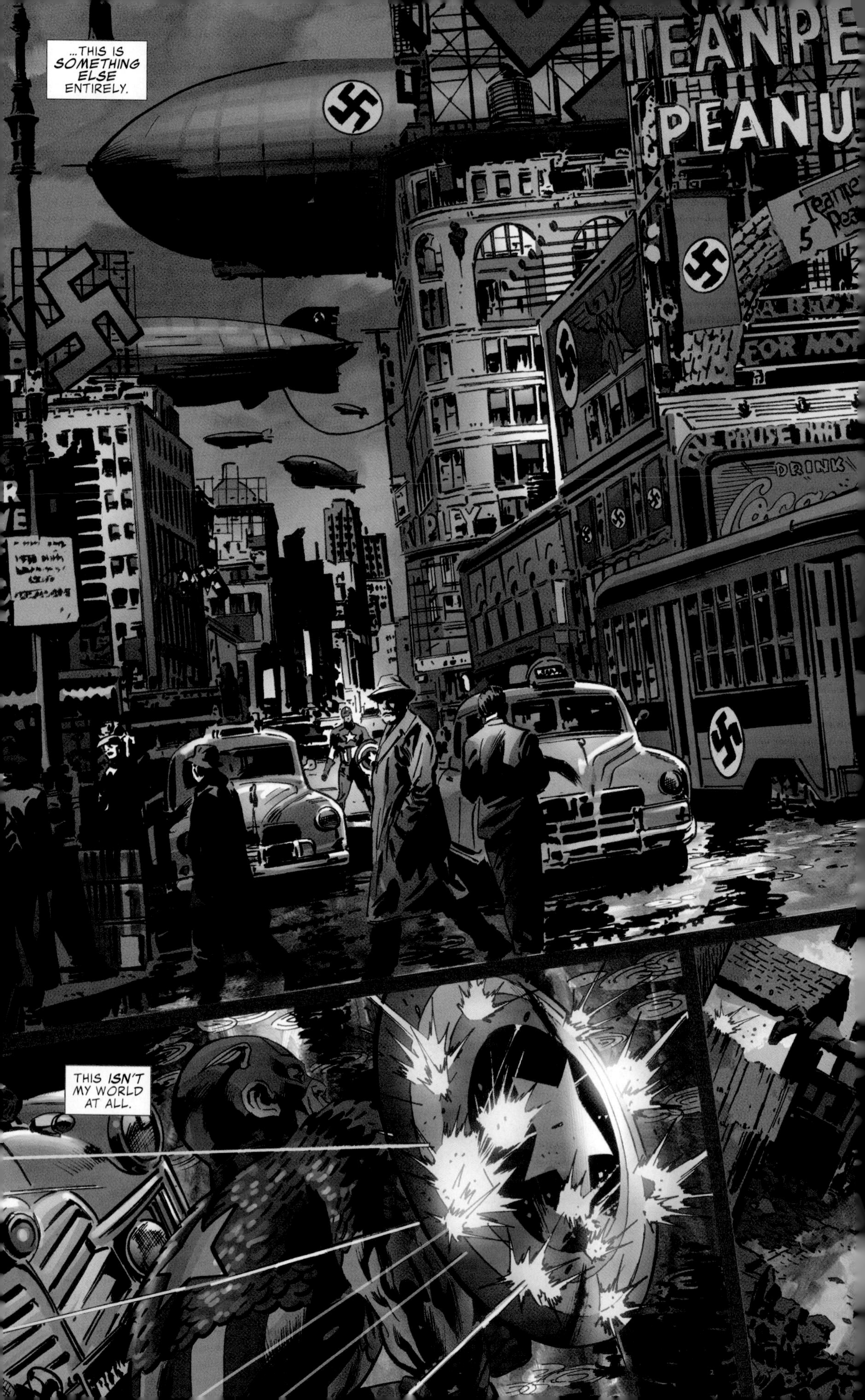
...THIS IS SOMETHING ELSE ENTIRELY.
TEANPE
PEANU
RIPLEY
DRINK
THIS ISN'T MY WORLD AT ALL.

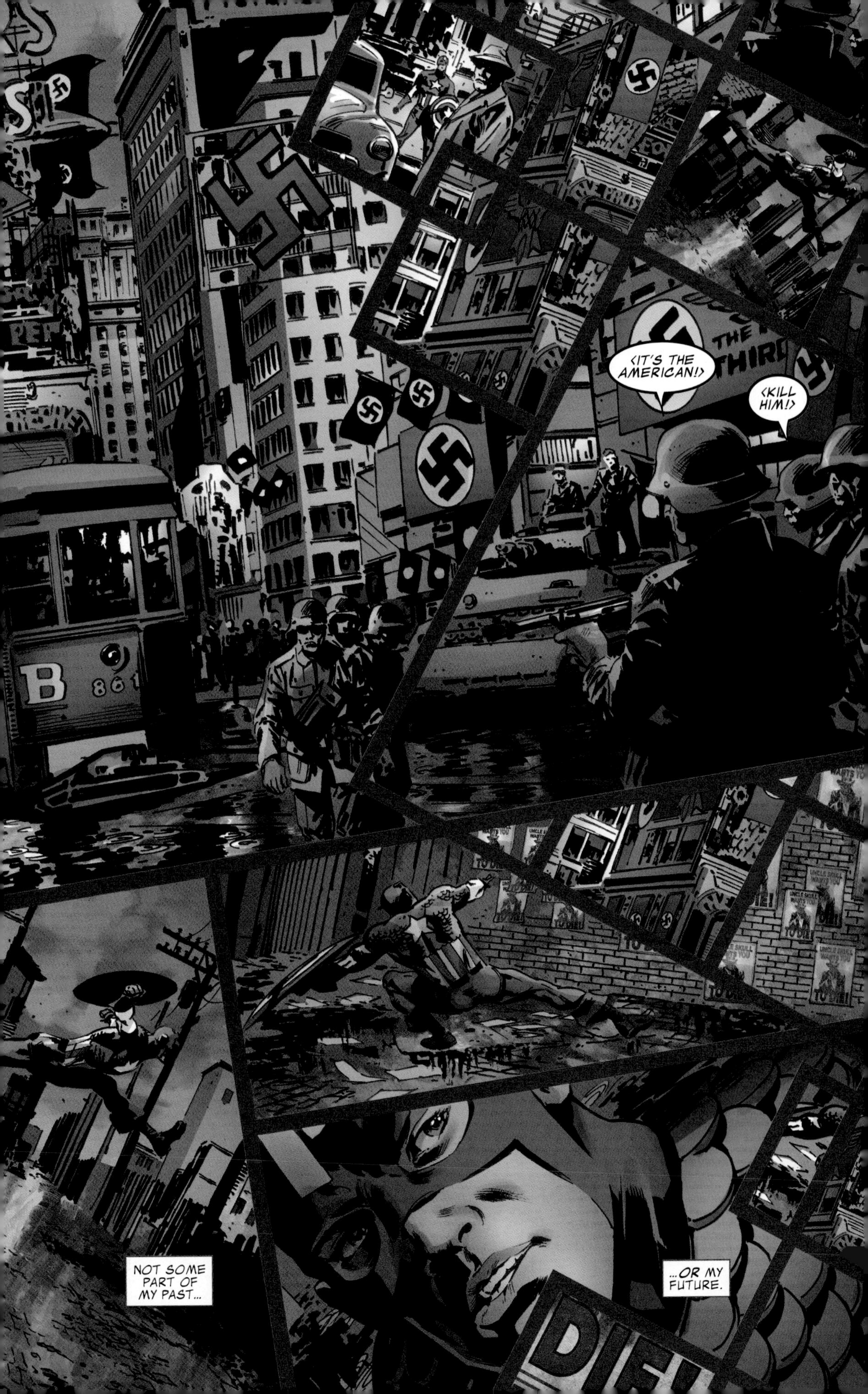

‹IT'S THE AMERICAN!›
‹KILL HIM!›
NOT SOME PART OF MY PAST...
...OR MY FUTURE.

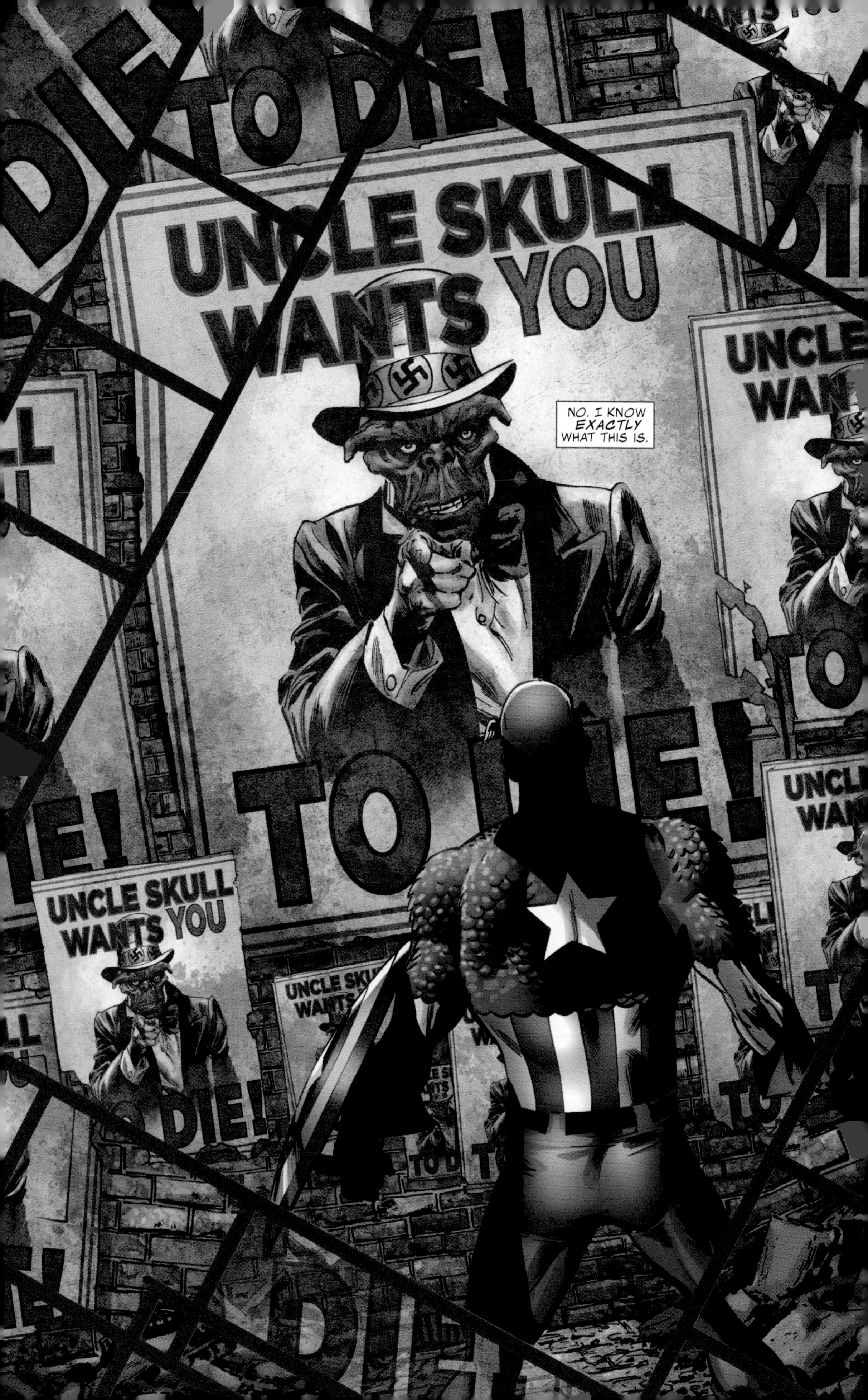
TO DIE!
UNCLE SKULL WANTS YOU
NO. I KNOW EXACTLY WHAT THIS IS.
UNCLE SKULL WANTS YOU
UNCLE SKULL WANTS YOU

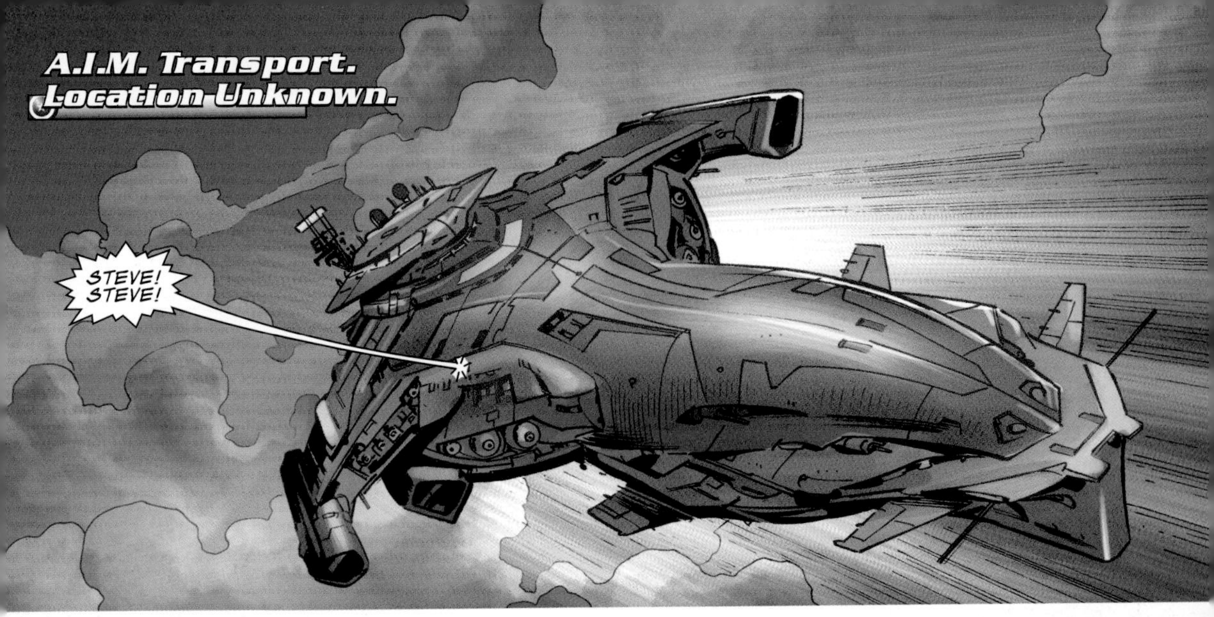
A.I.M. Transport.
Location Unknown.
STEVE! STEVE!

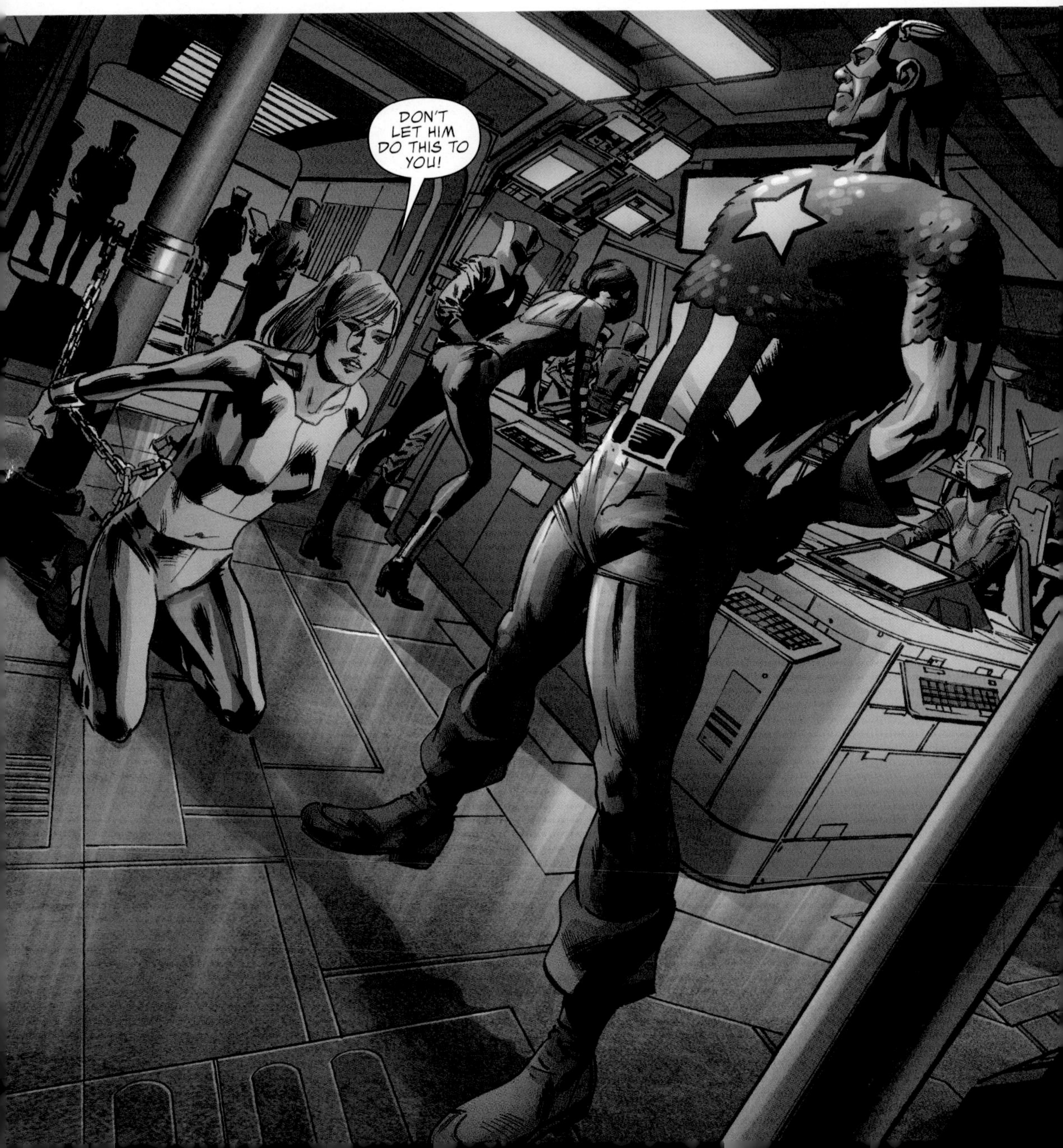
DON'T LET HIM DO THIS TO YOU!

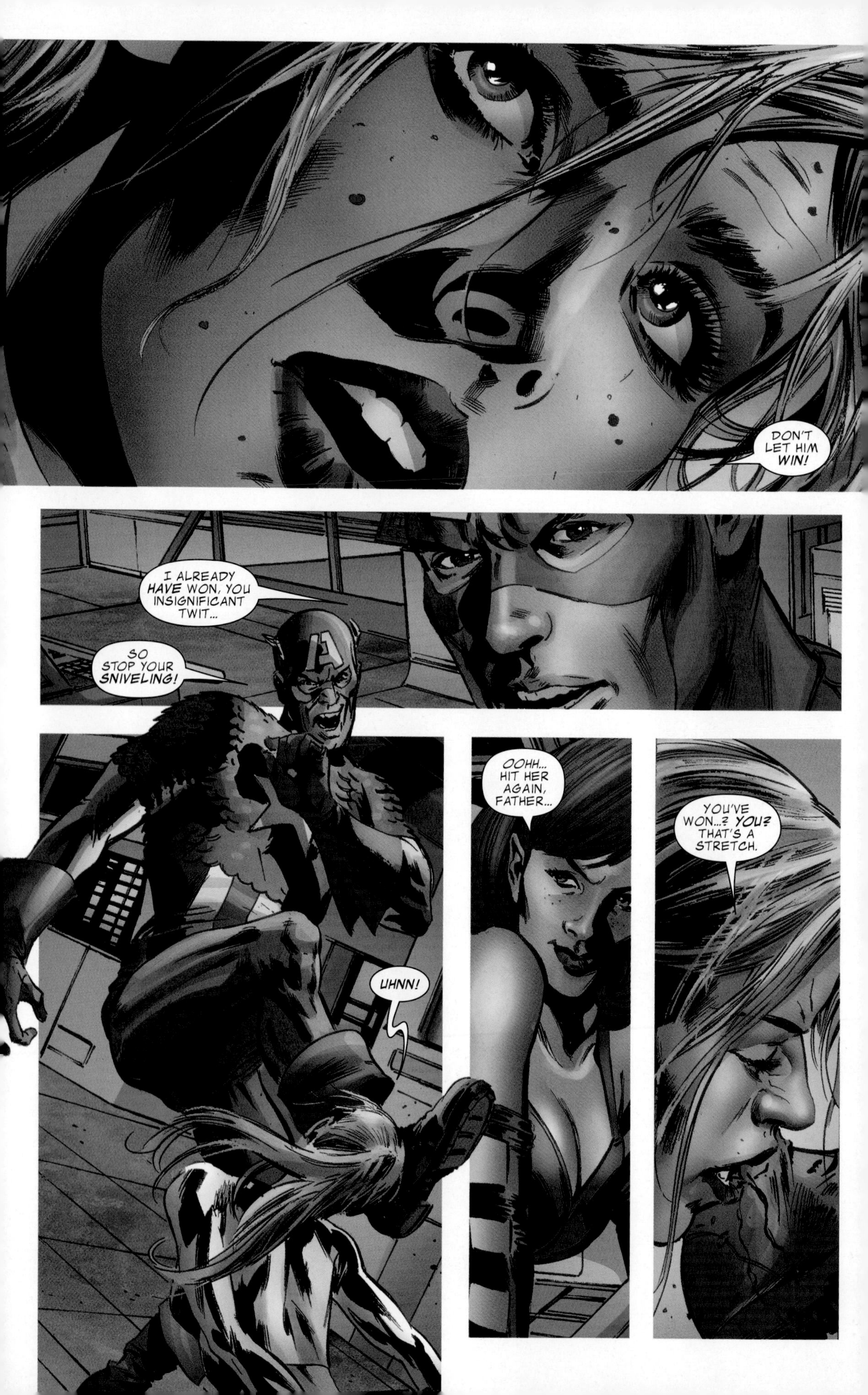
DON'T LET HIM WIN!
I ALREADY HAVE WON, YOU INSIGNIFICANT TWIT...
SO STOP YOUR SNIVELING!
UHNN!
OOHH... HIT HER AGAIN, FATHER...
YOU'VE WON...? YOU? THAT'S A STRETCH.

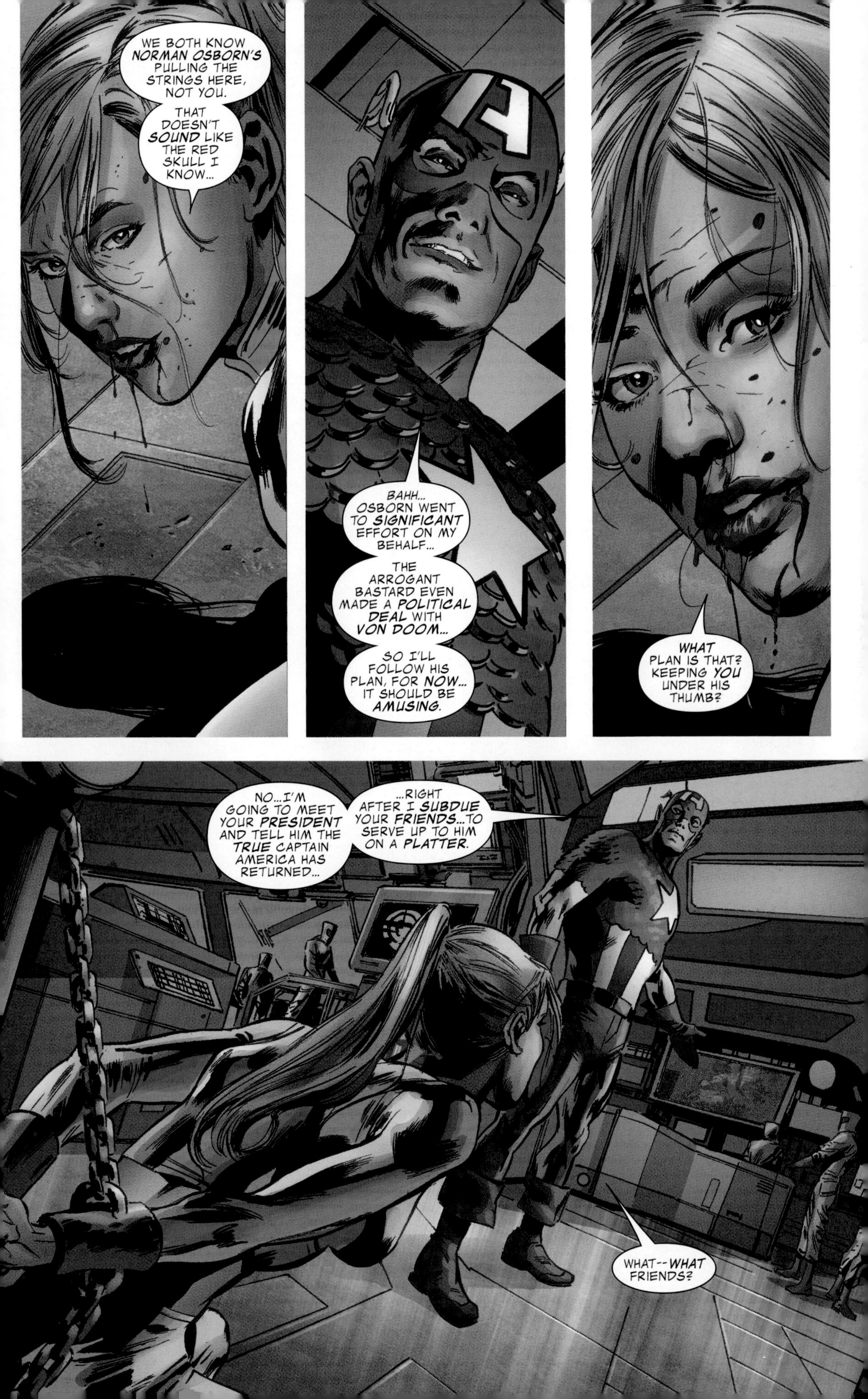
WE BOTH KNOW NORMAN OSBORN'S PULLING THE STRINGS HERE, NOT YOU.
THAT DOESN'T SOUND LIKE THE RED SKULL I KNOW...
BAHH... OSBORN WENT TO SIGNIFICANT EFFORT ON MY BEHALF...
THE ARROGANT BASTARD EVEN MADE A POLITICAL DEAL WITH VON DOOM...
SO I'LL FOLLOW HIS PLAN, FOR NOW... IT SHOULD BE AMUSING.
WHAT PLAN IS THAT? KEEPING YOU UNDER HIS THUMB?
NO...I'M GOING TO MEET YOUR PRESIDENT AND TELL HIM THE TRUE CAPTAIN AMERICA HAS RETURNED...
...RIGHT AFTER I SUBDUE YOUR FRIENDS...TO SERVE UP TO HIM ON A PLATTER.
WHAT--WHAT FRIENDS?

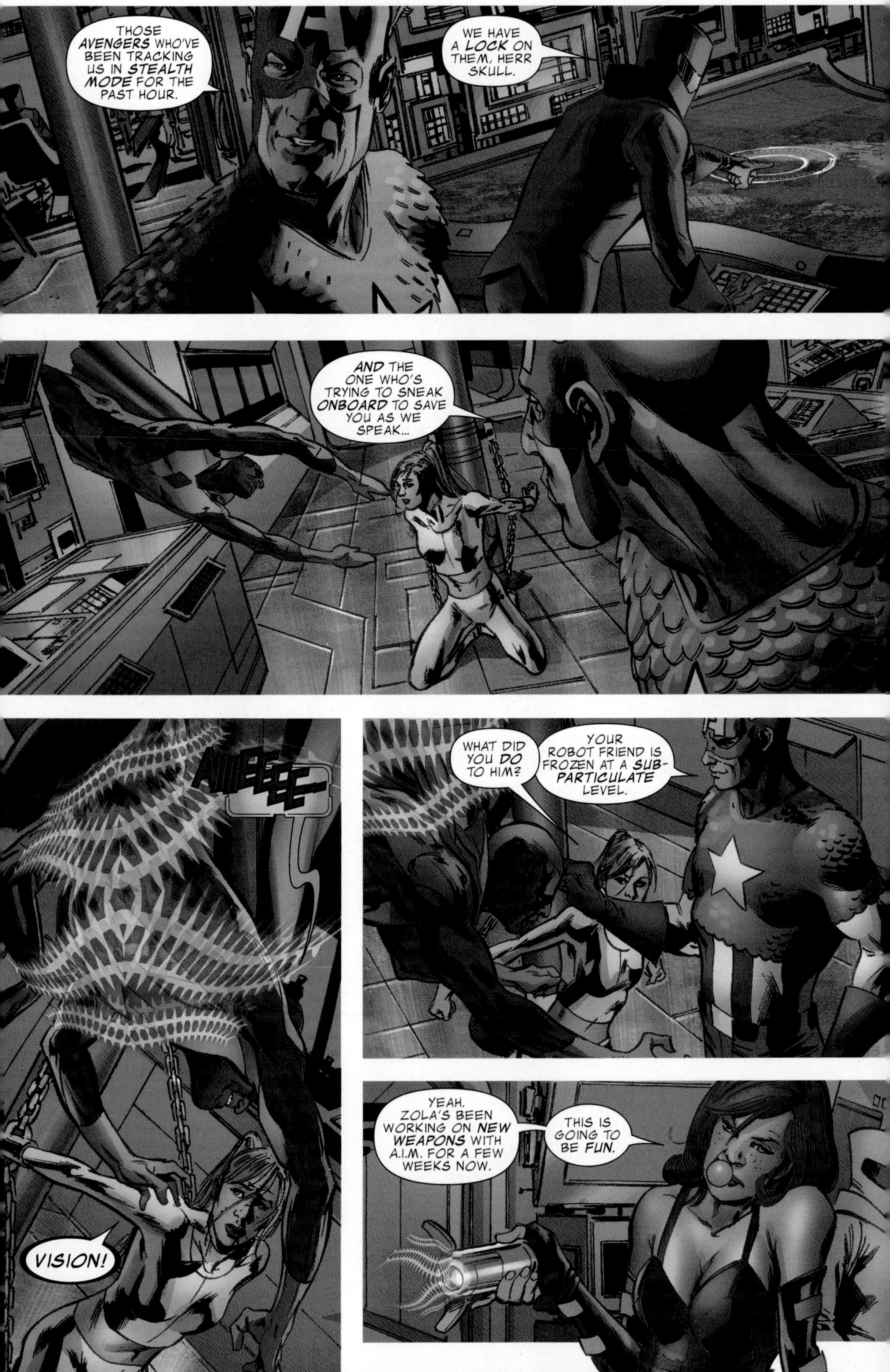
THOSE AVENGERS WHO'VE BEEN TRACKING US IN STEALTH MODE FOR THE PAST HOUR.
WE HAVE A LOCK ON THEM, HERR SKULL.
AND THE ONE WHO'S TRYING TO SNEAK ONBOARD TO SAVE YOU AS WE SPEAK...
AIIEEEEE
VISION!
WHAT DID YOU DO TO HIM?
YOUR ROBOT FRIEND IS FROZEN AT A SUB-PARTICULATE LEVEL.
YEAH. ZOLA'S BEEN WORKING ON NEW WEAPONS WITH A.I.M. FOR A FEW WEEKS NOW.
THIS IS GOING TO BE FUN.

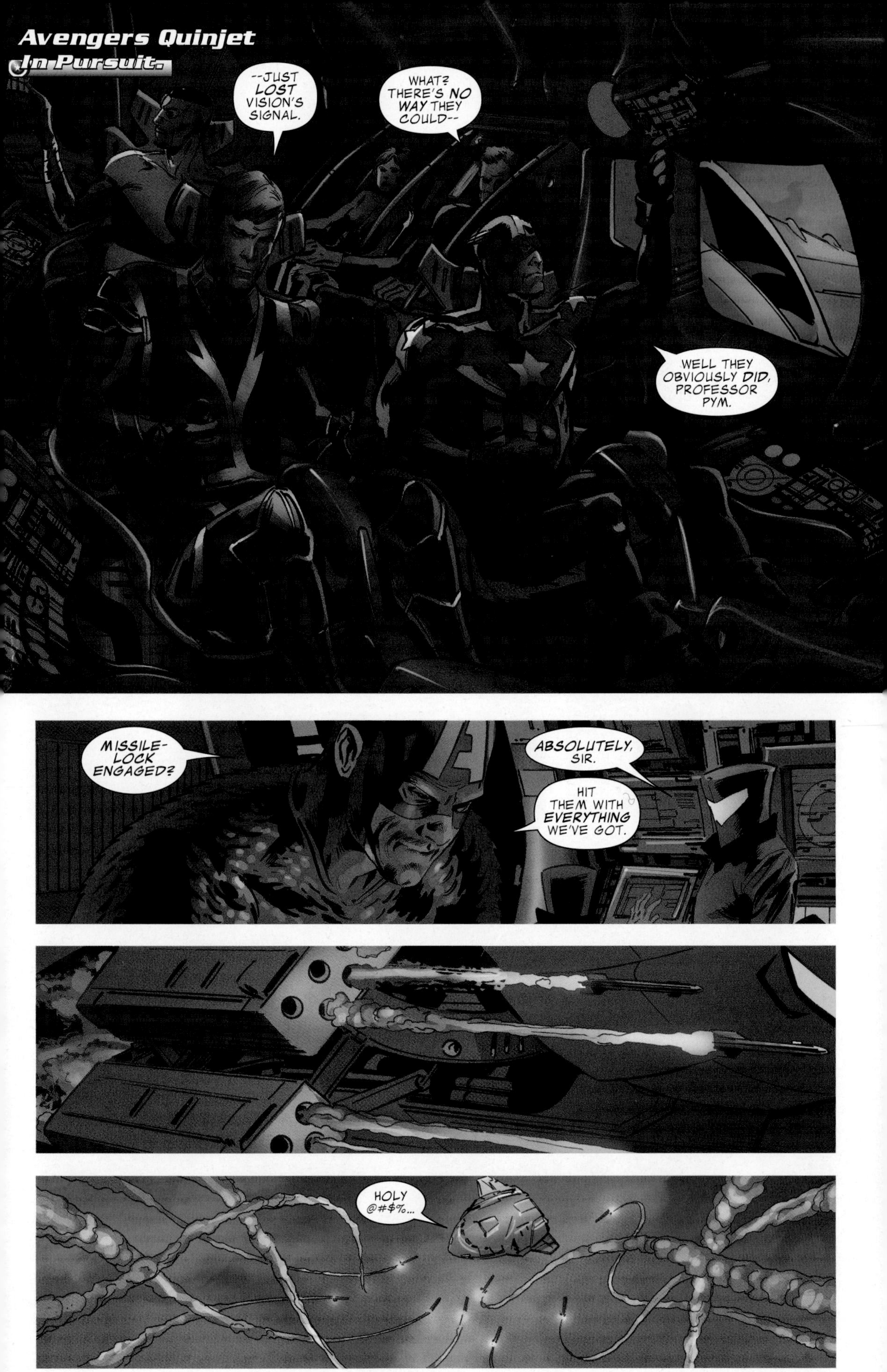
Avengers Quinjet In Pursuit.
--JUST LOST VISION'S SIGNAL.
WHAT? THERE'S NO WAY THEY COULD--
WELL THEY OBVIOUSLY DID, PROFESSOR PYM.
MISSILE-LOCK ENGAGED?
ABSOLUTELY, SIR.
HIT THEM WITH EVERYTHING WE'VE GOT.
HOLY @#$%...

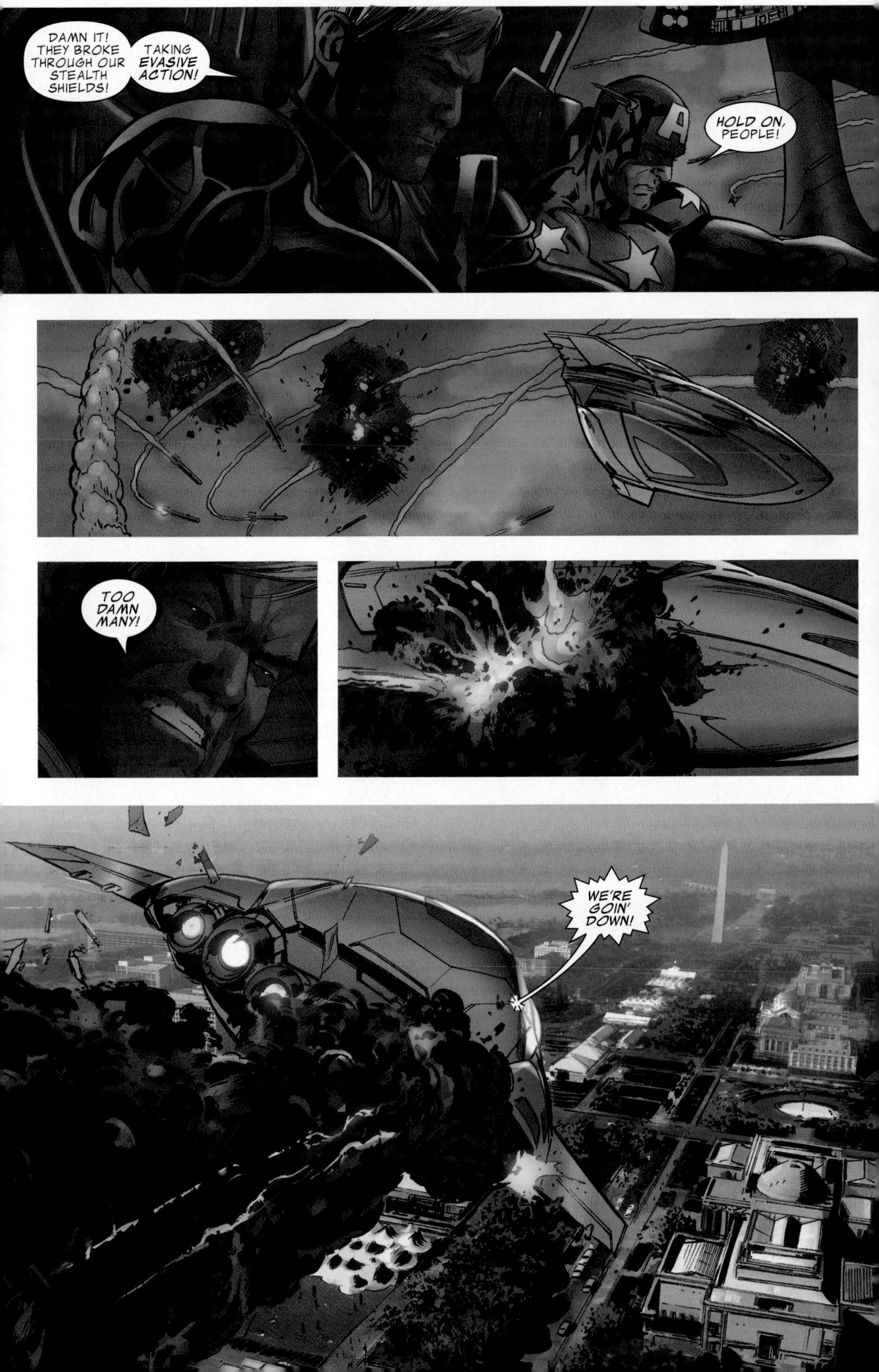
DAMN IT! THEY BROKE THROUGH OUR STEALTH SHIELDS!
TAKING EVASIVE ACTION!
HOLD ON, PEOPLE!
TOO DAMN MANY!
WE'RE GOIN' DOWN!

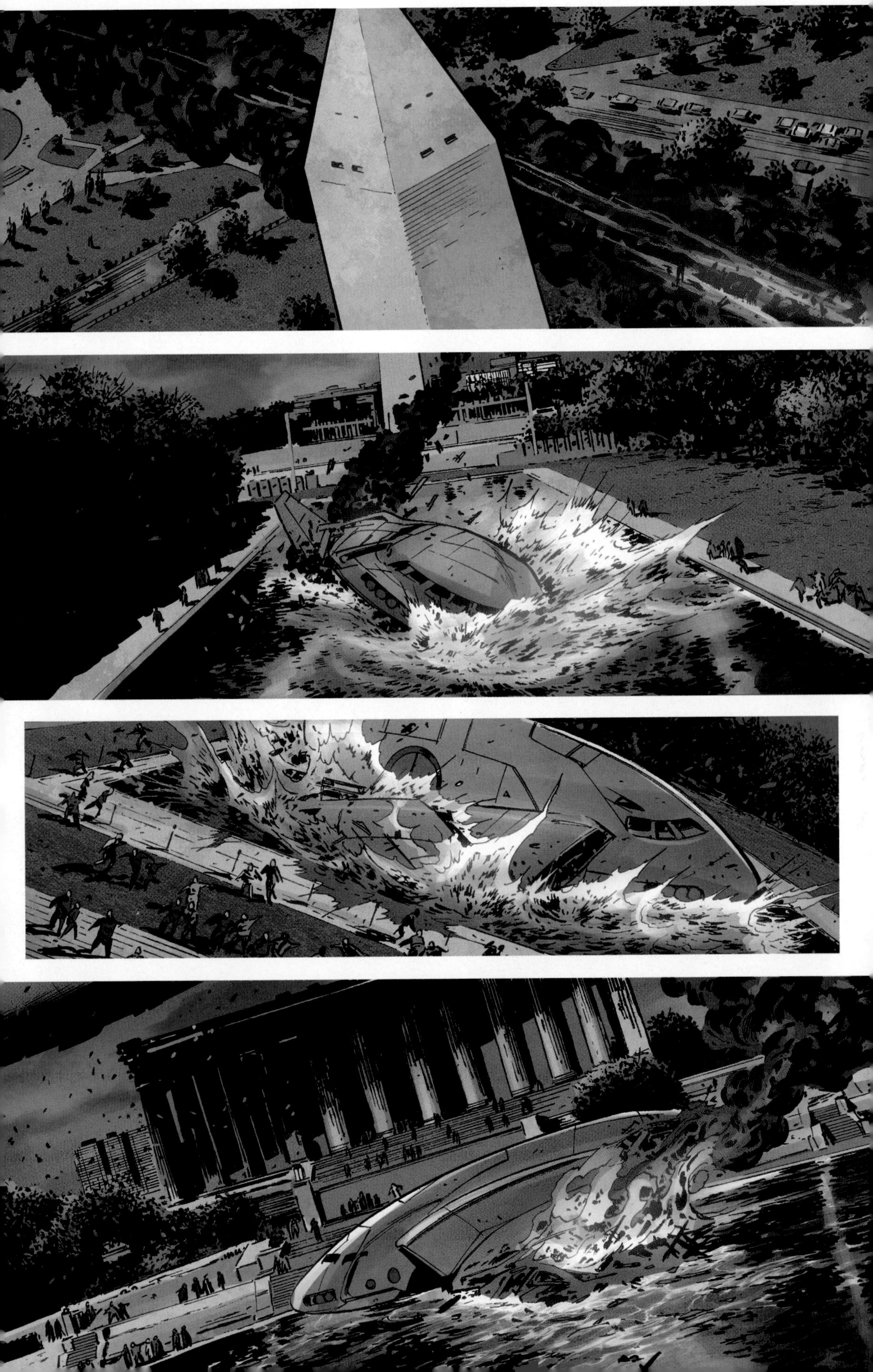

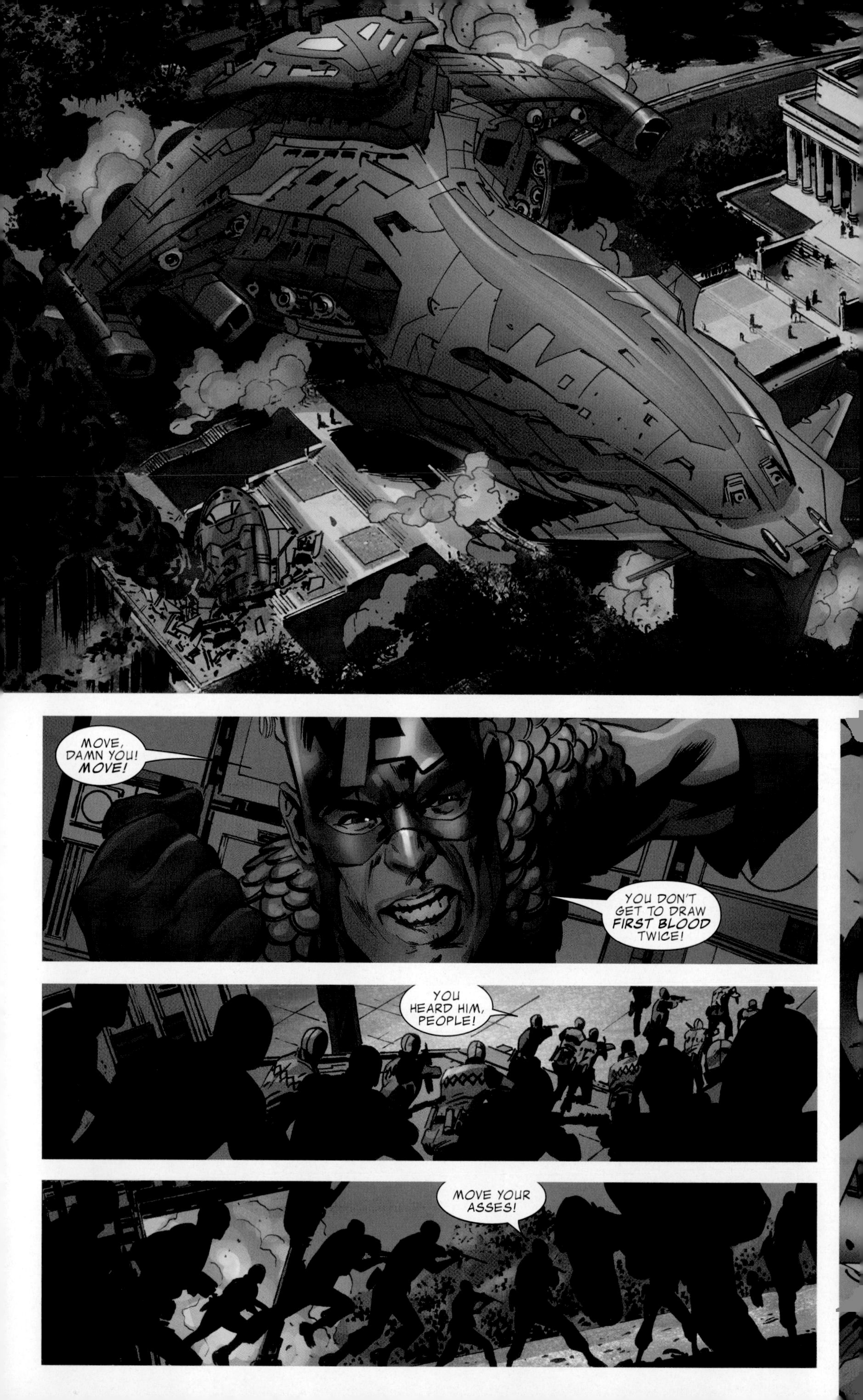
MOVE, DAMN YOU! MOVE!
YOU DON'T GET TO DRAW FIRST BLOOD TWICE!
YOU HEARD HIM, PEOPLE!
MOVE YOUR ASSES!

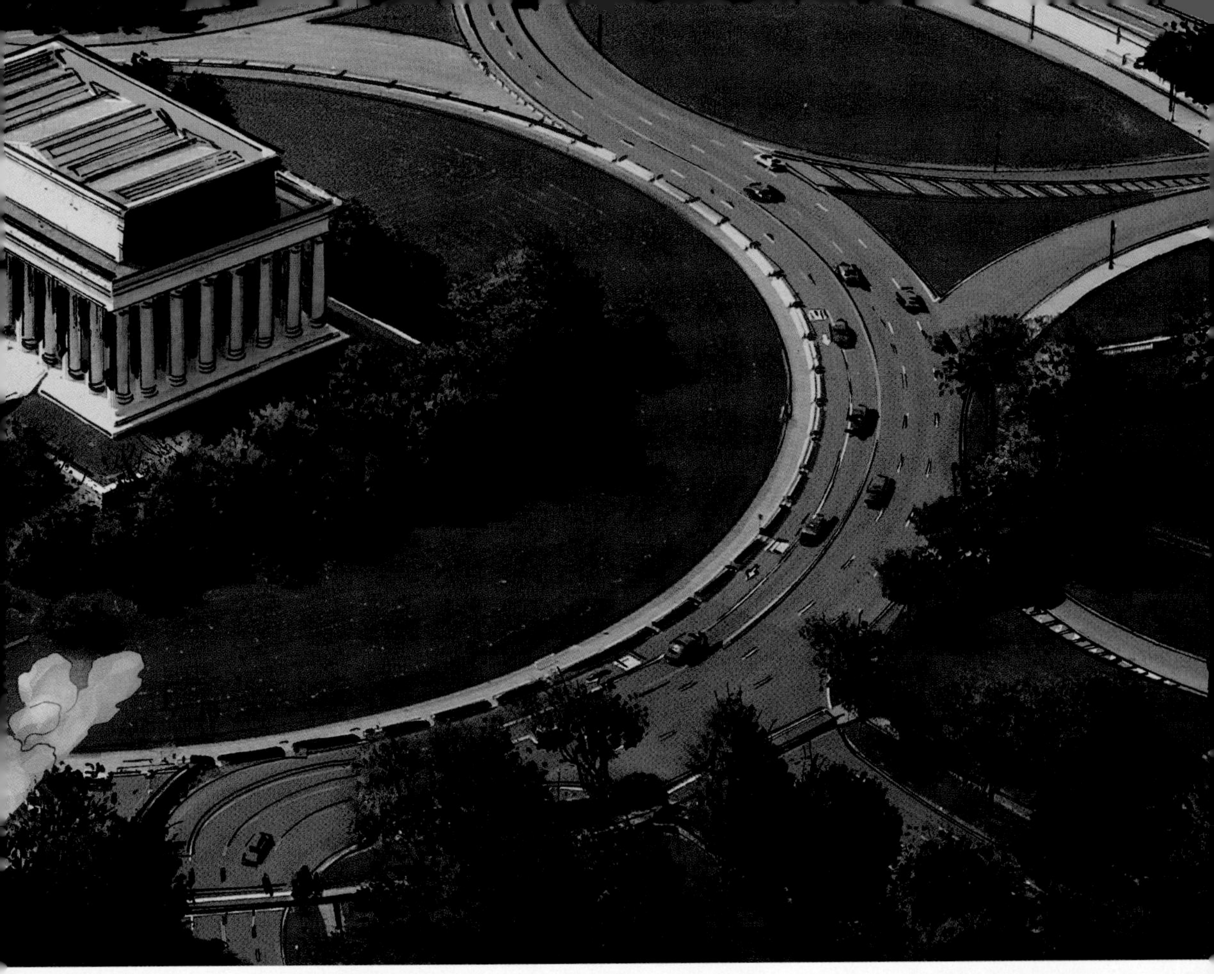

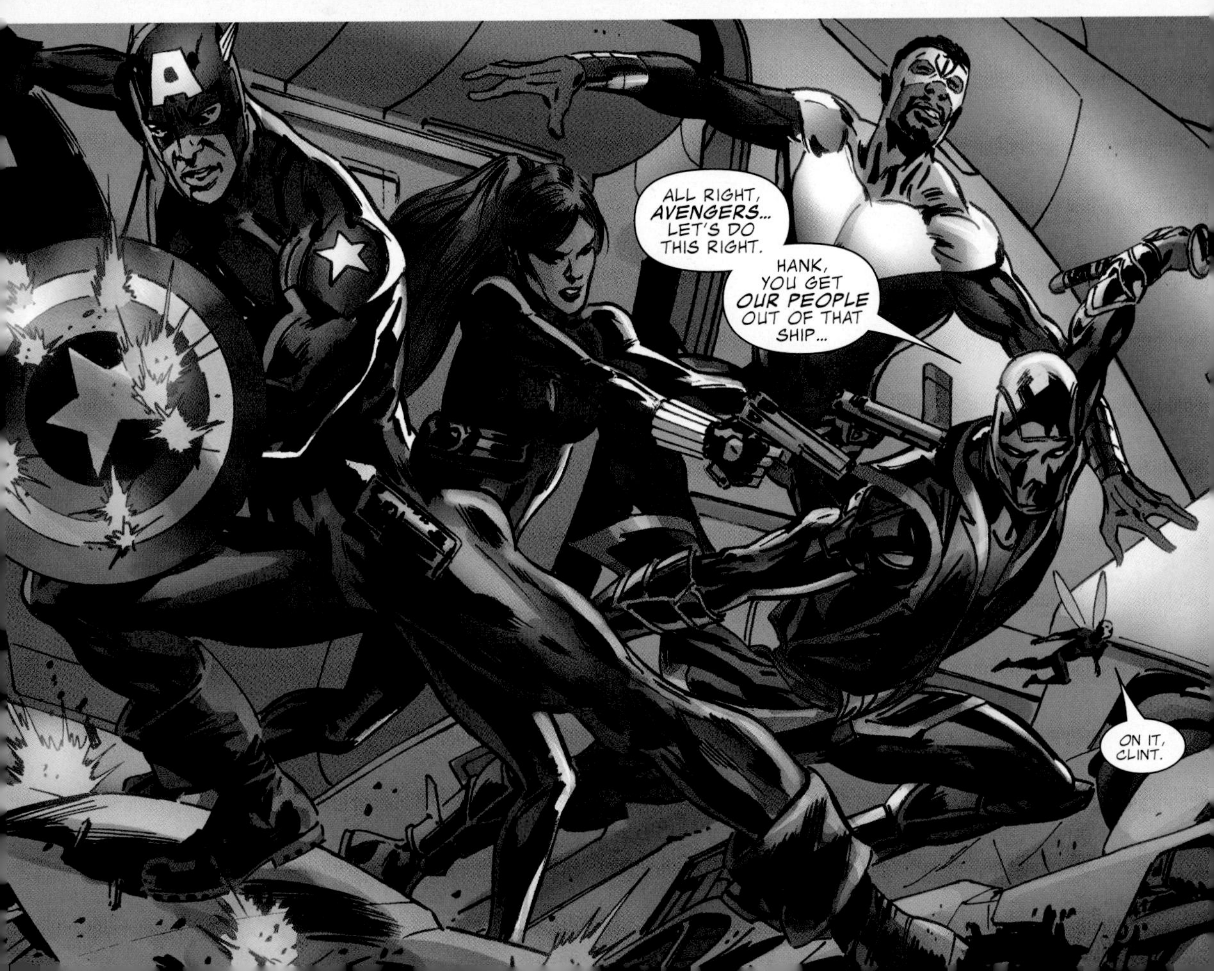
ALL RIGHT, AVENGERS... LET'S DO THIS RIGHT.
HANK, YOU GET OUR PEOPLE OUT OF THAT SHIP...
ON IT, CLINT.

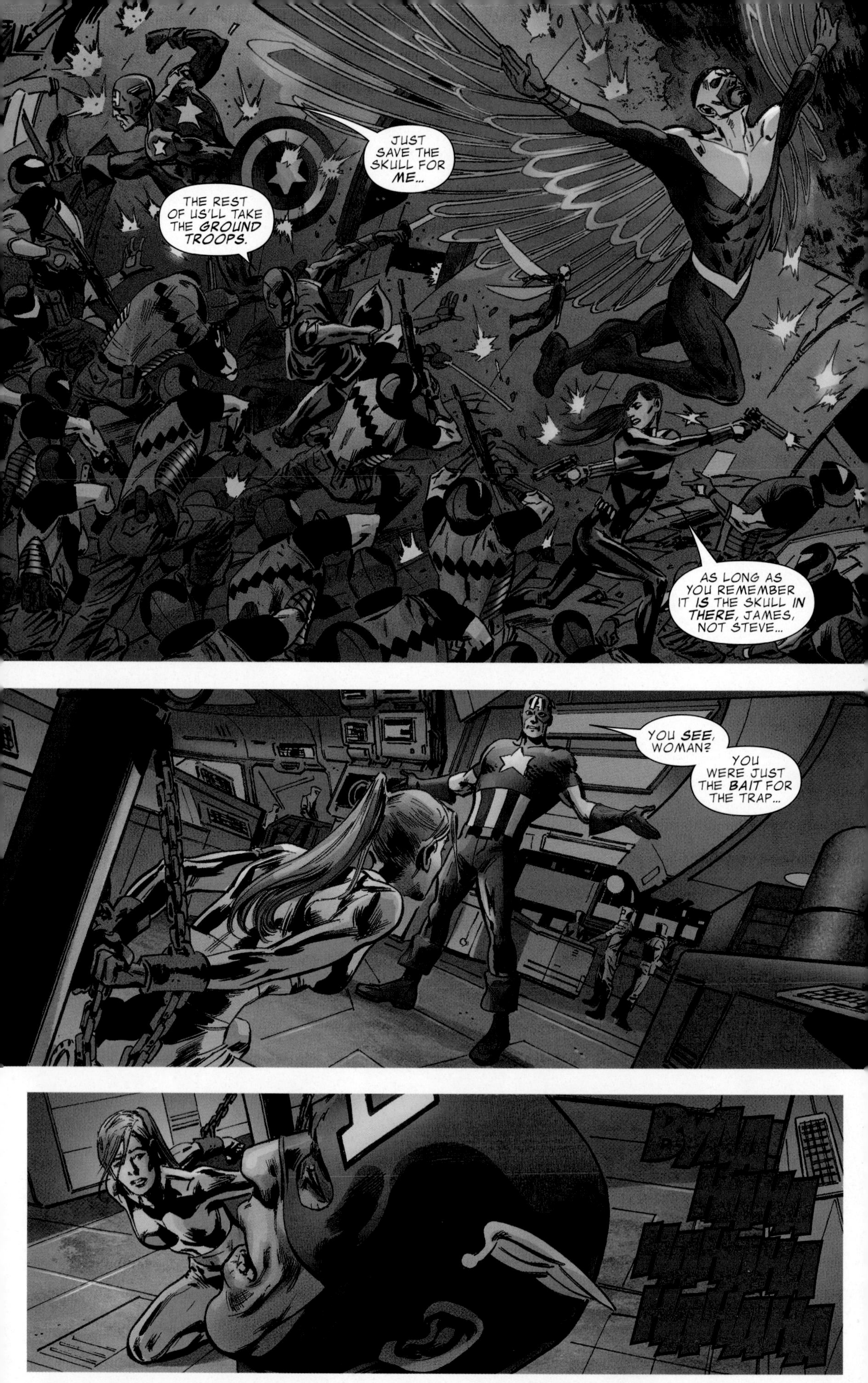
THE REST OF US'LL TAKE THE GROUND TROOPS.
JUST SAVE THE SKULL FOR ME...
AS LONG AS YOU REMEMBER IT IS THE SKULL IN THERE, JAMES, NOT STEVE...
YOU SEE, WOMAN?
YOU WERE JUST THE BAIT FOR THE TRAP...

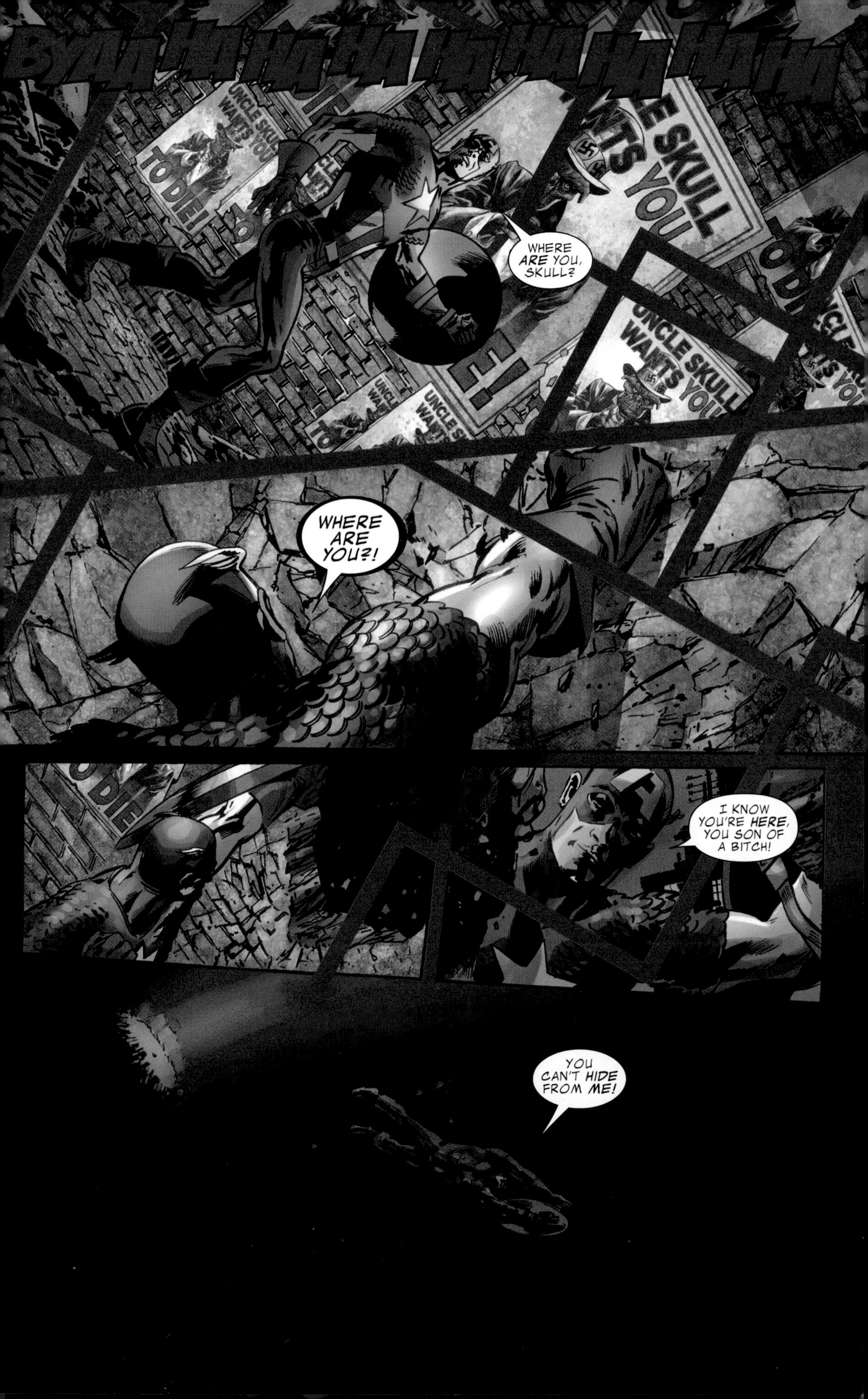

BWAH HA HA HA HA HA HA HA HA
UNCLE SKULL WANTS YOU TO DIE!
WHERE ARE YOU, SKULL?
WHERE ARE YOU?!
I KNOW YOU'RE HERE, YOU SON OF A BITCH!
YOU CAN'T HIDE FROM ME!

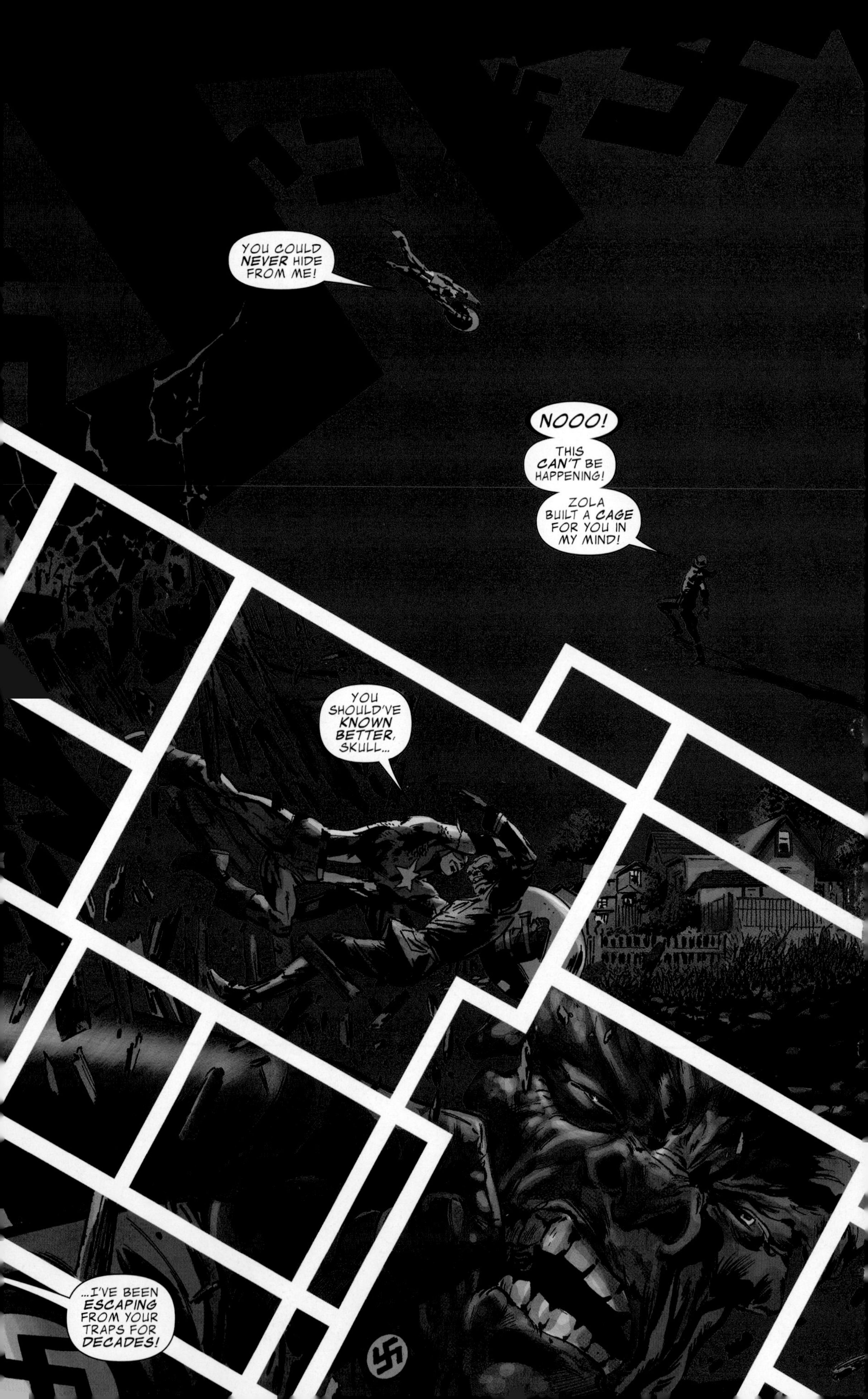
YOU COULD NEVER HIDE FROM ME!
NOOO!
THIS CAN'T BE HAPPENING!
ZOLA BUILT A CAGE FOR YOU IN MY MIND!
YOU SHOULD'VE KNOWN BETTER, SKULL...
...I'VE BEEN ESCAPING FROM YOUR TRAPS FOR DECADES!

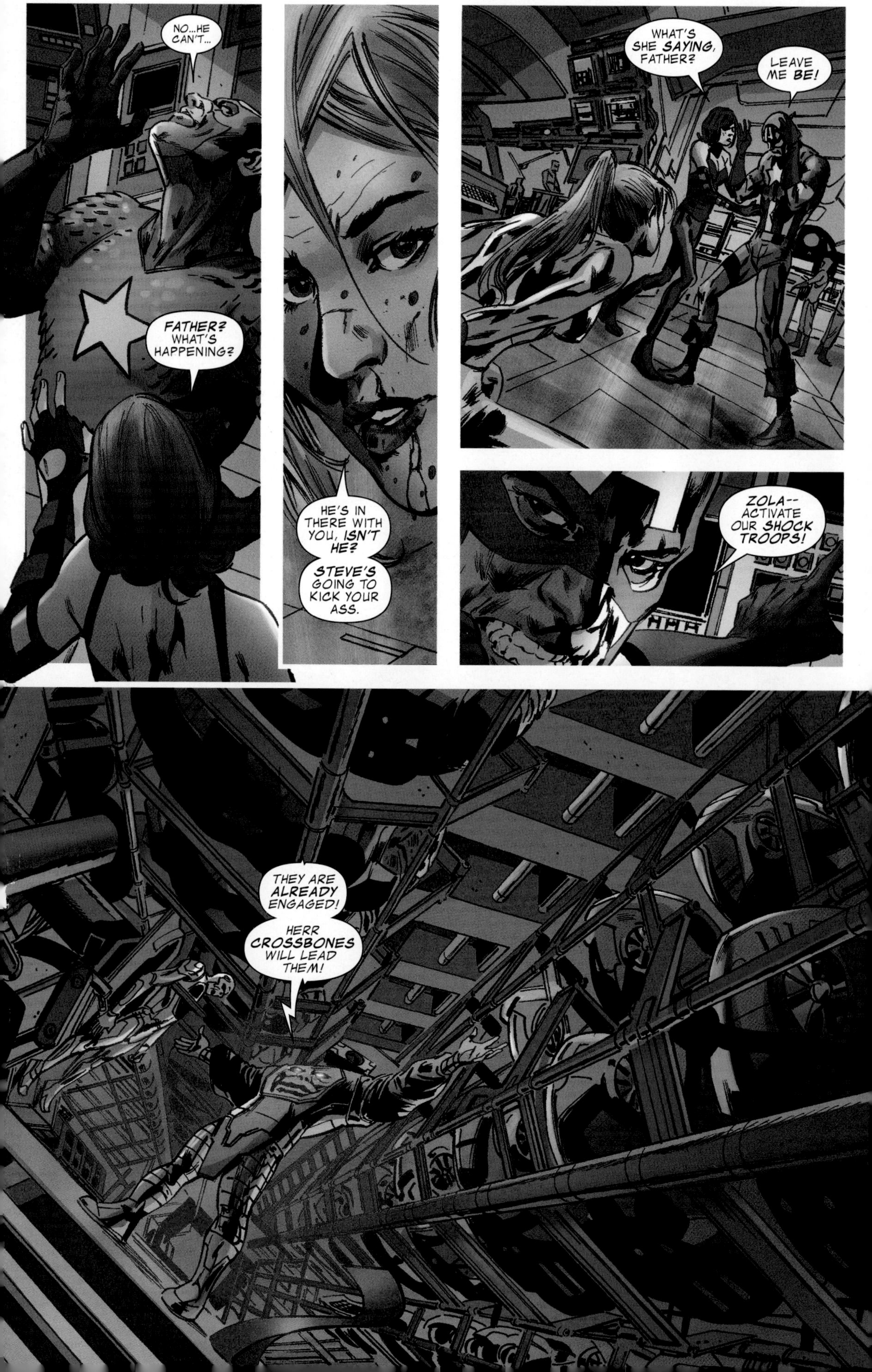
NO...HE CAN'T...
FATHER? WHAT'S HAPPENING?
HE'S IN THERE WITH YOU, ISN'T HE?
STEVE'S GOING TO KICK YOUR ASS.
WHAT'S SHE SAYING, FATHER?
LEAVE ME BE!
ZOLA-- ACTIVATE OUR SHOCK TROOPS!
THEY ARE ALREADY ENGAGED!
HERR CROSSBONES WILL LEAD THEM!

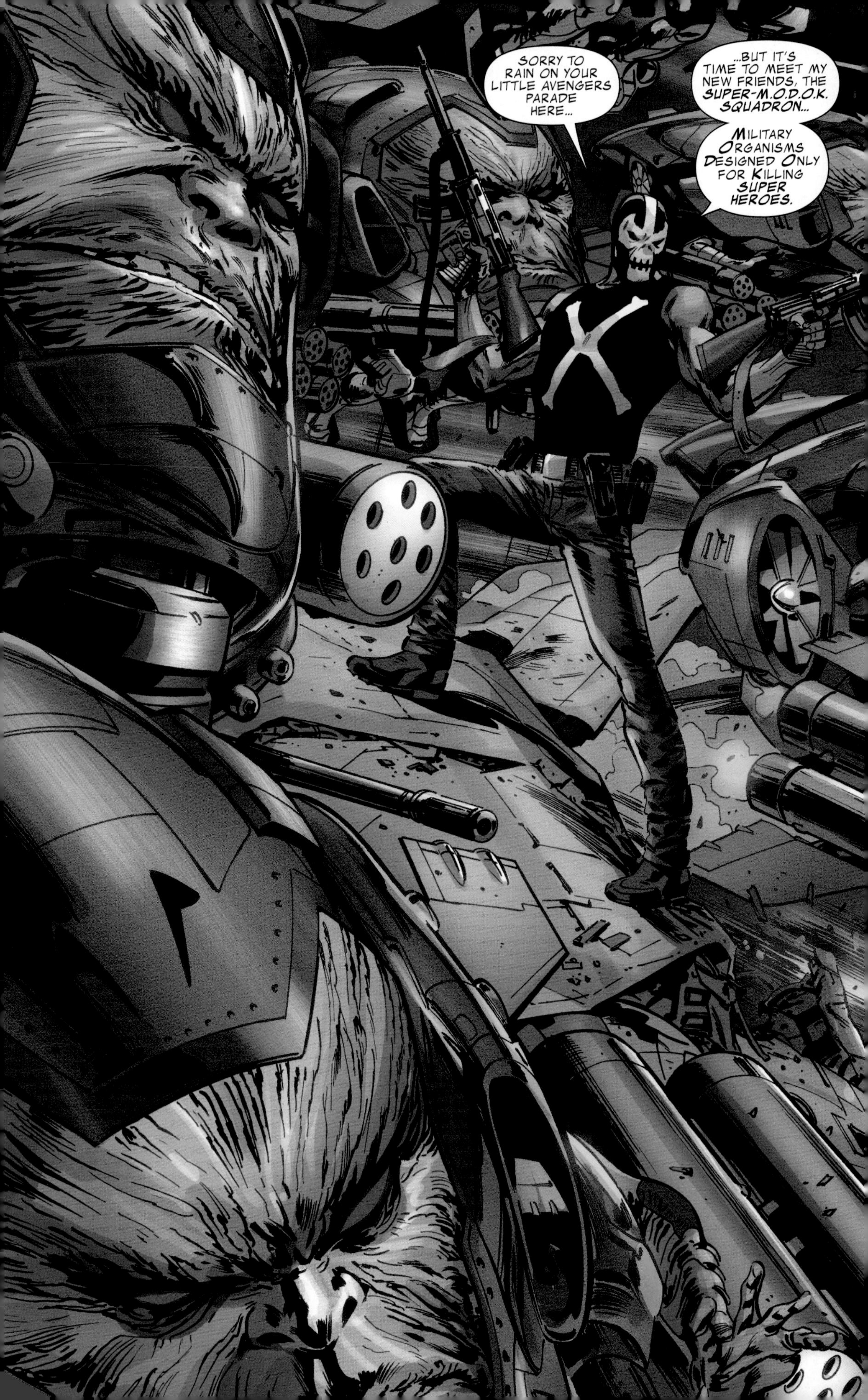

SORRY TO RAIN ON YOUR LITTLE AVENGERS PARADE HERE...
...BUT IT'S TIME TO MEET MY NEW FRIENDS, THE SUPER-M.O.D.O.K. SQUADRON...
MILITARY ORGANISMS DESIGNED ONLY FOR KILLING SUPER HEROES.

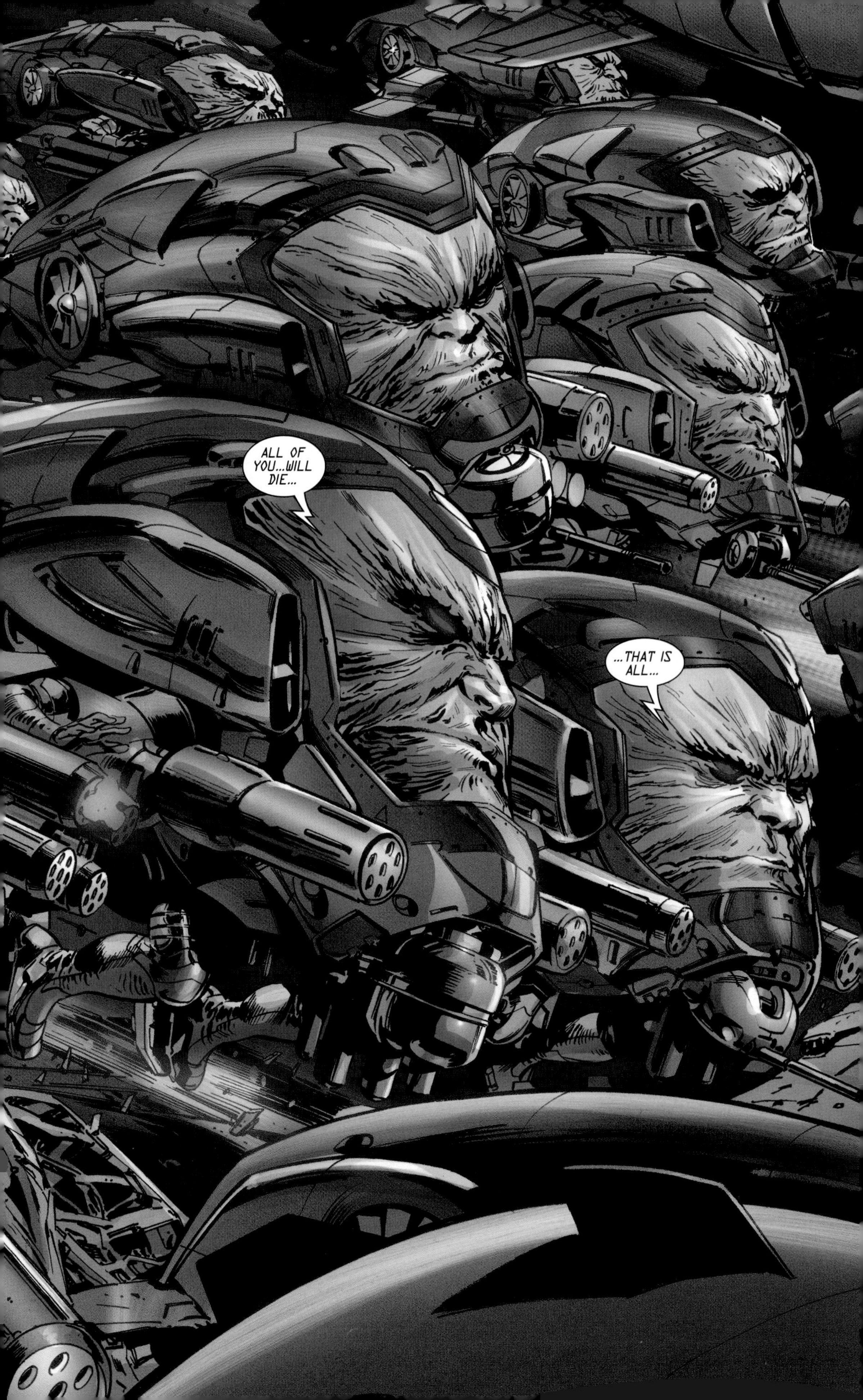
ALL OF YOU...WILL DIE...
...THAT IS ALL...

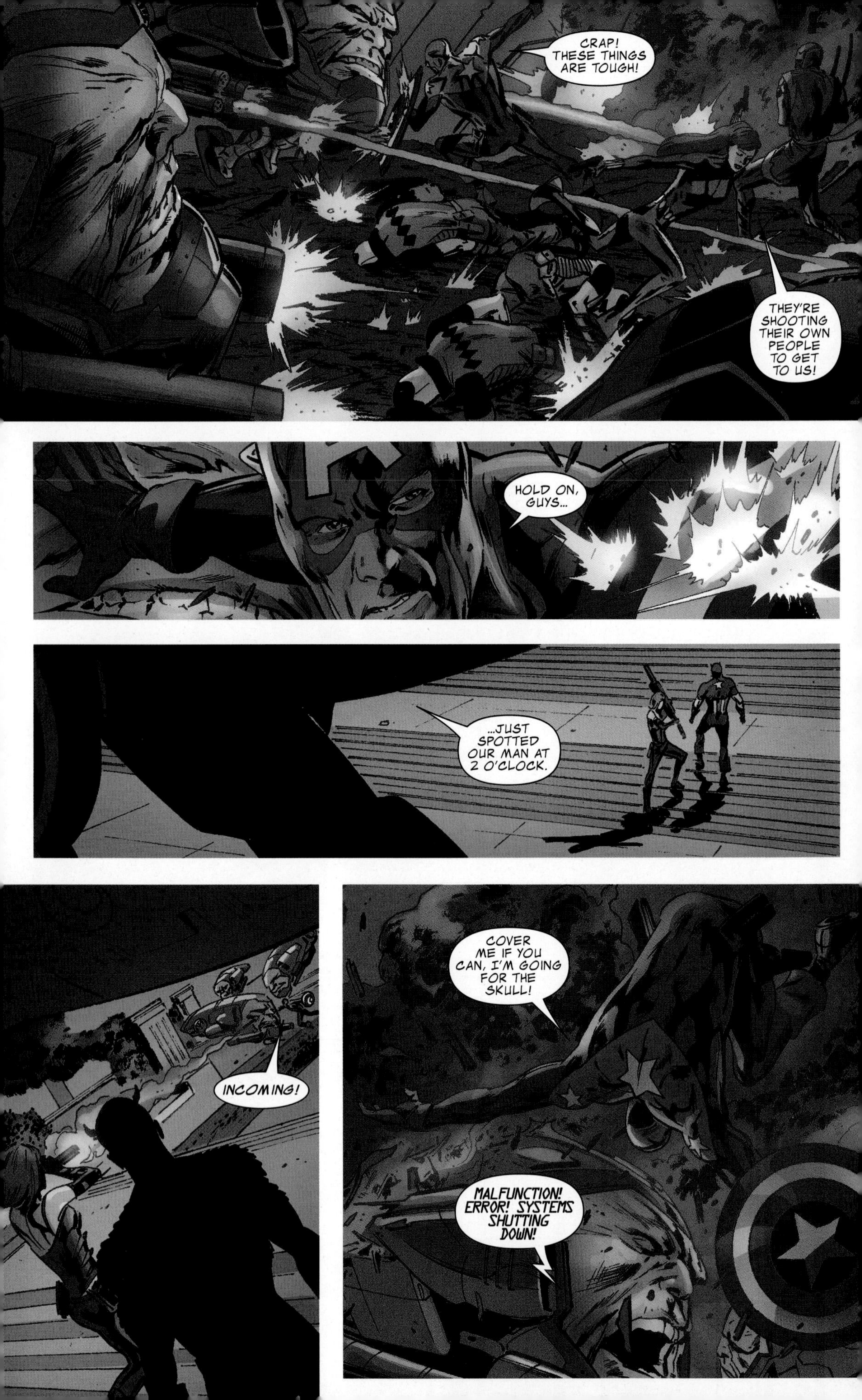
CRAP! THESE THINGS ARE TOUGH!
THEY'RE SHOOTING THEIR OWN PEOPLE TO GET TO US!
HOLD ON, GUYS...
...JUST SPOTTED OUR MAN AT 2 O'CLOCK.
INCOMING!
COVER ME IF YOU CAN, I'M GOING FOR THE SKULL!
MALFUNCTION! ERROR! SYSTEMS SHUTTING DOWN!

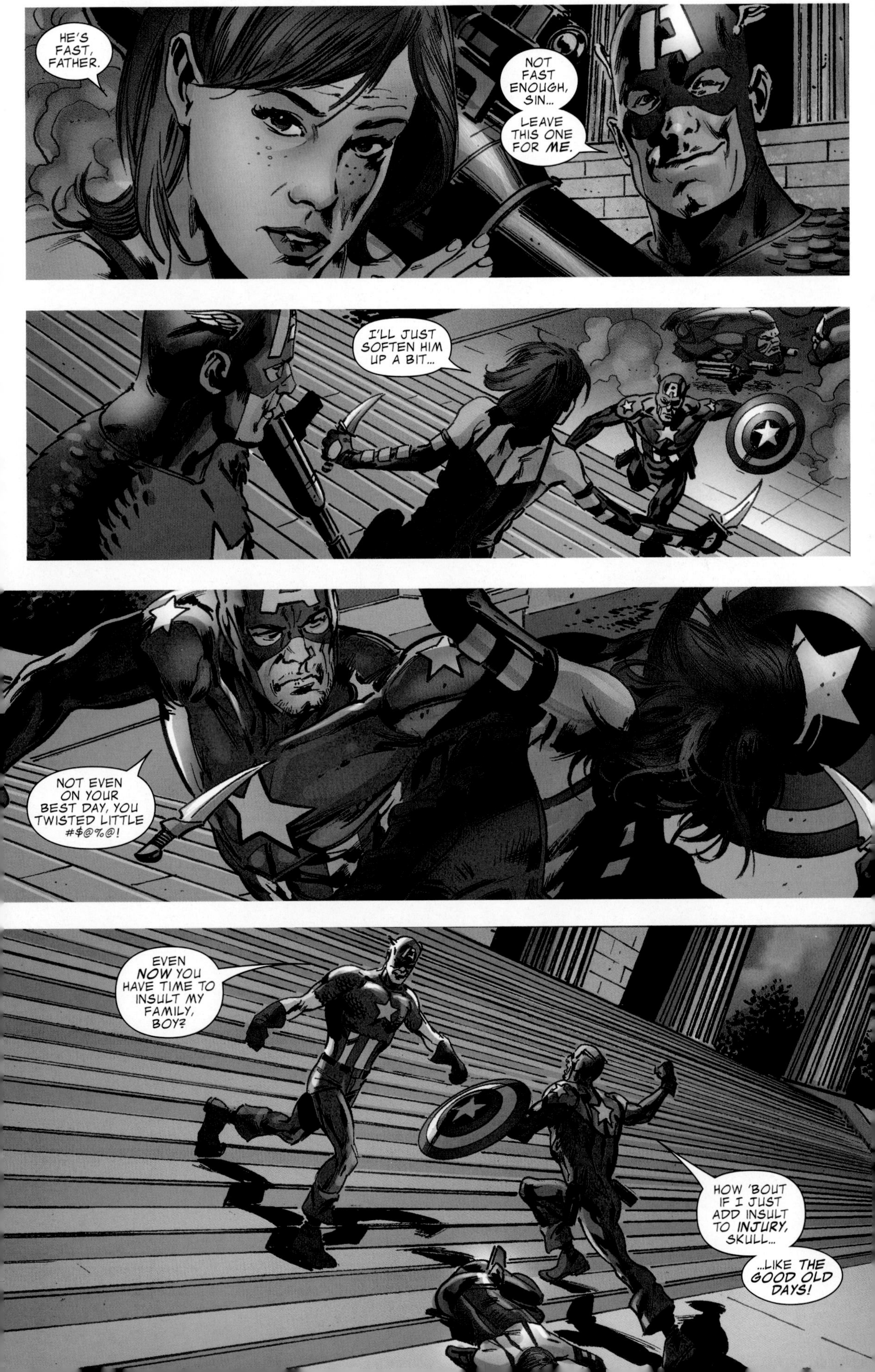
HE'S FAST, FATHER.
NOT FAST ENOUGH, SIN...
LEAVE THIS ONE FOR ME.
I'LL JUST SOFTEN HIM UP A BIT...
NOT EVEN ON YOUR BEST DAY, YOU TWISTED LITTLE #$@%@!
EVEN NOW YOU HAVE TIME TO INSULT MY FAMILY, BOY?
HOW 'BOUT IF I JUST ADD INSULT TO INJURY, SKULL...
...LIKE THE GOOD OLD DAYS!

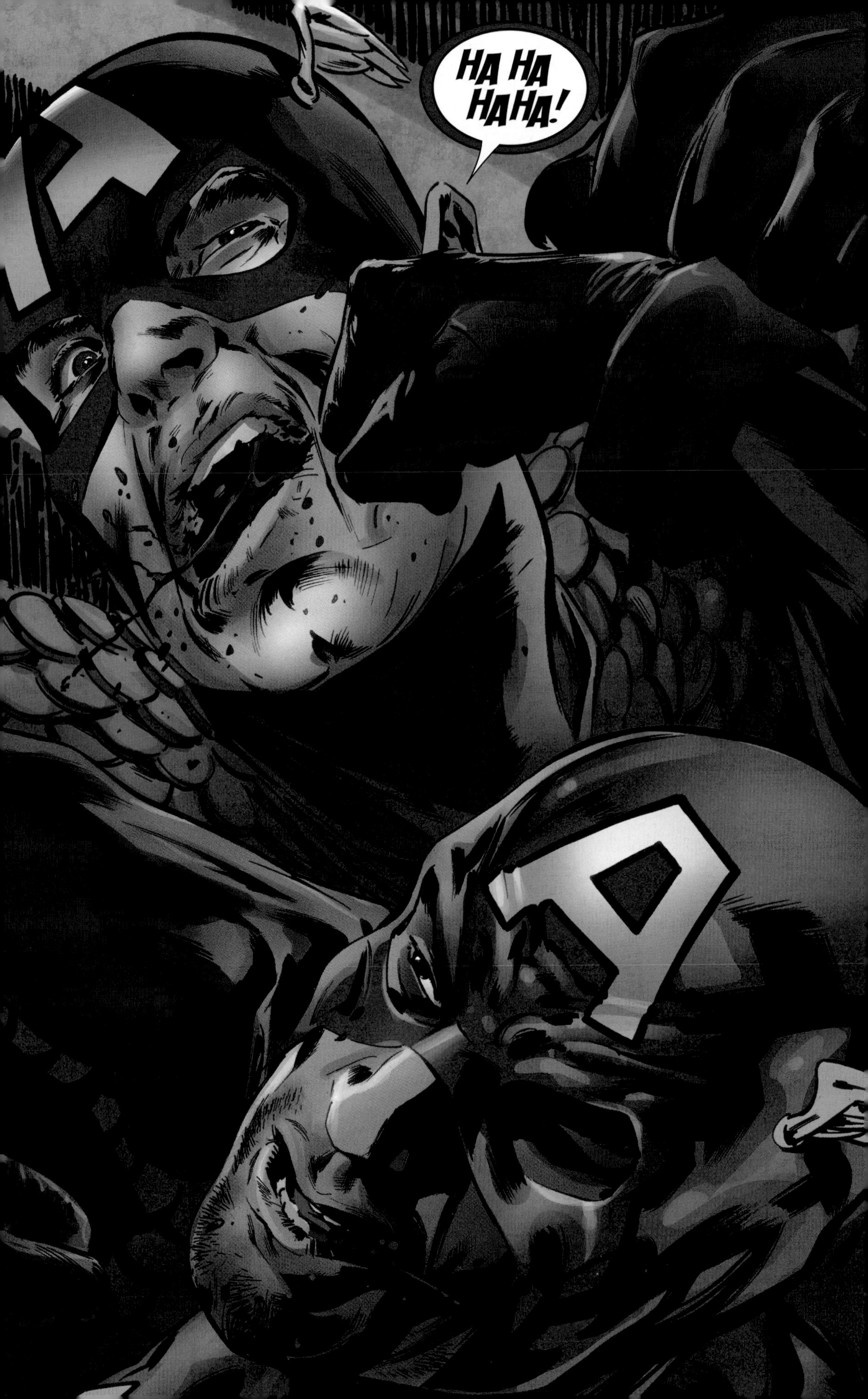
HA HA HAHA!

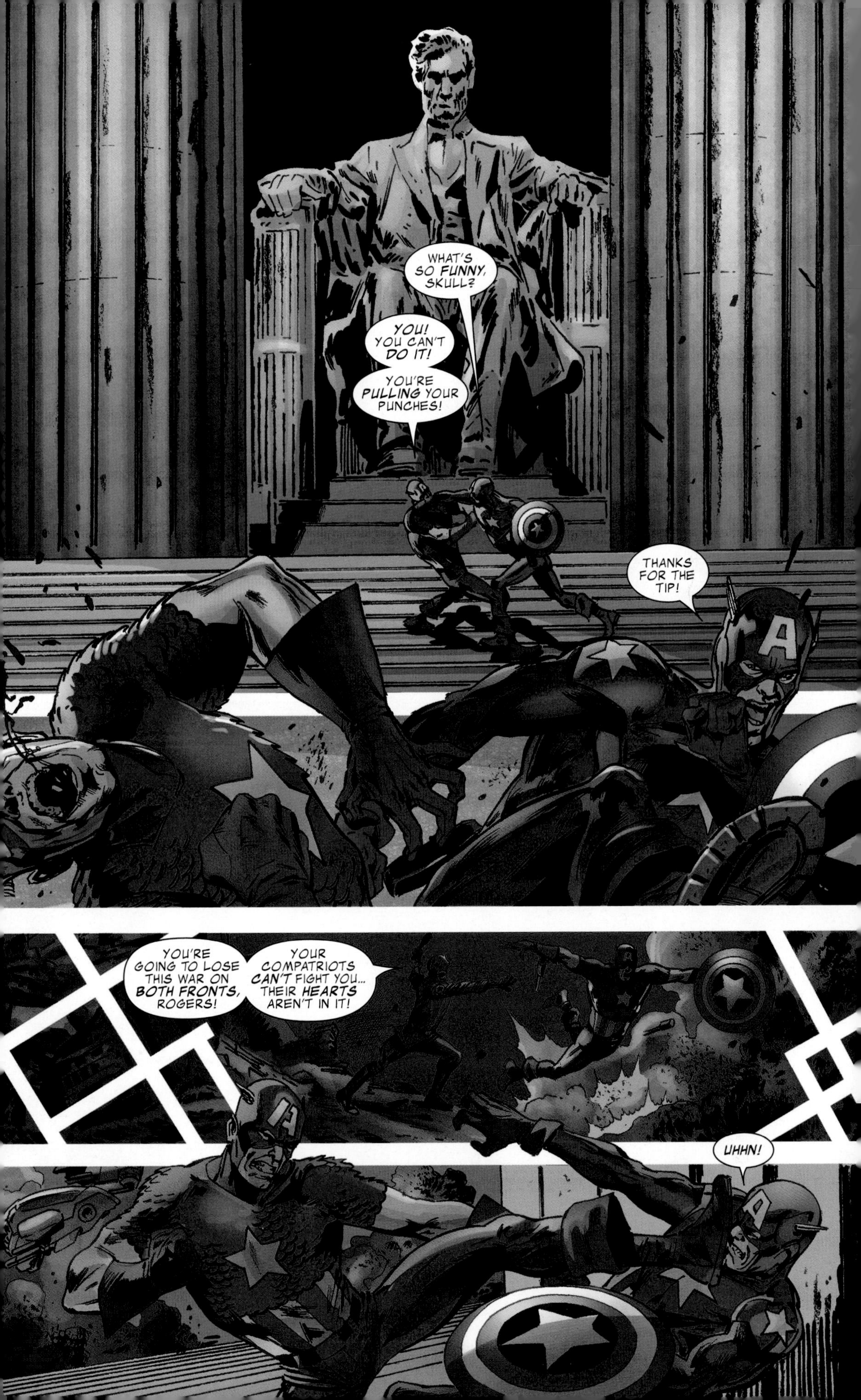
WHAT'S SO FUNNY, SKULL?
YOU! YOU CAN'T DO IT!
YOU'RE PULLING YOUR PUNCHES!
THANKS FOR THE TIP!
YOU'RE GOING TO LOSE THIS WAR ON BOTH FRONTS, ROGERS!
YOUR COMPATRIOTS CAN'T FIGHT YOU... THEIR HEARTS AREN'T IN IT!
UHHN!

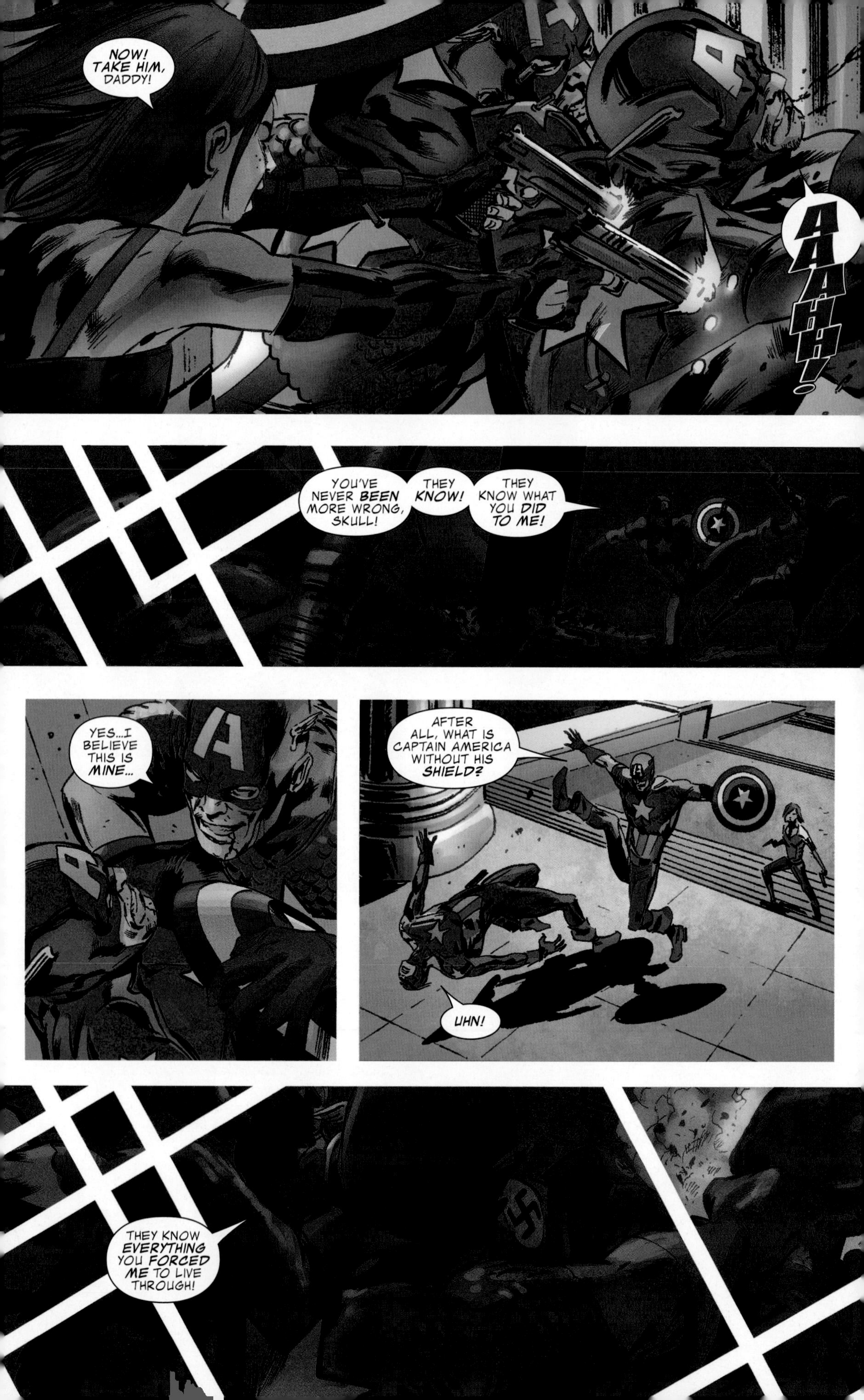
NOW! TAKE HIM, DADDY!
AAAHHH!
YOU'VE NEVER BEEN MORE WRONG, SKULL!
THEY KNOW!
THEY KNOW WHAT YOU DID TO ME!
YES...I BELIEVE THIS IS MINE...
AFTER ALL, WHAT IS CAPTAIN AMERICA WITHOUT HIS SHIELD?
UHN!
THEY KNOW EVERYTHING YOU FORCED ME TO LIVE THROUGH!

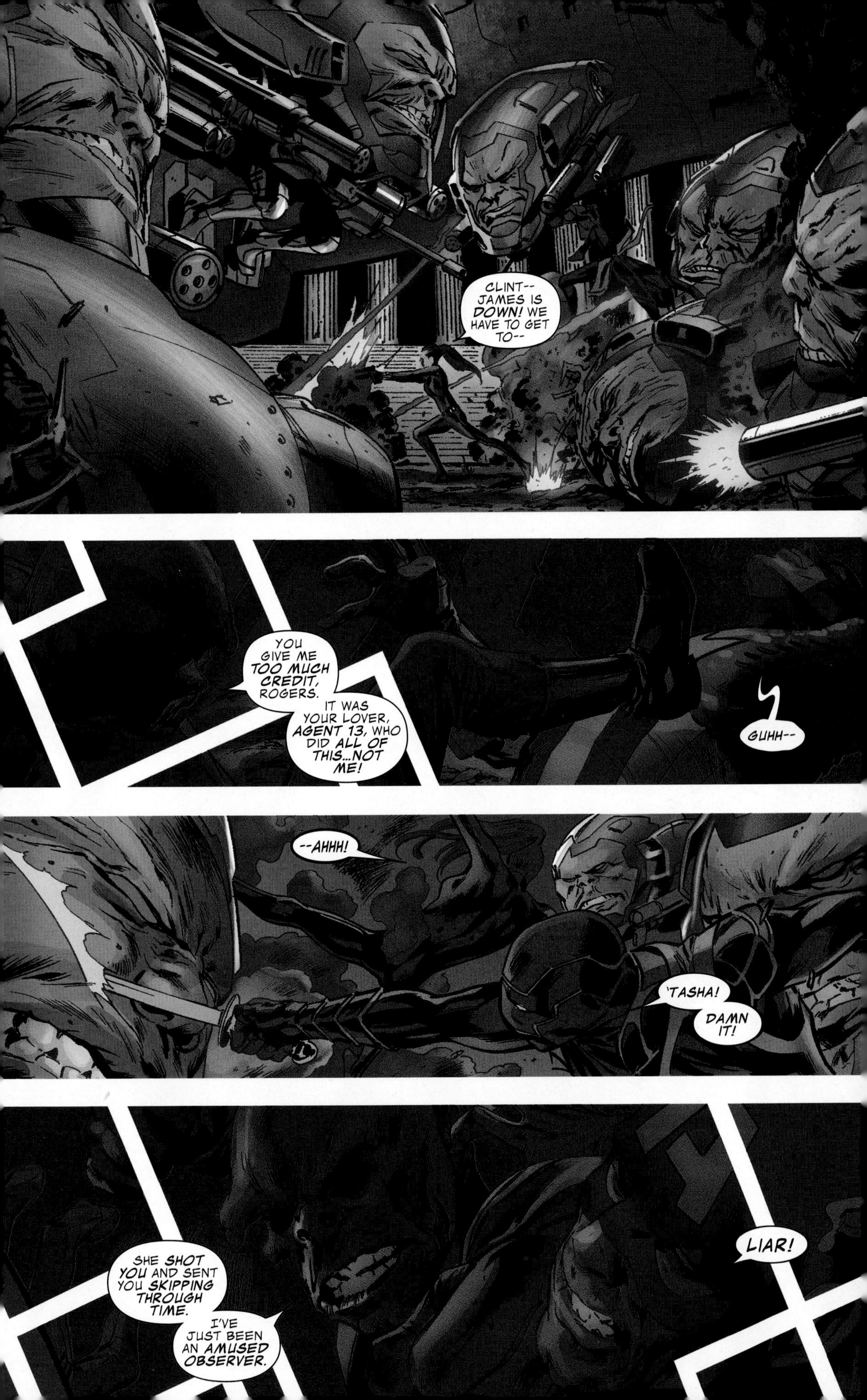
CLINT-- JAMES IS DOWN! WE HAVE TO GET TO--
YOU GIVE ME TOO MUCH CREDIT, ROGERS.
IT WAS YOUR LOVER, AGENT 13, WHO DID ALL OF THIS...NOT ME!
GUHH--
--AHHH!
'TASHA!
DAMN IT!
LIAR!
SHE SHOT YOU AND SENT YOU SKIPPING THROUGH TIME.
I'VE JUST BEEN AN AMUSED OBSERVER.

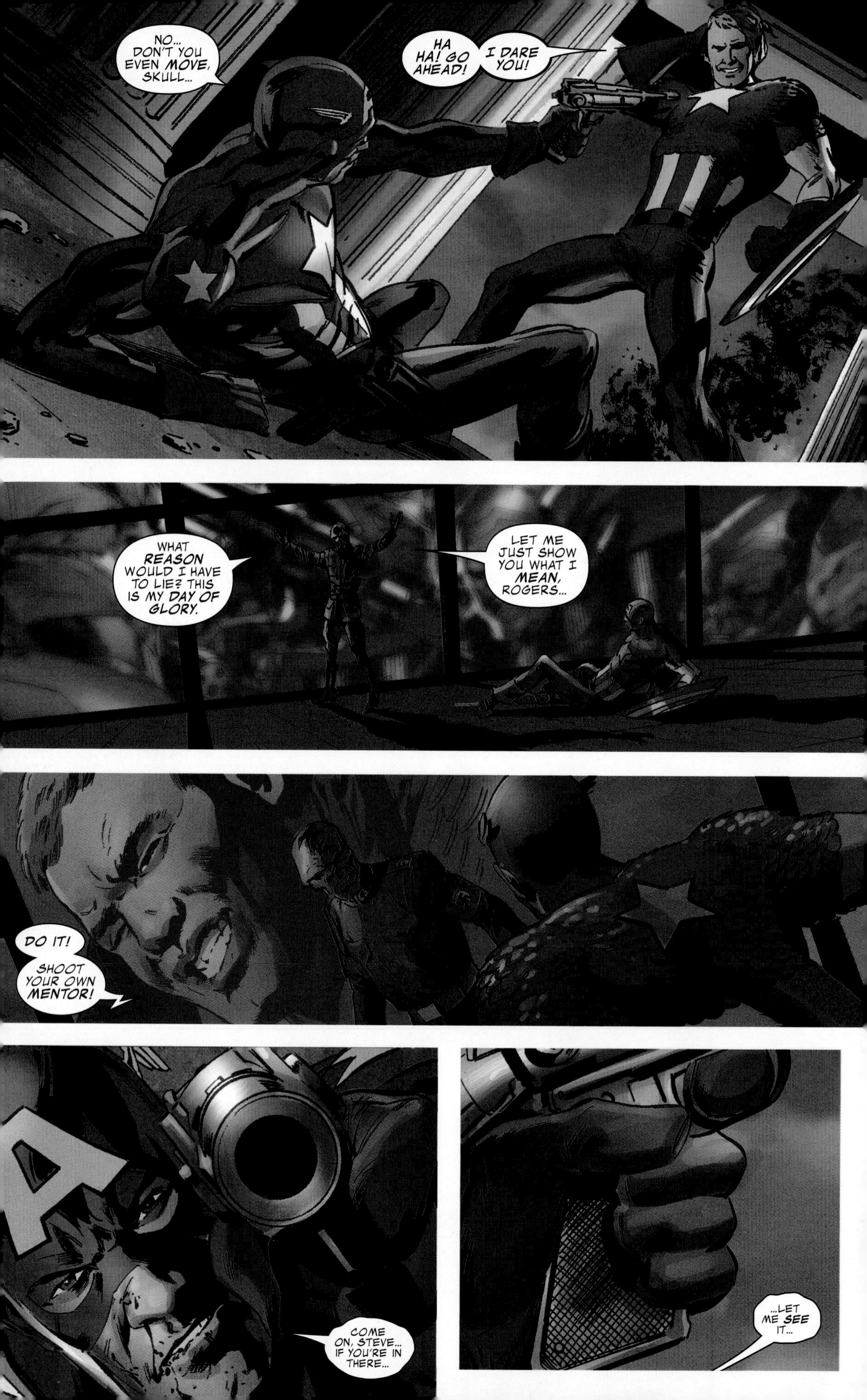
NO... DON'T YOU EVEN MOVE, SKULL...
HA HA! GO AHEAD!
I DARE YOU!
WHAT REASON WOULD I HAVE TO LIE? THIS IS MY DAY OF GLORY.
LET ME JUST SHOW YOU WHAT I MEAN, ROGERS...
DO IT! SHOOT YOUR OWN MENTOR!
COME ON, STEVE... IF YOU'RE IN THERE...
...LET ME SEE IT...

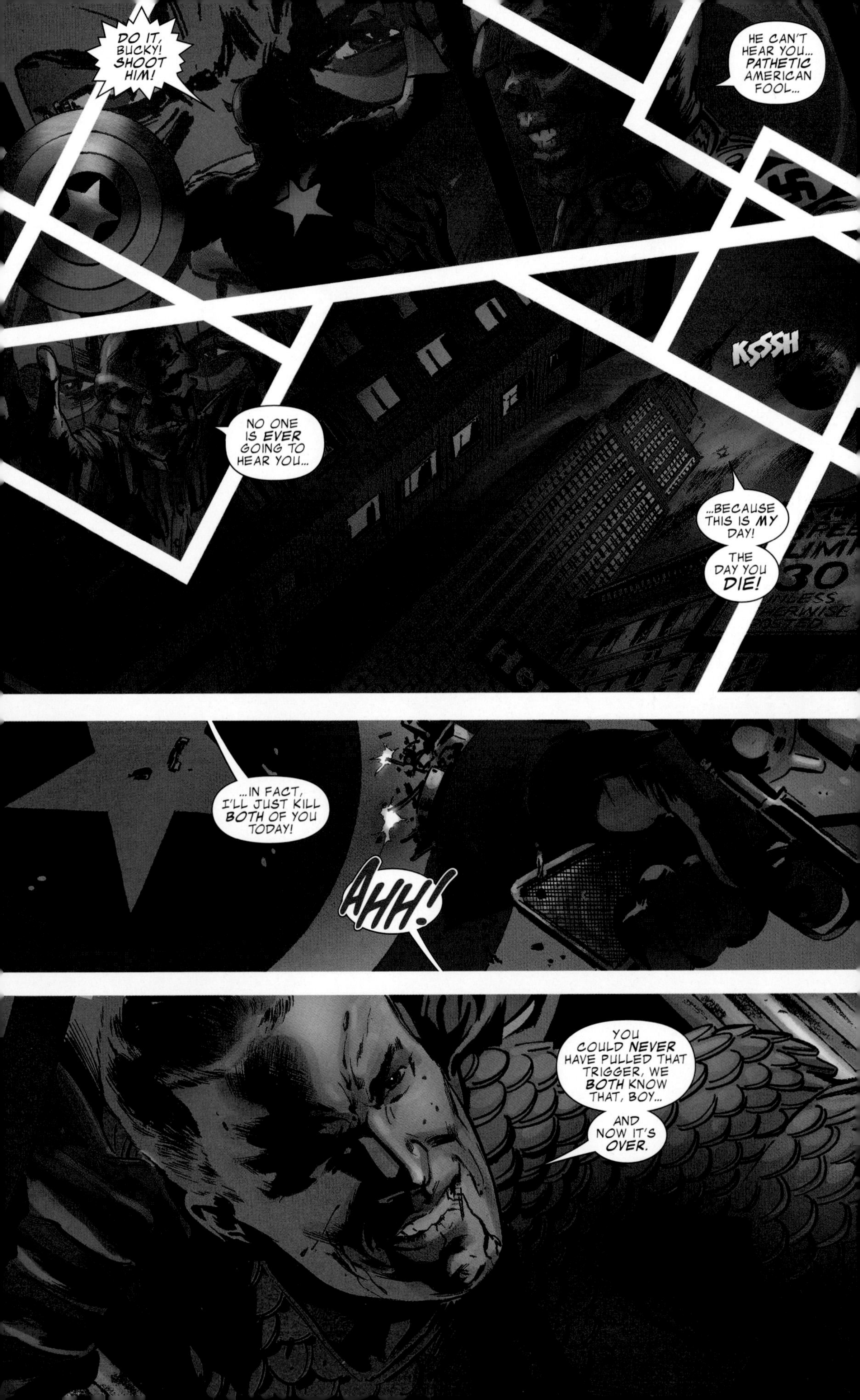
DO IT, BUCKY! SHOOT HIM!
HE CAN'T HEAR YOU... PATHETIC AMERICAN FOOL...
KSSSH
NO ONE IS EVER GOING TO HEAR YOU...
...BECAUSE THIS IS MY DAY!
THE DAY YOU DIE!
...IN FACT, I'LL JUST KILL BOTH OF YOU TODAY!
AHH!
YOU COULD NEVER HAVE PULLED THAT TRIGGER, WE BOTH KNOW THAT, BOY...
AND NOW IT'S OVER.

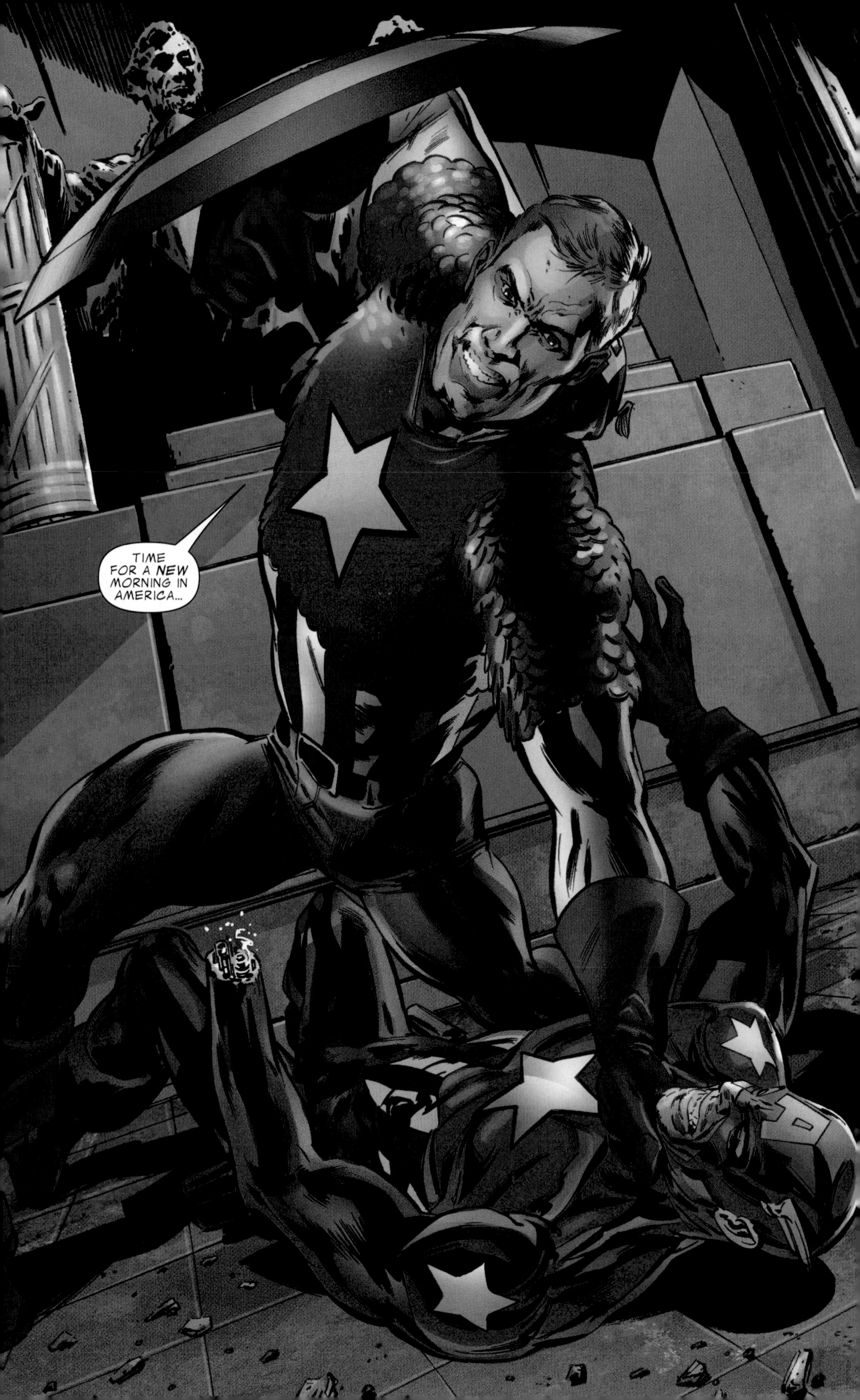
TIME FOR A NEW MORNING IN AMERICA...

"Ask not what your country can do for you –
ask what you can do for your country."

– John F. Kennedy

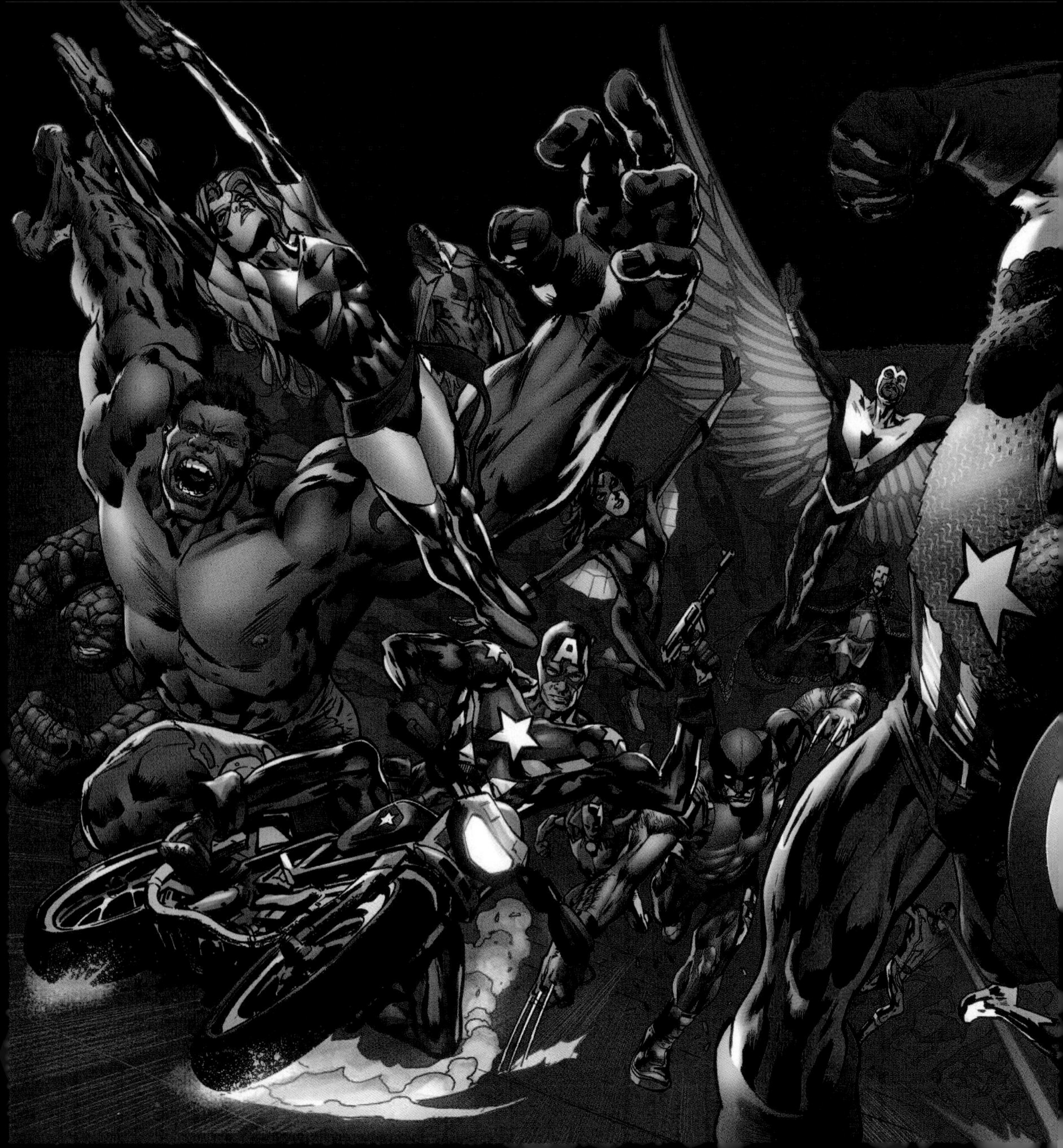

6

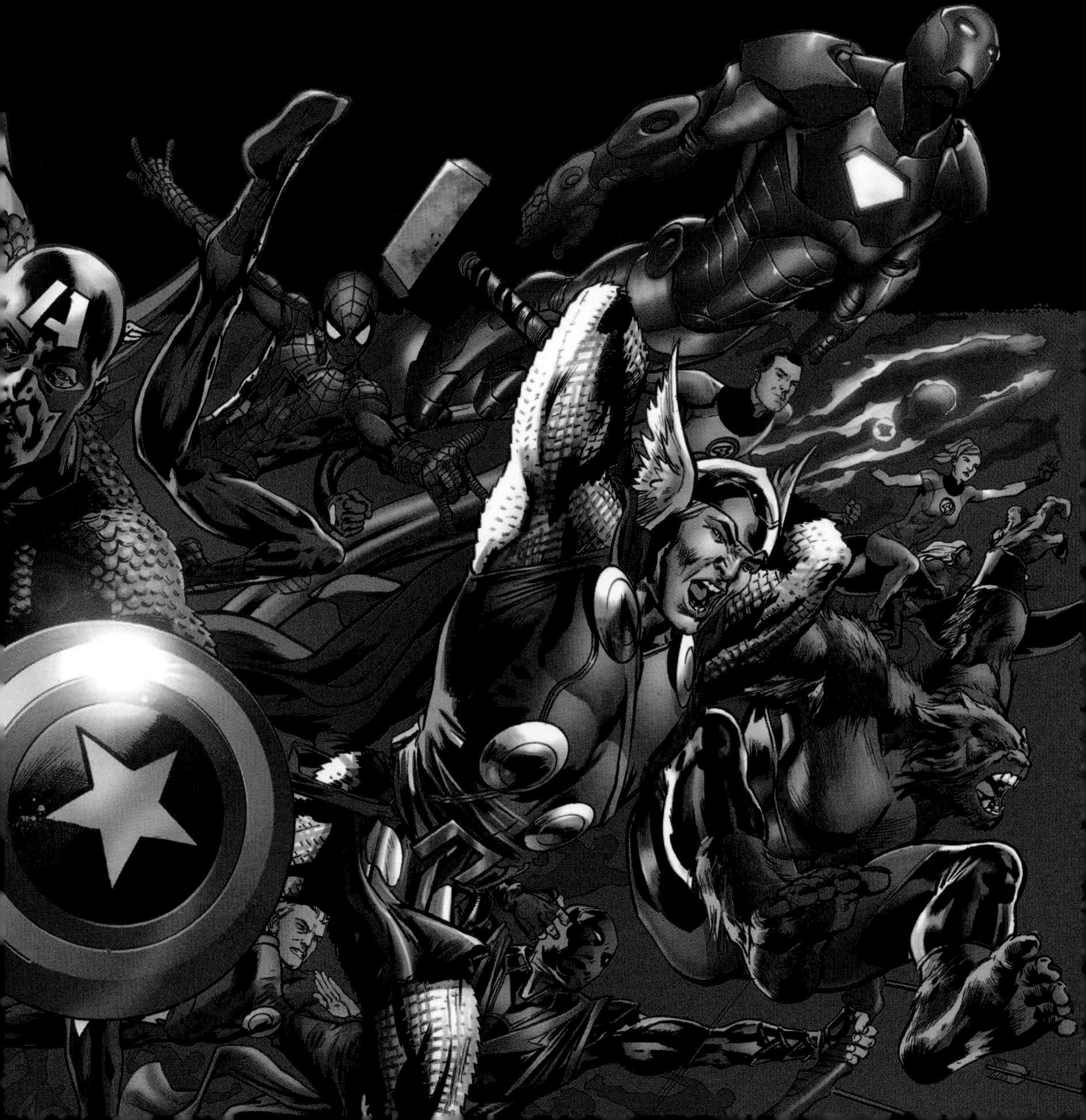

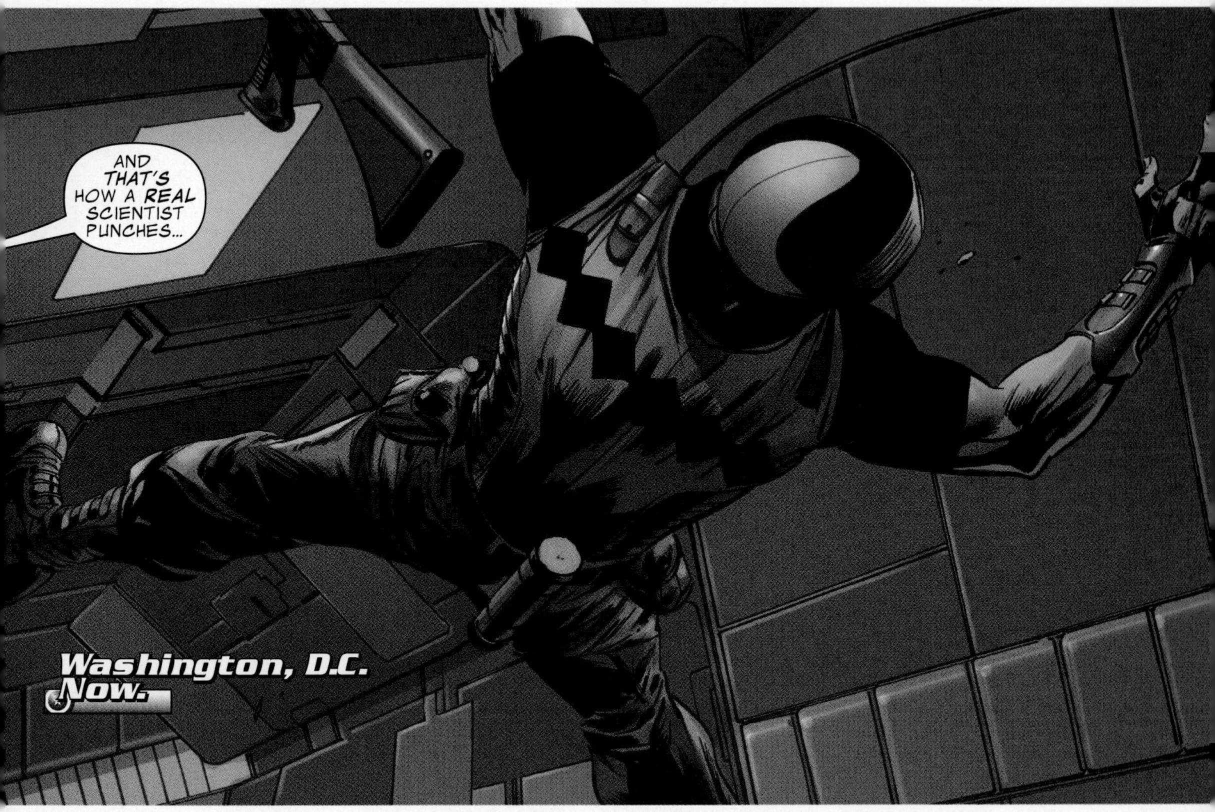
AND THAT'S HOW A REAL SCIENTIST PUNCHES...
Washington, D.C.
Now.

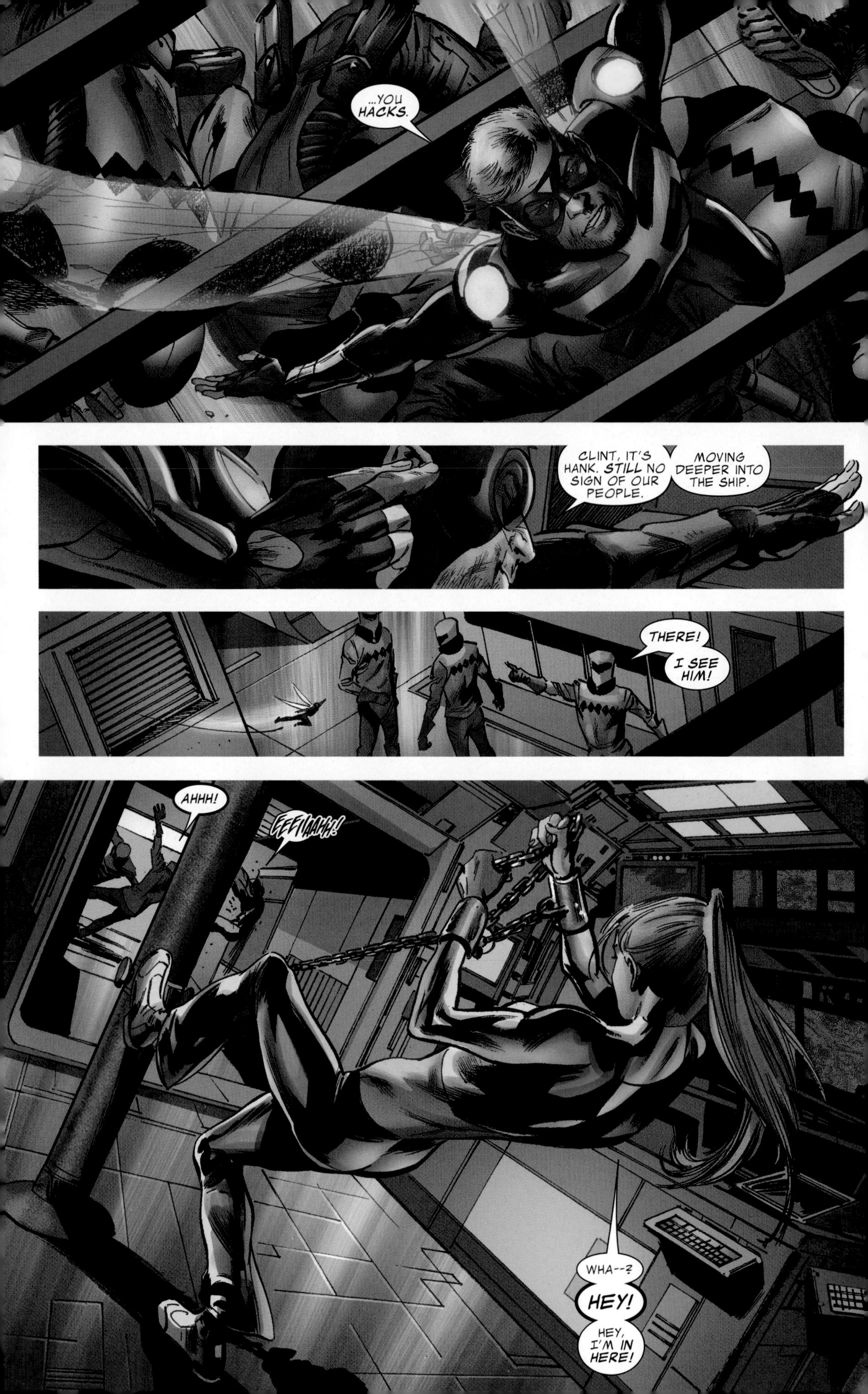

...YOU HACKS.
CLINT, IT'S HANK. STILL NO SIGN OF OUR PEOPLE.
MOVING DEEPER INTO THE SHIP.
THERE!
I SEE HIM!
AHHH!
EEEIAAHH!
WHA--?
HEY!
HEY, I'M IN HERE!

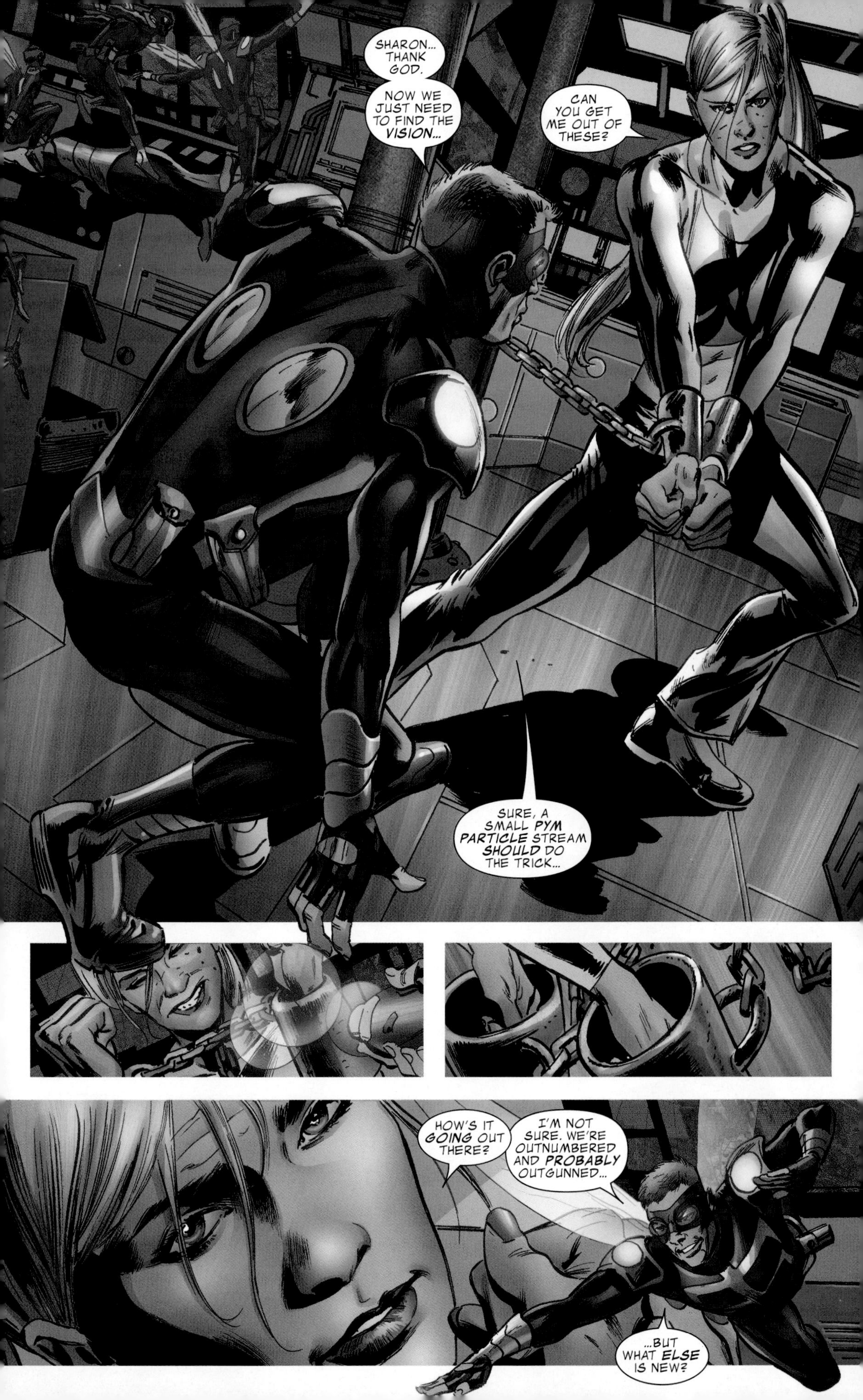
SHARON... THANK GOD.
NOW WE JUST NEED TO FIND THE VISION...
CAN YOU GET ME OUT OF THESE?
SURE, A SMALL PYM PARTICLE STREAM SHOULD DO THE TRICK...
HOW'S IT GOING OUT THERE?
I'M NOT SURE. WE'RE OUTNUMBERED AND PROBABLY OUTGUNNED...
...BUT WHAT ELSE IS NEW?

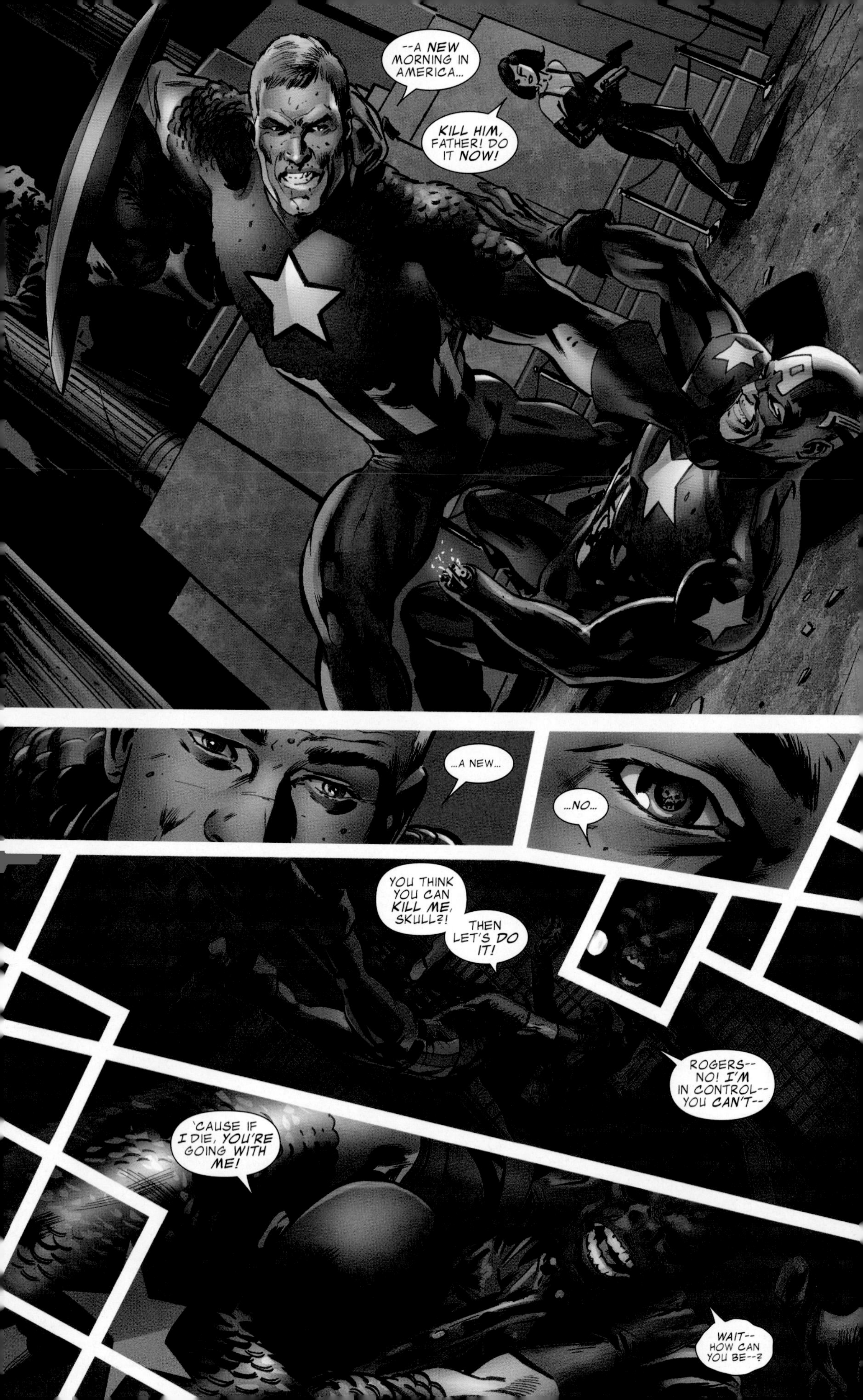
--A NEW MORNING IN AMERICA...
KILL HIM, FATHER! DO IT NOW!
...A NEW...
...NO...
YOU THINK YOU CAN KILL ME, SKULL?!
THEN LET'S DO IT!
ROGERS-- NO! I'M IN CONTROL-- YOU CAN'T--
'CAUSE IF I DIE, YOU'RE GOING WITH ME!
WAIT-- HOW CAN YOU BE--?

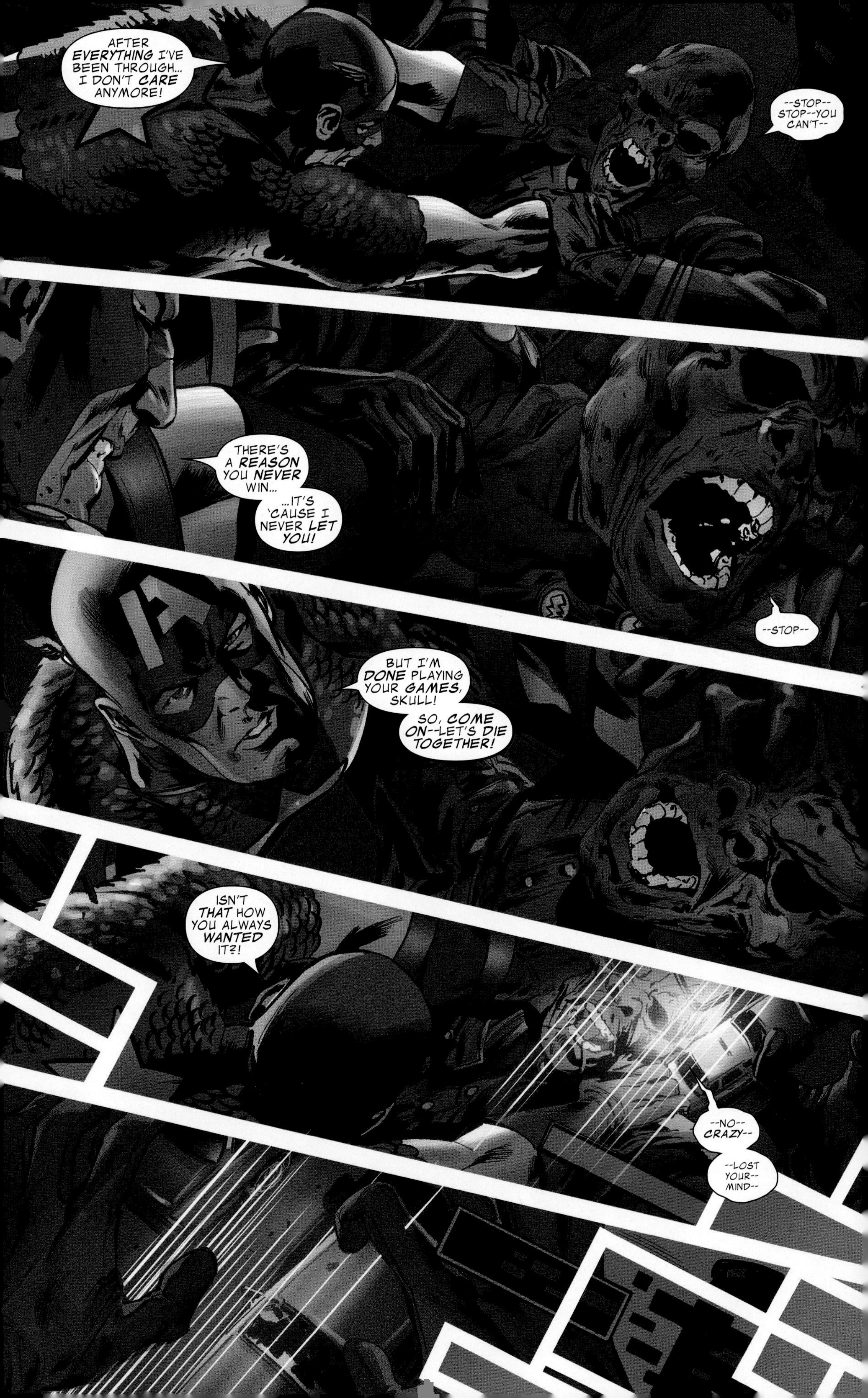
AFTER EVERYTHING I'VE BEEN THROUGH... I DON'T CARE ANYMORE!
--STOP-- STOP--YOU CAN'T--
THERE'S A REASON YOU NEVER WIN...
...IT'S 'CAUSE I NEVER LET YOU!
--STOP--
BUT I'M DONE PLAYING YOUR GAMES, SKULL!
SO, COME ON--LET'S DIE TOGETHER!
ISN'T THAT HOW YOU ALWAYS WANTED IT?!
--NO-- CRAZY--
--LOST YOUR-- MIND--

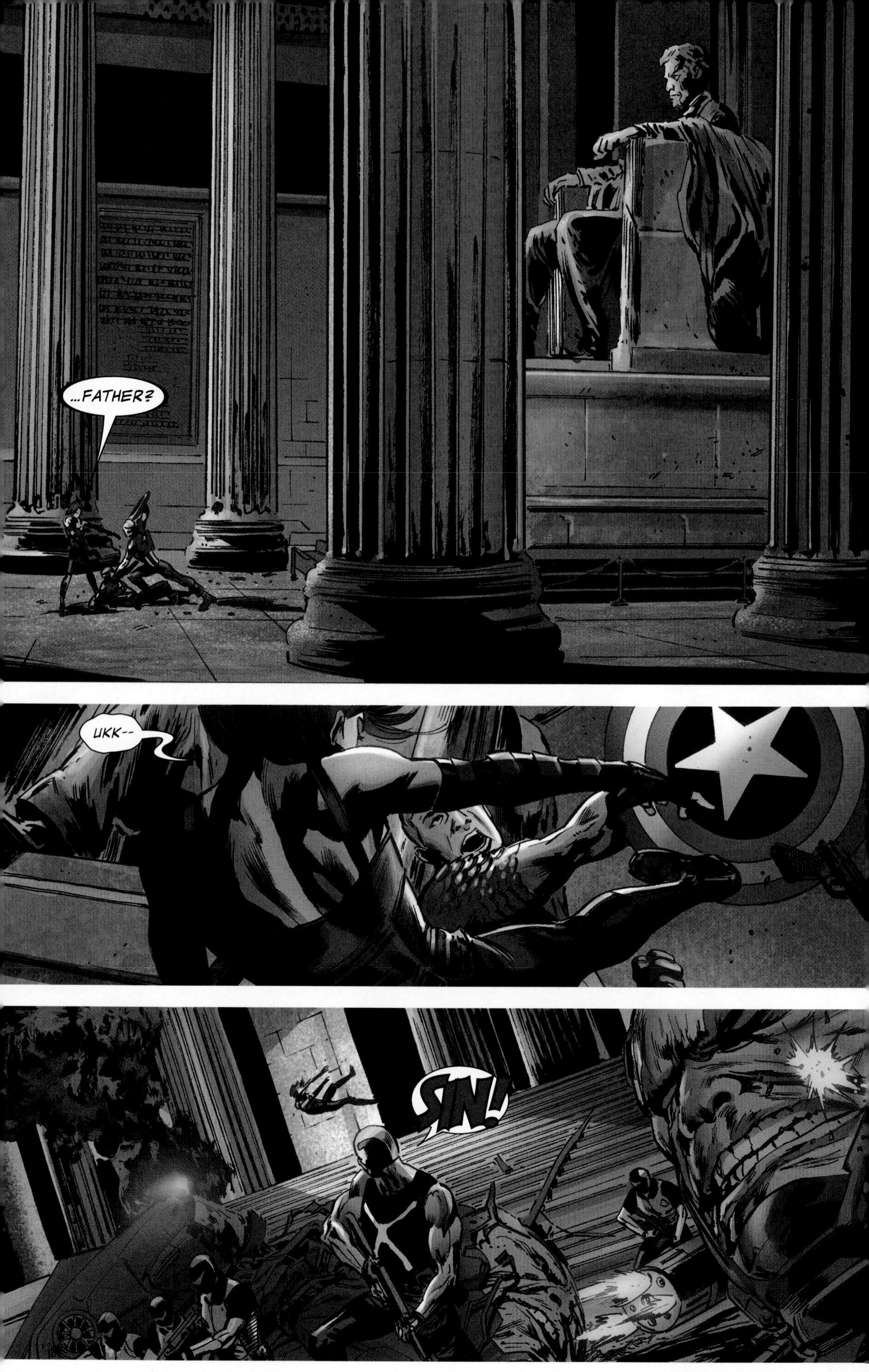
...FATHER?
UKK--
SIN!

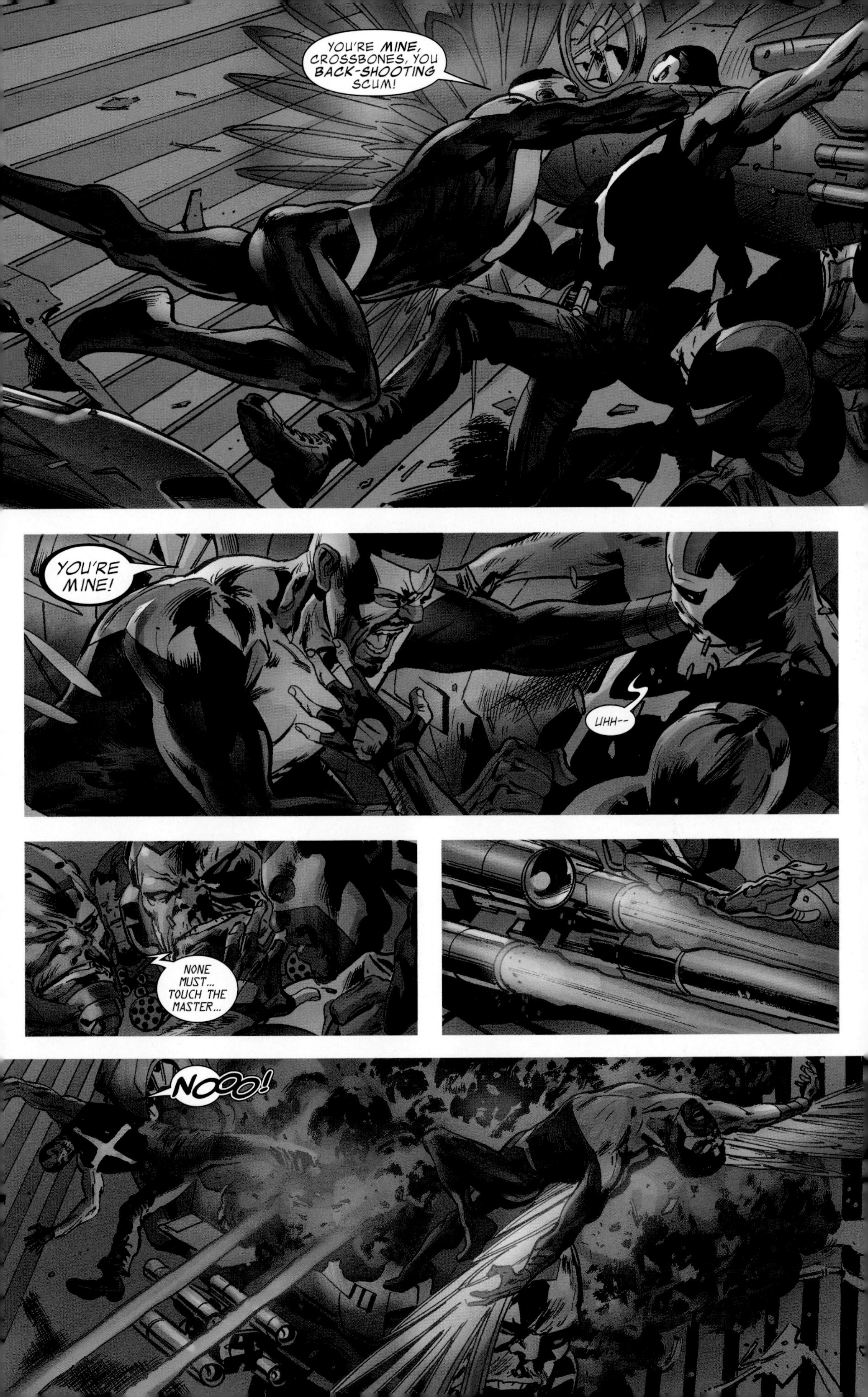
YOU'RE **MINE**, CROSSBONES, YOU **BACK-SHOOTING** SCUM!
YOU'RE MINE!
UHH--
NONE MUST... TOUCH THE MASTER...
NOOO!

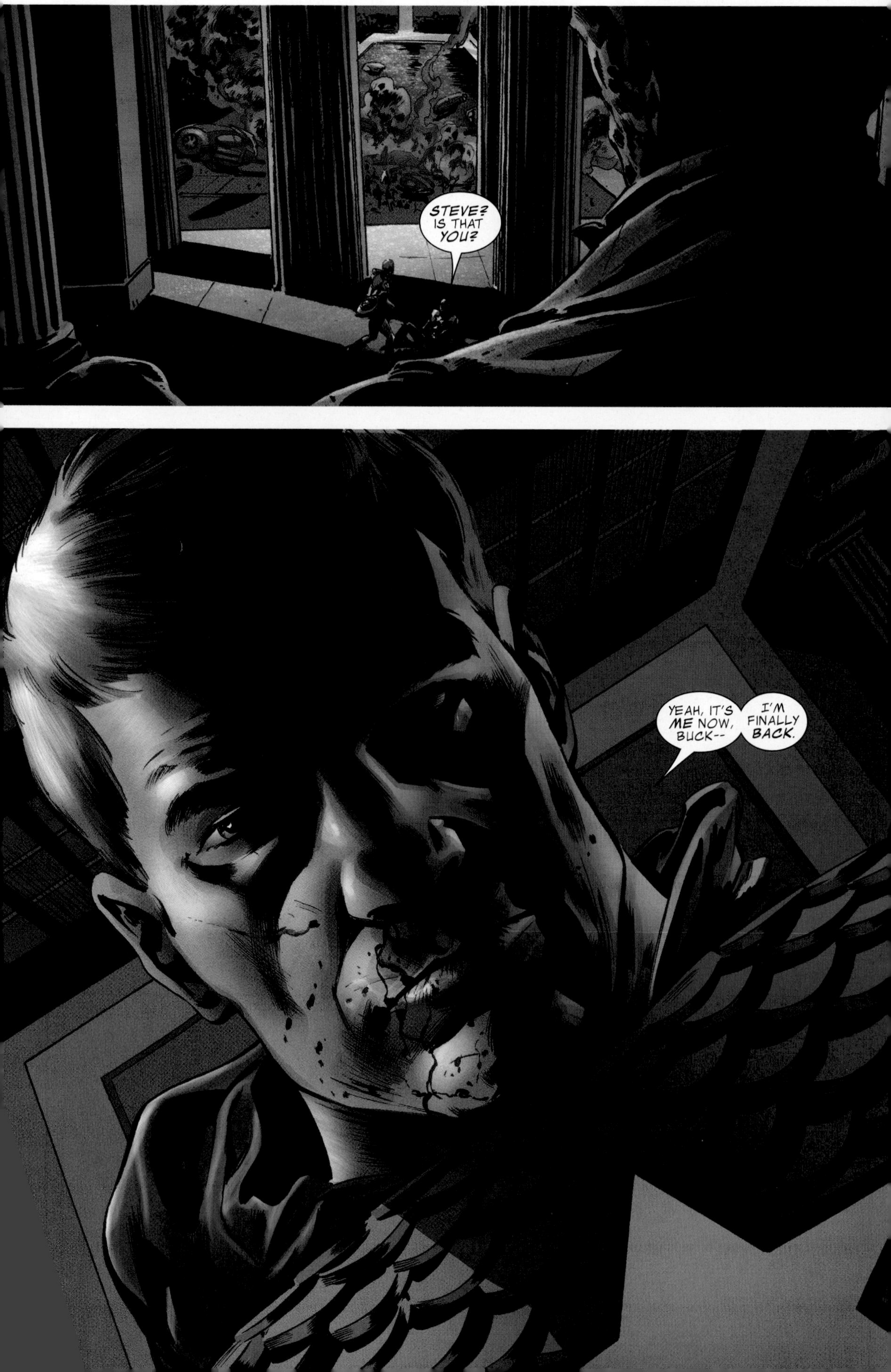
STEVE? IS THAT YOU?
YEAH, IT'S ME NOW, BUCK--
I'M FINALLY BACK.

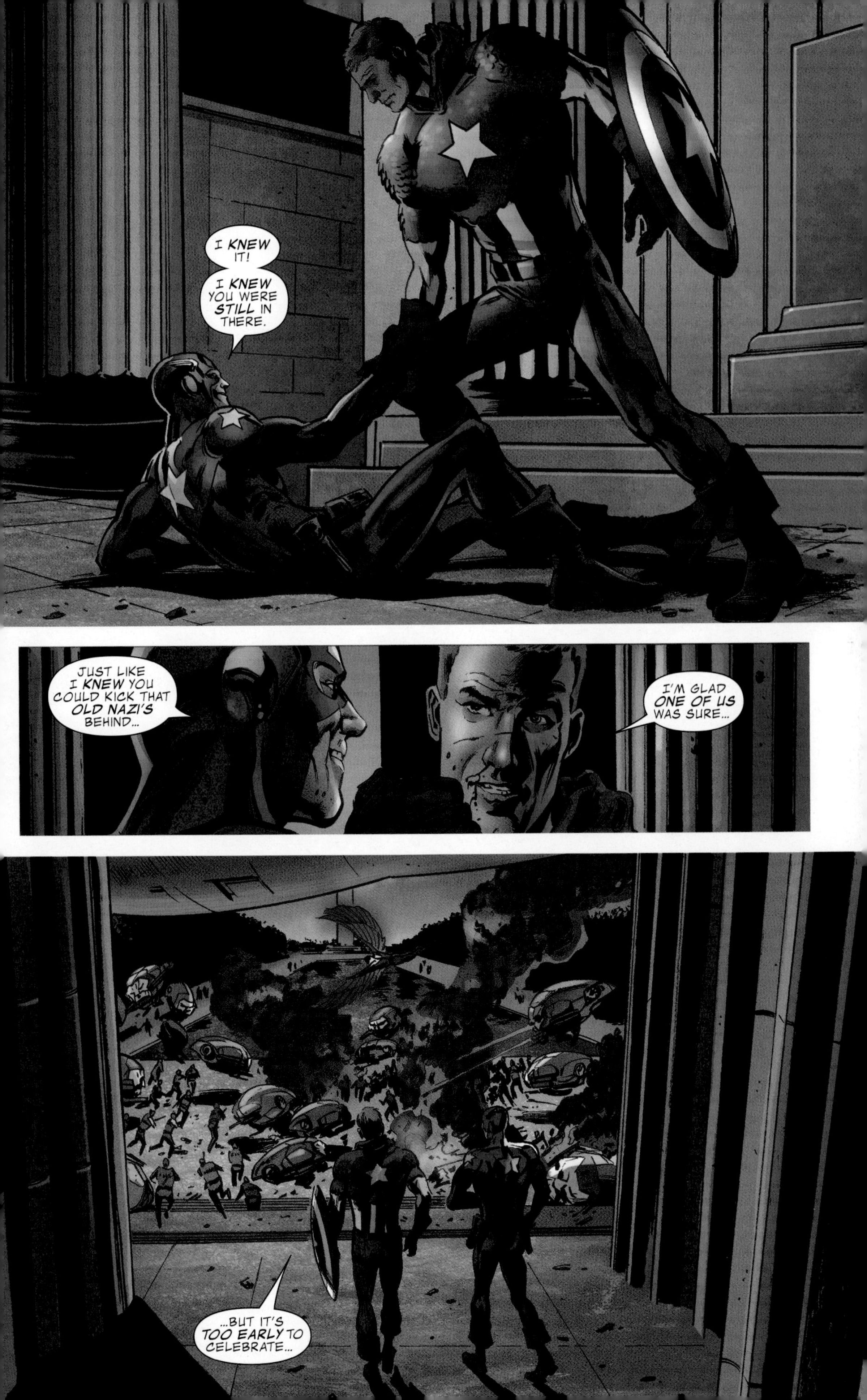
I KNEW IT!
I KNEW YOU WERE STILL IN THERE.
JUST LIKE I KNEW YOU COULD KICK THAT OLD NAZI'S BEHIND...
I'M GLAD ONE OF US WAS SURE...
...BUT IT'S TOO EARLY TO CELEBRATE...

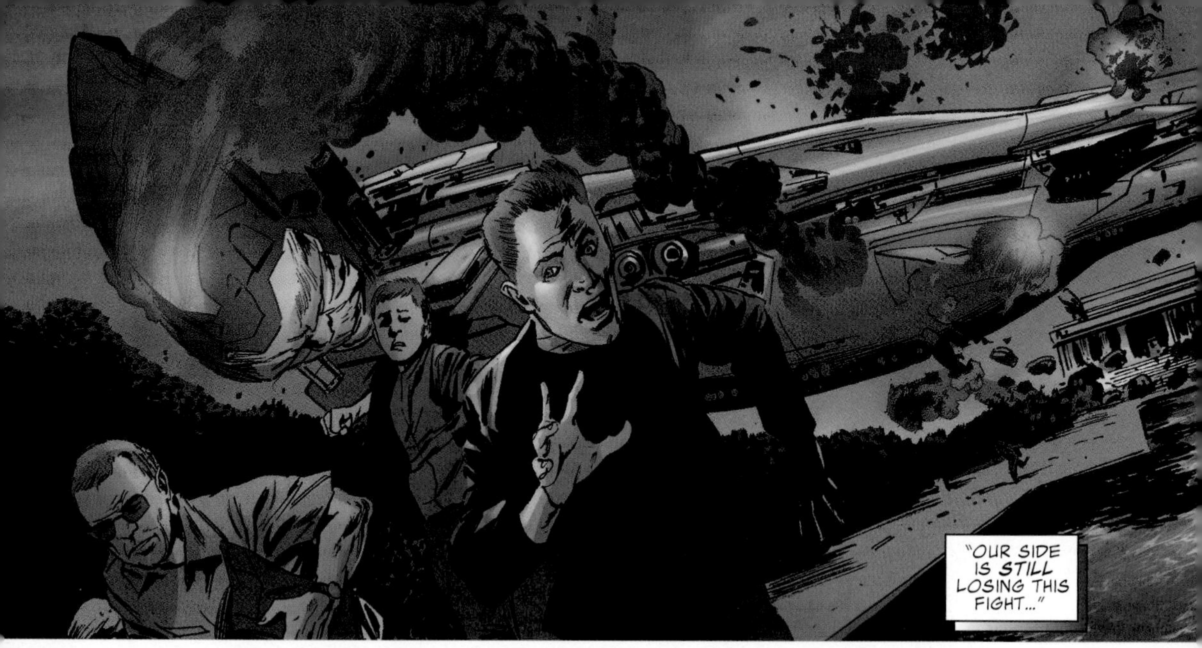
"OUR SIDE IS STILL LOSING THIS FIGHT..."

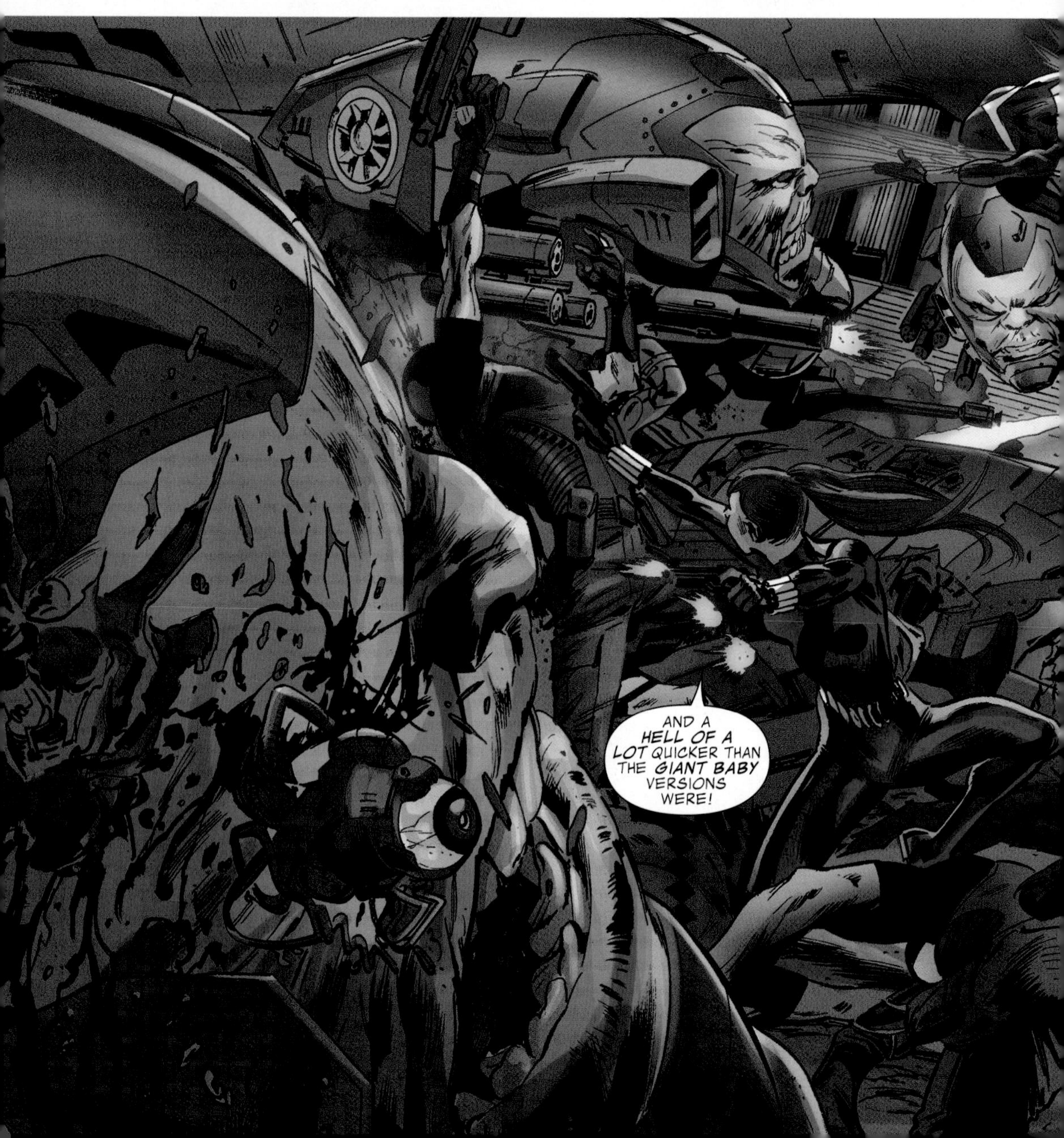
AND A HELL OF A LOT QUICKER THAN THE GIANT BABY VERSIONS WERE!

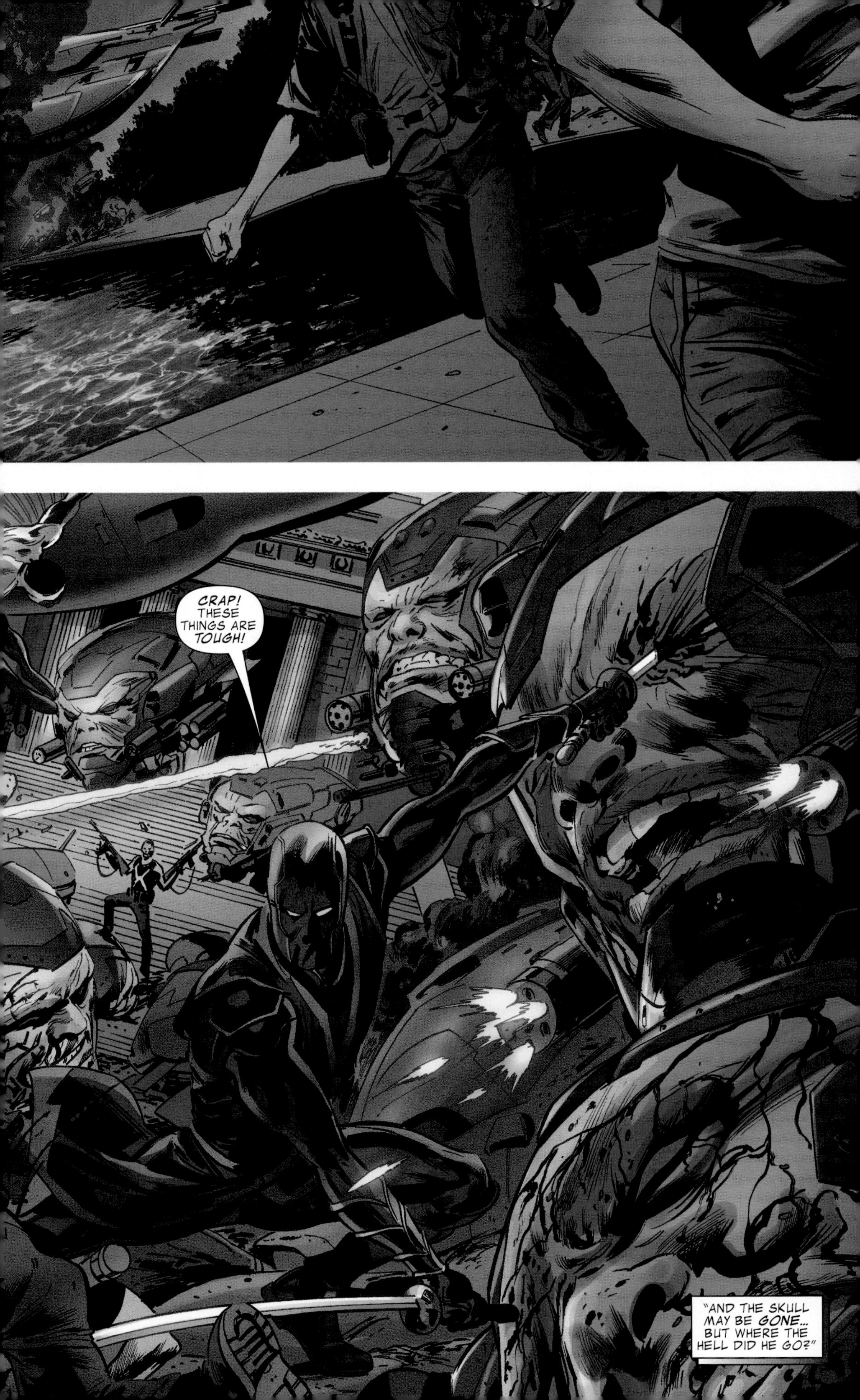
CRAP! THESE THINGS ARE TOUGH!
"AND THE SKULL MAY BE GONE... BUT WHERE THE HELL DID HE GO?"

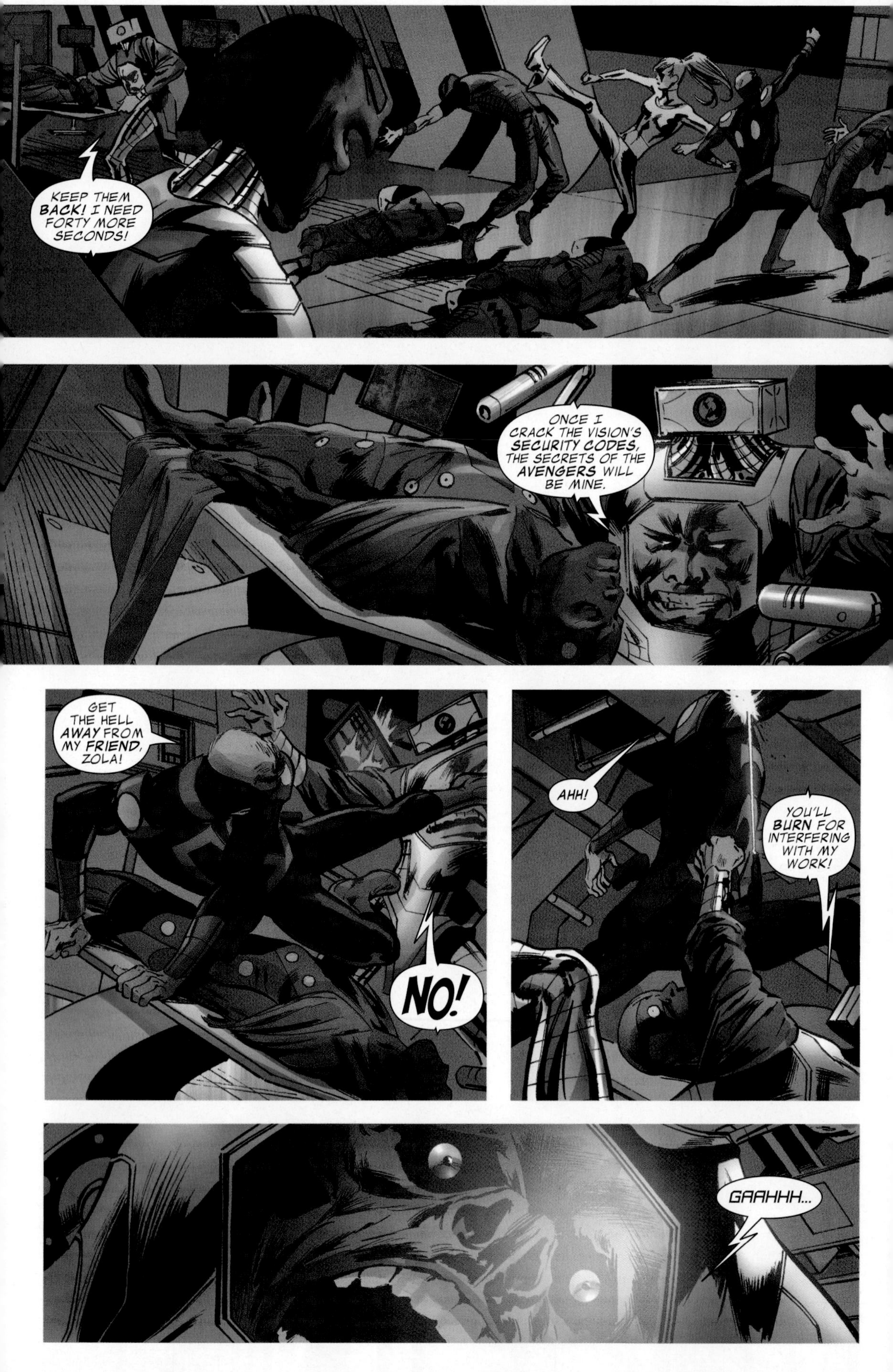
KEEP THEM BACK! I NEED FORTY MORE SECONDS!
ONCE I CRACK THE VISION'S SECURITY CODES, THE SECRETS OF THE AVENGERS WILL BE MINE.
GET THE HELL AWAY FROM MY FRIEND, ZOLA!
NO!
AHH!
YOU'LL BURN FOR INTERFERING WITH MY WORK!
GAAHHH...

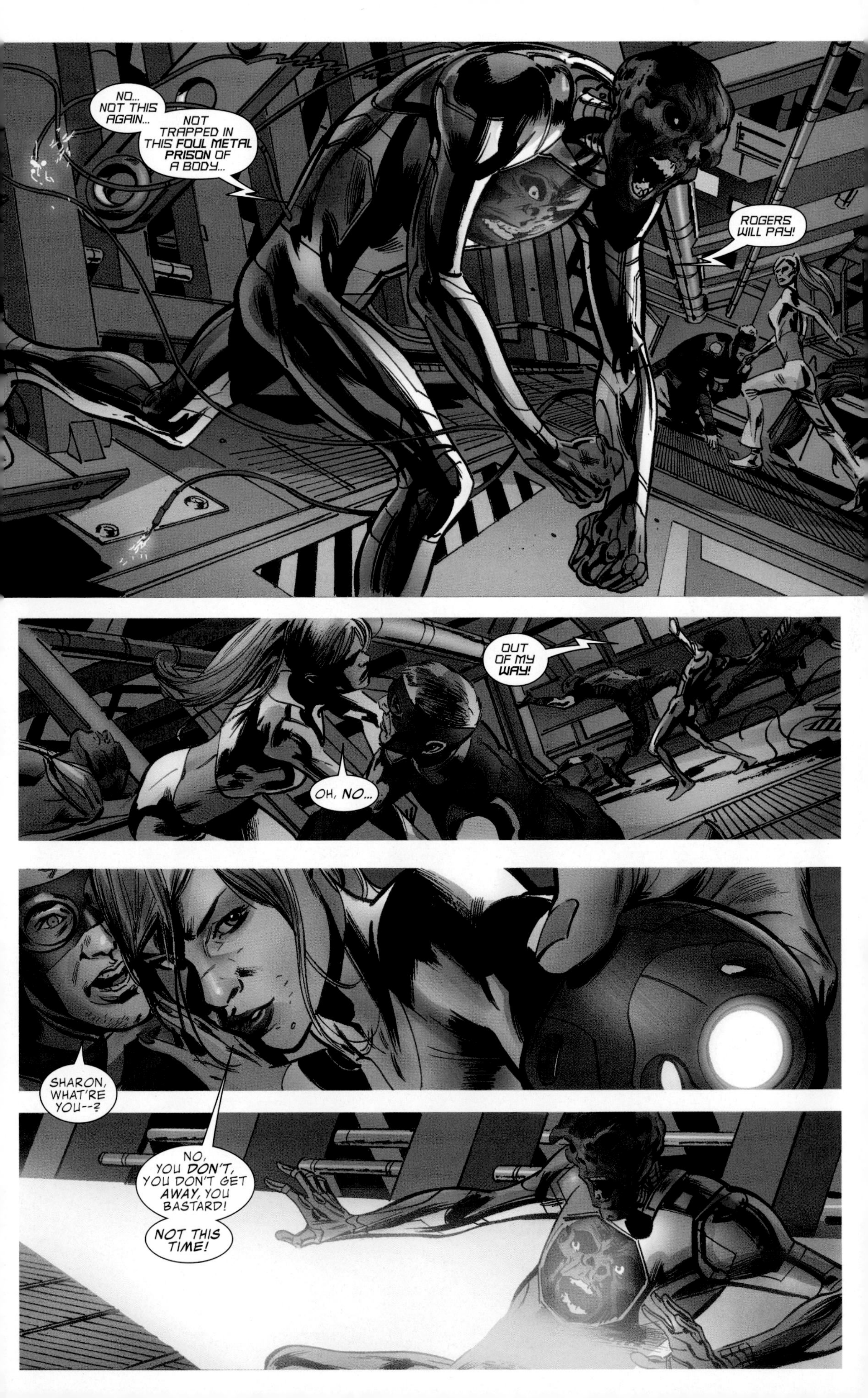
NO... NOT THIS AGAIN...
NOT TRAPPED IN THIS FOUL METAL PRISON OF A BODY...
ROGERS WILL PAY!
OUT OF MY WAY!
OH, NO...
SHARON, WHAT'RE YOU--?
NO, YOU DON'T, YOU DON'T GET AWAY, YOU BASTARD!
NOT THIS TIME!

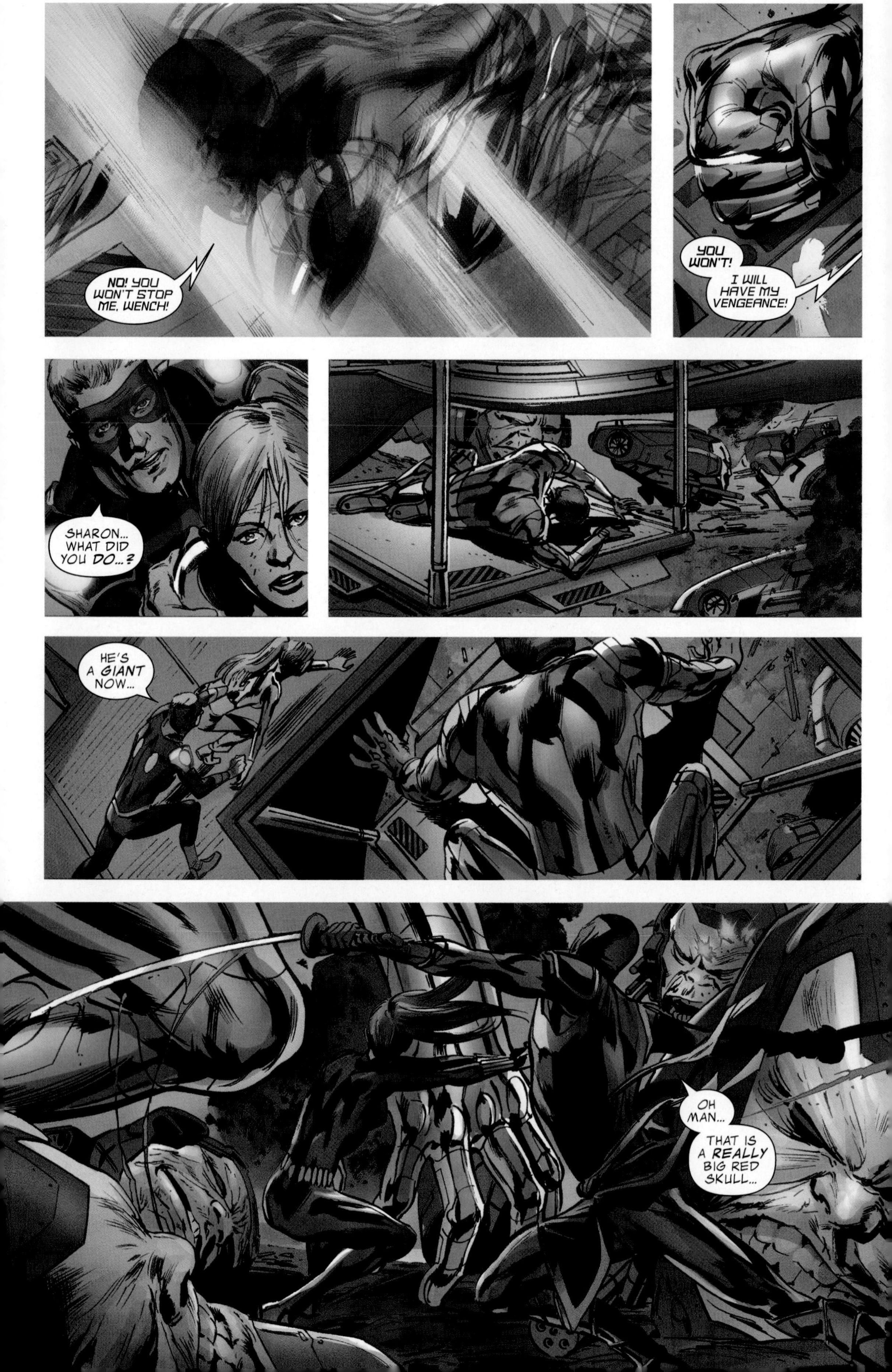
NO! YOU WON'T STOP ME, WENCH!
YOU WON'T!
I WILL HAVE MY VENGEANCE!
SHARON... WHAT DID YOU DO...?
HE'S A GIANT NOW...
OH MAN...
THAT IS A REALLY BIG RED SKULL...

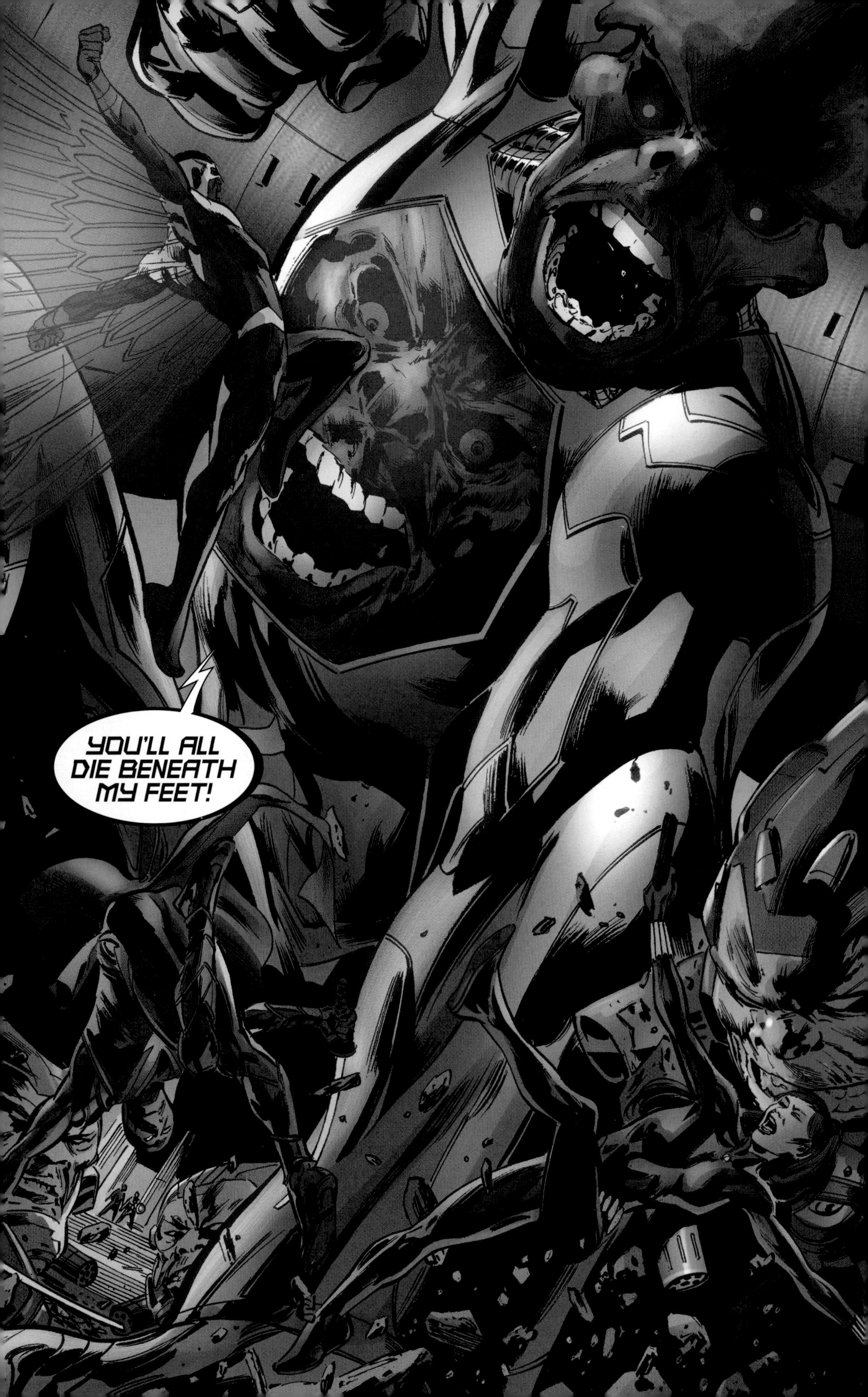
YOU'LL ALL DIE BENEATH MY FEET!

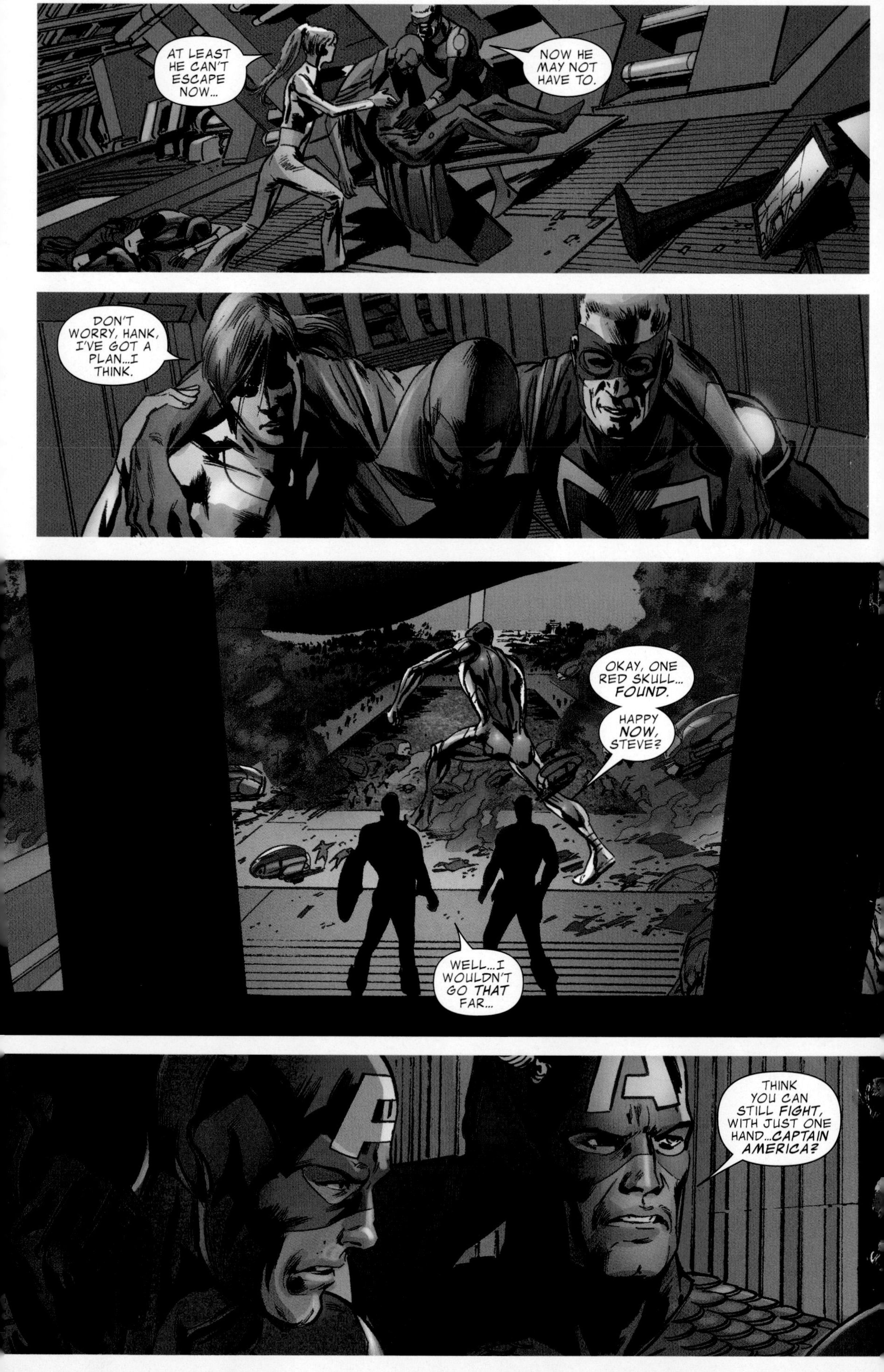
AT LEAST HE CAN'T ESCAPE NOW...
NOW HE MAY NOT HAVE TO.
DON'T WORRY, HANK, I'VE GOT A PLAN...I THINK.
OKAY, ONE RED SKULL... FOUND.
HAPPY NOW, STEVE?
WELL...I WOULDN'T GO THAT FAR...
THINK YOU CAN STILL FIGHT, WITH JUST ONE HAND...CAPTAIN AMERICA?

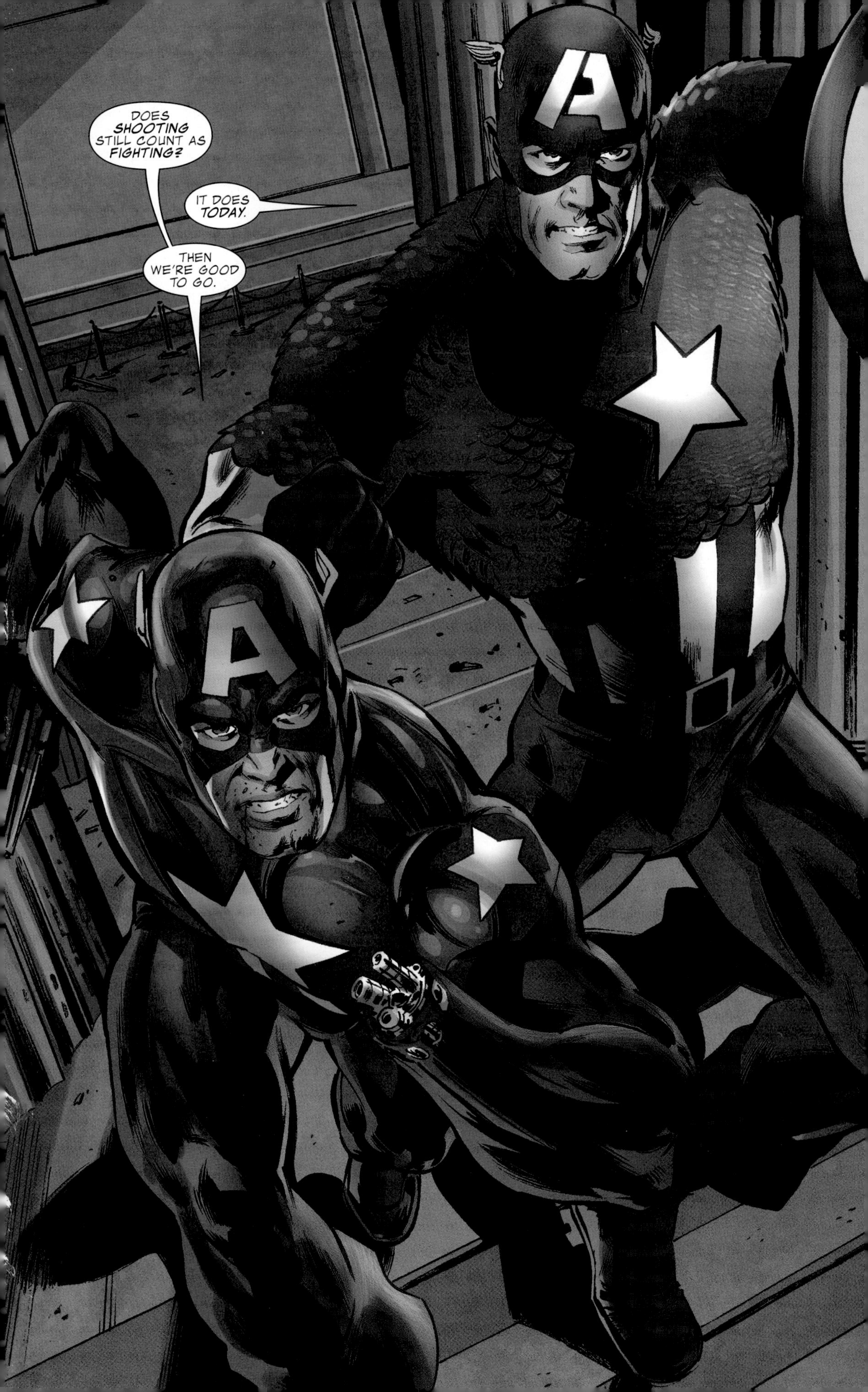
DOES SHOOTING STILL COUNT AS FIGHTING?
IT DOES TODAY.
THEN WE'RE GOOD TO GO.

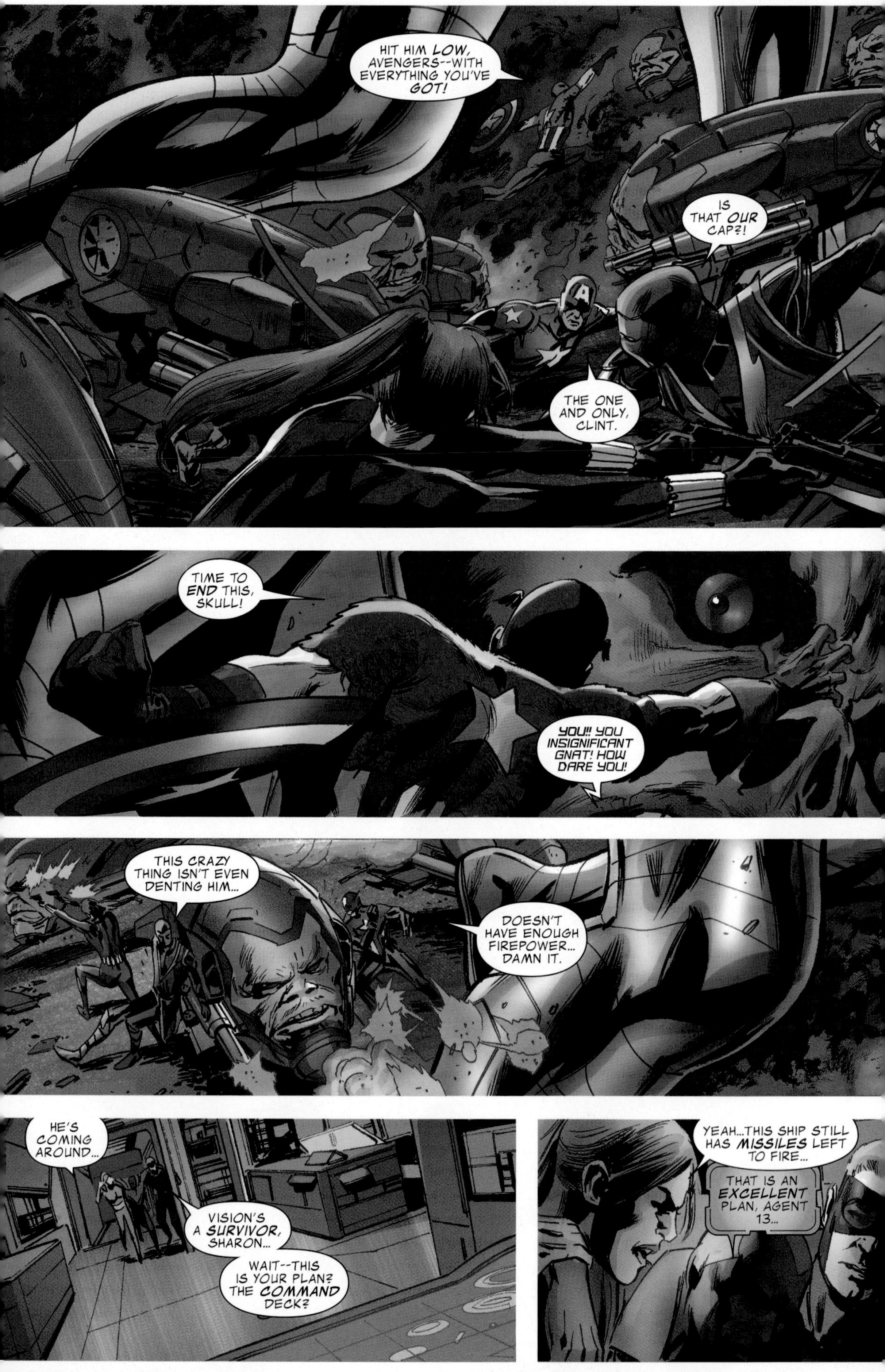
HIT HIM LOW, AVENGERS--WITH EVERYTHING YOU'VE GOT!
IS THAT OUR CAP?!
THE ONE AND ONLY, CLINT.
TIME TO END THIS, SKULL!
YOU!! YOU INSIGNIFICANT GNAT! HOW DARE YOU!
THIS CRAZY THING ISN'T EVEN DENTING HIM...
DOESN'T HAVE ENOUGH FIREPOWER... DAMN IT.
HE'S COMING AROUND...
VISION'S A SURVIVOR, SHARON...
WAIT--THIS IS YOUR PLAN? THE COMMAND DECK?
YEAH...THIS SHIP STILL HAS MISSILES LEFT TO FIRE...
THAT IS AN EXCELLENT PLAN, AGENT 13...

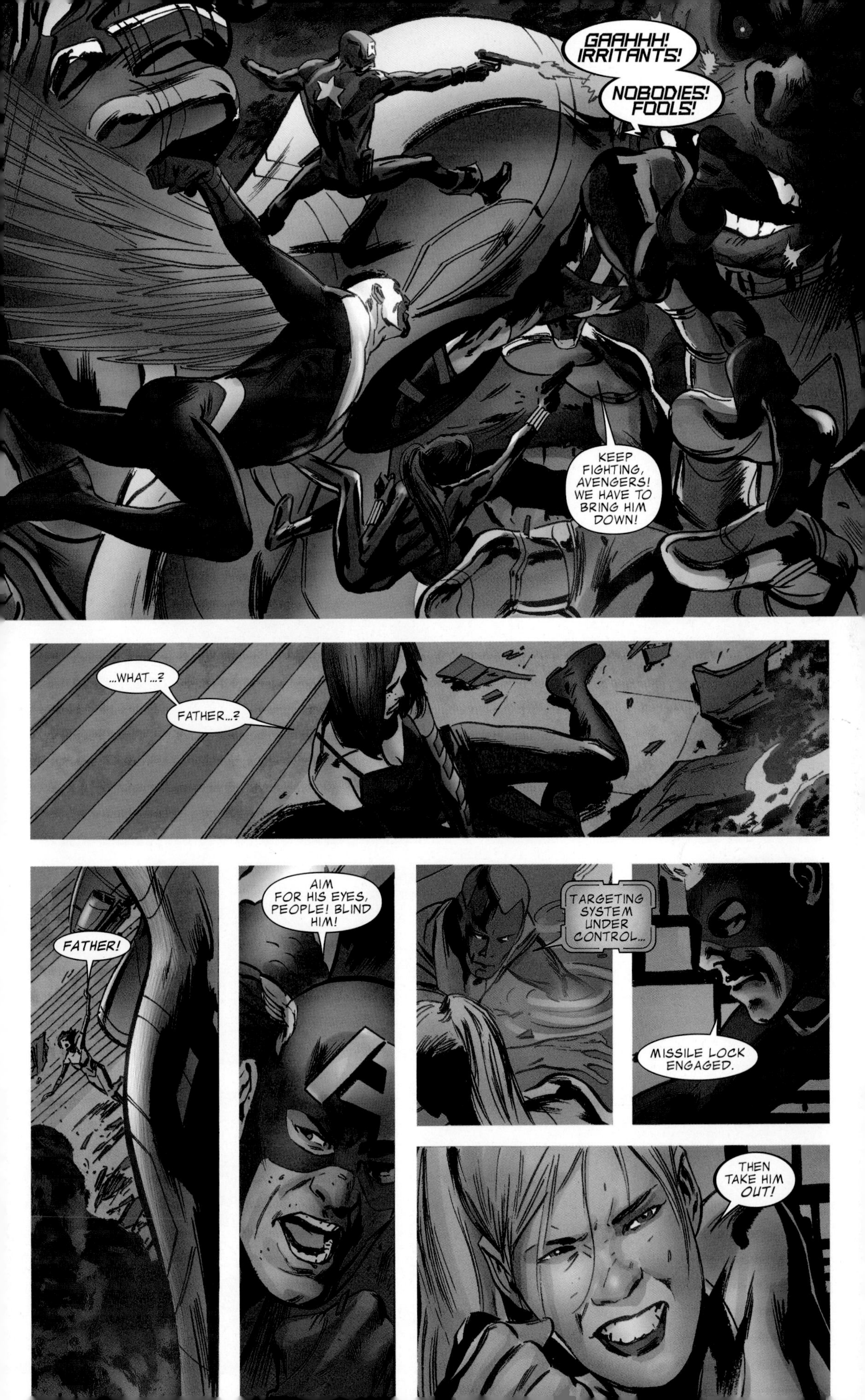
GAAHHH! IRRITANTS!
NOBODIES! FOOLS!
KEEP FIGHTING, AVENGERS! WE HAVE TO BRING HIM DOWN!
...WHAT...?
FATHER...?
FATHER!
AIM FOR HIS EYES, PEOPLE! BLIND HIM!
TARGETING SYSTEM UNDER CONTROL...
MISSILE LOCK ENGAGED.
THEN TAKE HIM OUT!

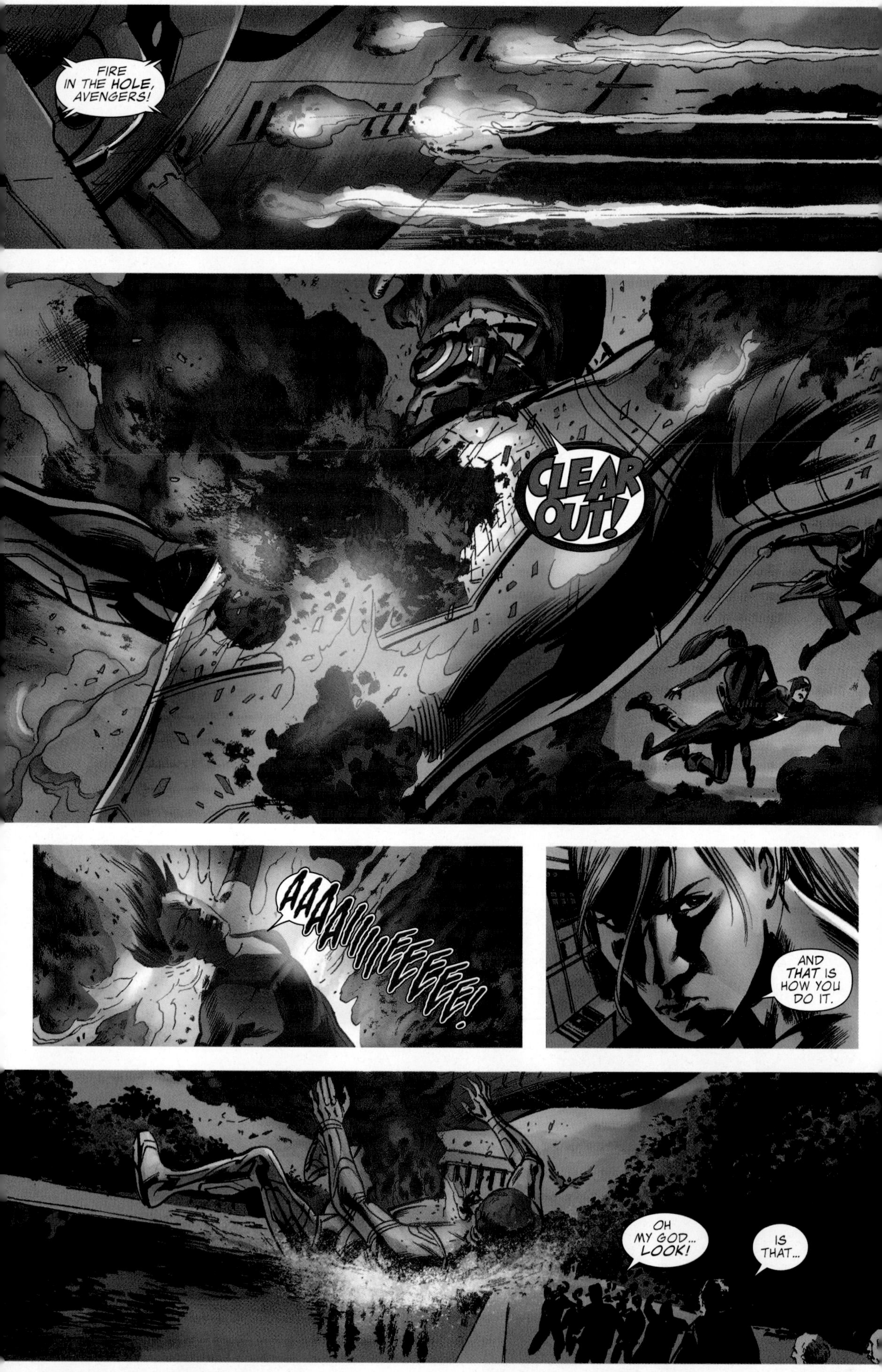
FIRE IN THE HOLE, AVENGERS!
CLEAR OUT!
AAAIIIIIEEEEEE!
AND THAT IS HOW YOU DO IT.
OH MY GOD... LOOK!
IS THAT...

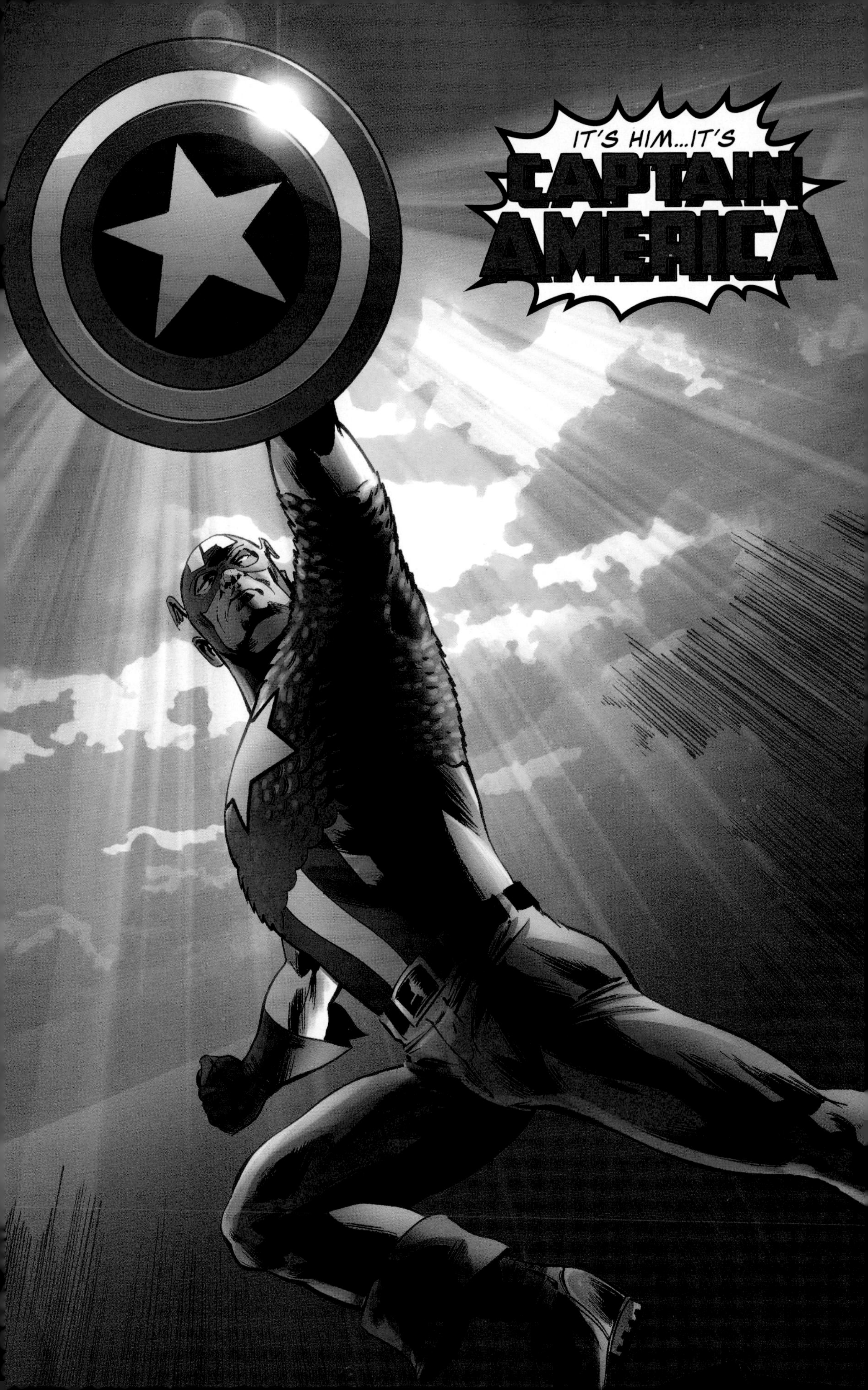
IT'S HIM...IT'S
CAPTAIN AMERICA

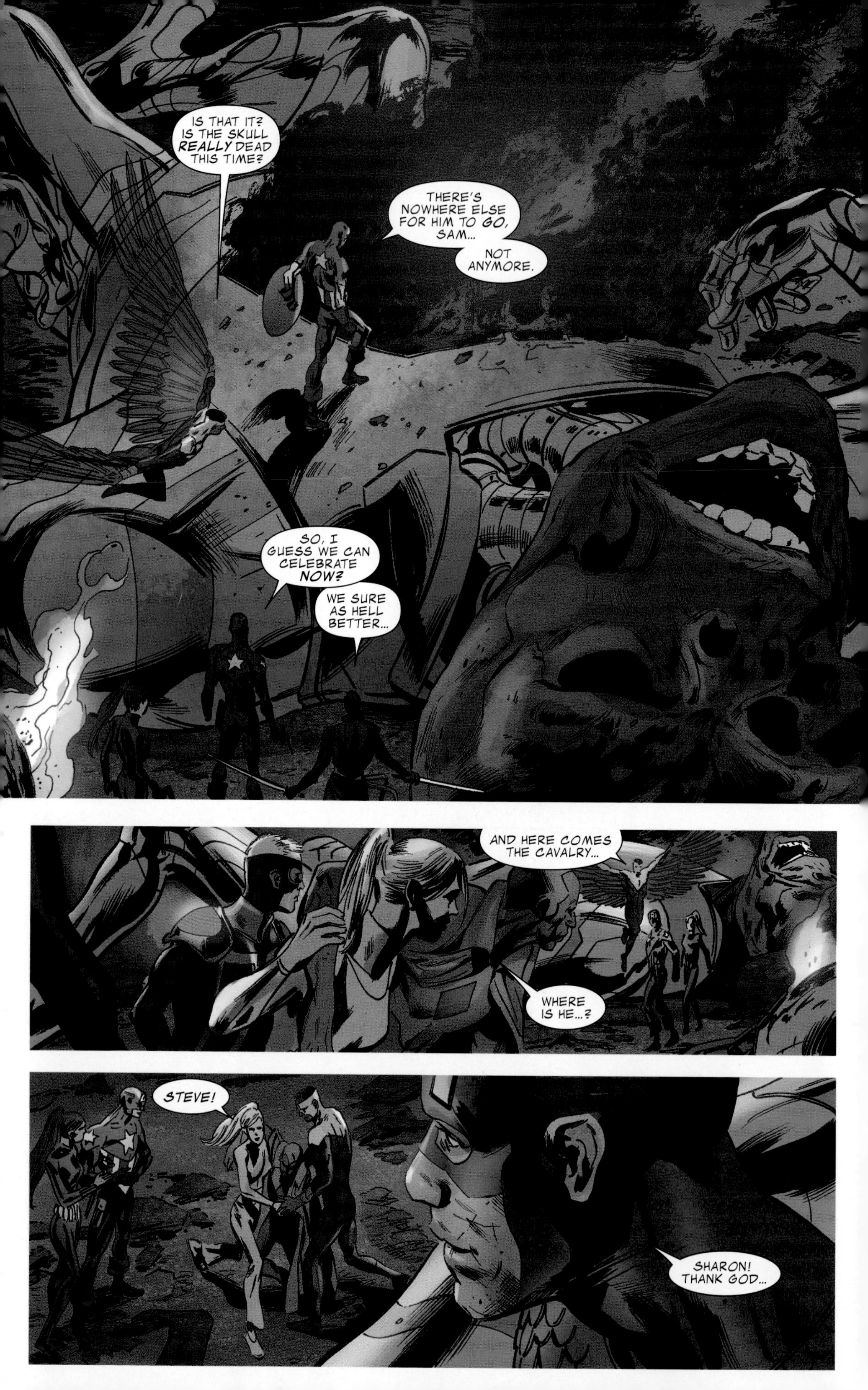
IS THAT IT? IS THE SKULL REALLY DEAD THIS TIME?
THERE'S NOWHERE ELSE FOR HIM TO GO, SAM...
NOT ANYMORE.
SO, I GUESS WE CAN CELEBRATE NOW?
WE SURE AS HELL BETTER...
AND HERE COMES THE CAVALRY...
WHERE IS HE...?
STEVE!
SHARON! THANK GOD...

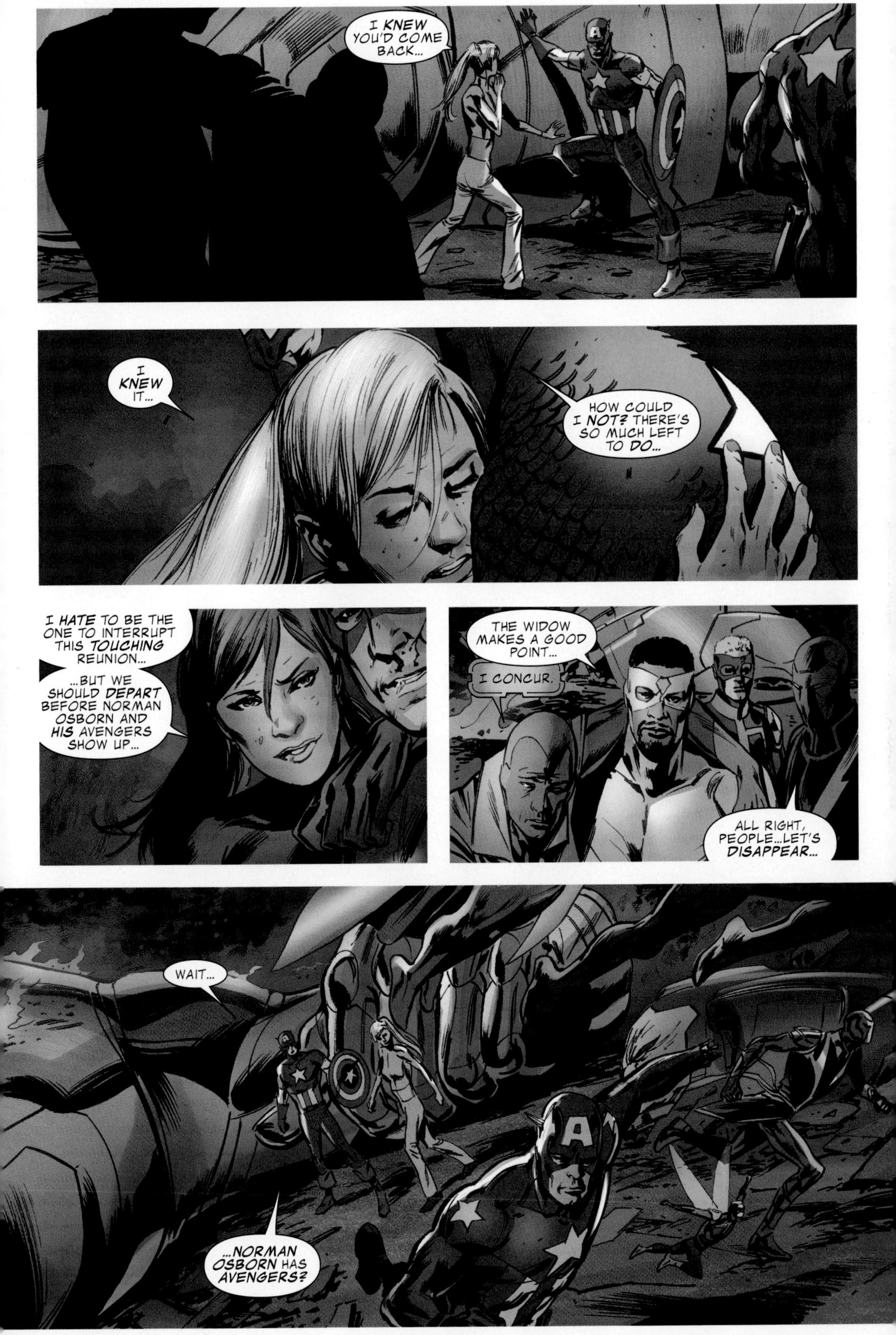
I KNEW YOU'D COME BACK...
I KNEW IT...
HOW COULD I NOT? THERE'S SO MUCH LEFT TO DO...
I HATE TO BE THE ONE TO INTERRUPT THIS TOUCHING REUNION...
...BUT WE SHOULD DEPART BEFORE NORMAN OSBORN AND HIS AVENGERS SHOW UP...
THE WIDOW MAKES A GOOD POINT...
I CONCUR.
ALL RIGHT, PEOPLE...LET'S DISAPPEAR...
WAIT...
...NORMAN OSBORN HAS AVENGERS?

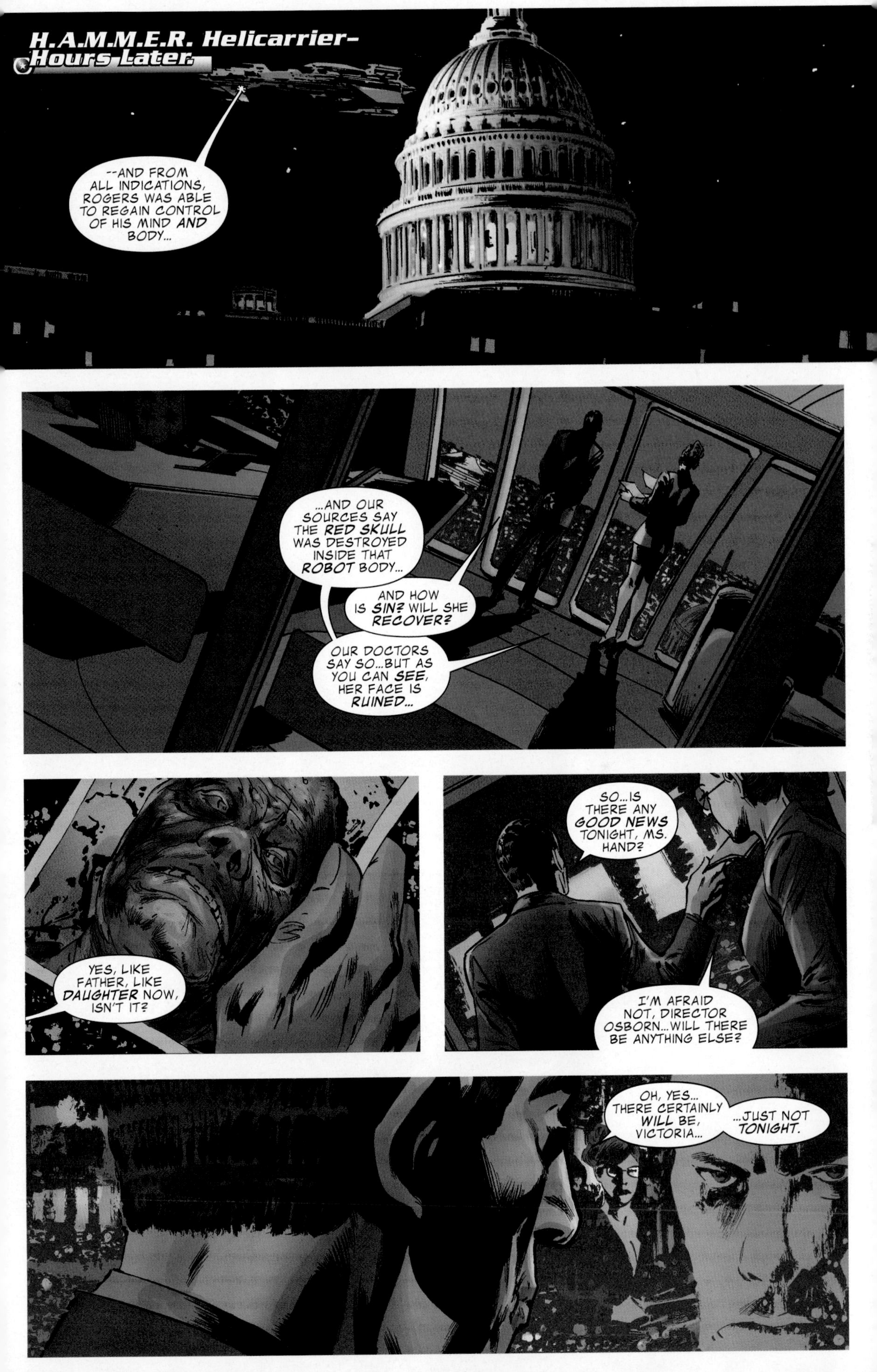
H.A.M.M.E.R. Helicarrier–
Hours Later.
--AND FROM ALL INDICATIONS, ROGERS WAS ABLE TO REGAIN CONTROL OF HIS MIND AND BODY...
...AND OUR SOURCES SAY THE RED SKULL WAS DESTROYED INSIDE THAT ROBOT BODY...
AND HOW IS SIN? WILL SHE RECOVER?
OUR DOCTORS SAY SO...BUT AS YOU CAN SEE, HER FACE IS RUINED...
YES, LIKE FATHER, LIKE DAUGHTER NOW, ISN'T IT?
SO...IS THERE ANY GOOD NEWS TONIGHT, MS. HAND?
I'M AFRAID NOT, DIRECTOR OSBORN...WILL THERE BE ANYTHING ELSE?
OH, YES... THERE CERTAINLY WILL BE, VICTORIA...
...JUST NOT TONIGHT.

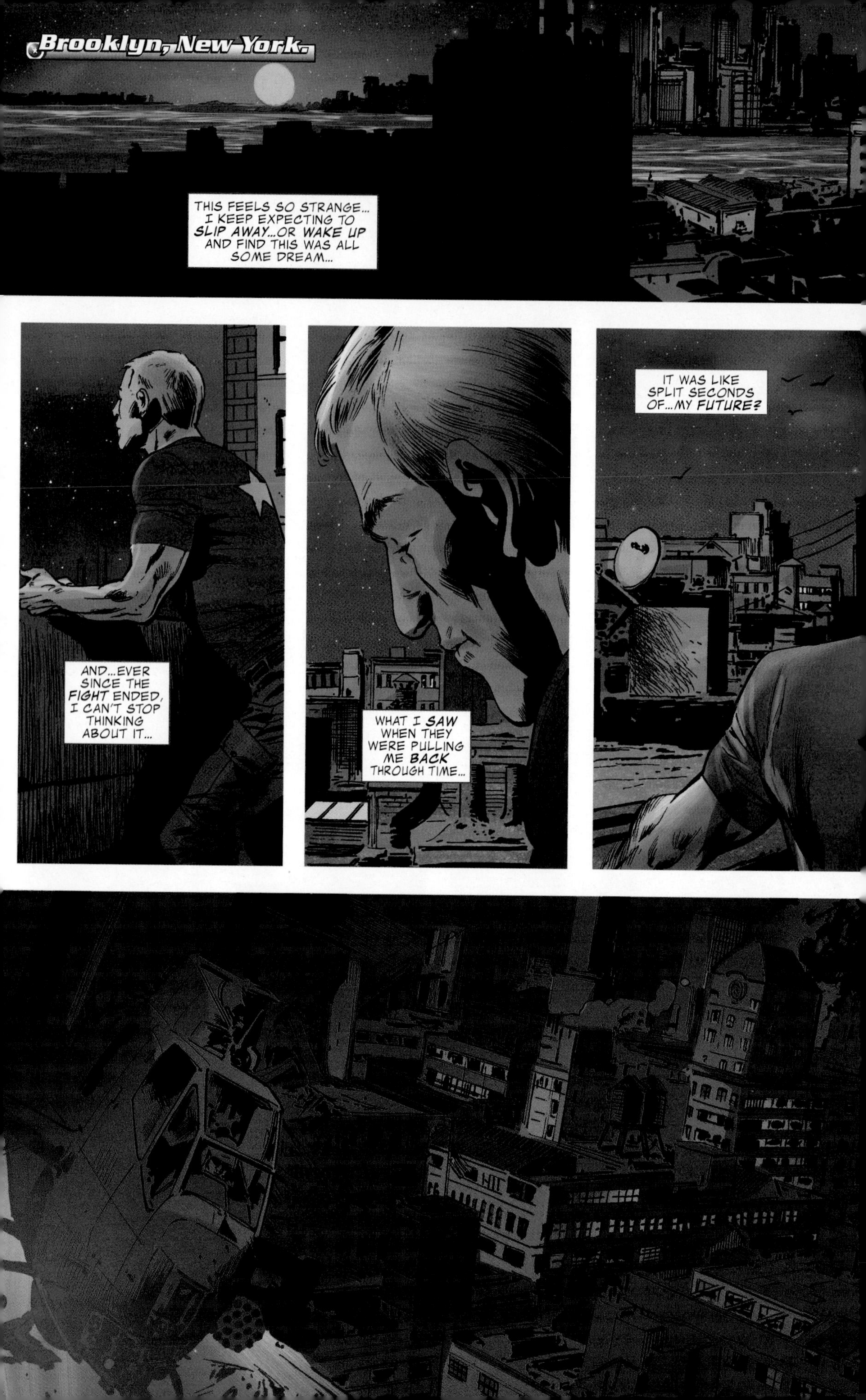
Brooklyn, New York.
THIS FEELS SO STRANGE... I KEEP EXPECTING TO SLIP AWAY...OR WAKE UP AND FIND THIS WAS ALL SOME DREAM...
AND...EVER SINCE THE FIGHT ENDED, I CAN'T STOP THINKING ABOUT IT...
WHAT I SAW WHEN THEY WERE PULLING ME BACK THROUGH TIME...
IT WAS LIKE SPLIT SECONDS OF...MY FUTURE?

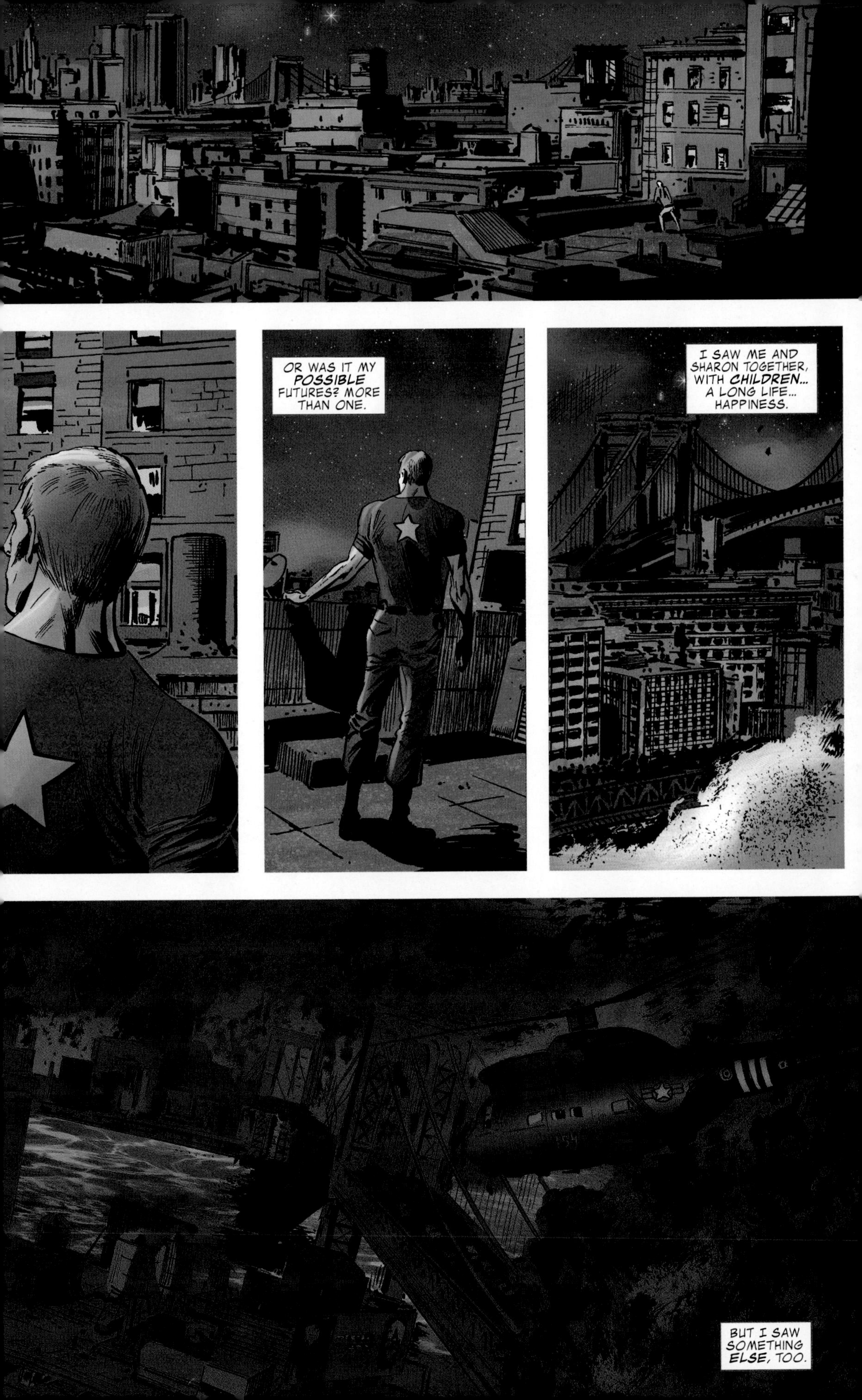
OR WAS IT MY POSSIBLE FUTURES? MORE THAN ONE.
I SAW ME AND SHARON TOGETHER, WITH CHILDREN... A LONG LIFE... HAPPINESS.
BUT I SAW SOMETHING ELSE, TOO.

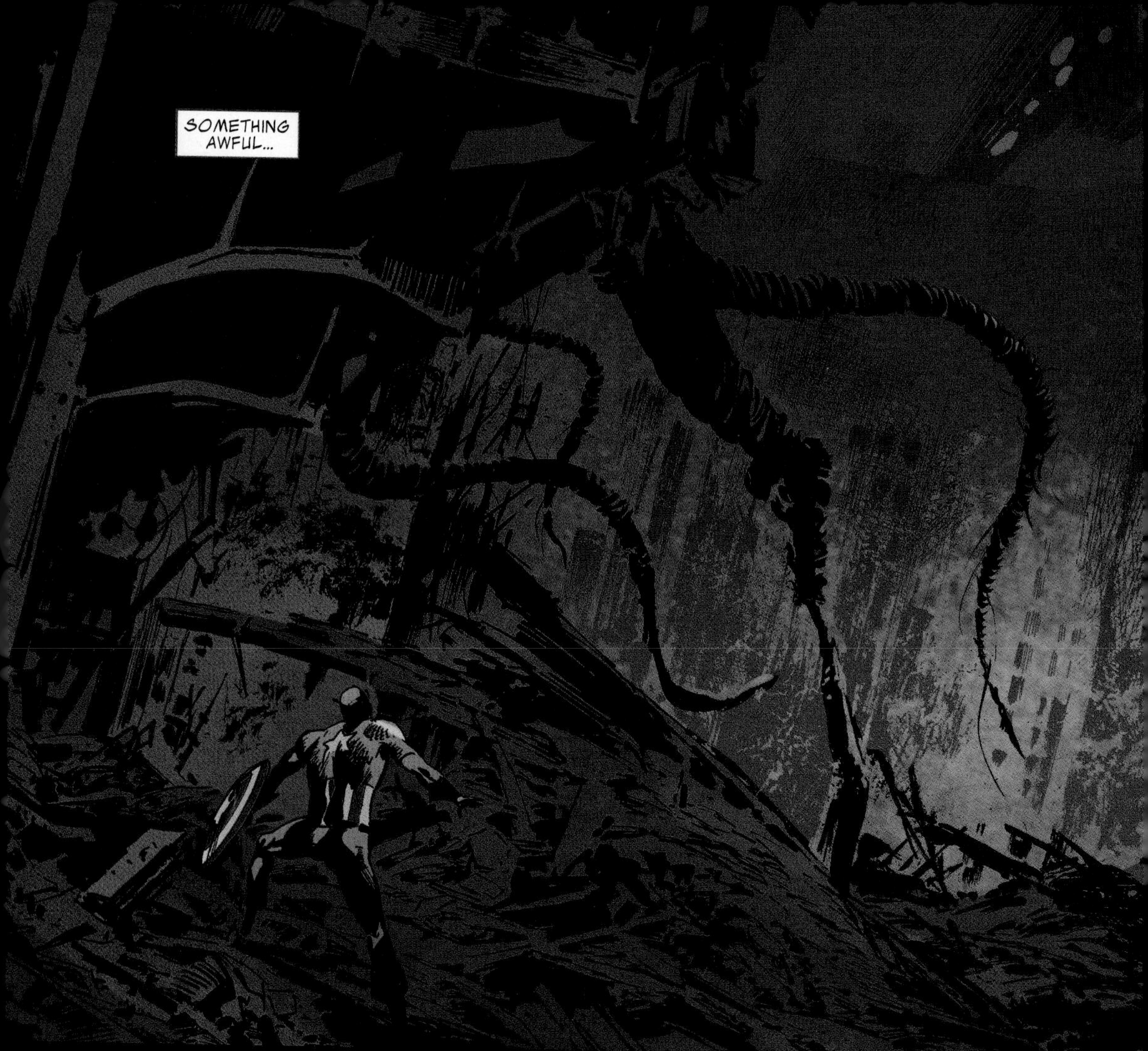
SOMETHING AWFUL...

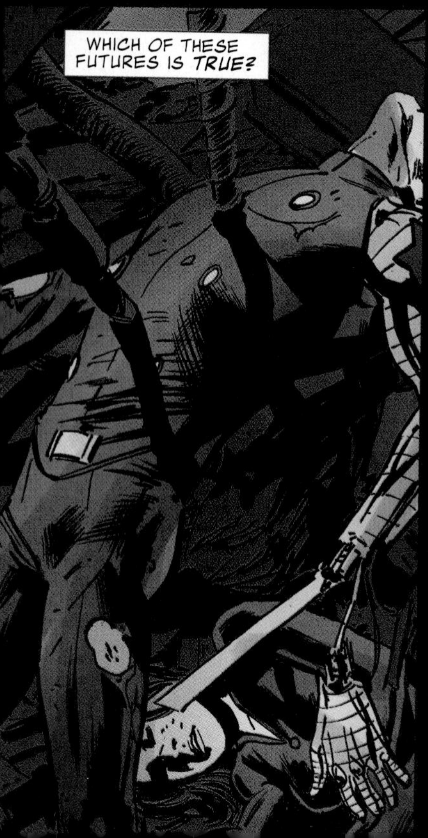
WHICH OF THESE FUTURES IS TRUE?

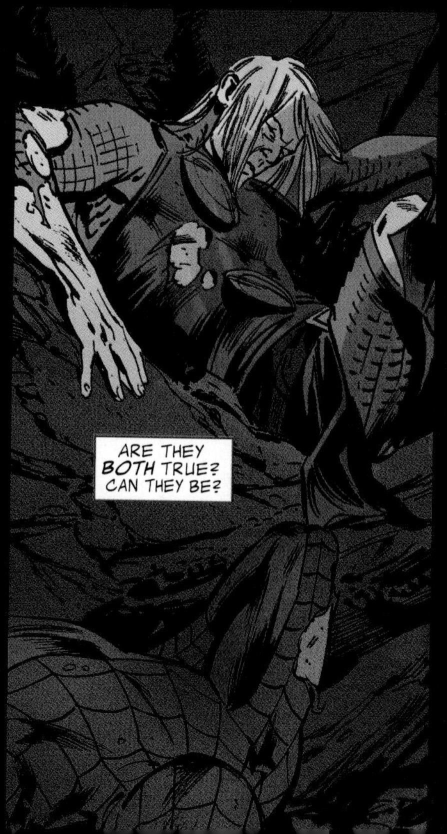
ARE THEY BOTH TRUE? CAN THEY BE?

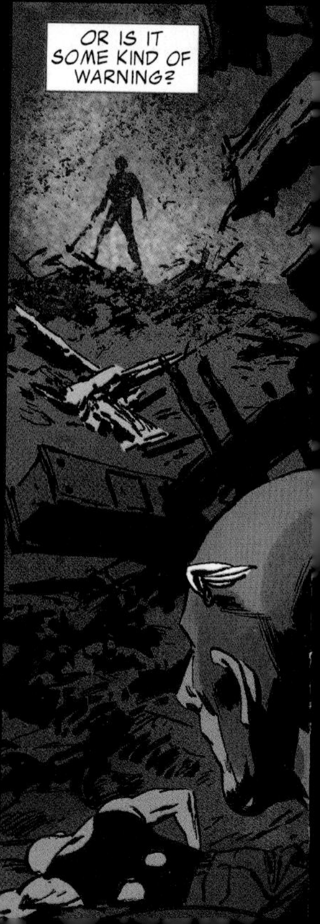
OR IS IT SOME KIND OF WARNING?

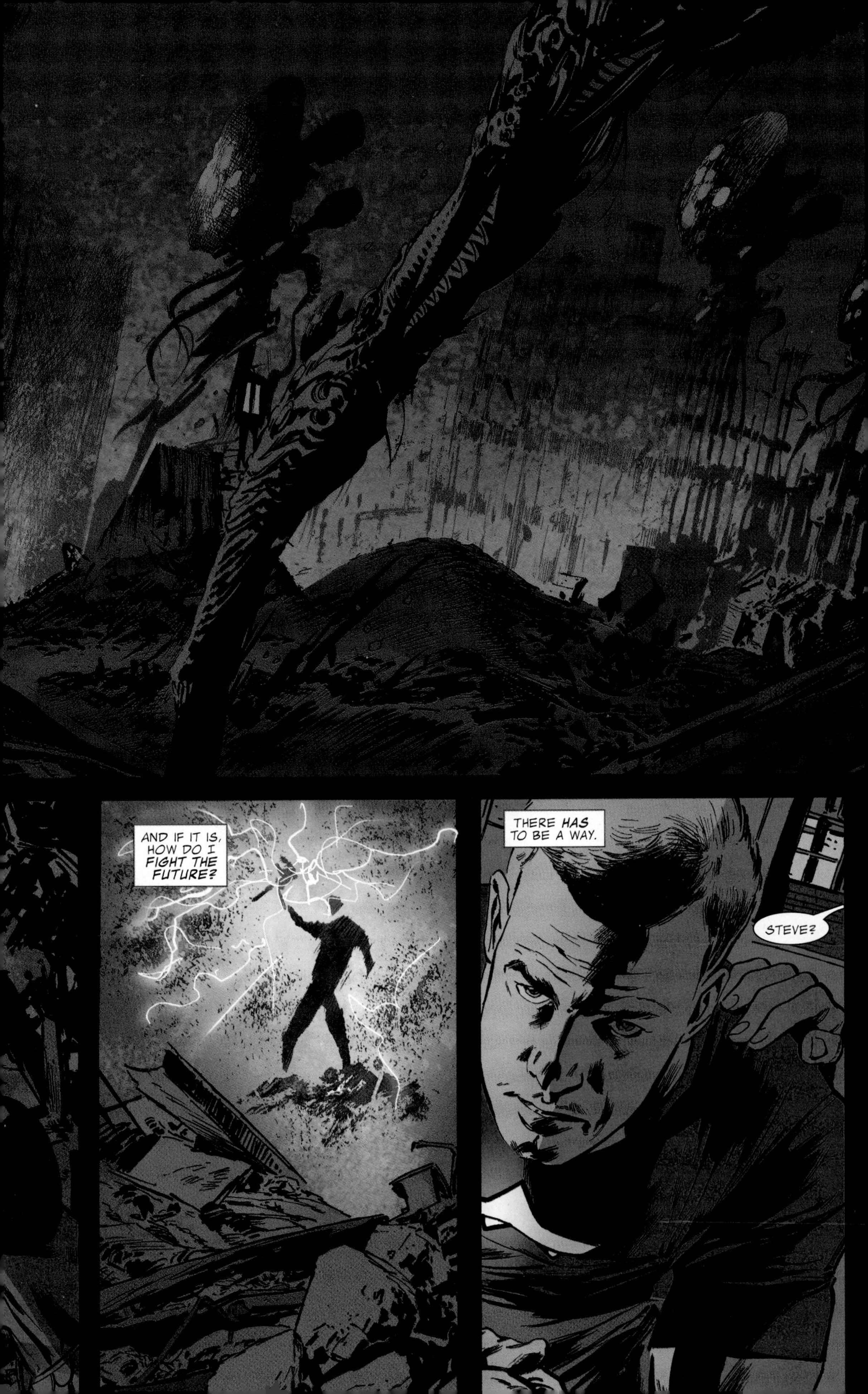
AND IF IT IS, HOW DO I FIGHT THE FUTURE?
THERE HAS TO BE A WAY.
STEVE?

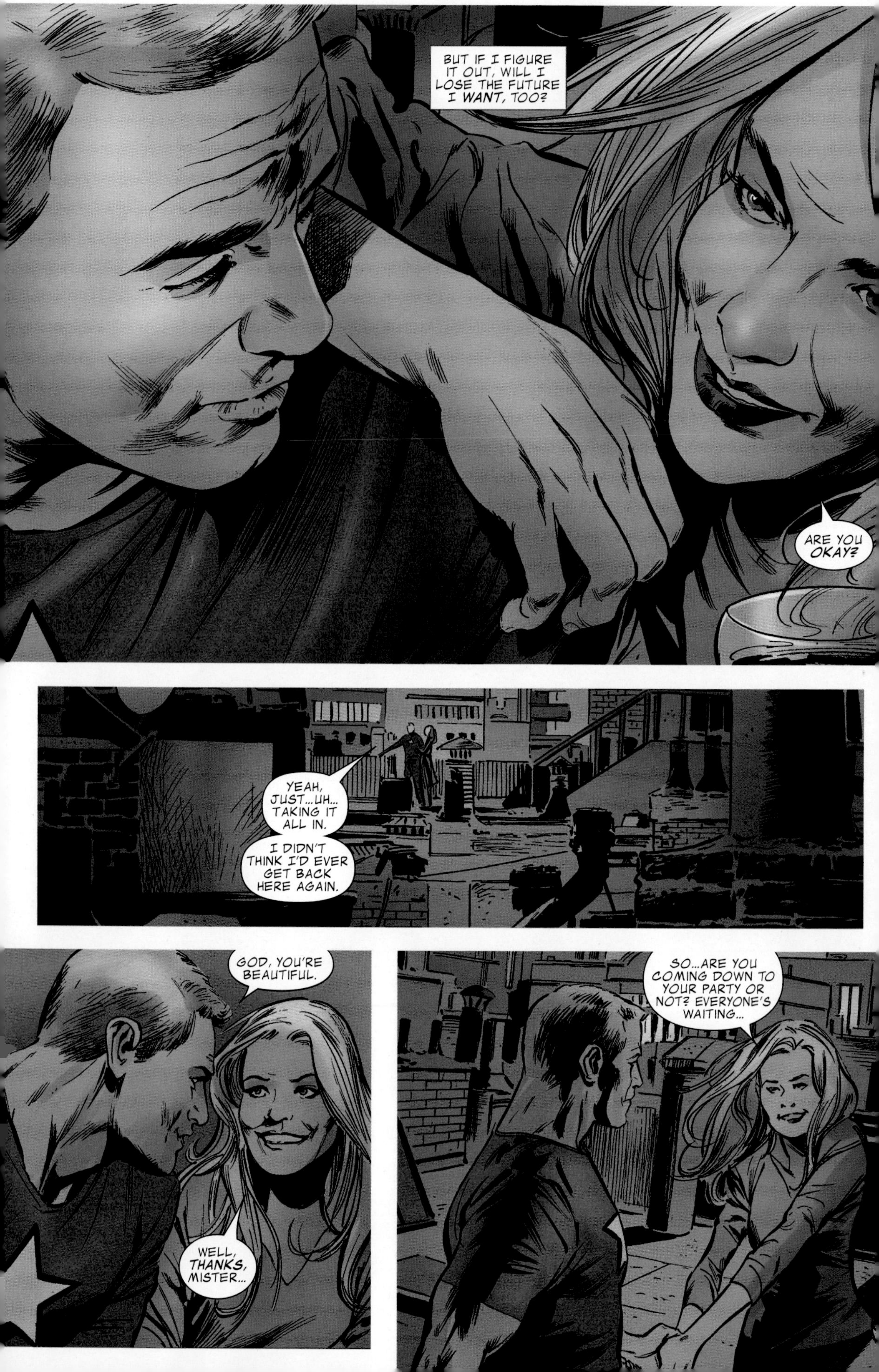
BUT IF I FIGURE IT OUT, WILL I LOSE THE FUTURE I WANT, TOO?
ARE YOU OKAY?
YEAH, JUST...UH... TAKING IT ALL IN.
I DIDN'T THINK I'D EVER GET BACK HERE AGAIN.
GOD, YOU'RE BEAUTIFUL.
WELL, THANKS, MISTER...
SO...ARE YOU COMING DOWN TO YOUR PARTY OR NOT? EVERYONE'S WAITING...

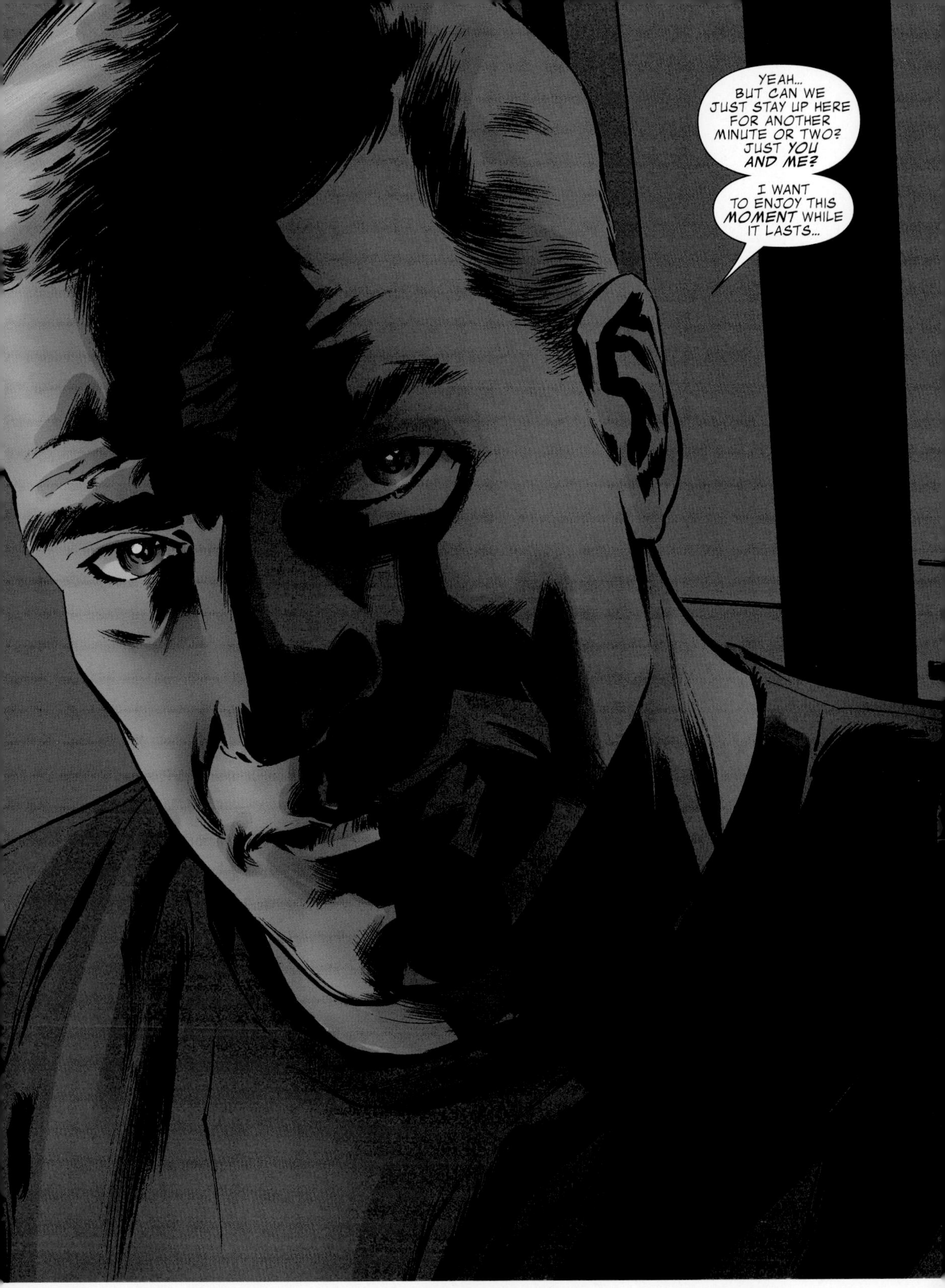
YEAH... BUT CAN WE JUST STAY UP HERE FOR ANOTHER MINUTE OR TWO? JUST *YOU AND ME?*
I WANT TO ENJOY THIS *MOMENT* WHILE IT LASTS...

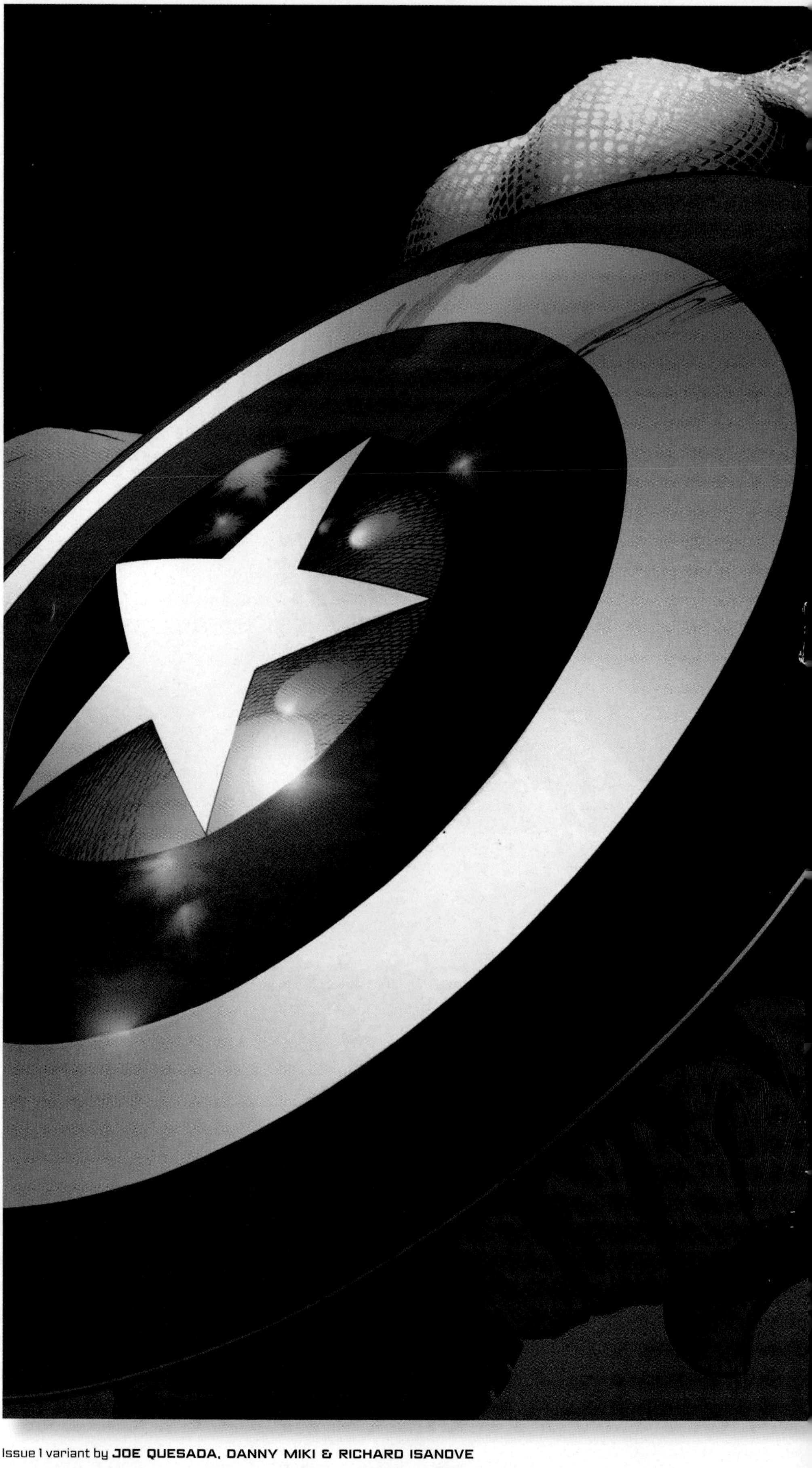

Issue 1 variant by **JOE QUESADA, DANNY MIKI & RICHARD ISANOVE**

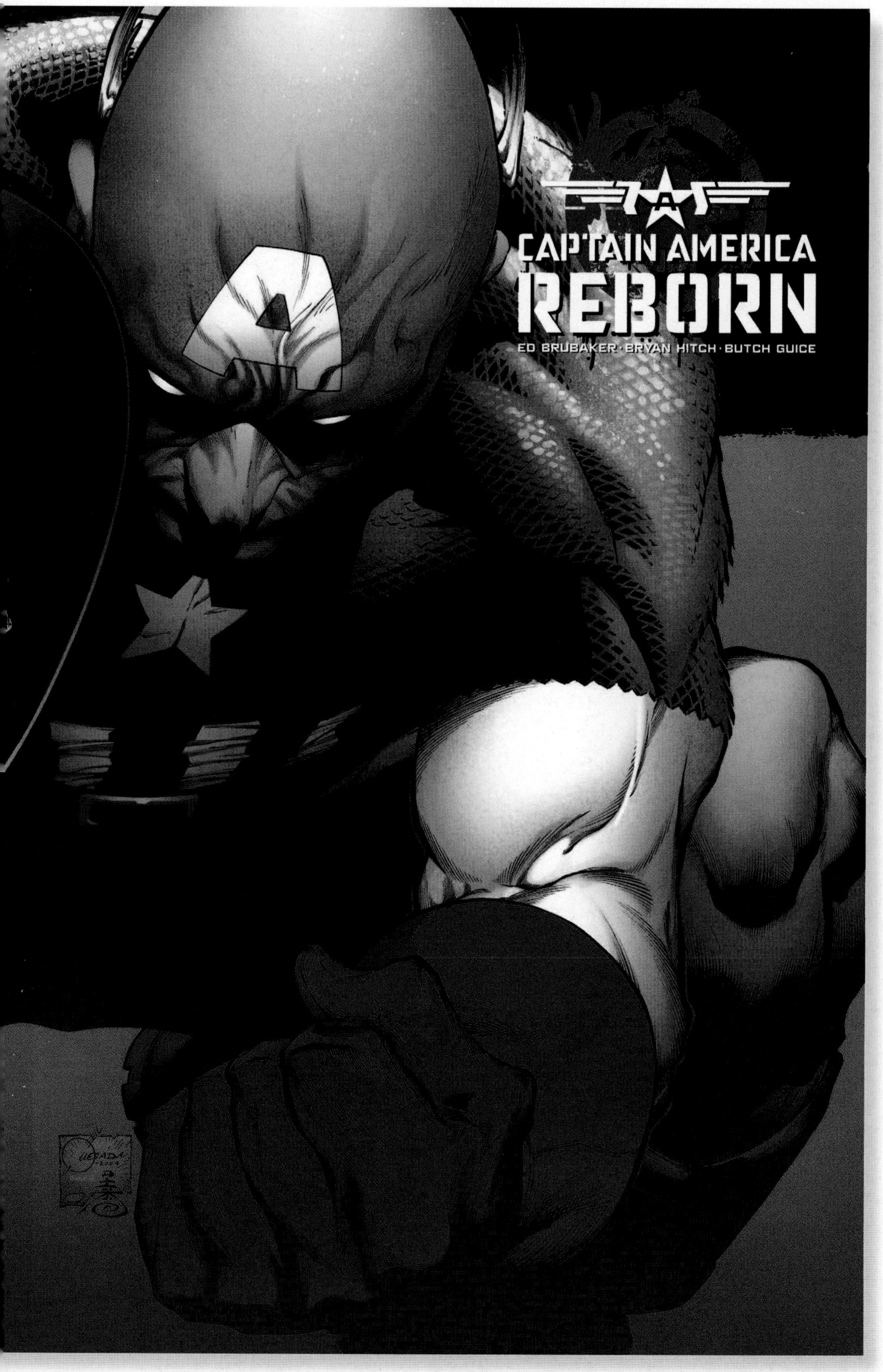
CAPTAIN AMERICA
REBORN
ED BRUBAKER · BRYAN HITCH · BUTCH GUICE

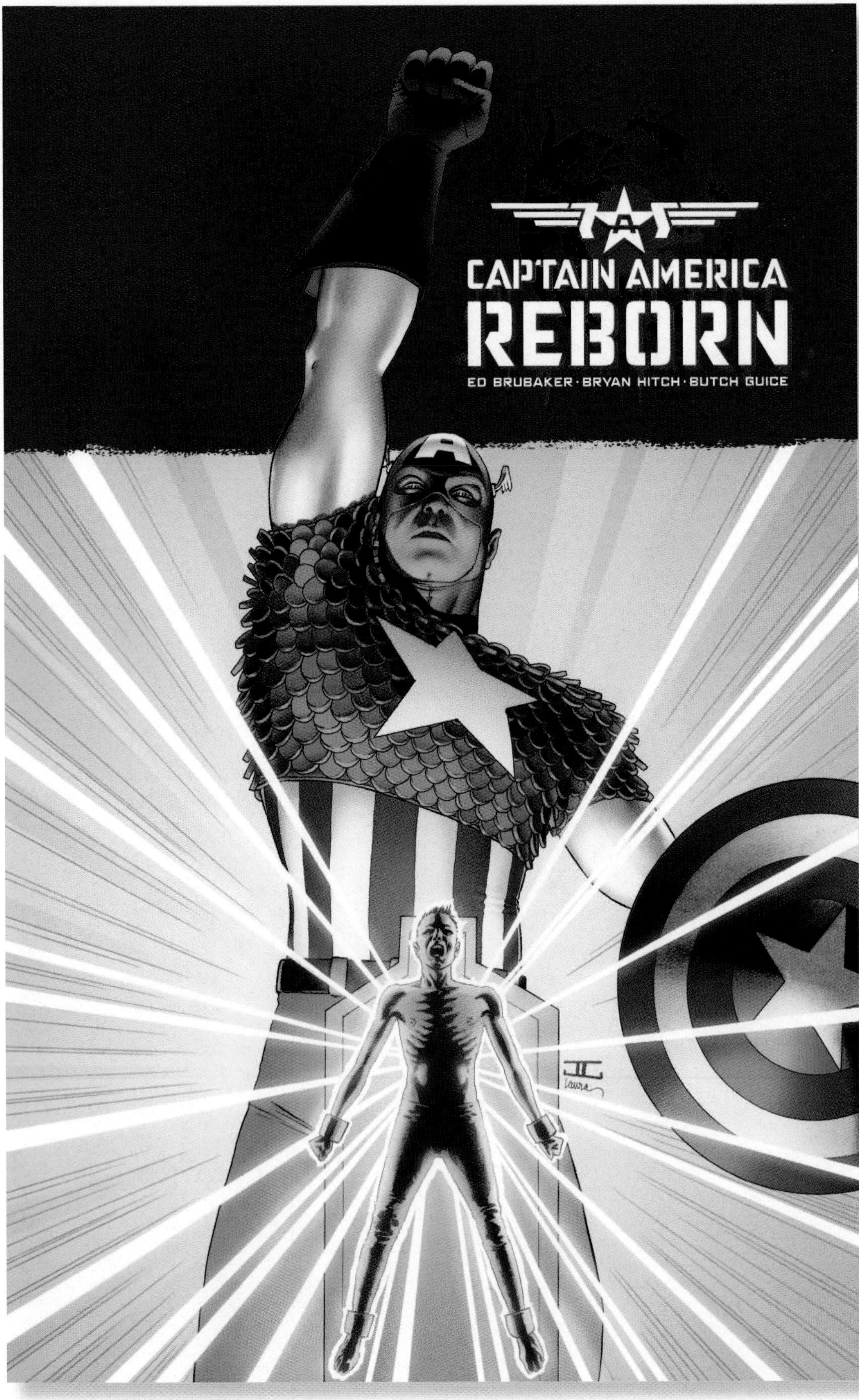
CAPTAIN AMERICA
REBORN
ED BRUBAKER · BRYAN HITCH · BUTCH GUICE
Issue 1 variant by **JOHN CASSADAY & LAURA MARTIN**

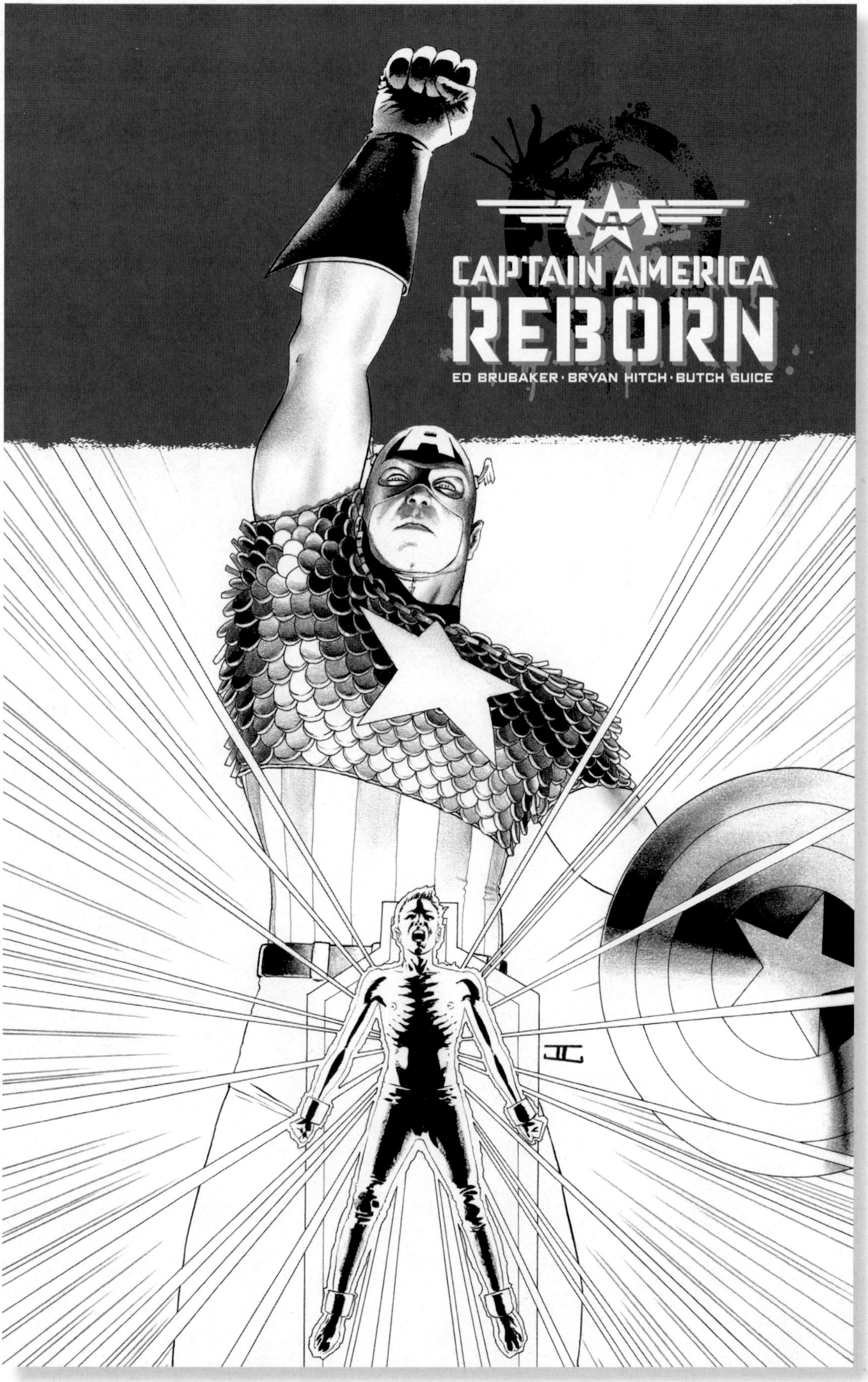
CAPTAIN AMERICA
REBORN
ED BRUBAKER · BRYAN HITCH · BUTCH GUICE

Issue 1 sketch variant by **JOHN CASSADAY**

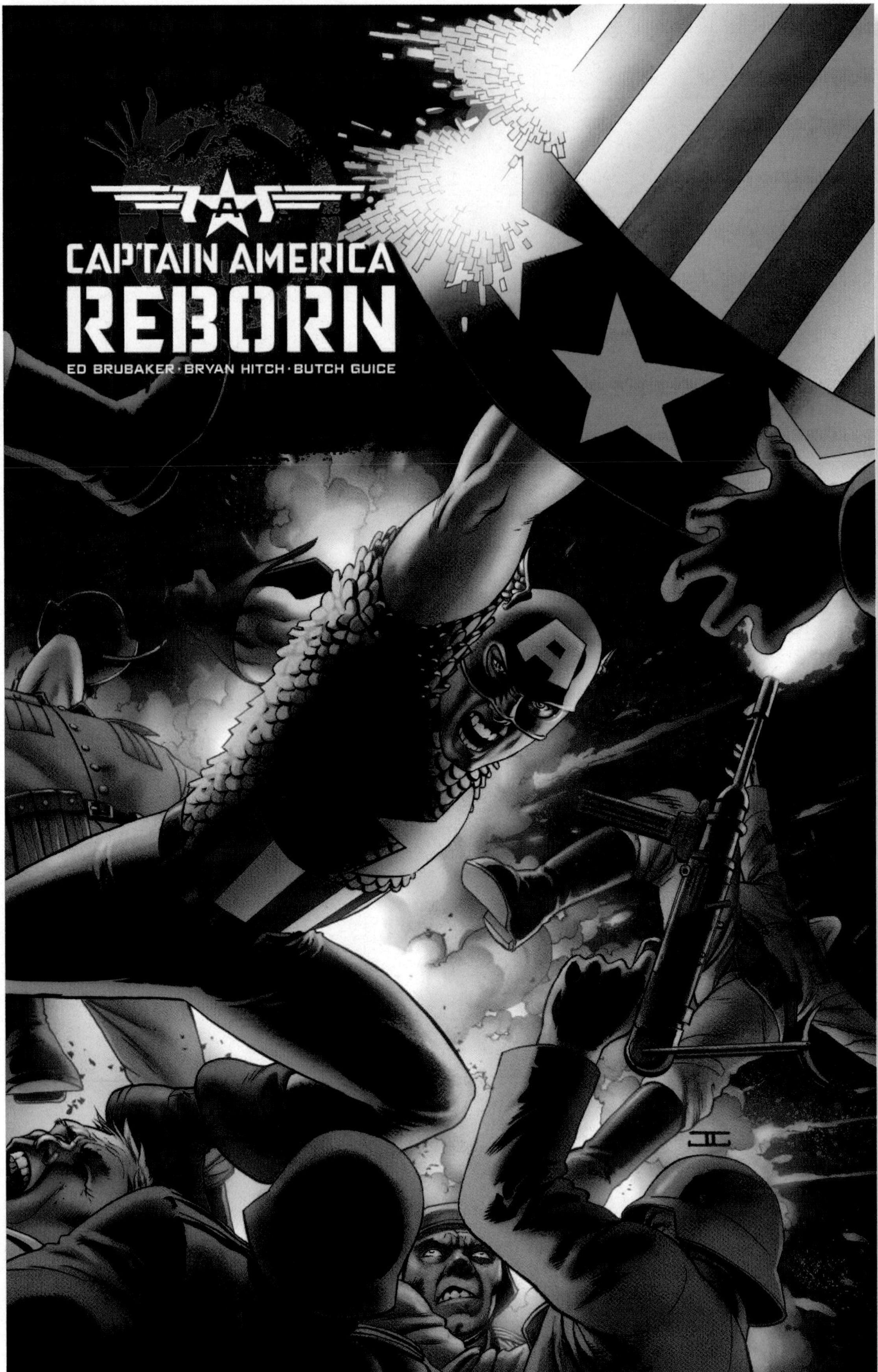

Issue 2 variant by **JOHN CASSADAY & LAURA MARTIN**

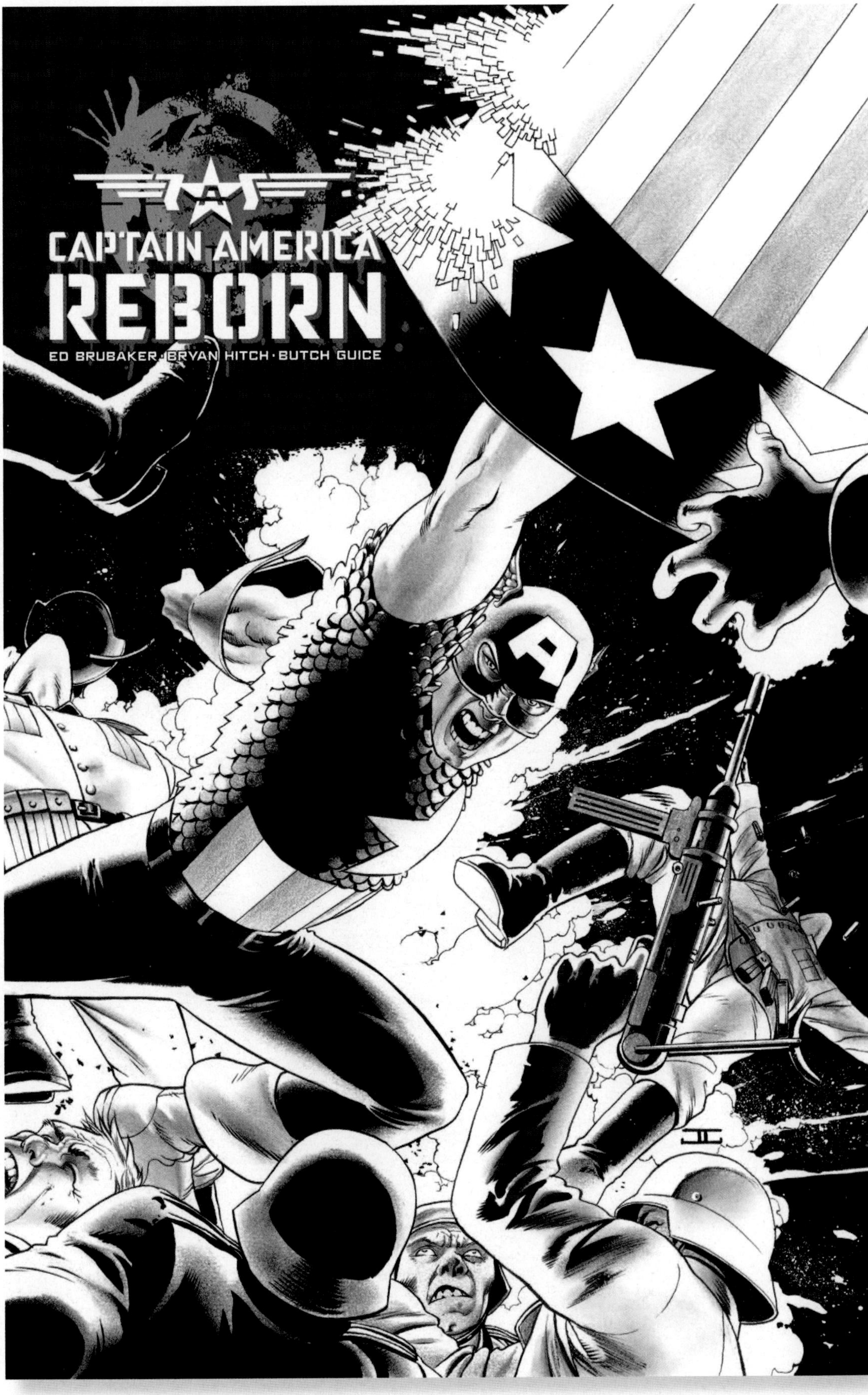
CAPTAIN AMERICA
REBORN
ED BRUBAKER · BRYAN HITCH · BUTCH GUICE

Issue 2 sketch variant by **JOHN CASSADAY**

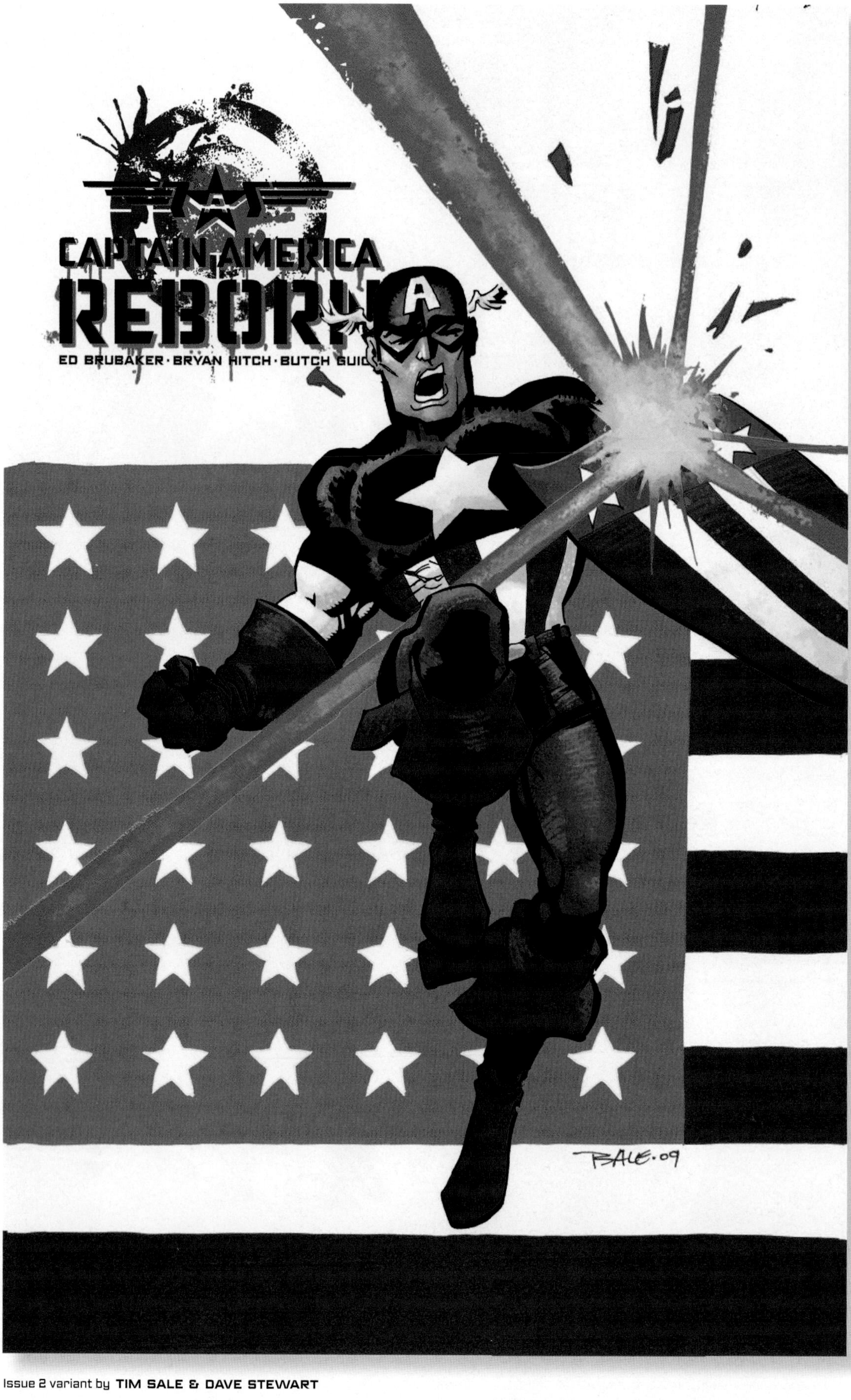

CAPTAIN AMERICA
REBORN
ED BRUBAKER · BRYAN HITCH · BUTCH GUIC
SALE·09

Issue 2 variant by **TIM SALE & DAVE STEWART**

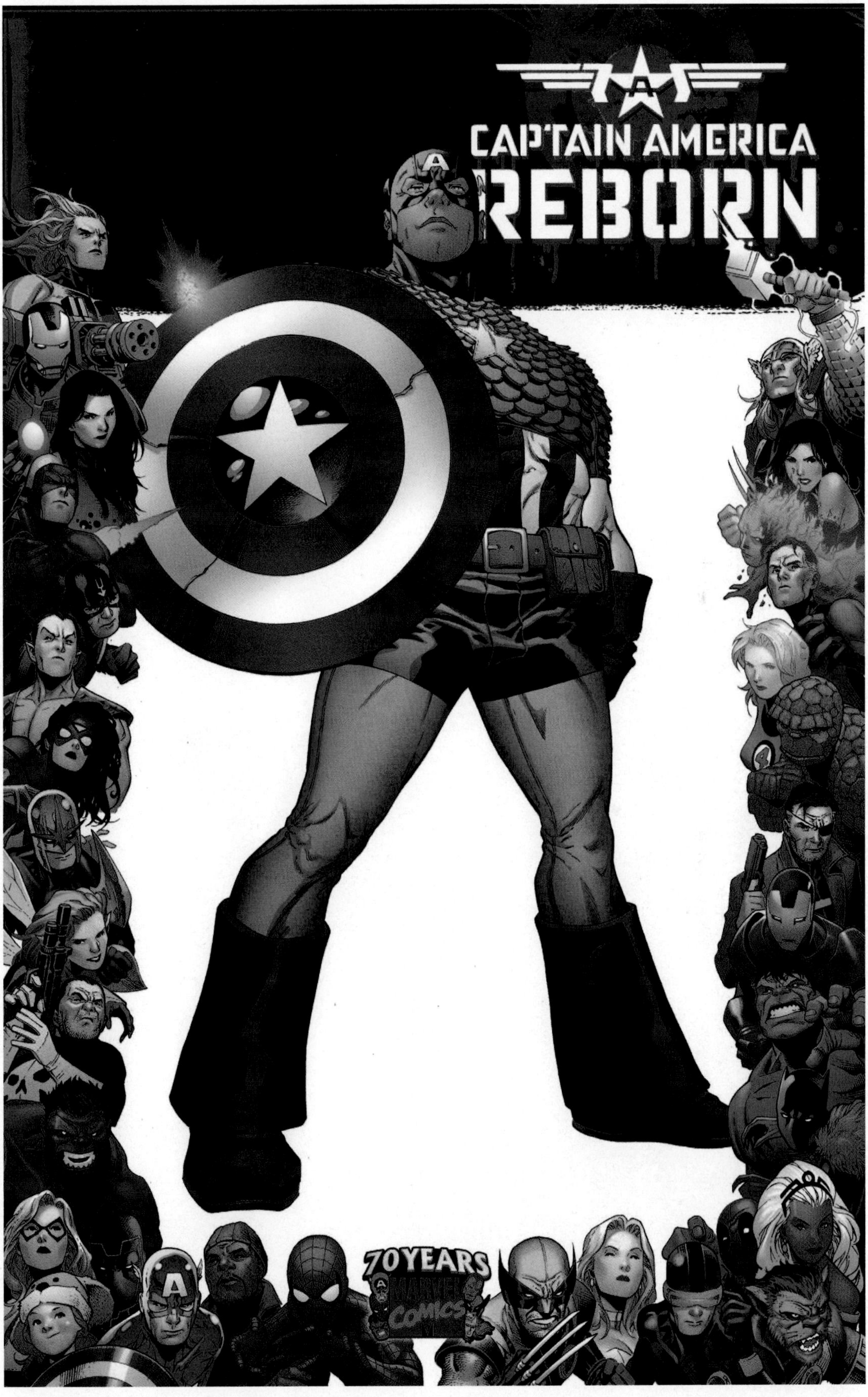
CAPTAIN AMERICA
REBORN
70 YEARS
MARVEL
COMICS

Issue 2 70th Anniversary Frame variant by **JOE QUESADA, DANNY MIKI & RICHARD ISANOVE**

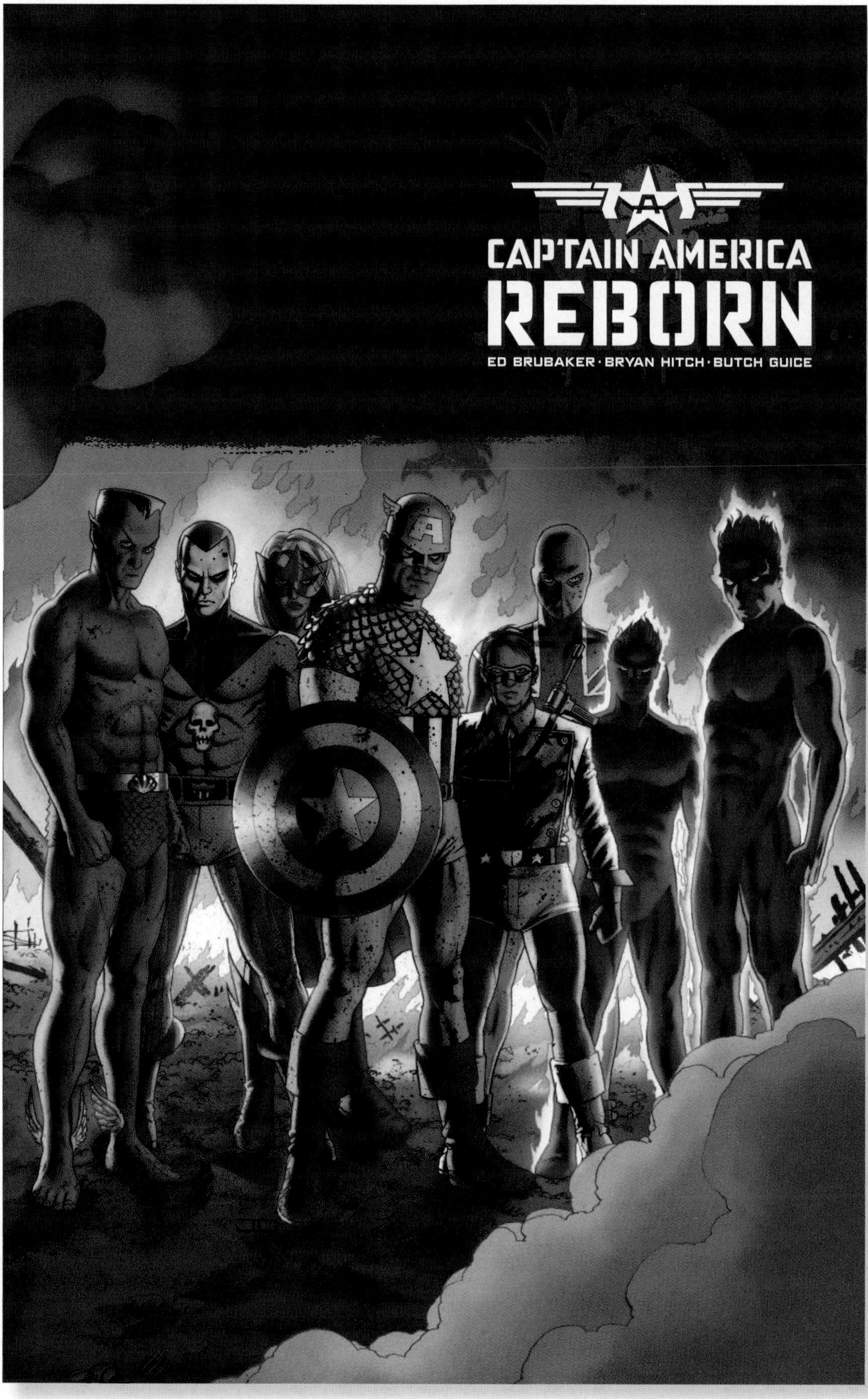
CAPTAIN AMERICA
REBORN
ED BRUBAKER · BRYAN HITCH · BUTCH GUICE

Issue 3 variant by **JOHN CASSADAY & LAURA MARTIN**

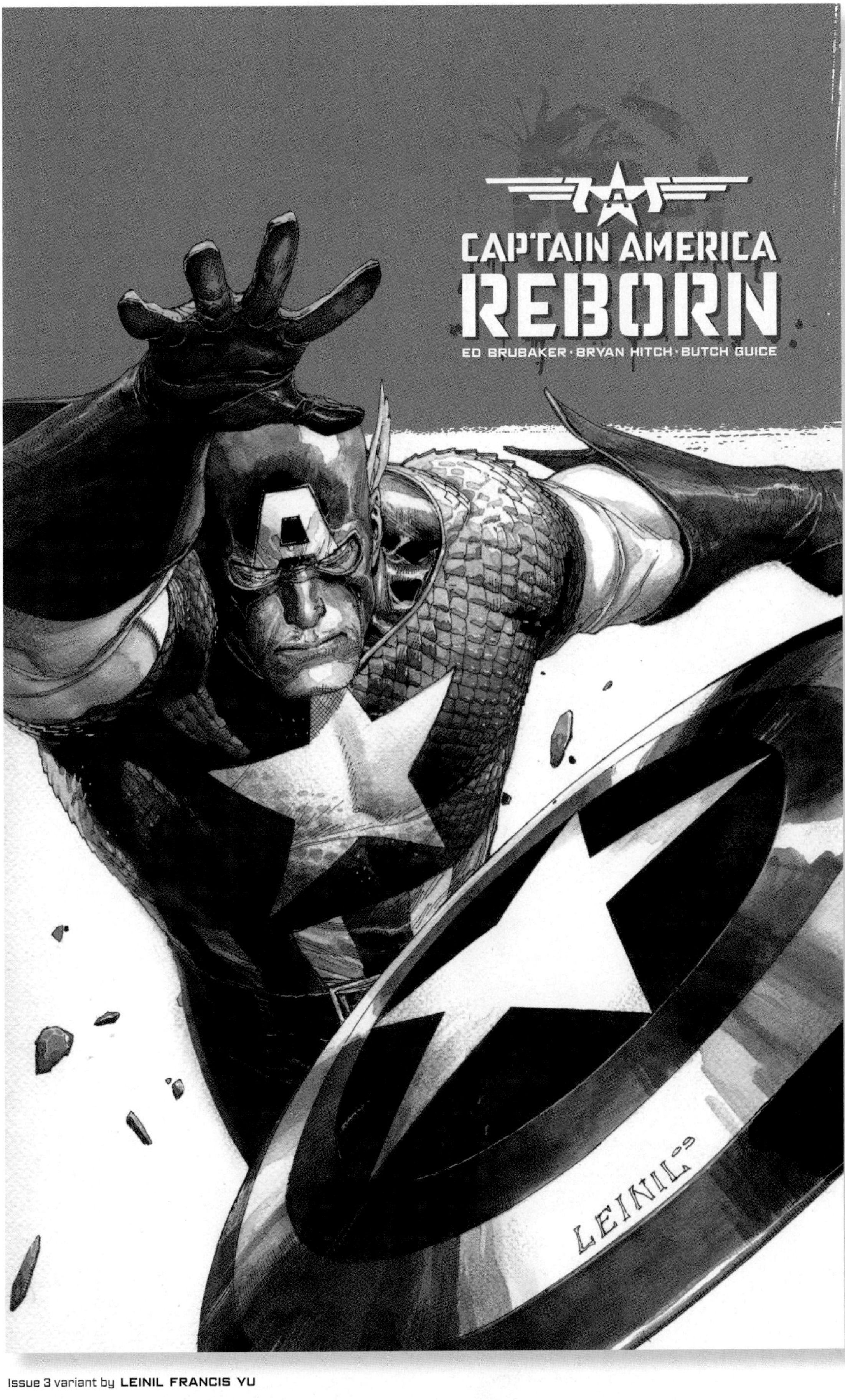
CAPTAIN AMERICA
REBORN
ED BRUBAKER · BRYAN HITCH · BUTCH GUICE
LEINIL '09

Issue 3 variant by **LEINIL FRANCIS YU**

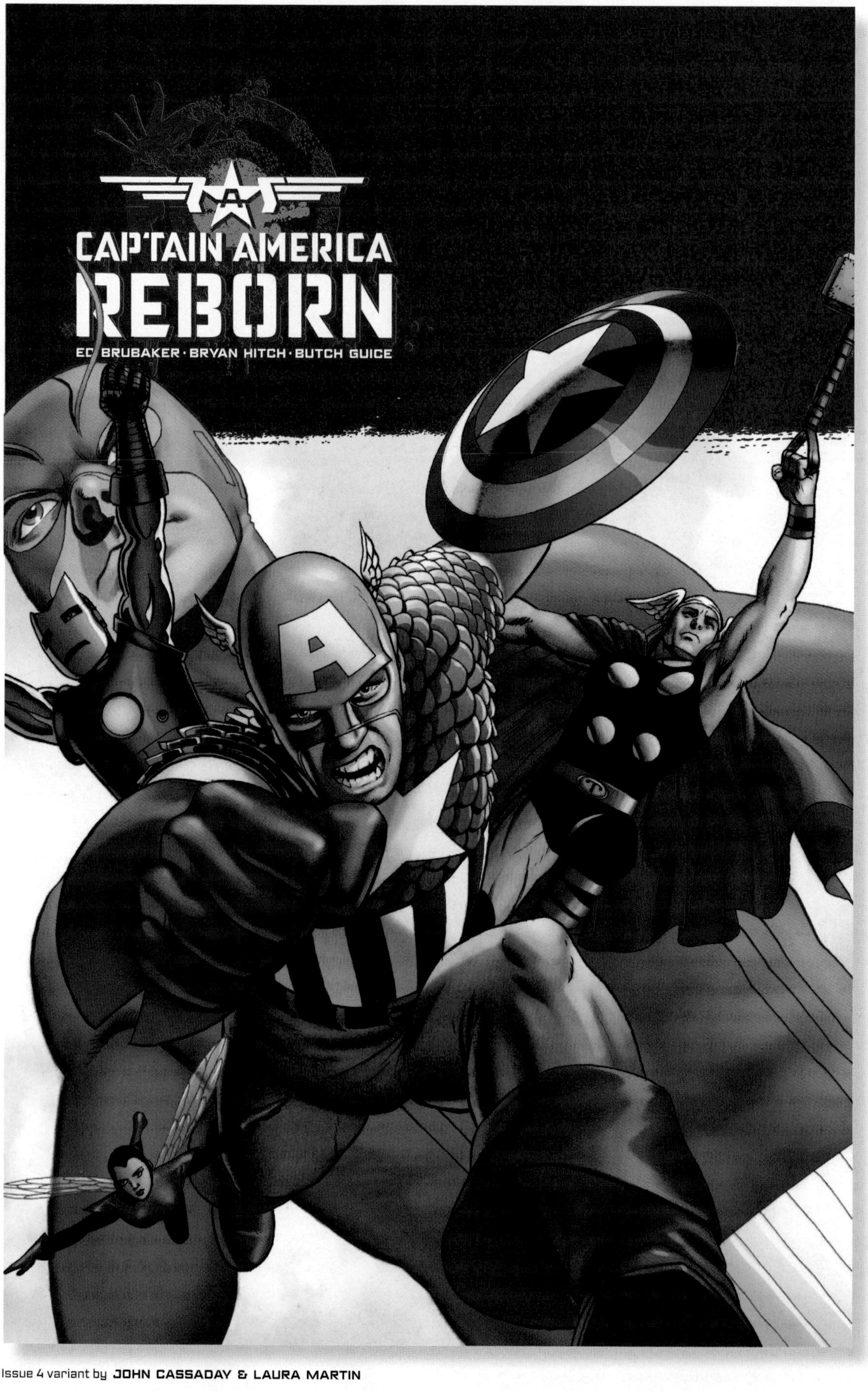
CAPTAIN AMERICA
REBORN
ED BRUBAKER · BRYAN HITCH · BUTCH GUICE

Issue 4 variant by **JOHN CASSADAY & LAURA MARTIN**

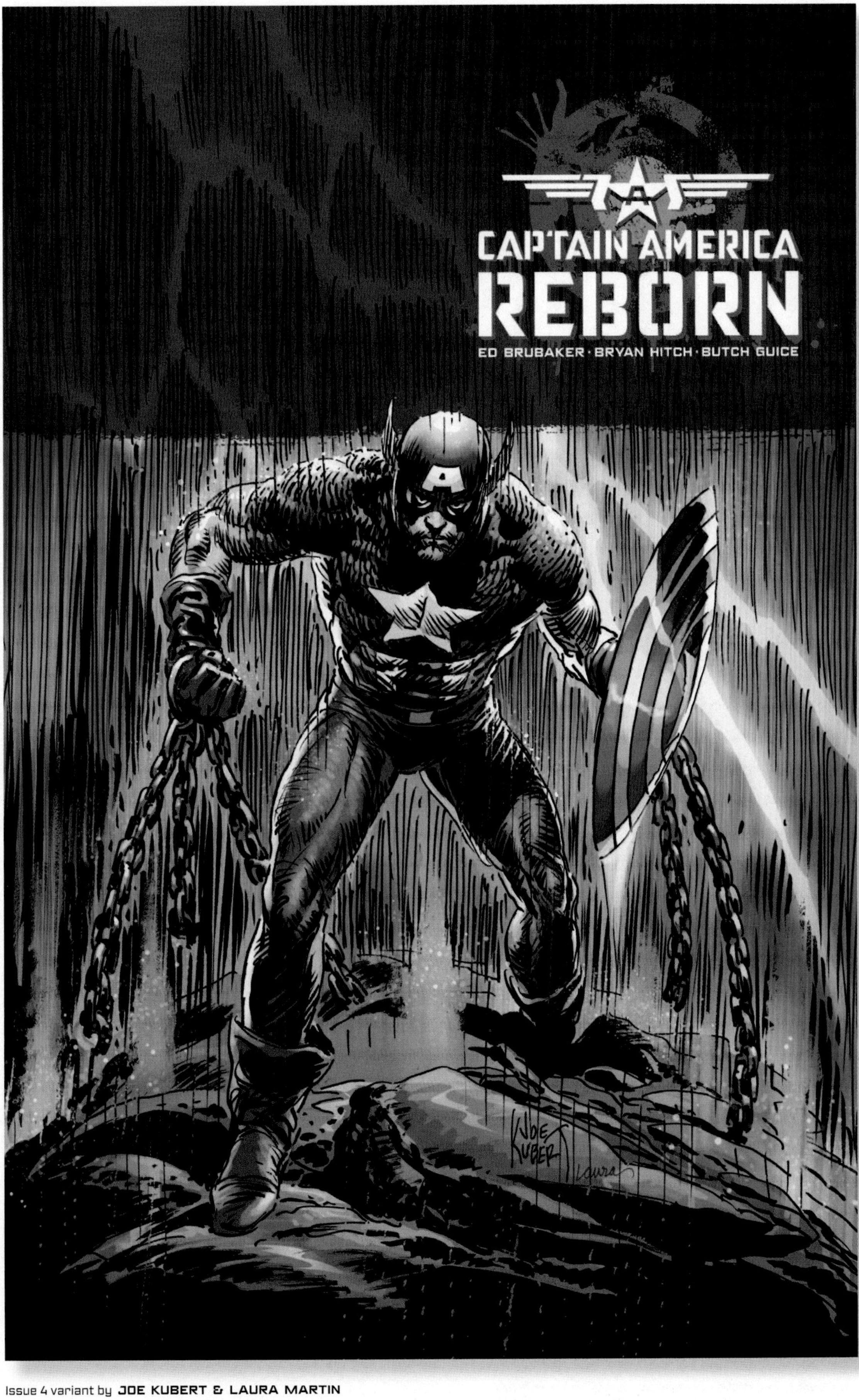
CAPTAIN AMERICA
REBORN
ED BRUBAKER · BRYAN HITCH · BUTCH GUICE

Issue 4 variant by **JOE KUBERT & LAURA MARTIN**

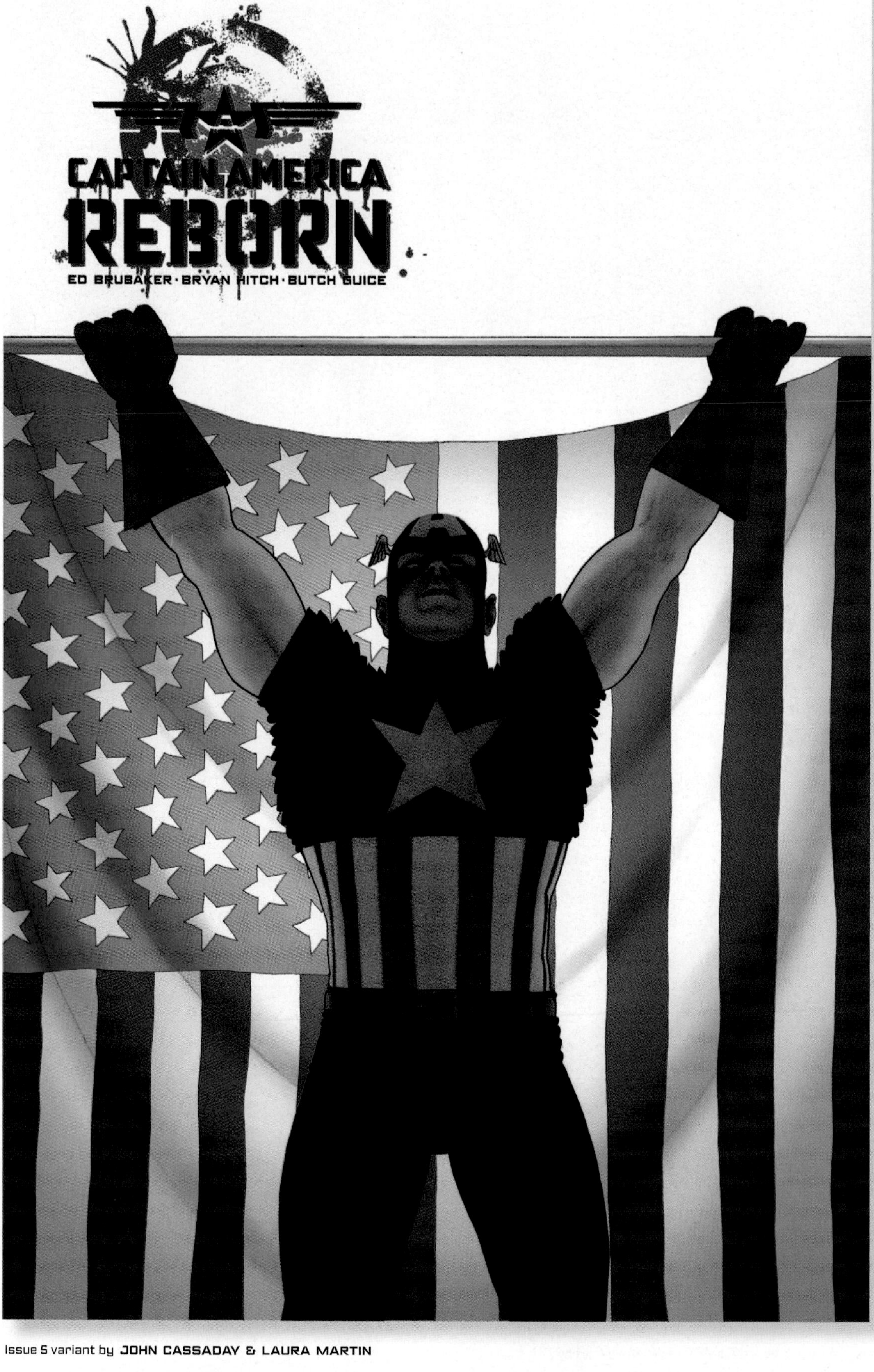
CAPTAIN AMERICA
REBORN
ED BRUBAKER · BRYAN HITCH · BUTCH GUICE

Issue 5 variant by **JOHN CASSADAY & LAURA MARTIN**

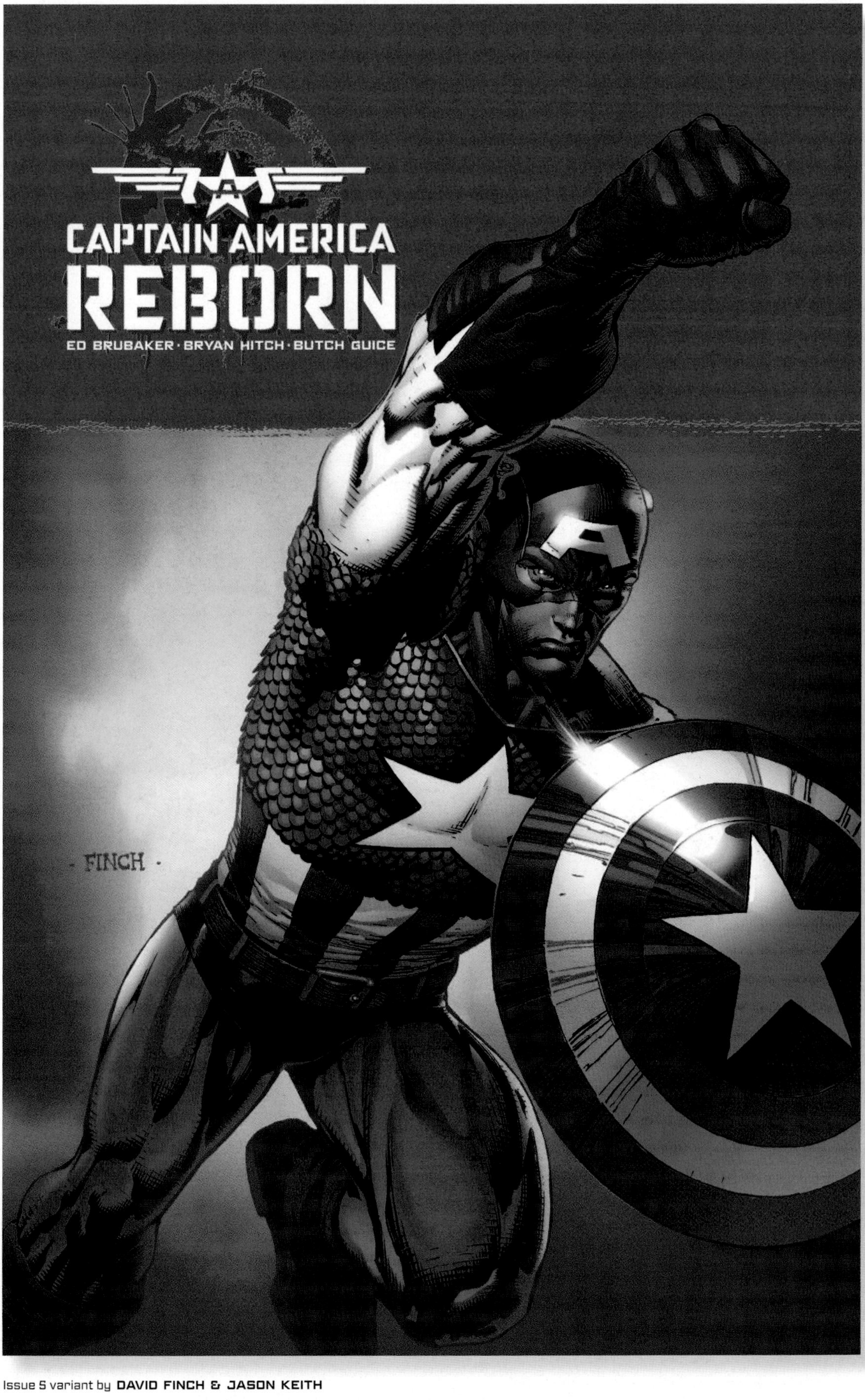
CAPTAIN AMERICA
REBORN
ED BRUBAKER · BRYAN HITCH · BUTCH GUICE
FINCH

Issue 5 variant by **DAVID FINCH & JASON KEITH**

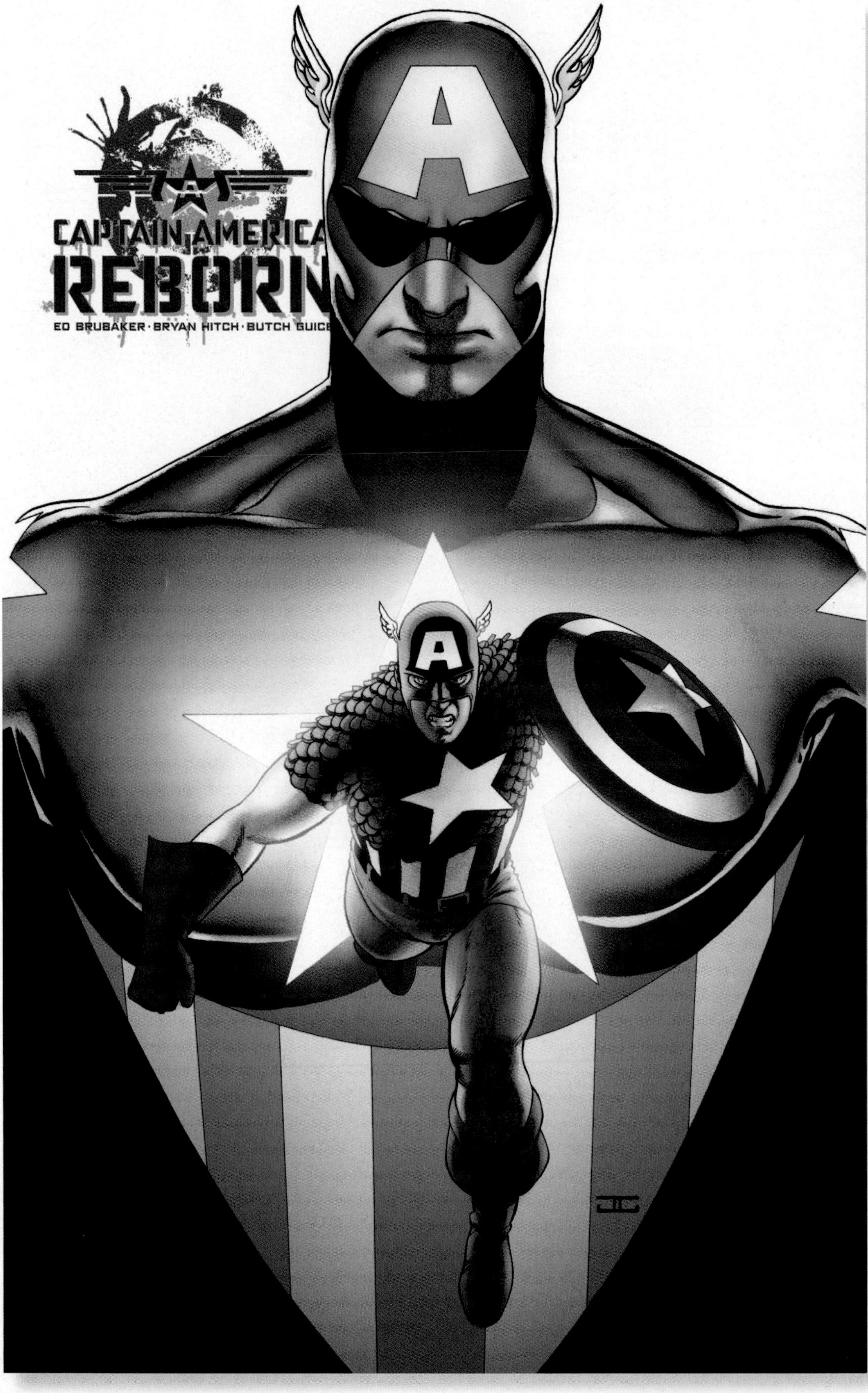
CAPTAIN AMERICA
REBORN
ED BRUBAKER · BRYAN HITCH · BUTCH GUICE
Issue 6 variant by **JOHN CASSADAY & LAURA MARTIN**

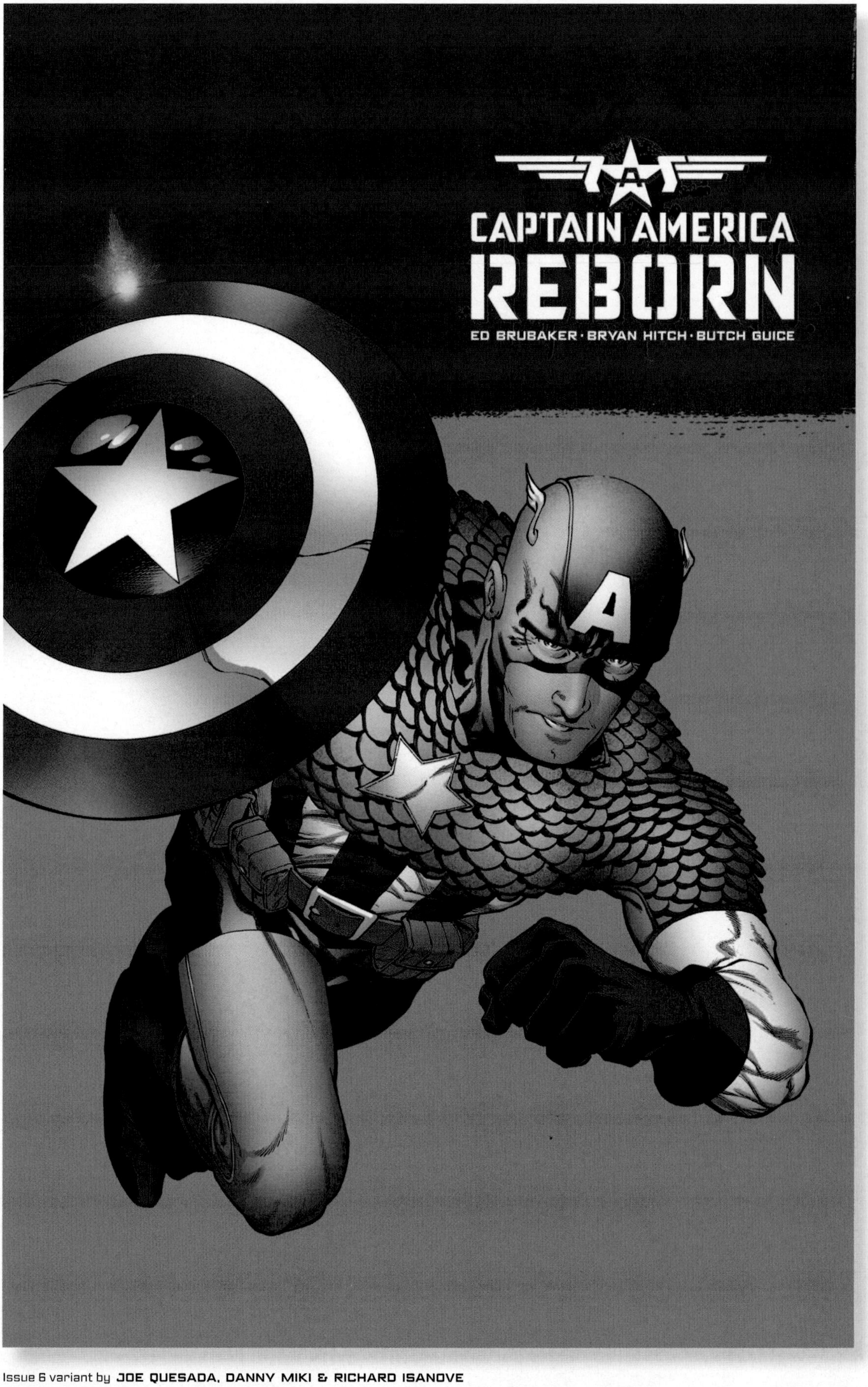
CAPTAIN AMERICA
REBORN
ED BRUBAKER · BRYAN HITCH · BUTCH GUICE

Issue 6 variant by **JOE QUESADA, DANNY MIKI & RICHARD ISANOVE**

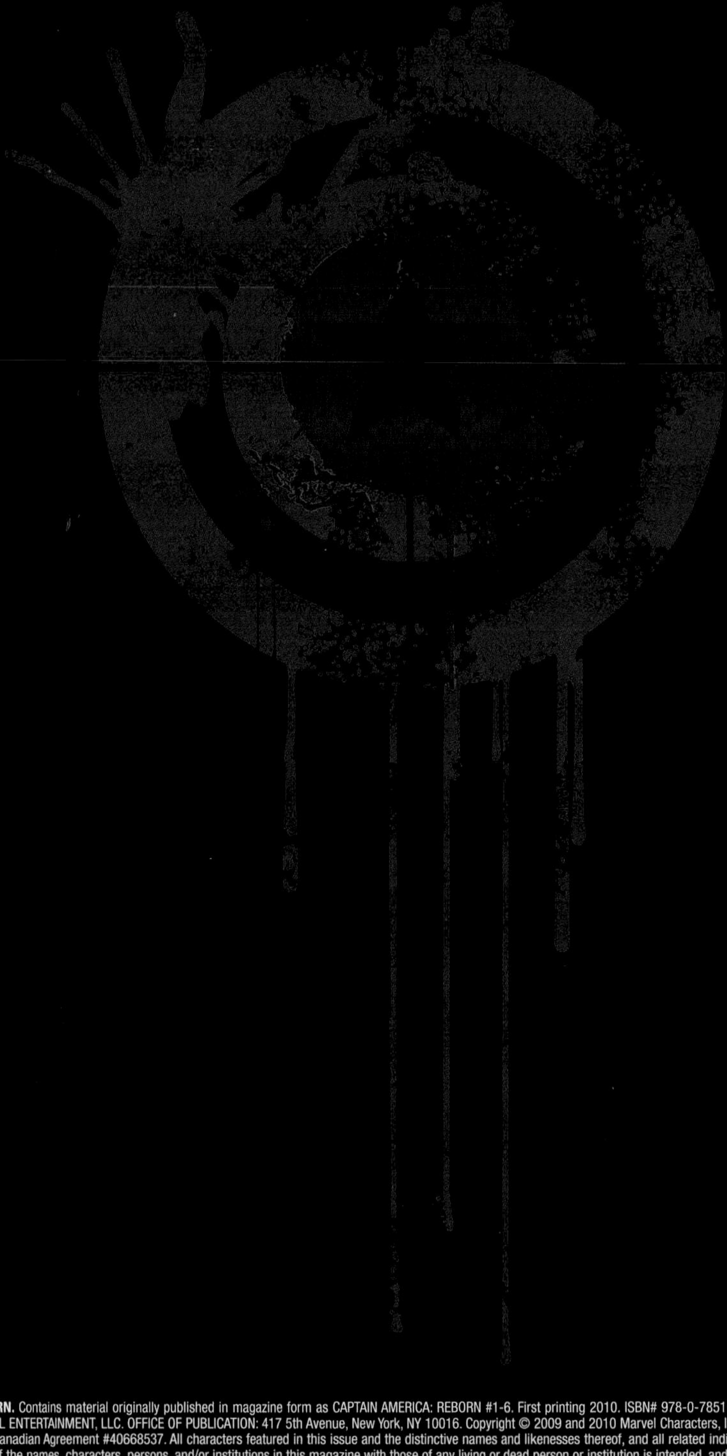

CAPTAIN AMERICA: REBORN. Contains material originally published in magazine form as CAPTAIN AMERICA: REBORN #1-6. First printing 2010. ISBN# 978-0-7851-3998-0. Published by MARVEL WORLDWIDE, INC., a subsidiary of MARVEL ENTERTAINMENT, LLC. OFFICE OF PUBLICATION: 417 5th Avenue, New York, NY 10016. Copyright © 2009 and 2010 Marvel Characters, Inc. All rights reserved. $24.99 per copy in the U.S. (GST #R127032852); Canadian Agreement #40668537. All characters featured in this issue and the distinctive names and likenesses thereof, and all related indicia are trademarks of Marvel Characters, Inc. No similarity between any of the names, characters, persons, and/or institutions in this magazine with those of any living or dead person or institution is intended, and any such similarity which may exist is purely coincidental. **Printed in the U.S.A.** ALAN FINE, EVP - Office of the President, Marvel Worldwide, Inc. and EVP & CMO Marvel Characters B.V.; DAN BUCKLEY, Chief Executive Officer and Publisher - Print, Animation & Digital Media; JIM SOKOLOWSKI, Chief Operating Officer; DAVID GABRIEL, SVP of Publishing Sales & Circulation; DAVID BOGART, SVP of Business Affairs & Talent Management; MICHAEL PASCIULLO, VP Merchandising & Communications; JIM O'KEEFE, VP of Operations & Logistics; DAN CARR, Executive Director of Publishing Technology; JUSTIN F. GABRIE, Director of Publishing & Editorial Operations; SUSAN CRESPI, Editorial Operations Manager; ALEX MORALES, Publishing Operations Manager; STAN LEE, Chairman Emeritus. For information regarding advertising in Marvel Comics or on Marvel.com, please contact Ron Stern, VP of Business Development, at rstern@marvel.com. For Marvel subscription inquiries, please call 800-217-9158. **Manufactured between 2/8/2010 and 3/10/2010 by R.R. DONNELLEY, INC., SALEM, VA, USA.**

10 9 8 7 6 5 4 3 2 1